PLATYPUS AND PARLIAMENT

The Australian Senate

in

Theory and Practice

DR STANLEY BACH has published extensively on the United States Congress and other legislatures and has worked as a consultant on parliamentary process in Asia, Africa, South America and Eastern Europe. For more than 30 years he worked with and provided advice to Senators and Representatives on the operations of the US Congress. From 1988 to 2002 he held the office of Senior Specialist in the Legislative Process for the Congressional Research Service of the Library of Congress.

In 2002 Dr Bach was awarded a Fulbright Senior Scholar Award to study bicameralism in Australia. While in Canberra he was a Fellow in the Political Science Program of the Research School of Social Sciences at the Australian National University. He was also awarded a fellowship in the Department of the Senate which enabled him to observe the operations of the Commonwealth Parliament at first hand.

This book is published as part of the Department of the Senate's program to promote public knowledge and awareness of the role and activities of the Senate. The views expressed in the book are those of the author and do not necessarily reflect those of the Senate or its staff.

PLATYPUS AND PARLIAMENT

The Australian Senate in Theory and Practice

STANLEY BACH

Department of the Senate

Published by
The Department of the Senate
Parliament House
Canberra ACT 2600 Australia

First published 2003

National Library of Australia
cataloguing-in-publication data

Bach, Stanley.
Platypus and parliament: the Australian Senate in
theory and practice.
Bibliography.
Includes index.
ISBN 0 642 71293 X.
ISBN 0 642 71291 3 (pbk.).

1. Australia. Parliament. Senate. I. Australia.
    Parliament. Senate. II. Title.

328.94

Printed in Australia by Canprint Communications
Fyshwick ACT

… having called into existence two strong houses, and especially a senate the like of which will not be found in any constitution that is in existence, or has ever been in existence in the world, we ought to make provision for great, important, probably historical occasions when those coordinate houses may be brought into serious conflict. … Now, in an ordinary constitution, where we have an upper house not elected by the people, or not elected on the same basis as the lower house, that second chamber would be disposed to yield to the pressure of the lower chamber elected upon a popular basis; but here, where we are creating a senate which will feel the sap of popular election in its veins, that senate will probably feel stronger than a senate or upper chamber which is elected only on a partial franchise, and, consequently, we ought to make provision for the adjustment of disputes in great emergencies.

Dr John Quick
Sydney, 1897

We are creating in these two chambers, under our form of government, what you may term an irresistible force on the one side, and what may prove to be an immovable object on the other side.

Alfred Deakin
Sydney, 1897

Contents

List of Tables

Preface

This is a book, as its subtitle explains, about the Senate of Australia in theory and in practice. Let me explain how and why I came to write it.

The best way to learn something is to explain it to others. I discovered this long ago when, after spending six years teaching about and then working in the United States Congress, I found myself at the Congressional Research Service (CRS) of the Library of Congress. Largely through happenstance, I became one of the CRS 'experts' who was tasked with explaining the legislative rules of the game to congressional staff and, less often, to the Representatives and Senators for whom they worked. I soon realized that I knew far less about Congress than I had thought, and I wondered how I could have persevered through all those years of studying political science, a few years of professing to be a professor, and a few more years of acting as if I were a savvy legislative operative, while knowing almost nothing about those very rules that I now was expected to master.

So I read and then read some more, and asked questions and more questions, and listened to my mentor explain the same things over and over again, with most of what I read and heard failing to sink in to my brain, as if all this information and insight were a cloudburst falling on desert soil. Again and again I thought that I had learned something only to discover otherwise when I tried unsuccessfully to explain it to someone else. It was at that point that I started to write. The audience for whom I really was writing was not Congress, and certainly not posterity; it was me. As I pounded away on my typewriter (it was many years ago), I was explaining my subject to myself. I was being paid to write these reports for Congress, of course, but I decided that if I could explain a subject lucidly and precisely enough for me to understand it, then my congressional audience certainly should be able to understand it as well. Sometimes I failed; more often than not, I succeeded.

I review this very ancient history to explain that what follows is an artefact of my efforts to learn something new and different. When I decided it was time to leave CRS after spending roughly 30 years in various incarnations on Capitol Hill, I chose to take advantage of my

...ew-found freedom by learning something about the counterparts of Congress in other regimes that can make a creditable claim to being called democracies. I was curious to learn more about how other national assemblies, operating in different constitutional contexts, worked in both theory and practice.

I soon realized that Australia would be the ideal venue to begin the next stage of my education. So I was extraordinarily fortunate to secure the support of the Australian-American Fulbright Commission and the J. William Fulbright Foreign Scholarship Board, enabling me to spend six months of 2002–2003 in Canberra, learning about the Commonwealth Parliament. While in Canberra, I was equally fortunate in being invited to enjoy the hospitality of Parliament, where I was a Fellow in the Department of the Senate, and of the Australian National University, where I was a Visiting Fellow in the Political Science Program of the Research School of Social Sciences.

In addition to giving me an unbeatable opportunity for what Richard Fenno has called research by 'soaking and poking'—poking around Parliament House and soaking up as much as I could—I also was able to do a lot of 'picking'—picking the brains of an impressive array of scholars and parliamentary officials, all of whom were surpassingly generous in sharing their time, knowledge, and insights. What follows is an extended essay on what I learned while in Canberra and from the additional research I was able to do both before and after my visit there. It is my attempt to explain to myself what I learned, in the guise of explaining it to you.

 One of the first things that struck me as I began to study the Australian Parliament was the quantity and quality of communication between political scientists and political practitioners. Senior parliamentary staff have taken time from the demands of their daily work to think and write about the health of Parliament as an institution and about its place in the Australian constitutional system. From the other direction, some of Australia's political scientists ask themselves important questions about Parliament and then write about those questions in terms that are both interesting and intelligible to Parliament's members and staff. For example, I encourage interested readers to explore the Senate's *Papers on Parliament* series, available electronically at www.aph.gov.au/senate/pubs/papers.htm. It is difficult to imagine American political scientists and political practitioners on Capitol Hill in Washington finding such common ground, or even making the effort to look for it.

I believe that an author should have clearly in mind the audience for whom he or she is writing. When I began to write what eventually became this book, I anticipated that my primary audience would be in the United States. If I am typical of American 'experts' on Congress, I expect that most of them know little or nothing about the Australian Parliament. When I started writing, it was with the hope that at least a few students of Congress would come to share my opinion that there are an intriguing array of similarities and differences between the two institutions, and that, in any event, Australia's Parliament is a fascinating place to visit, even if only vicariously. For American readers, therefore, this book is my way of offering them the fruits of the visit I was able to make—of sharing with them what I have learned and what I think it means.

I realized that there might be little in these chapters that is not already well-known to practitioners of parliamentary government in Canberra and to Australian political scientists with a special interest in Parliament. On the other hand, I also came to realize that there was no single book devoted solely to explaining essential facets of Australia's Senate and that was written with a general audience in mind. Although it might seem presumptuous for a non-Australian to try to fill that gap, I prefer to think that my initial ignorance of the subject has proven to be an advantage. In trying to explain the Senate to myself, I have had to start at the beginning and assemble the pieces of the puzzle in what, to me, is a logical, intelligible order. I hope that approach will make this book interesting and digestible to Australian readers who may not have thought very much about their Senate, as well as to readers in the United States or elsewhere.

Writing with two audiences in mind has been a challenge. I have included some references and comparisons intended to help American readers better understand some aspects of the Australian political system. When I was trying to understand cricket, I found it very useful to read an explanation that emphasized the game's similarities and differences with baseball. What works for cricket may work for politics as well. In turn, I also have included some references to ways in which the Parliament in Canberra resembles or differs from the Congress in Washington. These comparisons may help Australian readers understand why some aspects of their parliamentary practices are particularly intriguing to an American observer.

Except where my readers felt that my meaning would be unclear to Australian readers, I have used American spelling and grammatical conventions throughout. Australian readers also will note that I sometimes have used American rather than Australian nomenclature. For example, I refer to those elected to the House of Representatives (but not to the Senate) as 'Members', as Australians and Americans both do, and also as 'Representatives,' as Americans do but Australians do not. In other instances, I adopt both Australian and American usages—for example, by referring to a motion being moved (Australian) or offered or proposed (American). In addition, I capitalize certain words in some contexts but not in others. For example, I capitalize 'Representative' when referring to someone elected to the Australian or the US House of Representatives, but not when referring to someone serving in an unspecified representative capacity. Similarly, 'House' is capitalized when used as an abbreviation for 'House of Representatives,' as is 'Member' when used as an abbreviated form of 'Member of the House of Representatives' or 'Member of Parliament,' or 'Member of Congress,' but not, for example, when referring to a member of a committee or some other collectivity. I also capitalize 'Government' when referring to a specific ministry such as the Hawke Government, but not when referring to the government of Australia or the institutions of government in a broader or more generic sense.

In some of the chapters to come, I have quoted others frequently and sometimes at length. I have done so for three reasons. First, some of the books and articles on which I have relied are not likely to be widely available in the United States, so my quotations will give American readers some sense of the richness of this body of work. Second, Australian political analysts and political scientists usually write with a clarity and grace that is less often found in the work of their American counterparts. If an author already has made a point or an argument more elegantly than I could, I have chosen to let the author speak for himself or herself. And third, much of what I have to say is largely, though not entirely, my exposition of what I have learned from what others already have written. By quoting instead of paraphrasing, I am able to give credit where credit is due.

Readers will observe that this book has been published by the Department of the Senate, which pleases me greatly. But I am certain that everyone in the Senate—from the President, Senator Calvert, and the Clerk, Harry Evans, and on through the ranks of Senators and all those who work in and for the Senate (and, without any doubt, everyone associated with the House of Representatives as well)—would want me to emphasize that, in the pages that follow, I am speaking only for myself. The Senate has not endorsed the contents of this book, and it should not be assumed for a moment that any Senator or Senate officer necessarily agrees with any particular statement in it.

My first debt is to the good people of the Australian-American Fulbright Commission—Mark Darby, Judith Gamble, Melinda Hunt, and Sandra Lambert—not only for the Fulbright Senior Scholar Award which made my research possible, but for their continuing kindness during my time in Canberra. Without a little help from my friends— Alan Frumin, Charlie Johnson, Barbara Sinclair, and Steve Smith—I could not have hoped to receive the Fulbright award. I happily express my appreciation to Professor Marian Sawer and to Mary Hapel of the Political Science Program of the Research School of Social Sciences at the Australian National University for welcoming me as a Visiting Fellow and allowing me access to the resources and, even more important, the people of the RSSS and the ANU. Ken Coghill, Murray Goot, and John Hart also made important contributions to my education. My sojourn in Canberra would not have been possible without the cheerful support and assistance in Washington of Elizabeth Rybicki, Brian Merry, Mark Wigtil, Wendy Wigtil, and Ruth Widmann, who provided the umbilical cord that kept me connected. I am grateful to them all; my gratitude to Elizabeth is boundless.

Any errors of fact, analysis, or interpretation in what follows are my responsibility alone, of course. They would be far more numerous and much more serious, however, if not for the generous assistance of so many people in the Senate and outside, whose knowledge of the Senate and the Parliament exceeds mine by orders of magnitude and decades of experience, and who have been so willing to share with me their wisdom and advice. At the ANU, my friends John Uhr and Ian Marsh have been unstinting in their encouragement, support, and sound advice throughout this enterprise, from its inception to its completion. They have been my professors. In the Senate, Harry Evans, Anne Lynch, Rosemary Laing, Cleaver Elliott, Wayne Hooper and Kay Walsh, and Scott Bennett in the Parliamentary Library, all cheerfully undertook the laborious task of reading parts or all of this manuscript and improving it in countless ways. For their helpful comments, I also thank Elizabeth Rybicki, Marian Sawer, Campbell Sharman, and former Senator Michael Macklin. I will borrow a delightful comment that J.A. La Nauze made in the preface to his *The Making of the Australian Constitution*. La Nauze (1972: v–vi) wrote that his colleague, Geoffrey Sawer, 'most cheerfully gave me instruction, but it was not necessarily in his power to give me understanding.' One thing I do understand, though, is how much I owe to all of my teachers at both institutions.

I wish I knew how to express adequately my gratitude to all the wonderful men and women at Parliament House whose kindness and hospitality far exceeded anything I could have imagined before I arrived in Canberra. If I were to try to identify them all by name, the list would go on and on, and I still would commit serious sins of omission. So let me ask that my expression of appreciation to Ian Harris, Clerk of the House, and Robyn McClelland, Clerk Assistant (Table), extend to all their colleagues in the Department of the House of Representatives who welcomed me so warmly and shared with me their time and insights. And in the same manner, let me hope that everyone in the

Parliamentary Library and especially its Information and Research Services will understand that when I thank June Verrier and Judy Hutchinson for all their help and support, I mean for my thanks to flow to all of their colleagues as well.

Most important, of course, have been everyone in the Department of the Senate who welcomed me, helped me with my work, and made me feel at home. Never in my professional life have I encountered such a fine group of people all working together in the same place. I hope none of them will feel slighted when I express my profound thanks collectively to the officials and members of the Clerk's Office, the Procedure Office, Black Rod's Office, the Committee Office, and the Table Office. Finally, there is the mob in SG49 of the Senate wing whom I always will cherish as friends: Wayne Hooper, my host, my friend, and the godfather of this book; Kay Walsh and Rebecca Eames, who devoted so much time and care to bringing it to fruition; and (strictly in alphabetical order) Sarah Bannerman, Amanda Bennett, Sue Blunden, David Creed, Amanda Hill, Irene Inveen, Margaret Lindeman, Janice Paull, David Sullivan, and James Warmenhoven. When I have forgotten everything that I have written here, I will continue to remember them fondly.

All these people share a dedication to the Commonwealth Parliament and an interest in improving public understanding of what the Parliament, and especially the Senate, is and what it does. If this book is useful in that regard, then I shall be satisfied, because I will know that I have been able to offer some small repayment for the hospitality and kindness I was shown during my days in Canberra.

Stanley Bach
Canberra and Washington
2003

1

Introduction

On my first full day in Australia, I visited the Sydney Aquarium where my encounter with an energetic platypus reminded me of a comparison between the platypus and the Parliament of the Commonwealth of Australia.[1]

In his essay, 'To Be a Platypus,' in *Bully for Brontosaurus* (1991), Stephen Jay Gould judges that the platypus 'surely wins first prize in anybody's contest to identify the most curious mammal' because of 'its enigmatic mélange of reptilian (or birdlike), with obviously mammalian characters.' (Gould 1991: 270) Not surprisingly, there had been a debate among Nineteenth Century scientists about how best to classify the platypus:

> During the half-century between its discovery and Darwin's *Origin of Species*, the platypus endured endless attempts to deny or mitigate its true mélange of characters associated with different groups of vertebrates. Nature needed clean categories established by divine wisdom. An animal could not both lay eggs and feed its young with milk from mammary glands. (Gould 1991: 275)

Gould sympathizes with those who rejected attempts to force the platypus to fit into the then-prevailing taxonomic structure, arguing that 'Taxonomies are guides to action, not passive devices for ordering.' (Gould 1991: 274) He also disposes of the argument that, because of its mélange of characters, the platypus must be primitive, inefficient, or defective. Quite the contrary, he argues. The platypus is 'a bundle of adaptations' that make it 'a superbly engineered creature for a particular, and unusual, mode of life.' It is 'an elegant solution for mammalian life in streams—not a primitive relic of a bygone world.' (Gould 1991: 276-277)

It requires no great astuteness, especially on the part of any Australian readers, to understand the relevance of the platypus to this

---

1 The comparison was made by Melissa Langerman (in Bongiorno et al., 1999: 167), an astute observer of the latter, and perhaps the former as well, who had the good sense not to belabor the comparison, as I shall do here.

study of the Commonwealth Parliament and especially the Senate of
Australia. Both the platypus and the Parliament are uniquely Australian
creations. Both display characteristics of two categories of things
normally thought to be alternatives to each other: reptiles and mammals
in the case of the platypus; parliamentary and strong bicameral regimes
in the case of the Parliament. For this reason, both have been criticized
as defective or logically incoherent. Yet a more persuasive argument
can be made that the Parliament, like the platypus, also is 'a bundle of
adaptations' that make it 'an elegant solution' to the challenges posed
by the context of democratic governance in Australia.

So when I link the Commonwealth Parliament with the platypus, I
do so with no intent to disparage one or the other.[2] (Many Australians
are no more fond of their Parliament and its members than many
Americans are of their Congress and its members, so I might be thought
to be insulting the platypus, not the Parliament.) Instead, I choose this
characterization, first, to emphasize the combination of elements that
makes the Parliament a distinctive institution, and, second, to point to
the most interesting question about it: how well have these seemingly
inconsistent and even incompatible elements been joined together to
make a political system that works?

These elements are the combination of responsible government and
federalism, with the latter reflected in what Arend Lijphart calls 'strong
bicameralism'. In fact, Australia is one of five contemporary regimes
(the others being Colombia, Germany, Switzerland, and the United
States) that he categorizes under the heading of 'strong bicameralism'
because its two houses are symmetrical and incongruent. 'Symmetrical
chambers are those with equal or only moderately unequal
constitutional powers and democratic legitimacy.' 'Incongruent
chambers' are 'elected by different methods or [are] designed so as to
over-represent certain minorities.' (Lijphart 1999a: 206–207) If the two
houses of an assembly are more or less symmetrical in their powers,
neither has the constitutional authority to dominate the other. If they
also are incongruent in their mode of election, they are likely to differ
in their partisan composition. In a strong bicameral system, therefore,
there is the prospect of conflict between the two houses, neither of
which easily can impose its will on the other.

---

2   After adopting the comparison for the title of this book, I learned that, in 1895,
    Alfred Deakin had compared the platypus to the Australasian Federal Council, the
    predecessor of sorts of the Commonwealth, as 'a perfectly original development
    compounded from familiar but previously unassociated types.' (quoted in Irving
    1999: 132) Irving extends the comparison to the Constitution.

Such is the situation today in the Commonwealth Parliament of Australia, which has had symmetrical chambers since the beginning of the Federation in 1901 and incongruent chambers since the introduction in 1949 of proportional representation (PR) for electing Senators. Here is Lijphart on strong bicameralism in Canberra:

> The House of Representatives and the Senate in Australia do not have equal power, but by comparative standards the Senate is a very powerful body, and the relationship between the two houses can therefore be classified as only moderately asymmetrical; moreover, both houses are popularly elected. The two houses are also clearly incongruent in their composition. They already qualify for the label of strong bicameralism in this regard as a result of the equal representation of the states in the Senate in spite of the states' highly unequal populations—a feature of many federal systems. The difference in the methods of election—the majoritarian alternative-vote system for the House of Representatives and PR for the Senate—makes the two houses even more different in composition and reinforces their incongruence. STV [the single transferable vote] therefore has the effect of strengthening bicameralism and also the federalist character of Australian democracy on the second dimension. (Lijphart 1999b: 57–58)

An informed observer opened his generally sympathetic portrait of the Australian Parliament by writing of Prime Minister Gough Whitlam's 1972–1975 Labor Government that:

> At no stage did the Labor government have control of the Senate, so its legislative program was constantly under threat. In those three years the senate [sic] rejected more legislation than it had in its previous 71-year history. The government could never be certain that any particular bill would be passed, or even when it would be considered, by the upper house. This led to political as well as legislative problems for the government whose term could be threatened (and was eventually ended) by actions of the Senate. The timing of elections was largely dictated by questions of parliamentary tactics and by the government's opponents. (Solomon 1978: 9)

As this quotation suggests and as we shall explore in Chapter 4, the Whitlam Government was as unusual as was the manner of its demise. Nonetheless, this description is certainly not what we would expect to read about any government and parliament in the Westminster tradition. And in fact, what makes the Australian political system so interesting is precisely how it combines, by constitutional arrangement and statutory choice, some of the essential features of a parliamentary regime with other features that can put at risk a core relationship of such a regime— the responsibility of government to the house of Parliament which selects that government and invests it with its powers. Paradoxically enough, as I shall argue, the very features that jeopardize the responsibility of government to parliament are precisely those that hold out the possibility of ensuring the accountability of government to parliament.

Those features that put parliamentary responsibility at risk centre on the constitutional powers of the Senate, which in turn reflect the federal character of the Commonwealth that was established in 1901 by separate colonies sharing the same continent. Just as the 'grand compromise' of the American Constitution created a bicameral legislature in which the two houses enjoy almost the same powers, the authors of the Australian Constitution agreed to much the same arrangement (though the nature and extent of the Senate's powers have been and remain a source of contention). And just as one house of the US Congress has two members elected from each state, regardless of population, so too do the Australian states enjoy equal representation in its Senate even though they also differ dramatically in population. And just as the US Senate differs from the House of Representatives in other ways, especially the length of terms, that can contribute to inter-cameral tensions and legislative disagreements, so too are there potential sources of tension and conflict between the Senate and House of Representatives in Canberra, deriving not only from different lengths of terms but from different methods of election.

Within a decade after 1949, when Australia began electing its Senators by proportional representation, the government and its dependable majority in the House began confronting a Senate that usually has had a non-government majority. Yet all legislation, including all those measures nearest and dearest to the hearts of each prime minister and cabinet, must be approved in both houses. (A double dissolution is a device to circumvent the requirement for Senate approval but, as we shall see, it is a cumbersome one that has been invoked only once in a century.) In short, the government is responsible to the House but its ability to secure passage of its legislative program, even its budget, is at the mercy of both the House and the Senate.

One of the major themes in recent analyses of the US national political system has been the frequency and consequences of divided government—when a President of one political party confronts one or both houses of Congress controlled by the other party. In a classic parliamentary system, such divided government is impossible by definition: a government remains in office only so long as it enjoys the support, or at least the acquiescence, of a majority in Parliament or in the only house of Parliament that matters. But in Australia, with its strong bicameralism, both houses matter. So when the government lacks a secure majority in the Senate, that too is a form of divided government.

Richard Broome describes the climactic stage of enactme Australia's Parliament of the *Native Title Act 1993*, a landmark law affecting Aboriginal land rights:

> Because the Opposition [Liberal and National parties] opposed the entire Mabo bill its fate rested with two 'Green' Party senators, Christabel Chamarette and Dee Margetts who held the balance of power in the Senate. This effectively made the Bill more pro-Aboriginal as the 'Greens' pushed for amendments that had Aboriginal approval. As the nation watched, there were six days of emotion-charged scenes in Parliament as the Opposition filibusted [sic], the 'Greens' were pressured by radical and pragmatic Aboriginal opinion and horse-traded with the Government over 200 amendments, and the Keating [Labor Party] government threatened to sit till Christmas to pass the bill before 1994. On 21 December the Native Title Act was passed at 11:58 pm to ringing applause from Government, Green and Democrat members and the packed public gallery, after the longest debate in the Senate's history. (Broome 2002: 240)

Two Senators holding the balance of power? Six days of emotional debate? Filibustering in the Senate? Horse-trading with the government over 200 amendments? Threats to remain in session until Christmas? All this reads much more like a report from Capitol Hill in Washington than from a capital city that enjoys the efficiency of responsible parliamentary government.

As Solomon (1978: 9–10) observed, the parliamentary situation prevailing twenty years earlier, in 1972–1975, encouraged observers to conclude that 'a government must have a majority in the Senate if its very existence were not to be at risk.' The government is responsible to the House in that only the House can dismiss it through a vote of no confidence. As a matter of constitutional principle, the Senate cannot require the government to resign. However, as we shall see, the Senate demonstrated in 1975 that it could, if it had the will to do so, try to compel the government to resign or propel the nation into a political crisis. 'Thus only the House of Representatives can give a government life, but both houses can administer the death penalty, although the Senate may take a long time to put its wishes in to effect.'

This situation raises several questions: How has Australia managed to create and maintain a stable and effective democratic structure when it appears to have been designed by two different architects, one from London and the other from Washington, who appear not to have spoken with each other? Why was the structure designed as it was? And why did Australia exacerbate the problem embedded in its Constitution by amending its electoral laws in 1949 in ways that increased, and may have been expected to increase, the likelihood of there being different balances of partisan forces in the two houses?

In fact, the situation is even more intriguing. In the passage quoted above, we are told that the Senate rejected more legislation during the three-year tenure of the Whitlam Government 'than it had in its previous 71-year history.'

> Many governments had survived in the face of hostile Senates. Their legislative programs might have been (and often were) subject to harrassment [sic], but most proposed laws were passed. While the Senate was aware that it probably had the power to force a government to the polls, this power was rarely discussed and the threat of its use never made.[3]
> (Solomon 1976: 10)

Why did relations between the Labor Government and the Opposition-controlled Senate lead in 1974–1975 to what is almost ritualistically described as a constitutional crisis? And why does that conflict stand in dramatic contrast to the far more pacific relations (notwithstanding rhetoric to the contrary) that, both before and after, have characterized the cohabitation of the House and Senate under the roof of Parliament House?

These are among the questions that I shall address, if not answer to everyone's satisfaction. I begin, naturally enough, with a description of the constitutional context, which is particularly important in Australia because much of what is most significant about the Commonwealth Constitution of 1901 lies in what it does not say. I turn next to a discussion of double dissolutions and joint sittings, which are the constitutional devices for resolving bicameral deadlocks. I then examine how Australia's party system has developed and how its procedures for electing Representatives and Senators have changed. Virtually every student of the Australian political system seems to agree that the emergence of disciplined parliamentary parties and the introduction of proportional representation for Senate elections have combined to transform parliamentary government in Canberra.

With this context in mind, I review the sequence of events that brought down the Whitlam Government in 1975. The events of that year and the one preceding it undoubtedly stand as the most dramatic (and the most chronicled) events in the century-long political and constitutional history of the Commonwealth—events that demonstrate how much practical power the Senate can exercise, but power that it had never used before and has not used since. To understand how the

---

3 In 1970, however, Whitlam had said in debate that 'We all know that in British parliaments the tradition is that, if a money bill is defeated, as the receipt duties legislation was defeated last June [in the Senate], the government goes to the people to seek endorsement of its policies.' (*Commonwealth Parliamentary Debates* (House of Representatives), 1 October 1970: 1971–1972)

1975 crisis could occur, I look back to the constitutional debates of the 1890s and the parliamentary debates of 1948 to understand the thinking and expectations of the Constitution's authors, and the motives and expectations of the Labor Government that instigated PR for Senate elections beginning in 1949.

Next I explore some of the practical consequences and strategic possibilities that flow from the failure of successive governments to command a majority in the Senate. For the government, its core problem is the need to assemble majority coalitions by finding some votes from among non-government Senators. For the Opposition (or other parties represented in the Senate), it has the opportunity to assemble its own winning coalitions to defeat or amend government legislation. I look at the voting patterns in the Senate during recent years for evidence of the government's record of successes and failures, as well as the strategies and track record of the Opposition and other parties. For instance, which parties have joined together most often in winning coalitions? How often have non-government parties attempted to amend or defeat government legislation in the Senate, and how successful have these efforts been? Data on Senate divisions offer some purchase on these and related questions. Chapters 6 and 7, in which this analysis is presented, may be too detailed for the interests of some readers who may prefer just to skim them.

I then examine the Parliament's procedures for resolving whatever legislative differences arise between the House of Representatives and the Senate. This is only one dimension, though a critically important one, of a pattern of bicameral relations that I attempt to sketch. Finally, I address the question of electoral mandates and how it relates to the Senate, and then assess some of the proposals that have been made to 'reform' the Parliament, and especially the Senate, reflecting their proponents' conceptions of what the Senate is and should be. I conclude with some of my own thoughts about the political logic and health of the Commonwealth system of government, and whether Australians should view it with concern, satisfaction, or both.

The coverage of what follows is admittedly selective and incomplete; indeed, it is unapologetically idiosyncratic. One of the advantages of writing any book about such a big subject is that it cannot possibly be comprehensive in its coverage. Selectivity is unavoidable (as, of necessity, is an inability to plumb every subject to the depth it may deserve), so I have allowed myself to make a virtue of that necessity, devoting more attention to some subjects than to others because they strike me as particularly interesting or having particularly important implications for understanding the Australian political system.

The other side of selectivity, of course, is that there are important elements missing in what follows. For example, I devote little attention to the Senate in its first half-century because these were what Reid and Forrest (1989: 477) call its 'years of dependence' that 'did little to enhance its reputation for providing an effective scrutiny of proposed laws, or of the activities of the Executive Government.' More important is the absence here of a careful examination of the powers, activities, contributions, and both strengths and weaknesses of the Senate's committees. The Senate takes considerable pride in its committee system and with good reason, especially when it compares its committees with those of the House or of any true parliament. The current state and the future of the committee system, and whether it should be seen as a glass half-full or a glass half-empty, is a complex and multi-faceted subject that merits extended treatment in its own right. Among the other important subjects not addressed here are the Senate's leadership and especially its presiding officers, and the internal organization and activities of its parliamentary parties. These subjects also are worthy of much more study, and they combine to illustrate just how much more there is to be learned and conveyed to the interested public about not only the Senate but the Commonwealth Parliament as a whole.

2

The constitutional design

Constitutions explain only a fraction of how democratic governments actually work, but they do provide the organizational and procedural framework for government action. There are two aspects of the Australian Constitution that make it particularly interesting. One is the way in which it attempts to combine responsible government with strong bicameralism. The other is the number of critically important provisions that cannot be found in the Constitution—or that can be found only by implication, and then only by those who know where to look and how to read between the lines.

A 'Federal Commonwealth'

What is explicit in the Constitution is that Australia is a federal system. The preamble announces that 'the people of New South Wales, Victoria, South Australia, Queensland, and Tasmania [later joined by Western Australia] ... have agreed to unite in one indissoluble Federal Commonwealth under the Crown of the United Kingdom of Great Britain and Ireland ... ' The Commonwealth Constitution was the product of prolonged negotiations during the 1890s among representatives of colonies that had enjoyed self-government for decades and now were uniting voluntarily in a federation.

Not surprisingly, therefore, the powers of the Parliament, and consequently those of the Commonwealth, are enumerated in much the same manner as the legislative powers of the Congress are enumerated in the US Constitution. In addition, and unlike the American arrangements, sec. 51 of the Commonwealth Constitution authorizes one or more states to refer (or transfer) other matters to the Parliament in Canberra. The enumerated subjects on which the Parliament may legislate include:

> [M]atters referred to the Parliament of the Commonwealth by the Parliament or Parliaments of any State or States, but so that the law shall extend only to States by whose Parliaments the matter is referred, or which afterwards adopt the law.

The Commonwealth Constitution also contains, in sec. 109, a provision comparable to the 'Supremacy Clause' of the US Constitution. Section 109 states that 'When a law of a State is inconsistent with a law of the Commonwealth, the latter shall prevail, and the former shall, to the extent of the inconsistency, be invalid.'

Also like the American Constitution, room for expansion of Commonwealth power has been found in the Australian Constitution, perhaps in excess of what its authors had anticipated or would have approved. In the United States, it is found particularly in the 'Commerce Clause,' giving Congress the authority to regulate 'Commerce with foreign Nations, and among the several States, and with the Indian Tribes,' that has been interpreted to expand the reach of the federal government. In Australia, one place it is found is in the authority of Parliament to make laws respecting 'external affairs.' The High Court, exercising a power of constitutional interpretation much like that exercised by the US Supreme Court, has held that the Commonwealth Parliament may legislate to implement the terms of any valid treaty or other international agreement to which Australia is a party, even if the Parliament otherwise would lack the constitutional power to enact laws on the subject of that international compact.

In a well-known case, the Court upheld the Commonwealth's authority to pass legislation preventing construction of a dam in Tasmania, a matter that otherwise would have been within the exclusive authority of that state, because the Commonwealth was acting to implement an international convention. The result is an open-ended opportunity for the federal government to expand its legislative jurisdiction at the expense of the states. Whenever the Commonwealth enters into an international obligation, it also receives the power to legislate in order to satisfy that obligation. (It should be mentioned that, in Australia, the government can enter into a treaty or other international agreement without the consent of the Parliament, including the Senate in which all states are represented equally.) A cynic might even imagine the possibility of the Commonwealth deciding to become a party to some treaty or international agreement primarily because of the added domestic legislative power that would accompany it.

Another provision of the Commonwealth Constitution probably has affected federal-state relations over an even broader array of issues. Sec. 96 authorizes the Parliament to 'grant financial assistance to any State on such terms and conditions as the Parliament thinks fit.' Under this authority, the Parliament makes grants available to states for purposes within the states' jurisdiction, but sometimes these grants have been given only if the states met certain conditions. By this means, the

Commonwealth has been able to influence policies that are beyond its constitutional purview by influencing how the states legislate with respect to those matters. The basis for the Commonwealth's influence, obviously enough, is the states' desire for the funds that they can receive only if state policies satisfy federal conditions.

The executive government and Parliament

Of greater interest for our purposes are the constitutional provisions establishing the executive and legislative institutions of the Commonwealth, assigning powers to them, and defining the relations among them. It is on these matters that the Constitution is remarkably incomplete and misleading, and deliberately so.

Anyone who read and believed chapter II, on 'The Executive Government,' would be bewildered by the practical operation of Australia's government. Consider secs 61–64:

61. The executive power of the Commonwealth is vested in the Queen and is exercisable by the Governor-General as the Queen's representative, and extends to the execution and maintenance of this Constitution, and of the laws of the Commonwealth.
62. There shall be a Federal Executive Council to advise the Governor-General in the government of the Commonwealth, and the members of the Council shall be chosen and summoned by the Governor-General and sworn as Executive Councillors, and shall hold office during his pleasure.
63. The provisions of this Constitution referring to the Governor-General in Council shall be construed as referring to the Governor-General acting with the advice of the Federal Executive Council.
64. The Governor-General may appoint officers to administer such departments of State of the Commonwealth as the Governor-General in Council may establish.
    Such officers shall hold office during the pleasure of the Governor-General. They shall be members of the Federal Executive Council, and shall be the Queen's Ministers of State for the Commonwealth.
    After the first general election no Minister of State shall hold office for a longer period than three months unless he is or becomes a senator or a member of the House of Representatives.

From reading these provisions, we learn that Australia is indeed a monarchy. All executive power of the Commonwealth is vested in the Queen (and her successors) acting through her appointed agent, the Governor-General.[4] The Governor-General is advised by the Federal

4   The Constitution was enacted as sec. 9 of the *Commonwealth of Australia Constitution Act 1900*. Sec. 2 states that 'The provisions of this Act referring to the

Executive Council and sometimes is required to seek the Council's advice (but not its consent). However, he appoints the members of the Council and may dismiss any of them if and when he chooses. The Governor-General also determines the organization of the executive government by establishing ministries ('departments of State'). He appoints ministers to head these departments from among members of the Executive Council, and the Governor-General may dismiss any minister just as he may remove any member from the Council itself. The only restriction on the Governor-General's discretion in selecting ministers is that they must be (or within three months, must become) members of the Senate or the House of Representatives. However, this requirement applies only to ministers, not to all members of the Federal Executive Council.

Now consider what we have not learned from these provisions. If we relied on their plain meaning, we would not know that, in practice, the Governor-General exercises exceedingly little discretionary power (with some ill-defined reserve powers, such as the power that was at the heart of the 1975 crisis discussed in Chapter 4). We would not know that it is the majority party or coalition in the Parliament, or its leader, and certainly not the Governor-General, that selects the members of the Federal Executive Council, one of whom is designated the prime minister; that it is the prime minister, and certainly not the Governor-General, who decides which minister will head which departments; that all ministers hold their offices at the discretion of the prime minister or his party or coalition in the Parliament, and certainly not 'during the pleasure of the Governor-General'; that the only active members of the Federal Executive Council are the Representatives and Senators selected by the current prime minister or his party caucus in the Parliament; and that the Governor-General is most unlikely to ignore the advice his ministers give him. As Brian Galligan (1980b: 266) has put it, 'In normal circumstances ministers are not his advisers; they are his masters. If the Governor-General can do almost anything according to law, he can do virtually nothing according to convention.'

Nowhere does the Constitution mention the prime minister, the Cabinet, or the concept or practice of responsible government by which the prime minister and Cabinet continue in office only so long as they continue to enjoy the confidence of a majority of the Members of the House of Representatives. The only hint of such things is the requirement that each minister must be, or soon become, a member of the House or Senate. Instead, the cardinal principles of responsible

Queen shall extend to her Majesty's heirs and successors in the sovereignty of the United Kingdom.'

government that Australia inherited from Great Britain, and to which it intended to adhere, are conventions. These conventions are shared understandings of what the Constitution really means, not what it actually says. As we shall see when we look briefly in Chapter 5 at the constitutional debates of the 1890s, some thought it was unnecessary to spell out intentions and expectations that were universally shared; others thought the conventions of responsible government were too subtle and nuanced to be captured adequately in flat assertions of constitutional text.[5] We shall return to the subject of conventions in Chapter 4 and again in Chapter 10.

What the Constitution has to say about the location and exercise of legislative power does little to cast doubt on the power of the monarch, acting through the Governor-General. The Australian Parliament comprises the monarch as well as both houses. The Governor-General summons Parliament to meet; he may prorogue it (thereby ending a parliamentary session and terminating all pending legislative business); and he may dissolve the House of Representatives (and under certain conditions, the Senate as well) before the expiration of the term for which its Members are elected. When Parliament passes a bill, the Governor-General may exercise a veto that Parliament cannot override, or he may propose his own amendments to the bill, or he may 'reserve the law for the Queen's pleasure.' In the last case (in theory) the monarch has two years to decide whether to give her assent, just as she may, within one year, disallow any law to which the Governor-General has assented.

In short, the Governor-General's legislative powers are nominally greater than those of the American President. Contrary to the American notion of separation of powers (or in Richard Neustadt's more accurate formulation, separated institutions sharing powers), the Governor-General is an integral component of the Parliament. For example, the Parliament cannot even consider a spending proposal unless the Governor-General recommends it (sec. 56). He also has constitutional authorization to propose amendments to any bill that Parliament already has approved, unless he chooses instead to veto that bill absolutely (sec. 58).

Again, of course, there is little connection between these constitutional formalities and the operations of Australian government. The Governor-General summons and prorogues Parliament, and dissolves the House of Representatives, when the government asks him to do so. Likewise, when the Governor-General does propose

5 Still others, such as Richard Baker, who became the first President of the Senate, held out hope that some other system might evolve once the Federation was born.

amendments to bills that Parliament has sent him for his assent, they are the government's amendments that he sends to Parliament House at the government's request. Since 1901, Governors-General have returned with amendments a total of 14 bills, only three of them since 1948 (*House of Representatives Practice* 2001: 805).

So in the definition of the Commonwealth's legislative and executive institutions, and in the allocation of legislative and executive powers between them, there is a striking disjunction between what the Constitution says and what it was intended and understood to mean.[6] As Kirby observes (2001: 593), 'If one were to read the Australian Constitution, without knowledge of the conventions by which it operates, one could be forgiven for concluding that Australia was a kind of personal fiefdom of the British monarch [acting through her agent, the Governor-General].' Yet notwithstanding the explicit terms of the Constitution, there is no question that its authors considered the conventions of cabinet responsibility and responsible government to be Australia's great political inheritance from Great Britain, an inheritance that they fully intended to honour and continue.

The Senate and its powers

It also was understood that responsible government meant responsibility not to Parliament but to one-half of Parliament, the House of Representatives, just as in London it meant responsibility only to the House of Commons, not to the House of Lords as well. Just as in the United States in the 1780s, however, the agreement among the Australian states in the 1890s required the creation of a bicameral Parliament.

Like American Senators, most Australian Senators are elected for six-year terms, compared with the two-year terms of American Representatives and the maximum three-year terms for Members of

---

6   Winterton (1983: 72) explains that:

      The task of spelling out the details of responsible government had never before been undertaken, and the delegates [to the two constitutional Conventions of 1891 and 1897–1898] decided not to attempt to write down all the practical constitutional understandings, holding that it was unnecessary to do so. Responsible government operated satisfactorily in Canada and the Australian Colonies without explicit constitutional entrenchment, so it was considered unnecessary, and even bad form, to spell out all the details. Even so, the Commonwealth Constitution was more explicit in establishing responsible government than any other contemporary colonial constitution; to have gone further and specifically enacted all its conventions, practices and understandings would undoubtedly have made the operation of responsible government in the Commonwealth unduly rigid and inflexible.

Australia's House of Representatives.[7] In both bodies, the terms of Senators are staggered. In the US, one-third of the Senate is elected every two years. In Australia half of the Senators usually are elected every three years at what are called half-Senate elections. At the request of the government, the Governor-General regularly dissolves the House before the end of its maximum three-year term of office; the Senate, by contrast, can be dissolved only in the case of a double dissolution (which is a constitutional possibility discussed below).

Also as in the United States, each state has the right to elect the same number of Senators, regardless of the differences in their populations. Each of the original Australian states (and so far there are no others) is guaranteed not two but a minimum of six Senators, a number that was increased to the current number of 12 by the *Representation Act 1983*. Furthermore, the Commonwealth Constitution of 1901 provided for direct popular election of Senators, a development that would not come to the United States until the US Constitution was amended in 1913. Finally, Australia's Constitution includes what has become known as the 'nexus' provision of sec. 24: 'the House of Representatives shall be composed of members directly chosen by the people of the Commonwealth, and the number of such members shall be, as nearly as practicable, twice the number of the senators.' Thus, any increase in the membership of the House—to reflect population growth, for example—requires a corresponding increase in the membership of the Senate.

As we shall see, the nexus between the size of the House and that of the Senate gives the House an important advantage if and when the Constitution's procedures for resolving legislative disagreements are invoked. On the other hand, members of the constitutional Conventions who supported the Senate's influence could well have felt that the nexus was to be preferred to leaving the size of the houses to later legislation. It was reasonable to surmise that Parliament would enact legislation to increase the House's membership in order to keep pace with Australia's increasing population, but also that the House (and governments) would not have much incentive to support legislation making comparable increases in the membership of the Senate. In fact, in 1948 and again in 1983, when the number of Senators per state was increased, it was not because there was a felt need for more Senators. It was the size of the House that governments of the day wanted to expand, and increasing the size of the Senate was the constitutional cost of doing so.

---

7   Four Senators, two each from the ACT and the Northern Territory, are elected for the same term as Members of the House of Representatives.

In the Introduction, I referred to Lijphart's concept of strong bicameralism, characterized by two chambers that are symmetrical, in that they have more or less comparable powers, but that are incongruent, in that they are selected in significantly different ways. I will defer discussion of how Australia's House and Senate are elected and how their modes of election have changed, and focus here on the Senate's constitutional powers, especially compared with those of the House of Representatives.

The controlling provisions are in sec. 53 of the Constitution which states that, 'Except as provided in this section, the Senate shall have equal power with the House of Representatives in respect of all proposed laws.' So the two houses are equal partners in the legislative process, with three exceptions relating, not surprisingly, to financial legislation:

> Proposed laws appropriating revenue or moneys, or imposing taxation, shall not originate in the Senate.

> The Senate may not amend proposed laws imposing taxation, or proposed laws appropriating revenue or money for the ordinary annual services of the Government.

> The Senate may not amend any proposed law so as to increase any proposed charge or burden on the people.

As we might expect, the meaning of these prohibitions has required some interpretation and involved some negotiation over the years.[8] What, for instance, constitutes 'the ordinary annual services of the Government' or a 'proposed charge or burden on the people'? We will touch on these questions later. For the moment, what is important is the general principle that financial legislation, both taxing and spending, is the primary responsibility of the House and, through it, the government.[9]

---

8   The contrasting positions that the House and Senate Clerks have taken regarding sec. 53 are reflected in papers published in *Papers on Parliament* No. 19, May 1993, under the title 'Constitution, Section 53.'

9   'Legislation which requires appropriations or the imposition of taxation for its operation may be introduced in the Senate with an indication that the necessary appropriation or imposition of taxation is to be inserted into the legislation in the House of Representatives ... ' (*Odgers' Australian Senate Practice* 2001: 293). *Odgers' Australian Senate Practice* and *House of Representatives Practice* are written and published respectively by the Department of the Senate, under the direction of the Clerk of the Senate, and by the Department of the House of Representatives, under the direction of the Clerk of the House. Each is generally accepted to be an authoritative statement of Senate or House procedure and practice. However, neither house acts formally to approve the text of its book, so it

Emblematic of the government's primacy in financial matters is sec. 56, which provides that 'A vote, resolution, or proposed law for the appropriation of revenue or moneys shall not be passed unless the purpose of the appropriation has in the same session been recommended by message of the Governor-General to the House in which the proposal originated.' In explanation, Moore (1910: 138D) argues that 'It is an essential part of our Parliamentary system that every grant of money for the public service shall be based upon the request or recommendation of the Crown.' He goes on to quote Erskine May that 'The foundation for all Parliamentary taxation is its necessity for the public service as declared by the Crown through its Constitutional advisors.'

However, the effect of these restrictions on the Senate regarding financial legislation is mitigated by the provisions of secs 54 and 55, which are intended to prevent the House of Representatives from taking undue advantage of the prerogatives it enjoys under sec. 53. With regard to spending bills, sec. 54 requires that 'The proposed law which appropriates revenue or moneys for the ordinary annual services of the Government'—a bill that the Senate cannot amend—'shall deal only with such appropriations.' This condition is primarily intended to protect against what is known in Canberra as 'tacking': including in the appropriation bill a non-appropriation provision (what in the Washington vernacular would be called a legislative 'rider') to prevent the Senate from being able to amend it.

With regard to revenue bills, sec. 55 provides that:

> Laws imposing taxation shall deal only with the imposition of taxation, and any provision therein dealing with any other matter shall be of no effect.
>
> Laws imposing taxation, except laws imposing duties of customs or of excise, shall deal with one subject of taxation only; but laws imposing duties of customs shall deal with duties of customs only, and laws imposing duties of excise shall deal with duties of excise only.

The first clause again protects the Senate against 'tacking'—in this context, being presented with a bill containing non-tax provisions that the Senate cannot amend because they have been included in a tax bill. The second clause prevents the House from sending to the Senate a bill that deals with more than one aspect of Australia's Commonwealth tax system, except that there can be omnibus customs bills and omnibus excise bills so long as those bills do not contain provisions on other subjects, tax-related or otherwise. To the Senate the Constitution says

should not be assumed that every Senator or Member concurs in every assertion and judgment to be found in either of them.

that initiating financial legislation is a prerogative of the House; to the House the Constitution says that it must not abuse its privileged position regarding that legislation.[10]

Even more important, the Senate is far from being powerless with respect to financial legislation. First, when the Senate cannot amend a bill from the House, it can request that the House agree to the amendments that the Senate would have made if sec. 53 did not prevent it from doing so:

> The Senate may at any stage return to the House of Representatives any proposed law which the Senate may not amend, requesting, by message, the omission or amendment of any items or provisions therein. And the House of Representatives may, if it thinks fit, make any of such omissions or amendments, with or without modifications.

Thus, the Senate need not stand mute when it receives a spending or tax bill from the House. In fact, when the Senate agrees to request that the House make one or more amendments to such a bill, the Senate does so before the third reading of the bill (which marks its passage). So the two houses must dispose of the request in a mutually agreeable way before the bill reaches the third reading stage in the Senate, which it must do before it can become law.[11] In other words, the House may resist Senate requests for amendments, but the House cannot ignore them nor can it reject them summarily unless it is prepared to allow the bill to die. Second, even though the Senate cannot amend certain financial bills, it does not have to pass them, and it may reject them either by direct vote or by its refusal to bring them to a vote.[12]

---

10 In *Odgers' Australian Senate Practice* (2001: 298), it is pointed out that secs 53 and 54 refer to proposed laws whereas sec. 55 refers to laws. Therefore, it is argued, the first two sections are not justiciable but the third one is.

11 Sometimes the Senate returns a bill to the House with both amendments and requests, when some of the amendments the Senate wants to make would violate sec. 53. In that case, the two houses first must reach agreement regarding the requests; then the Senate reads the bill for a third time and returns it to the House. Only after these actions have been completed can the House formally act on the amendments that the Senate made to the bill.

12 There are other reasons why the constraints on the Senate's legislative powers regarding money bills are not as severe as they might seem, as Pearce (1977: 123) illustrates: 'Where it is desired to include a standing appropriation in a bill rather than in separate legislation, it is possible to introduce the bill into the Senate without an appropriation clause. The requisite clause can then be inserted in the bill by way of amendment by the House of Representatives.'

These constitutional authorities that the Senate enjoys have led it to reject any notion that the House enjoys a general primacy over money-related bills.[13]

> The provisions of section 53 are usually described as limitations on the power of the Senate in respect of financial legislation, but they are procedural limitations only, not substantive limitations on power, because the Senate can reject any bill and can decline to pass any bill until it is amended in the way the Senate requires. In particular, the distinction between an amendment and a request is purely procedural; in one case the Senate amends a bill itself, in the other it asks the House of Representatives to amend the bill. In both cases the bill is returned to the House of Representatives for its agreement with the proposed amendment. In the absence of agreement the Senate can decline to pass the bill.
>
> The provisions of section 53 therefore have a purely procedural application, to determine whether amendments initiated by the Senate should take the form of amendments made by the Senate or requests to the House of Representatives to make amendments. The only effect of choosing a request instead of an amendment is that a bill makes an extra journey between the Senate and the House ... .
>
> While appropriation bills and bills imposing taxation may not originate in the Senate, this does not mean that the Senate is not an equal partner with the House of Representatives in actually making appropriations. (*Odgers' Australian Senate Practice* 2001: 292)

Not surprisingly, some commentators disagree. For example, Rydon (1985: 68) contends that 'The Senate was made directly subordinate to the House in regard to money bills—which it could not originate or amend but could reject—and indirectly subordinate in all legislation through the provisions for the settlement of disputes between the houses.'

When the Commonwealth Constitution was written, the British House of Lords still enjoyed more than a suspensive veto over legislation; its veto power was limited by the *Parliament Act 1911*, which was enacted ten years after the first Commonwealth Parliament convened. Perhaps if Federation had come a decade later, the Australian Senate also might have been denied the power to block passage of tax and spending bills, not just to delay them and suggest amendments.

---

13 'The practical implication of the Senate's power of rejection of a bill coupled with its power to make a request is that the government in the House of Representatives is compelled to pay as much heed to a request as it has to an amendment. If the request is refused and the bill rejected by the Senate there is very little difference in result between the House of Representatives refusing to consent to amendments and the Senate thereupon rejecting the bill. The bill is lost in either case. If a government wishes its legislation to be passed, it may have to modify it to meet Senate demands no matter in what form they are expressed.' (Pearce 1977: 126)

Perhaps not, however. Colin Hughes quotes Redlich as having written (in his *The Procedure of the House of Commons*) in 1908, the year before the events that precipitated the 1911 law, that:

> Amendment of the single money bill was constitutionally impossible. For two hundred years the House of Lords had ceased to claim any such right. In the face of the alternative presented to them, the Lords could do nothing else than accede to the aggregate of financial proposals without exception. They could not bring themselves to reject the whole financial scheme of the year. And so the matter ended. For more than a generation now the Commons' right to sole management of the country's finance has been asserted in this way; it is now both true in fact and accepted as a principle of constitutional law that the House of Lords is excluded from influence on money matters and it can never expect to reassert a claim to possess any. (Hughes 1980: 45)

The implication is that the authors of the Commonwealth Constitution surely would have been aware that, although the Lords had not (yet) been denied the power to amend or defeat supply bills, it was well-established that they did not do so. In addition, however, the American example was readily at hand; Bryce's *The American Commonwealth* was popular reading at the time, though by no means the only source of information available to delegates about American constitutional arrangements and their practical operation. In any event, and as we shall see in Chapter 4, the Senate's discretion with regard to money bills eventually gave rise to the greatest political and constitutional controversy in Australian history.

Pressing requests

There also has been an ongoing disagreement about how insistent on its requested amendments the Senate can and should be (Edwards 1943; *House of Representatives Practice* 2001: 433–438; *Odgers' Australian Senate Practice* 2001: 325–327).

Both houses accept that the Senate may request that the House make amendments to money bills; sec. 53 leaves no doubt on that score. However, there have been disagreements about the interpretation and application of this section (*House of Representatives Practice* 2001: 428–433). As early as 1903, questions arose as to whether a particular Senate proposal could be made as an amendment or whether it needed to be embodied in a request. And as recently as 1995 and 1996, the two houses received committee reports on the appropriate interpretation of this section. The two reports, however, were less than compatible. Since then, 'the preference in the House has been to avoid delaying the business of the Parliament with debates on the matter. On occasions when the Chair has drawn the attention of the House to Senate amendments where the position was unclear, the House has thought it appropriate not to take any objection.' (*House of Representatives Practice* 2001: 431, 436–437)

This issue was at the heart of an early test of the Senate's legislative strength, which took place barely a year after the Commonwealth Parliament was inaugurated in May 1901. In April of the following year, the House sent the Senate the Customs Tariff Bill, certainly the most contentious measure the Parliament had tackled to date (Souter 1988: 69–72). The Senate was constitutionally barred from amending the bill but not from recommending amendments and requesting that the House concur in them. After debating the bill for more than a month, the Senate requested 93 amendments. The House responded by accepting 33 of them, amending 11 others, and rejecting the remaining 49 Senate amendments.[14] The Senate then 'pressed' its request that the House concur in 26 of the 49 amendments that the House had rejected.

There was some uncertainty and disagreement about whether the Senate had exceeded its constitutional rights in pressing some of its amendments once the House had rejected them. The issue never has been resolved in principle. In 1902, Senator Symon argued for the Senate's right to press a request:

> Surely, when a person is given the power to make a request—unless the contrary is expressly stated—he is not debarred from civilly and courteously repeating it a second time. Power to request means to request as often as necessary till the request is granted ... (*Commonwealth Parliamentary Debates*, 9 September 1902: 15824)

However, the Attorney-General argued to the contrary in 1933, that 'Repetition of the requests converts it into a demand', and concluded that:

> The Senate should recognize that the only practical way in which effect may be given to the words of the section which draw a distinction between making a request at any stage of a bill, and amending a bill, is by taking the view that a request can be made only once, and that, having made it, the Senate has exercised all the rights and privileges allowed by the Constitution. (*Commonwealth Parliamentary Debates*, 30 November 1933: 5249)

It is an interesting debate, the kind that constitutional scholars relish, but life and the work of the Parliament must go on. So in 1901, rather than risk delaying what was considered to be essential legislation, the

---

14 This is a simplified summary of the Senate and House actions, as given by Gavin Souter (1988: 71).

House acceded to the Senate's requests for some of the remaining amendments, and again refused to agree to others of them, but the House reserved the constitutional issue for another day:

> Having regard to the fact that the public welfare demands the early enactment of a Federal tariff, and pending the adoption of Joint Standing Orders, the House of Representatives refrained from the determination of its constitutional rights or obligations in respect of the Senate's Message of 3rd September, 1902, and resolved to receive and consider it forthwith. (*Journals of the Senate*, 4 September 1902: 545)

The Senate was not to be outdone. While agreeing to the House's latest message, the Senate also approved a motion asserting that 'the action of the House of Representatives in receiving and dealing with the reiterated requests of the Senate is in compliance with the undoubted constitutional position and rights of the Senate.' (*Journals of the Senate*, 9 September 1902: 552)

So it did not take long for the two houses to confront each other over a problem that at least some authors of the Constitution knew they had left embedded in it.[15] Much the same sequence of events took place in 1908, when the Senate requested 238 amendments to another customs tariff bill. Once more the House chose not to engage in a constitutional dispute, but instead stated that it was considering the Senate amendments without prejudice. The Senate responded with its assertion that the House simply was acting in recognition of the Senate's constitutional powers.

By 1933, when the Parliament undertook a major tariff revision, the two houses evidently had reached an uncomfortable but mutually-understood *modus vivendi* on this matter.[16] Souter (1988: 294–295)

---

15 Nor did it take long to demonstrate the limitations of sec. 57 (discussed in the next chapter) and the joint sittings for which it provides. With the new Commonwealth's revenue depending on prompt enactment of tariff legislation, going through all the time-consuming stages that must precede a joint sitting, including a double dissolution and a new election, was not a realistic option.

16 The other side of the sec. 53 coin are the protections in sec. 55 of the Constitution that are designed to protect the Senate against the House abusing its constitutional authority to pass certain bills that the Senate cannot amend. In 1943, the Senate successfully resisted what Souter (1988: 352–353) identifies as the first alleged instance of 'tacking'. The House had included in an income tax bill a provision establishing a National Welfare Fund. The Senate requested that the House omit the provision, having concluded that including it constituted tacking in violation of sec. 55, which states that 'Laws imposing taxation shall deal only with the imposition of taxation, and any provision therein dealing with any other matter shall be of no effect.' The House disagreed but the Senate was adamant, so the House ultimately deleted the provision while insisting that, in doing so, it was not accepting the Senate's interpretation of sec. 55. The Senate, of course, responded by reiterating

reports that the Senate requested amendments to 47 of the 1800 tariff items in the bill. The House agreed to make 33 of the amendments, made seven others with modifications, and rejected the remaining seven of the requested amendments. When the Senate pressed three of the seven amendments—affecting rabbit traps, dates, and spray pumps—'the House of Representatives responded in accordance with the unwritten rules of the game.'

> After resolving that public interest demanded early enactment of the tariff, and carefully refraining 'from the determination of its constitutional rights or obligations', the House agreed to the pressed requests, with modifications. On receipt of this message the Senate resolved that the House's dealing with its reiterated requests was 'in compliance with the undoubted constitutional position and rights of the Senate', and agreed to the Bill as amended.

The issue persists to the present, and the current state of play is aptly summarized in *House of Representatives Practice* (2001: 434): 'There has been a difference of opinion as to the constitutionality of the action of the Senate in pressing requests. However, the House, while passing a preliminary resolution refraining from determining its constitutional rights or obligations, has on most occasions taken the Senate's message into consideration.'[17] However the House is anxious to reject any implication (drawn by the Senate, for example) that it has, by usage, accepted the Senate's right to press requests. Instead, *House of Representatives Practice* (2001: 436) quotes approvingly the observation that 'a government has often been prepared to forfeit constitutional niceties for the sake of getting its legislation made,' especially when the alternatives are to lose the bill or use it to begin satisfying the requirements for a double dissolution. In the 1933 case, one Member concluded 'that the three items rabbit traps, spray pumps, and dates, however important they may be, hardly justify a double dissolution.'

---

that its action had been 'in compliance with the undoubted constitutional position and rights of the Senate.'

17 On the House position generally, see *House of Representatives Practice* 2001: 433–438. The ritual in which the House engages brings to mind the similar practical arrangement that the US House of Representatives and Senate have made with regard to the House's insistence that the Constitution requires all appropriations bills to originate in the House. The Senate never has accepted this interpretation of the 'Origination Clause' which states that 'All bills for raising revenue shall originate in the House of Representatives' (Art. I, sec. 7, cl. 1). Nonetheless, the Senate has acquiesced in practice, recognizing the House's determination to insist on its position.

House of Representatives Practice responds to a summary of the arguments advanced in *Odgers' Australian Senate Practice* with a quotation from Quick and Garran's seminal *The Annotated Constitution* to the effect that pressed requests have no constitutional standing. 'A House which can make an amendment can insist on the amendment which it has made; but a House which can only "request" the other House to make amendments cannot insist upon anything.' In their view, if the House decides not to make an amendment the Senate has requested, 'the Senate must take the full responsibility of accepting or rejecting the bill as it stands.' (Quick and Garran 1901: 672)

One of the other arguments offered in support of Quick and Garran's position is that 'the consequence of the opposite view [is] that the distinction between the power to request and the power to amend [is] merely formal.' (*House of Representatives Practice* 2001: 435)[18] As we have seen, that is precisely the view that the Senate has taken. The discussion of this subject in *Odgers' Australian Senate Practice* (2001: 327) concludes that:

> Section 53 being ... a procedural section, prescribing procedural rules for the Houses to observe, it is for the Houses, in their transactions with each other, to interpret those rules by application. It is suggested that, in their dealings with Senate requests over the years, the Houses have supplied the required interpretation so far as the pressing of requests is concerned, and that interpretation is that requests may be pressed.

This is precisely the argument of agreement by usage that the House has been at pains to refute. Elsewhere, in insisting on the 'Effective equality of the Senate and the House in the making of laws and the performance of all other parliamentary responsibilities', *Odgers' Australian Senate Practice* (2001: 3–4) notes simply that 'The only qualification is that certain types of financial legislation must originate in the House of Representatives, and in some cases the Senate is limited to suggesting *and, if necessary, insisting on* amendments.' (emphasis added)

---

18 Similarly: 'A different opinion, expressed in the Senate by Sir Josiah Symon, that the Constitution gave the Senate substantially the power to amend, though in the form of a request meant that the Constitution, in declaring that the Senate might not amend but might request amendments, was contradicting itself, cancelling in the fourth paragraph of section 53 what it had enacted in the second. In respect of this view the opinion tabled in the House stated that the Constitution did intend a substantial difference; it was thought clear that the Constitution did not intend to stultify itself by giving back in one clause what it had taken away in another.' (*House of Representatives Practice* 2001: 435)

In effect, the two houses have agreed to disagree.[19] Should the House ever decide to stand and fight on this ground, I expect that the ensuing battle would be bloody indeed.

Double dissolutions and joint sittings

When the Commonwealth Constitution was being designed, it required little imagination to anticipate that Parliament could encounter legislative deadlocks. At the 1897 Sydney Convention, Deakin stressed the powers of the Senate and the prospects for deadlock:

> [W]e must take into account the different quality of these two houses, and the enormously greater power of resistance we are giving to the second chamber in this federal constitution, far greater than any second chamber possesses in our several colonies. It is on the broadest franchise. Representing the people in every sense of the term, that chamber will be a far more formidable opponent of the chamber of representatives than any [colonial or state] legislative council could possibly be. Under this constitution we are creating on the one side a senate and on the other side a house of representatives with its executive—and the executive is the important element in most of these considerations. We are creating in these two chambers, under our form of government, what you may term an irresistible force on the one side, and what may prove to be an immovable object on the other side, and the problem of what might happen if these two were brought into contact. (*Convention Debates*,[20] 15 September 1897: 582)

The Constitution's provisions

To resolve such problems, the Constitution's authors provided, as a last resort, an elaborate procedure that involves a 'double dissolution' of both houses of Parliament under sec. 57, which states in part that:

> If the House of Representatives passes any proposed law, and the Senate rejects or fails to pass it, or passes it with amendments to which the House of Representatives will not agree, and if after an interval of three months

---

19 To the end of 2002, the Senate had requested amendments on 163 occasions and pressed requests 21 times (*Odgers' Australian Senate Practice* 2001, and December 2002 supplement)

20 *Convention Debates* refers to the records of the debates of the Australian Constitutional Conventions of 1891 and 1897–98. The debates of the National Australasian Convention, held in Sydney in 1891, were published in one volume in 1891; and four volumes of the debates of the Australasian Federal Convention, held in three sessions in Adelaide, Sydney and Melbourne during 1897 and 1898, were published 1897–98. These debates are available online at www.aph.gov.au/ Senate/pubs/records.htm

the House of Representatives, in the same or the next session, again passes the proposed law with or without any amendments which have been made, suggested, or agreed to by the Senate, and the Senate rejects or fails to pass it, or passes it with amendments to which the House of Representatives will not agree, the Governor-General may dissolve the Senate and the House of Representatives simultaneously. But such dissolution shall not take place within six months before the date of the expiry of the House of Representatives by effluxion of time [i.e., within six months of the end of the three-year term for which Representatives are elected].

Then, if after the House and Senate elections following a double dissolution, the House passes the bill for a third time and the two houses still are unable to reach agreement on it, the Governor-General may convene a joint sitting of the two houses, also under provisions of sec. 57:

> If after such dissolution the House of Representatives again passes the proposed law, with or without any amendments which have been made, suggested, or agreed to by the Senate, and the Senate rejects or fails to pass it, or passes it with amendments to which the House of Representatives will not agree, the Governor-General may convene a joint sitting of the members of the Senate and of the House of Representatives.
>
> The members present at the joint sitting may deliberate and shall vote together upon the proposed law as last proposed by the House of Representatives, and upon amendments, if any, which have been made therein by one House and not agreed to by the other, and any such amendments which are affirmed by an absolute majority of the total number of the members of the Senate and House of Representatives shall be taken to have been carried, and if the proposed law, with the amendments, if any, so carried is affirmed by an absolute majority of the total number of the members of the Senate and House of Representatives, it shall be taken to have been duly passed by Houses of the Parliament, and shall be presented to the Governor-General for the Queen's assent.

Thus, before Parliament can decide the ultimate fate of a bill at a joint sitting, first the two houses must reach a deadlock over it. This deadlock can arise if the Senate defeats a House-passed bill, or if the Senate fails to vote on passing it, or if the Senate passes the bill after making amendments to it (or requesting amendments in the case of a bill that the Senate is barred from amending) that are unacceptable to the House. Then, after an interval of at least three months following the point at which deadlock was reached, and whether during the same or the subsequent session of Parliament, the same process must be repeated with the same result.[21] The House again must pass the same

---

21   The three-month interval is measured not from the date on which the House first passes the bill, but from the date on which deadlock is reached. According to the

proposal, with or without any amendments that the Senate had made or requested or to which the House had agreed before the first deadlock was reached; and the Senate again must defeat the proposal, fail to vote on passing it, or insist on amendments that the House refuses to accept.

Only after the House and Senate have reached a second deadlock over the same proposal may the Governor-General, acting at the request of the government, dissolve both houses simultaneously (a double dissolution), leading to new elections for all seats in both the House and the Senate.[22] After the new Parliament convenes following those elections, and if the same deadlock then occurs for a third time, the Governor-General may convene the two houses in a joint sitting. At this joint sitting, there are to be votes on the bill and on any amendments that one house has approved and the other has not. An absolute majority of the membership of both houses is required to approve any amendment and to pass the bill, if and as amended.[23]

It bears emphasizing that a joint sitting can consider only a bill that satisfies the requirements of sec. 57 and only those amendments to it that in the US Congress would be called 'amendments in disagreement'—i.e., amendments that one house has proposed and that the other house has taken action on that constitutes an unwillingness to

High Court in *Victoria v Commonwealth* (1975 7 ALR 1, quoted in *Odgers' Australian Senate Practice* 2001: 81), the time interval is 'measured not from the first passage of a proposed law by the House of Representatives, but from the Senate's rejection or failure to pass it. This interpretation follows both from the language of section 57 and its purpose which is to provide time for the reconciliation of the differences between the Houses; the time therefore does not begin to run until the deadlock occurs.' While this certainly is a reasonable interpretation, it does require a determination to be made as to exactly when the deadlock has occurred, which in turn can depend on when the Senate can be said to have failed to pass the bill in question or on when a stalemate has been reached over the disposition of the Senate's amendments to the bill. If, for instance, the Senate has passed a bill with amendments, the government and its majority in the House of Representatives can control the time at which the House considers those amendments and, therefore, the time at which it can be said that the Senate had passed the bill with amendments that were unacceptable to the House. As the events leading to the double dissolution in 1951 revealed, such determinations may not be as obvious as they might seem at first blush.

22 However, sec. 57 bars a double dissolution from taking place within six months of the end of the three-year elected term of the House.

23 Moore (1910: 156–157) attributes the use of joint sittings to 'the Norwegian system, according to which the two Chambers (or rather the two parts into which the House is divided) meet as one for the purpose of composing their differences.' He also notes that sec. 15 of the Commonwealth Constitution provides for joint sittings of state parliaments to elect Senators to fill casual vacancies and that, in the United States at that time, joint sittings were used 'by the State Legislatures in case the Chambers have in separate sittings chosen different persons as Senators.'

agree to them. Neither house can propose additional amendments at the joint sitting, nor may any compromises be proposed. The joint sitting may only choose among alternatives that already had been defined and considered by the two houses acting separately.[24]

Clearly, then, this procedure cannot be invoked quickly, and those who designed it cannot have expected that it would be used frequently.[25] In devising it, the Constitution's authors could not look for inspiration to either America's written constitutions or Britain's constitutional conventions. The US Constitution requires bicameral differences to be resolved if a law is to be enacted, but it is silent on the procedures for doing so. And when the Australian Constitution was written, the British Parliament had no formal procedures for resolving the legislative deadlocks that could occur before passage of the *Parliament Act 1911*.

---

24 On the day before the joint sitting in 1974 (discussed in the context of the crisis of that and the following year), the High Court held that the joint sitting could consider more than one bill. It also held that the Governor-General's proclamation could not, and did not, control what actions the joint sitting might take. However, that ruling did not mean that the joint sitting could do whatever it wished. Instead, the Court meant that the agenda of the joint sitting was controlled by the express terms of sec. 57 of the Constitution, and so could not be expanded or contracted by the Governor-General, by either or both houses acting separately, or by the members of Parliament meeting in the joint sitting. At the joint sitting, the Speaker of the House (who had been elected Chairman) also ruled, and his ruling was upheld on appeal, that it was not in order for the joint sitting to consider (even debate) any matter other than those for which the joint sitting had been convened (*House of Representatives Practice* 2001: 466).

25 If the requirements of sec. 57 are satisfied, joint sittings can be convened to resolve differences over legislation, but not over proposed constitutional amendments. Sec. 128 of the Constitution requires a proposed amendment to be approved by an absolute majority in each house; then it is submitted to a national referendum. However, sec. 128 continues:

> if either House passes any such proposed law by an absolute majority, and the other House rejects or fails to pass it, or passes it with any amendment to which the first-mentioned House will not agree, and if after an interval of three months the first-mentioned House in the same or the next session again passes the proposed law by an absolute majority with or without any amendment which has been made or agreed to by the other House, and such other House rejects or fails to pass it or passes it with any amendment to which the first-mentioned House will not agree, the Governor-General may submit the proposed law as last proposed by the first-mentioned House, and either with or without any amendments subsequently agreed to by both Houses, to the electors in each State and Territory qualified to vote for the election of the House of Representatives.

Moore (1910: 157) comments that 'the provisions of sec. 128 for avoiding the obstacle of disagreement between the Houses are less cumbrous than those applicable to ordinary legislation. The reason is that the alteration of the Constitution is treated as pre-eminently a matter to be determined by direct vote of the electors.'

Odgers' Australian Senate Practice (2001: 80) characterizes sec. 57 as 'a concession of federalism to democracy':

> Provided that the whole process set out in section 57 is followed, the normal double majority for the passage of laws may be dispensed with, only for the legislation causing the deadlock, and laws may be passed in accordance with the wishes of the majority of the representatives of the people as a whole, if that majority is not too narrow. In cases of significant disagreement, democratic representation prevails over the geographically distributed representation of the people provided by the Senate.

If and when push finally comes to shove, the Constitution favours the ultimate legislative supremacy of the House of Representatives. In light of the 'nexus' requirement of sec. 24 that 'the number of [Representatives] shall be, as nearly as practicable, twice the number of senators,' the procedure for voting in joint sittings all but ensures that the House and, therefore, the government eventually can prevail in a legislative dispute with the Senate if each house is united in support of its position.[26] In a House of Representatives document intended to explain Parliament to the Australian public, double dissolutions are characterized as an opportunity for the voters to break the deadlock by changing the composition of the Senate to more closely conform with that of the House. 'In effect, the legislation may be put to the people, presenting the electorate with the opportunity to change the composition of the Senate following a full Senate election.' It is also noted, however, that 'There is also, of course, the possibility of a change in the composition of the House—the deadlock may be broken in either direction.'[27]

In practice, however, any differences between the two houses that might emerge from the difference in their bases of representation or in their modes of election—both of which are discussed in the next chapter—have been overwhelmed by the strength of party discipline in both houses. The possibility of sec. 57 coming into play now depends almost entirely on whether the government enjoys majority control of the Senate. Party discipline now trumps any sense of obligation to support the position of one's chamber. What matters is the voting

---

26 Note that sec. 57 concerns double dissolutions to resolve legislative differences on bills that originated in the House. It does not apply to bills originating in the Senate. So the Constitution seems to assume that legislation (or at least important legislation) will originate in the House, suggesting a subordinate or reactive legislative role for the Senate. See Moore (1910: 155)

27 'Double Dissolution', House of Representatives *Infosheet* No. 18, April 2002, p. 2 [www.aph.gov.au/house/info/factsht/fs18.htm].

strength of government and non-government forces in the two houses combined.

Four double dissolutions

In more than a century, there have been only six double dissolutions: in 1914, 1951, 1974, 1975, 1983, and 1987—but only one joint sitting to consider legislation—in 1974.[28] The events of 1974 and 1975 merit extended discussion in a later chapter. A summary of the causes and consequences of the other four double dissolutions will bring the double dissolution procedures to life and highlight some of the questions that have arisen in interpreting and implementing sec. 57.

1914

As a result of the 1913 elections (for the entire House and half the Senate), the Liberal Government of Prime Minister Joseph Cook had a one-vote majority in the House but held only 7 of 36 seats in the Senate. The government found this situation untenable; new elections to both houses either would strengthen its position or put it out of its political misery.

To that end, according to Souter, the Government Preference Prohibition Bill

> was introduced in October [1913] for the specific purpose of provoking a disagreement between the houses and in due course providing constitutional grounds for a dissolution of them both ... . By no stretch of the imagination was this [bill] central to the Cook Government's programme; but it was certain to be rejected by the Senate a second time when re-submitted after an interval of three months. That would give [Prime Minister] Cook his grounds for going to the Governor-General. (Souter 1988: 133)

That the procedural requirements of sec. 57 were met was not in question. However, there was a dispute as to whether the bill giving rise to the deadlock justified a double dissolution. Should the Governor-General take into account the significance of the legislation in question in passing on the government's request for a double dissolution? (Sawer 1956: 115–117, 121–124; Zines 1977: 218–222)

---

28 Joint sittings also were held, in 1981 and 1988, to fill vacant Senate seats for the Australian Capital Territory (ACT) before it was granted self-government in 1989. Additional joint sittings for such purposes are unlikely, the electoral law now providing for a joint sitting only to fill a Senate vacancy for a territory other than the ACT or the Northern Territory, in the unlikely event that some other territory receives representation in the Senate. See *House of Representatives Practice* 2001: 851, footnote

In his letter to the Governor-General requesting the double dissolution, the Prime Minister explained that the dearth of Liberal Senators 'has for two successive sessions made the parliamentary machine unworkable' (quoted in *House of Representatives Practice* 2001: 448), implying that the situation would not change until new elections took place. However, the Prime Minister did not contend that the fate of the Commonwealth hung on the fate of the bill in question. In fact, it was the uncontested insignificance of the bill that led the Senate to advise against granting the double dissolution.

The Senate expressed its position in an Address to the Governor-General, arguing in part that:

> The Constitution deliberately created a House in which the States as such may be represented, and clothed this House with co-ordinate powers (save in the origination of Money Bills) with the Lower Chamber of the Legislature. These powers were given to the Senate in order that they might be used; but if a Senate may not reject or even amend any bill because a Government chooses to call it a 'test' bill, although such bill contains no vital principle or gives effect to no reform, the powers of the Senate are reduced to a nullity. We submit that no constitutional sanction can be found for the view, which is repugnant to one of the fundamental bases of the Constitution, viz., a Legislature of two Houses, clothed with equal powers, one representing the people as such, the other representing the States.
>
> And we respectfully submit that the dissolution of the Senate ought not to follow upon a mere legitimate exercise of its functions under the Constitution, but only upon such action as makes responsible government impossible, *e.g.* the rejection of a measure embodying a principle of vital importance necessary in the public interest, creating an actual legislative dead-lock and preventing legislation upon which the Ministry was returned to power. (*Journals of the Senate*, 17 June 1914: 3)

The Chief Justice, Sir Samuel Griffith, took essentially the same position in his advice to the Governor-General, in which he argued that the power that sec. 57 gives to the Governor-General should be regarded as 'an extraordinary power':

> to be exercised only in cases in which the Governor-General is personally satisfied, after independent consideration of the case, either that the proposed law as to which the Houses have differed in opinion is one of such public importance that it should be referred to the electors of the Commonwealth for immediate decision by means of a complete renewal of both Houses, or that there exists such a state of practical deadlock in legislation as can only be ended in that way. (quoted in *Odgers' Australian Senate Practice* 2001: 88–89)

Both the Senate and the Chief Justice could find support for their position in an argument that had been made to those engaged in writing the Constitution by the Leader of the Convention, Edmund Barton:

> '[D]eadlock' is not a term which is strictly applicable to any case except that in which the constitutional machine is prevented from properly working. I am in very grave doubt whether the term can be strictly applied to any case except a stoppage of the legislative machinery arising out of conflict upon the finances of the country. ... a stoppage which arises on any matter of ordinary legislation, because the two houses cannot come to an agreement at first, is not a thing which is properly designated by the term 'deadlock', because the working of the constitution goes on—the constitutional machine proceeds notwithstanding a disagreement. ... it is only when the fuel of the machine of government is withheld that the machine comes to a stop and that fuel is money. (*Convention Debates*, 15 September 1897: 620)

Notwithstanding such arguments, the Governor-General granted the double dissolution. In doing so, he made no reference to the legislation at issue or to the prospects for future legislation. Evidently he thought it unnecessary or inadvisable either to weigh those factors or to acknowledge what part, if any, they played in his decision. Furthermore, he did not address how much discretion a Governor-General should exercise in deciding whether or not to grant a requested double dissolution. In contrast to the opinion of the Chief Justice, quoted above, that the Governor-General should give his 'independent consideration' to the importance of the bill or the parliamentary situation more generally, the Prime Minister had asserted that the Governor-General's discretion under sec. 57 'can only be exercised by him in accordance with the advice of his Ministers representing a majority in the House of Representatives' (quoted in *House of Representatives Practice* 2001: 448), implying that it also would be inappropriate for the Governor-General to declare a double dissolution unless advised to do so.

The Cook Government was defeated at the ensuing elections, so the bill died and no joint sitting took place. However, the precedent had been established 'that sufficient cause for double dissolution could be deliberately engineered.' (Souter 1988: 137) Subsequent prime ministers have stressed the significance of the legislation giving rise to their requests for double dissolutions and, as Cook had, the likelihood that similar problems would arise again if the composition of the Parliament remained unchanged. On occasion, governors-general have referred to such considerations in announcing double dissolutions. However, no Governor-General has refused to grant a double dissolution that the government of the day has requested if the requirements of sec. 57 have been satisfied.

1951

It was not until 37 years later that the next double dissolution occurred. When it did, it was under different political circumstances and it raised a different issue about the application of sec. 57 (Whitington 1969: 152–159).

In 1950, the Menzies Government, comprising a coalition of the Liberal and Country parties, held a 74–48 majority in the House (with one Independent) but was in the minority, 26–34, in the Senate. In May of that year, the House passed the Commonwealth Bank Bill. In June, the Senate passed it with amendments, but the House disagreed with the Senate amendments and asked the Senate to reconsider them. Instead of withdrawing its amendments, the Senate insisted on them. In response, the House insisted on its disagreement to the amendments and the Senate then reaffirmed its insistence on them. At that point, the House failed to take further action. Instead, and a week before the House received a message of the Senate's final action, an identical bill was introduced in the House. The House passed this second bill on the same day in October on which it received the Senate's message of its final action on the first bill. In the Senate, the second bill was referred to a select committee with instructions to report in four weeks. Several days later (and well before the four-week period expired), the Prime Minister requested a double dissolution, which the Governor-General proceeded to grant. (For the chronology of events, see *Odgers' Australian Senate Practice* 2001: 90–94, and *House of Representatives Practice* 2001: 449–450.)

In Menzies' advice to the Governor-General, the Prime Minister addressed the basis for his request and justified the need for a double dissolution less in terms of the specific bill at issue than in terms of the more general situation in Parliament:

> ... the Government, with a new mandate from the people, has been in major affairs, constantly delayed and frustrated by the facts that the two Houses are of opposite political complexions and that in consequence the legislative machine, except in respect of relatively minor matters, has been materially slowed down and rendered extremely uncertain its operation.
>
> Under these circumstances, if the only condition upon which a Double Dissolution could be granted was, broadly expressed, that a serious conflict between the two Houses ought to be ended by the votes of the electors, then I would have no doubt whatever that as Prime Minister I should be more than justified in asking you to take the necessary steps to have determined by those electors a disagreement which tends so strongly against the giving of prompt expression to the public will. (quoted in Nethercote 1999: 12)

To appreciate the reason for Menzies' argument, it helps to understand that, as we shall discuss in the next chapter, these events occurred during the first Parliament after enactment in 1948 of the law that provided for Senators to be elected thereafter by proportional representation. One reason that the Labor Government of the day had proposed the change was to ensure that it would retain a majority in the Senate if, as expected, it lost control of the House, as it did, to Menzies and the Coalition. In 1950, consequently, the Coalition Government was, for one of the very few times in the Federation's first half-century, faced with a Senate that it did not control. Securing a double dissolution, therefore, gave Menzies and his Government the opportunity to gain control of the Senate while retaining control of the House of Representatives. With these same possibilities in mind, the Australian Labor Party (ALP), which did control the Senate, had to think twice before creating the grounds for a double dissolution and an election that might leave it in the minority in both houses.

> Although the ALP platform called for abolition of the Senate, the tactical value of the upper house was undeniable at times like the present. But careful judgment was required as to how that advantage could be used against the Government without provoking a double dissolution election at which Labor was likely to be savaged again. Some unpalatable measures would therefore be allowed through the Senate ... (Souter 1988: 411)

The Commonwealth Bank Bill, however, was not allowed through, and Labor's worst fears were realized. At the ensuing election, the Liberals were returned with majorities in both houses and the ALP was banished to the political wilderness. With respect to the banking bill, no third deadlock occurred, no joint sitting was necessary, and a different bill on the same subject subsequently became law.

In connection with these events, the question arose as to whether the Senate's decision to refer the second bill to a select committee constituted a 'failure to pass' it within the meaning of sec. 57. As the Solicitor-General argued at the time (quoted in *House of Representatives Practice* 2001: 451–452), 'The expression "fails to pass" is clearly not the same as the neutral expression "does not pass", which would perhaps imply mere lapse of time.' So 'Perhaps the principle involved can be expressed by saying that the adoption of Parliamentary procedures for the purpose of avoiding the formal registering of the Senate's clear disagreement with a Bill may constitute a 'failure to pass' within the meaning of the section.' That was precisely the Prime Minister's contention. Menzies argued that the Senate had demonstrated sufficiently its intent to procrastinate so that its inaction constituted conclusive evidence of its determination not to pass the bill:

[T]here is clear evidence that the design and intention of the Senate in relation to this Bill has been to seek every opportunity for delay, upon the principle that protracted postponement may be in some political circumstances almost as efficacious, though not so dangerous, as straight-out rejection. Since failure to pass is, in section 57, distinguished from rejection or unacceptable amendment, it must refer, among other things, to such a delay in passing the Bill or such a delaying intention as would amount to an expression of unwillingness to pass it. (quoted in *House of Representatives Practice* 2001: 450)

When the Senate rejects a bill, its 'failure to pass' it is obvious. But when the Senate either takes no action or takes some other action, such as referring a bill to a select committee, it becomes more a matter of judgment as to whether the 'failure to pass' requirement has been met. In this case, the Senate averred that referring the bill to a committee did not imply an unwillingness to consider the bill further, or even to pass it. However, the Governor-General granted the double dissolution, as the government had requested. So the government's arguments prevailed in practice, and the High Court did not have occasion to rule on their merits.

1983

There were other bills on which the two houses had disagreed in 1950–1951, but the government did not seek to have any of the others satisfy the requirements of sec. 57 so that they could have been eligible for consideration if there had been a joint sitting following the 1951 double dissolution and elections. In 1983, Parliament confronted, albeit in a different form, the issues that had arisen in connection with the 1914 and 1951 double dissolutions, as well as additional questions surrounding a double dissolution that involved multiple bills.

The 1980 elections had produced a House in which the Fraser Liberal-National Party coalition had an 82–66 majority, but was narrowly in the minority in the Senate. As a result of legislative actions and inactions beginning in August 1981, the government requested a double dissolution in February 1983. In so doing, the government asserted that a total of 13 bills had completed the procedural stages laid out in sec. 57 and so might become eligible for consideration at a joint sitting if one were to take place after the intervening election (*House of Representatives Practice* 2001: 461–463).

Of particular interest were nine of the bills that were Sales Tax Amendment bills that the Senate could not amend. Instead, the Senate had requested amendments that the House had resolved not to make. 'The Senate considered the House's position and declined to pass a resolution "that the requests be not pressed", the effect of which was to press the requests' (*Odgers' Australian Senate Practice* 2001: 109), an action that, the government argued, constituted a 'failure to pass'.

In dissolving both houses, the Governor-General took note of the Prime Minister's assertions regarding the importance of the bills in question and the implications of the deadlocks for the ability of the sitting Parliament to function effectively in the future. However, the Governor-General was unwilling to grant the double dissolution when the government first requested it, asking instead for additional evidence that Parliament had in fact become 'unworkable' and that there was no effective alternative to the double dissolution. The government was able to satisfy the Governor-General on this score. However, the Governor-General's request and the government's compliance with it strengthened the contention that the Governor-General can and even should make an independent determination as to whether requests for double dissolutions should be granted.

For Uhr, there were cautionary lessons to be drawn from this incident by both the government and Opposition. It implied that there were limits on the ability of an Opposition-controlled Senate to force a double dissolution and new elections,[29] though no one in Canberra seems anxious to test those limits after having experienced the events of 1975, which we will review in Chapter 4. What may prove more important in practice is a message to governments not to assume that they can artificially create the basis for a double dissolution by passing one or more non-money bills that they know the Senate will not accept, and do so primarily for the purpose of being able to achieve a double dissolution at a subsequent time of the government's choosing—that is, whenever obstruction or opposition in the Senate becomes too inconvenient. However, the issue has yet to arise again (it was not an issue in 1987), so we cannot know whether a future Governor-General will be prepared to refuse a government's request for a double dissolution when there is no alternate government available to replace it.

The elections replaced Fraser's Liberal-National Government with an ALP majority of 75–50 in the House and a plurality of 30–28 over the Coalition in the Senate, with five Senate seats in other hands. Consequently, the new government did not pursue passage of the bills in question and no joint sitting was convened.

---

29 'The circle had come as complete as it ever would, Fraser's appointee [as Governor-General] now put the prime minister and his followers on public notice that the constitution provided an avenue for requests, not demands, for double dissolutions.' (Uhr 1992: 94–95)

Two other issues arose in connection with this double dissolution, issues on which the two houses evidently do not see eye-to-eye to this day. One was what *Odgers' Australian Senate Practice* (2001: 110), more than a quarter-century later, calls the 'stockpiling' of bills in anticipation of a double dissolution so that they might be salvaged by passage in a joint sitting. The author editorializes that, 'At least in circumstances where there is no withholding of supply by the Senate, such a use of stockpiled bills, perhaps stale and unrelated to a particular situation, does not appear to be within the intent of section 57 of the Constitution.' This position is not surprising since this practice so obviously works to the advantage of the government and the House it controls, and to the corresponding disadvantage of the Senate.

The second issue was whether the two houses had reached the required impasse on the sales tax bills—the House having decided not to make the requested Senate amendments and the Senate having decided not to not press them. The House did not address this question directly; instead, it took the position that the Senate should not have pressed its requests in the first place. When the House received the message relating that the Senate had done so:

> Mr. Speaker made a statement on the constitutional issues involved, noting that the right of the Senate to repeat and thereby press or insist on a request for an amendment had never been accepted by the House. The House then agreed to a resolution inter alia endorsing the statement of the Speaker in relation to the constitutional questions raised by the Senate message and declining to consider the message in so far as it purported to press amendments contained in the earlier message. (*House of Representatives Practice* 2001: 461)

The Senate's authoritative treatise on its procedures emphasizes instead that 'the initial parliamentary consideration of these bills ended in the House, not the Senate,' and argues that 'The fault lay with the House in deliberately and wrongly breaking off communication with the Senate and shelving the bills.' (*Odgers' Australian Senate Practice* 2001: 111)

Neither issue was adjudicated because the bills died with the defeat of the Fraser Government at the 1983 elections. Should either issue arise again, the differing positions of the two houses, which seem to have persisted for so long, might well be argued again.

1987

Four years later, there was no doubt that the House had twice passed the Hawke Government's Australia Card Bill 1986 and that the Senate had twice rejected it by refusing second reading (Sugita 1997: 163-166). The elections that followed the double dissolution left the political complexion of Parliament essentially unchanged: the government was in a solid majority in the House and in a solid minority in the Senate. The government did have enough votes to prevail in a joint sitting. In preparation for a joint sitting to pass the bill, therefore, the House passed it for a third time.

During Senate debate, however, a convincing argument was made that implementation of the bill, if enacted, would require regulations that the Senate, acting unilaterally, without the concurrence of the House, could vote to disallow. Furthermore, an equally compelling argument was made that the Senate would do just that, given the non-government majority in the Senate. At the government's instigation, therefore, the Senate eventually took action on the bill that surely constituted 'failure to pass'. But then, instead of requesting a joint sitting, the government let the bill die. It knew that it could anticipate victory in a joint sitting, but that its victory would be fruitless because of the likelihood (or virtual certainty) that the Senate would veto the necessary implementing regulations. Also, it was too late to amend the bill in a way that would have circumvented this problem because sec. 57 permits a joint sitting to vote only on the bill and any amendments that one house or the other already has passed (and the other has not accepted).

Implications and interpretations

As we shall discover in Chapter 5, the Constitution's authors laboured long and hard to decide whether to include provisions to resolve legislative deadlocks and, if so, how to design those provisions. Yet there was only one double dissolution in the first half-century of Federation, and a total of only six in a century. Why?

Double dissolutions rarely have been necessary because governments almost always have had enough votes in the Senate to see their legislation enacted. As we shall see in the next chapter, governments usually had majorities in the Senate from the formation of the party system until the mid-1950s. Even when governments have faced Opposition majorities or, in recent decades, non-government majorities, non-government Senators have been reluctant to press their legislative powers out of a combination of respect for the principles of responsible government as well as a desire to avoid having to face the electorate before the natural expiration of their six-year terms. Furthermore, governments have had at least two reasons for preferring to reach compromises with the Senate rather than remaining adamant and resorting to double dissolutions: first, a recognition that Senate amendments often have improved government legislation, and have even been made by the Senate at the government's initiative or with its support or acquiescence; and second, a calculation that compromise with the Senate is preferable to the risk of a new election at which its own majority in the House would be at risk.[30]

Of the four double dissolutions we have just reviewed, none led to a joint sitting and none led to enactment of the specific bill in question. In 1914 and 1983, the elections brought the defeat of the sitting government and, therefore, the demise of the legislation at issue. Governments must exercise caution in invoking sec. 57; double dissolutions and the elections that follow involve risks as well as potential rewards. In 1987, the Hawke Government, which was returned to office, did not pursue the bill that led to the double dissolution when it concluded that doing so ultimately would prove futile. In 1951, the Menzies Government, which also remained in office, dropped the specific bill in favour of other legislation on the same subject (though if the government had been determined to enact the same bill that gave rise to the double dissolution, presumably it could have done so after having won control of the Senate).

As we have seen, these four double dissolutions triggered several disagreements about how sec. 57 is to be interpreted and applied. One issue concerns what constitutes the Senate's failure to pass a bill, which is an essential ingredient of deadlock. In 1951, it was established that the Senate did not have to defeat a bill in order for that bill to qualify under sec. 57. But uncertainty remains about what other Senate actions (such as referring a bill to a select committee) do satisfy the constitutional requirement. In Chapter 4, we will examine another double dissolution that occurred in 1974. In that context, the High Court ruled that the Senate had not 'failed to pass' a bill when, on the same day in December that it received the bill from the House, it voted to adjourn debate on it until the first sitting day in February of the following year. 'The Senate has a duty to properly consider all Bills and cannot be said to have failed to pass a Bill because it was not passed at the first available opportunity; a reasonable time must be allowed.' (*Victoria v Commonwealth* 1975 7 ALR 1, quoted in *Odgers' Australian Senate Practice* 2001: 82) But what constitutes 'a reasonable time'?

In the same decision, the Chief Justice commented that when the Senate has amended a House bill, the equivalent of what in congressional parlance is known as the 'stage of disagreement' should be reached before the 'failure to pass' threshold has been crossed. In

---

30   These and other aspects of the relations between the two houses are discussed in later chapters.

other words, it is not sufficient for the Senate to have amended a bill it has received from the House. The House should disagree to the amendments, and the Senate should insist on its amendments instead of receding from them at the House's request. Only then can it be said that deadlock has occurred; only then should the three-month clock begin to run. Although this issue was not before the High Court in the 1975 case, the Chief Justice's comments (quoted in *Odgers' Australian Senate Practice* 2001: 87) still are instructive:

> At the least, the attitude of the House of Representatives to the amendments must be decided and, I would think, must be made known before the interval of three months could begin. But the House of Representatives, having indicated in messages to the Senate why it will not agree, may of course find that the Senate concurs in its view so expressed, or there may be some modification thereafter of the amendments made by the Senate which in due course may be acceptable to the House of Representatives. It cannot be said, in my opinion, that there are amendments to which the House of Representatives *will* not agree until the processes which parliamentary procedure provides have been explored. (emphasis in original)

The same reasoning could be applied to determining when there is a second deadlock for the purpose of declaring a double dissolution and then a third deadlock for the purpose of convening a joint sitting. The question which the Chief Justice suggests but does not address is whether the processes to which he referred must be exhausted, or whether it suffices for each house to have made known its rejection of the position taken by the other with respect to the Senate's amendments. Unsettled questions remain.

We also have seen how governments can provoke double dissolutions, or control when they take place, for their political advantage. In requesting a double dissolution, the government of the day naturally emphasizes the importance of the bill or bills that have been blocked by the Senate's 'failure to pass' (*Odgers' Australian Senate Practice* 2001: 84). However, this is done for political, not constitutional, reasons. As noted above, the first double dissolution, in 1914, was the result of a deadlock that the government deliberately created over relatively minor legislation when, according to Prime Minister Cook, it had become 'abundantly clear' that the Opposition had taken control of the Senate. Cook explained that the government then 'decided that a further appeal to the people should be made by means of a double dissolution, and accordingly set about forcing through the two short measures for the purpose of fulfilling the terms of the Constitution.' (quoted in *Odgers' Australian Senate Practice* 2001: 83)

Although any government will deny that it would even think of requiring a new election solely for political reasons, the Senate still must recognize that its failure to pass *any* bill twice might be used by the government as grounds for calling new Senate and House elections. Moreover, once the requirements for a double dissolution have been satisfied, it falls to the government to decide if and when the Governor-General declares the double dissolution, which gives the government the flexibility to choose a politically advantageous moment. Sec. 57 states that the Governor-General 'may,' not 'must,' declare a double dissolution, leaving open the possibility that he or she could reject a government's advice to do so. In practice, however, I think it quite unlikely, in the foreseeable future and especially in light of the events of 1975, that a Governor-General would exercise this discretion and thereby enmesh himself in a highly charged partisan political controversy.

The use of double dissolutions for electoral advantage at propitious moments is linked to another application of sec. 57 that has inspired controversy: basing a double dissolution on the Senate's 'failure to pass' more than one bill (Zines 1977: 222–224). In 1983, as many as 13 bills were said to have satisfied the requirements of sec. 57. So if a government waits until each of two or more bills has twice reached deadlock, and then calls for a double dissolution, each of those bills then is eligible for consideration and passage at a subsequent joint sitting (assuming a third, post-election, deadlock also occurs) at which the position of the House and the government is likely to prevail. According to the High Court, 'a joint sitting of both Houses of Parliament convened under s. 57 may deliberate and vote upon any number of proposed laws in respect of which the requirements of s. 57 have been fulfilled.' One Justice put it nicely: 'One instance of a double rejection suffices but if there be more than one it merely means that there is a multiplicity of grounds for a double dissolution, rather than grounds for a multiplicity of double dissolutions.' (*Cormack v Cope* 1974 131 CLR 432, quoted in *Odgers' Australian Senate Practice* 2001: 83)[31]

The Senate has objected, especially because of the opportunities governments may be able to create that enable them to 'stockpile' bills in order to trigger a double dissolution, even if many months, or even

---

31 See Comans (1985) for a discussion of (1) whether two or more bills that qualify for consideration at a joint sitting must be considered at the same joint sitting, and (2) whether a bill provides grounds for a double dissolution, or could be considered at a joint sitting, if the law that the bill would amend was changed between the several times the bill was passed.

years, later. If the House can construct any bill that the Senate is certain to reject, and reject again, it gives the government the ability to secure a double dissolution, not just a dissolution of the House, whenever it chooses and regardless of the merits or importance of the bill.

More generally, the ways in which sec. 57 has been interpreted and applied has caused the Senate heartburn for several reasons. The criticisms and suggestions made on behalf of the Senate in *Odgers' Australian Senate Practice* 2001: 117 deserve quotation at length:

> Section 57 of the Constitution was intended to provide a mechanism for resolving deadlocks between the two Houses in relation to important legislation. By judicial interpretation, and by the misuse of the section by prime ministers over the years, it now appears that simultaneous dissolutions can be sought in respect of any number of bills; that there is no time limit on the seeking of simultaneous dissolutions after a bill has failed to pass for the second time; that a ministry can build up a 'storehouse' of bills for simultaneous dissolutions; that the ministry which requests simultaneous dissolutions does not have to be the same ministry whose legislative measures have been rejected or delayed by the Senate; that virtually any action by the Senate other than passage of a measure may be interpreted as a failure to pass the measure, at least for the purposes of the dissolutions; and that the ministry does not need to have any intention to proceed with the measures which are the subject of the supposed deadlock after the elections. By putting up a bill which is certain of rejection by the Senate on two occasions, a ministry, early in its life, can thus give itself the option of simultaneous dissolutions as an alternative to an early election of the House of Representatives. *This gives a government a de facto power of dissolution over the Senate which it was never intended to have, and greatly increases the possibility of executive domination of the Senate as well as of the House of Representatives.* (emphasis added)
>
> Consideration should be given to a reform of section 57 to restrict the power of a ministry to go to simultaneous dissolutions as a matter of political convenience. In order to restrict section 57 to its intended purpose, a limitation should be placed on the number of measures which may be the subject of a request for dissolutions, time limits should be placed upon such dissolutions in relation to the rejection of the measures in question, and a prime minister should be required to certify that the measures in question are essential for the ministry to carry on and that it is the intention of the ministry to proceed with the measures should it remain in office, and the Governor-General should be required to be satisfied independently as to those matters.

Although a double dissolution puts members of both houses—and, of course, the government—at risk, Uhr suggests that governments may calculate that the elections following a double dissolution may well be worth that risk. Referring to the 1951 double dissolution, he argues (1992: 100) that 'it introduced into the armoury of prime ministers the threat of a double dissolution in parliamentary circumstances judged as 'unworkable' by an ambitious executive.'[32]

So the House of Representatives can try to confront Senators with the choice between capitulation—approving government legislation that a majority of them may oppose—and double dissolution—facing the electorate well before the expiration of their six-year terms of office. There is a certain irony to this argument, as we shall see, because at the heart of the events of 1974 and 1975 were attempts by Senators to use their authority to 'fail to pass' government legislation in order to force Representatives to face the electorate before the expiration of the terms for which they had been elected. Before turning to those events, however, we first need to review the party and electoral systems that have done so much to shape the relations between the Parliament and the government and, within the Parliament, between the House of Representatives and the Senate.

---

32 There is another consideration that a government must take into account as it calculates whether it should request a double dissolution in the hope that the ensuing election will produce majorities for it in both houses of the Parliament. As we shall discover in the next chapter, when all of a state's Senate seats are contested at the same election, the quota of votes that a minor party or independent candidate needs to win one of those seats is much less than it is at a normal half-Senate election. So even if a government thinks that its popularity is high, it still must ask itself whether it is the minor parties that could be most likely to gain seats in the Senate and find themselves in a stronger position when the new Parliament convenes.

3

The electoral and party systems

The Commonwealth Constitution does not govern in detail how members of the House of Representatives and the Senate are to be elected, nor could it dictate the number and strength of Australia's national political parties and the dynamics of competition among them. The electoral and party systems have a profound impact on the political dynamics in Canberra, including the roles of the two houses of Parliament and the relations between them, so both are summarized here. Special attention is given to a development that has fundamentally affected the balance of power among the parties, the implementation of principles of responsible government, and the practical dynamics of politics in Parliament: the decision made in 1948 that thereafter Senators would be elected by proportional representation.

Electing Representatives and Senators

The procedures for electing Australian Representatives and Senators are considerably more complicated than the procedures for electing their American counterparts. US Representatives and Senators all are elected in essentially the same way—in what often is called the 'first-past-the-post' system, but which I prefer to call the constituency plurality system. Each voter casts one vote for the candidate whom he or she prefers to represent the voter's constituency, whether state or congressional district, and the candidate who receives the most votes is the winner. In Australia, by contrast, members of the Commonwealth Parliament are chosen by a combination of constituency majority and proportional representation (PR) systems, with the use of preferential voting (also known as the alternative vote) for elections to both houses. Also, voting has been compulsory since the general election of 1925.[33]

---

33 What actually is compulsory is that the voter go to his or her polling place and cast a ballot; there is no way the government can compel a voter to cast a valid ballot (called in Australia a formal vote).

As in the United States, seats in the Australian House of Representatives are allocated among the states according to their respective populations, and each state then is divided into as many districts (electoral divisions, in Australian parlance) as the number of Representatives allocated to it, so that each division elects a single Representative. The populations of divisions within each state are to be roughly equal, though each original state is guaranteed (by sec. 24 of the Constitution) a minimum of five seats in the House. (By law, each of the two territories is guaranteed at least one seat.) Representatives all are elected at the same time and for a maximum term of three years, though, as we have seen, the House may be dissolved earlier—at some time before its life otherwise would end, in the words of sec. 57, 'by effluxion of time'.[34]

Until 1918, elections to the House were conducted using the district plurality system.[35] In that year, Parliament decided to continue electing one Representative per district, but also decided to switch from plurality elections to majority elections with preferential voting. Under this system, which has been in place for House elections ever since, each voter marks his or her ballot by numbering all the candidates in order of preference—marking '1' for the voter's first choice, '2' for his or her second choice, and so on. If a candidate receives an absolute majority of all the first preference votes, that candidate is elected. If not, the votes received by the candidate with the fewest first preference votes are distributed among the other candidates according to the second preferences of that candidate's supporters. If this redistribution still does not produce a candidate with an absolute majority of votes, the second-least popular candidate is excluded and his or her votes are redistributed in similar fashion, and so on until one candidate does receive a majority of the votes.

The rationale for preferential voting is that it protects against the election of a candidate who receives a plurality, but not a majority, of the votes cast. If more than two candidates run for the same seat, it is quite possible that none of them will receive a majority; most voters

---

34 Only one House served its full three year term and then expired by effluxion of time, and that was in 1910.

35 Actually, the first parliamentary elections, held in 1901, were conducted under state laws, sec. 31 of the Constitution providing that, until Parliament provided otherwise, 'the laws in force in each State for the time being relating to elections for the more numerous House of the Parliament of the State shall, as nearly as practicable, apply to elections in the State of members of the House of Representatives.' Parliament did provide otherwise with enactment of the *Commonwealth Electoral Act 1902*, which was followed by the *Commonwealth Electoral Act 1918*.

will select someone other than the candidate who receives a plurality of the votes. A closely related effect of preferential voting is to encourage more than two candidates to run for the same seat—or to put it differently, for more than two parties to field candidates for the same seat. In plurality district elections, it is typically argued that anyone who contemplates voting for a third or minor party candidate is, in effect, throwing away his or her vote. If the candidate whom a voter truly prefers has no realistic chance of winning, so the argument goes, any voter who selects that candidate thereby gives up the opportunity to affect the choice between the two candidates who actually might win. Under a preferential voting system, a voter can vote for the candidate he or she truly prefers, and then mark his or her second preference for a candidate with a better prospect of winning—the political equivalent of having one's cake and eating it too. Precisely because of this logic, of course, preferential voting can have the effect of encouraging a multiplicity of candidates and so reducing the likelihood that any one of them will receive a majority of the first preference votes cast.[36]

Senators representing the states are elected for six year terms, with half to be elected every three years at what are known as half-Senate elections, except following a double dissolution of both houses. The six original states (and so far the only ones) are guaranteed equal representation in the Senate and a minimum of six Senators per state. Until 1949, Senators were elected in much the same way as Representatives, except that three or more Senators were chosen in each state at each election. Sec. 7 of the Constitution provides for Senators to be elected on a statewide basis—each state voting 'as one electorate'— unless Parliament provides otherwise, which it has not done. Thus, until the 1949 election, between three and six Senators were elected statewide at each election, by a plurality system that often led, as we shall see, to one party winning most or all of the seats being contested.[37]

Then, in 1948, Parliament determined that Senators henceforth would be elected by a form of proportional representation involving use of the 'single transferable vote.' Under this complicated system, as originally designed, each voter assigns numbers, reflecting that voter's preferences, to all candidates for however many Senate seats are to be filled; the voter has only one first preference vote, one second

---

36 Over time, there has been an increase in the average number of candidates in each House electorate, with the greatest increases occurring during the past three decades.

37 Before the 1951 election, there had been only two occasions on which all Senators were elected at the same time: at the first election in 1901and at the election following the double dissolution of 1914.

preference vote, and so on, even though more than one Senator is to be elected. A 'quota' then is calculated that reflects the total number of first preference votes cast and the number of Senate seats being contested. A candidate is elected if he or she receives at least that many first preference votes. If that candidate receives 'surplus' votes—i.e., more votes than the quota—those surplus votes are distributed according to the second or subsequent preferences of those who voted for the elected candidate. Then, if after all surplus votes have been distributed and not enough candidates have received the required quota of votes, the votes of the least popular candidate are redistributed according to his or her supporters' second preferences, and so on, until a number of candidates sufficient to fill all the seats being contested have received the required quota of votes.

When six Senators are elected in a state at the same time, which would be the case today at a normal half-Senate election (six being half of each state's complement of twelve Senators), the required quota for election is 14.3 per cent of the votes cast. This is one-seventh of the votes cast, or one divided by the number of seats being contested (six), plus one. To be elected, however, a candidate does not have to receive 14.3 per cent of all the first preference votes: 'a quota of votes may be made up of first preference votes, or of votes transferred from the surpluses of successful candidates and from the transferred votes of excluded candidates, or any combination of these three sources ... ' Between 1949 and 1984, Sharman calculates, minor party and Independent Senators received roughly two-thirds of the votes needed to constitute a quota in the form of first preference votes, receiving the remaining one-third of their quota 'from transfers from excluded candidates of the major parties and other minor parties' (Sharman 1986: 21). During that period, however, a minor party candidate was elected to the Senate having received barely six per cent of the required quota in first preference votes. In 2001, Kerry Nettle, a Green candidate, won a Senate seat in New South Wales with only 4.4 per cent of the first preference votes, beating the Australian Democrat candidate who received 6.2 per cent (Grattan 2002).

The details make the process of electing Senators even more complex than this brief summary might suggest. To illustrate, Sharman (1986) predicted that the 1984 decision to increase the number of Senators per state from ten to twelve would work to the disadvantage of minor party and Independent candidates. One might think otherwise, because increasing the number of seats has the effect of reducing the percentage of votes necessary to win one of those seats: if five Senators are elected, the quota needed to win each of those seats is 16.7 per cent (one divided by six), whereas, as we have seen, with six elected, the quota is 14.3 per cent (one divided by seven). However, Sharman argued, it also is necessary to take into account the difference between electing an even or an odd number of Senators. If an even number is elected (e.g., six), he calculated, there are likely to be fewer major party surplus votes that are available for transfer to minor party and Independent candidates than if an odd number are elected. Therefore, he concluded, increasing the number of Senators elected from five to six actually should damage the prospects of minor party and Independent Senate candidates, not improve them.

Reid and Forrest (1989: 125) quote the Joint Select Committee on Electoral Reform, which recommended the change, as stating in its first report to the Parliament that this is precisely what its members expected would happen, leading Reid and Forrest to infer that the committee 'clearly had the interest of one or other of the major parties at heart. It assumed that one of the major parties had a right to a Senate majority and that the essential purpose of elections was to determine which one.' However, Uhr (2002a: 23) argues, the committee and the Parliament 'failed to take account of the trend in Senate voters' tactical support away from the major parties to the minor parties, made considerably easier by the reduction in the size of the quota required to win a Senate seat.'

For our purposes, there are two simple points to be emphasized. First, since the general election of 1949, Representatives and Senators have been elected in different ways. And second, this difference in modes of election usually has resulted in different party balances in the two houses. From the perspective of the officers of the House of Representatives (*House of Representatives Practice* 2001: 94):

> The result of proportional representation has been that since 1949 the numbers of the Senate have been fairly evenly divided between government and opposition supporters with the balance of power often being held by minority parties or Independents, whose political influence has increased as a consequence. Governments have frequently been confronted with the ability of the Opposition and minority party or Independent Senators to combine to defeat or modify government measures in the Senate.

There is the not-very-well disguised implication here that the advent of PR for Senate elections has caused a problem. Contrast the characterization in the above quotation with the following statement in *Odgers' Australian Senate Practice* (2001: 120):

> The 1948 electoral settlement for the Senate mitigated the dysfunctions of the single member electorate basis of the House of Representatives by enabling additional, discernible bodies of electoral opinion to be represented in Parliament. The consequence has been that parliamentary government of the Commonwealth is not simply a question of majority rule

but one of representation. The Senate, because of the meth
composition, is the institution in the Commonwealth which reconciles
majority rule, as imperfectly expressed in the House of Representatives,
with adequate representation.

Those who work on one side of Parliament House can argue that the
House of Representatives is the more representative body because the
weight of each vote cast in House elections is roughly the same,
whereas the equal representation of states in the Senate means that the
electoral power of a Tasmanian voter, for instance, is much greater than
that of a voter living in the much more populous states of Victoria or
New South Wales, the homes of Melbourne and Sydney respectively.
But those who work on the other side of the building are only too happy
to point out that, in their opinion, it actually is the Senate that is the
more representative body because the distribution of voters' preferences
among the parties is more accurately reflected in the distribution of
Senate seats among the parties than in the distribution of House seats
(Evans 1997b: 22–23).

However differently the two houses may assess the electoral
'reform' of 1948, they certainly can agree that the introduction of
proportional representation for Senate elections reshaped the political
relations between the Senate, on the one hand, and both the House and
the government, on the other. Consider the view of the Senate that
Partridge (1952: 175) expressed before the first minor party Senators
arrived on the scene following the 1955 election:

> [T]he working of parliamentary and cabinet government has not been
> substantially affected by its federal setting. The fact is that the element of
> responsible cabinet government has prevailed over the federal principle for
> the most part, and cabinet and parliamentary government in this country
> has not developed in a manner different from British development. If there
> are important differences between Australian and British parliaments and
> cabinets, they are traceable rather to differences in the history and the
> character of the two societies than to problems or conditions created by the
> existence of federalism in this country.

Table 3.1 documents that the advent of PR created new possibilities
for the Senate. The table divides general elections into pre-1948 and
post-1948 periods. As it shows, between the emergence of the modern
party system in 1910 and the 1948 Act, there were only two brief
periods (following the 1913 and 1929 elections) when the government
did not hold a majority of seats in both houses. Thirteen of the 15
general elections during this period resulted in one-party (or coalition)
control of the House and Senate. Contrast this pattern with the 26
general elections held between 1949, the first time that Senators were
elected by PR, and 2001.

TABLE 3.1: Government strength in the House of Representatives
and the Senate, 1901–2001

Year of election	Government	% of seats held by government	
		House of Reps	Senate
1901	Protectionist	41.33	30.56
1903	Protectionist	34.67	22.22
1906	Protectionist	21.33	16.67
1910	*ALP*	*57.33*	*63.89*
1913	Liberal	50.67	19.44
1914	*ALP*	*56.00*	*86.11*
1917	*National*	*70.67*	*66.67*
1919	*National*	*49.33*	*97.22*
1922	*National/Country*	*52.63*	*66.67*
1925	*National/Country*	*67.11*	*77.78*
1928	*National/Country*	*55.26*	*80.56*
1929	ALP	61.84	19.44
1931	*UAP*	*52.63*	*58.33*
1934	*UAP/Country*	*62.67*	*91.67*
1937	*UAP/Country*	*58.67*	*55.56*
1940	*UAP/Country*	*49.33*	*52.78*
1943	*ALP*	*65.33*	*61.11*
1946	*ALP*	*57.33*	*91.67*
1949	Liberal/Country	60.16	43.33
1951	*Liberal/Country*	*56.10*	*53.33*
1953	*Liberal/Country*	*56.10*	*51.67*
1954	*Liberal/Country*	*52.03*	*51.67*
1955	Liberal/Country	60.48	50.00
1958	*Liberal/Country*	*62.10*	*53.33*
1961	Liberal/Country	50.00	50.00
1963	Liberal/Country	58.06	50.00
1964	Liberal/Country	58.06	50.00
1966	Liberal/Country	66.13	50.00
1967	Liberal/Country	66.13	46.67
1969	Liberal/Country	52.80	46.67
1970	Liberal/Country	52.80	43.33
1972	ALP	53.60	43.33
1974	ALP	51.97	48.33
1975	*Liberal/National Country*	*70.87*	*54.69*
1977	*Liberal/National Country*	*68.55*	*54.69*
1980	Liberal/National Country	58.40	48.44
1983	ALP	60.00	46.87
1984	ALP	55.41	44.74
1987	ALP	58.11	42.11
1990	ALP	52.70	42.11
1993	ALP	54.42	39.47
1996	Liberal/National	62.84	47.37
1998	Liberal/National	54.05	44.74
2001	Liberal/National	54.66	46.05

Italics indicate a government majority in the Senate.
Source: Adapted from *Parliamentary Handbook of the Commonwealth of Australia*
(29th ed.), Department of the Parliamentary Library, 2002: 588–589.

TABLE 3.2: Votes and seats won by minor parties in
Senate elections, 1949–2001

Year of election	Party	% of vote	Number of seats	% of seats
1949	None	—	—	—
1951	None	—	—	—
1953	None	—	—	—
1955	ALP (Anti-Communist)	6.1	1	3.3
1958	Democratic Labor	8.4	1	3.1
1961	Democratic Labor	9.8	1	3.2
1964	Democratic Labor	8.4	2	6.7
1967	Democratic Labor	9.8	2	6.7
	Others	2.4	1	3.3
1970	Democratic Labor	11.1	3	9.4
	Others	5.6	2	6.3
1974	Democratic Labor	3.6	—	—
	Liberal Movement	1.0	1	1.7
	Others	2.9	1	1.7
1975	Democratic Labor	2.7	—	—
	Liberal Movement	1.1	1	1.5
	Others	3.6	1	1.5
1977	Australian Democrats	11.1	2	5.9
	Others	4.9	—	—
1980	Australian Democrats	9.3	3	8.8
	Others	3.1	1	2.9
1983	Australian Democrats	9.6	5	7.8
	Others	3.2	1	1.6
1984	Australian Democrats	7.6	5	10.9
	Nuclear Disarmament	7.2	1	2.2
1987	Australian Democrats	8.5	7	9.2
	Nuclear Disarmament	1.1	1	1.3
	Others	3.1	2	2.6
1990	Australian Democrats	12.6	5	12.5
	Greens	2.8	1	2.5
	Others	2.7	—	—
1993	Australian Democrats	5.3	2	5.0
	Greens	2.9	1	2.5
	Others	3.8	1	2.5
1996	Australian Democrats	10.8	5	12.5
	Greens	2.4	1	2.5
	Others	6.7	—	—
1998	Australian Democrats	8.5	4	10.0
	Greens	2.7	—	—
	One Nation	9.0	1	2.5
	Others	4.8	1	2.5
2001	Australian Democrats	7.2	4	10.0
	Greens	4.8	2	5.0
	One Nation	5.5	—	—
	Others	6.1	—	—

Source: *Odgers' Australian Senate Practice* 2001: 23–25, and the June 2002 Supplement.

Twenty of those elections produced governments that did not hold a majority of Senate seats. Since the election of 1961, the only time that governments have had majorities in the Senate was during the period following the elections of 1975 and 1977. The introduction of PR for Senate elections unquestionably led to major and lasting changes in the distribution of House and Senate seats among the political parties and, consequently, major and lasting changes in the dynamics of Australian national politics.

Only the first PR elections for the Senate, in 1949, produced divided government in the sense that one of the two major parties (or coalitions) controlled the House and the government while the other controlled the Senate. The pattern in contemporary Canberra has not been one of *Opposition* control of the Senate, but one of *non-government* control with 'the balance of power' resting with a small number of minor party or Independent Senators who may support the government or the Opposition, or who may swing between one and the other, depending on the issue and the willingness of the government to negotiate compromises with, or make concessions to, them.[38] Table 3.2 shows the percentage of the vote and the number and percentage of Senate seats won by minor party and Independent candidates since the general election of 1949.

Increases in the size of the Senate and, therefore, in the number of Senators to be chosen in each state at each election, have made it increasingly easy for minor parties to win seats (but see Sharman 1986). As we have seen, at a normal half-Senate election at which six Senators are elected in each state, the quota of votes needed to win one of those seats is only 14.3 per cent of the state-wide vote. And when there is an election following a double dissolution and all twelve of each state's Senate seats are at stake, the quota is cut almost in half, to 7.7 per cent. As the size of the Senate has increased, the magnitude of both quotas has declined. However, the absence of one-party control of the Senate depends as well on the relatively equal support that the two major political forces have enjoyed since the 1949 election. Modern Australian politics has not been characterized by landslide elections. For a party to win four of the six seats contested in a state at a half-Senate election, it would have to win 57.2 per cent of the vote—that is, four times the quota of 14.3 per cent of the votes that is required to win each seat—and, since the increase in the size of the Senate in 1984, no

---

38   In later chapters we will explore how often in recent years it has been accurate to say that minor party and Independent Senators really have exercised a balance of power.

party ever has won such a large majority in any state's half-Senate election.

TABLE 3.3: Party affiliations following
Senate elections, 1910–2001

Date of Election	Labor	Non-Labor Party/Coalition[1]	Other Parties	Independents
1910	23	13		
1913	29	7		
1914	31	5		
1917	12	24		
1919	1	35		
1922	12	24		
1925	8	28		
1928	7	29		
1931	10	26		
1934	3	33		
1937	16	20		
1940	17	19		
1943	22	14		
1946	33	3		
1949	34	26		
1951	28	32		
1953	29	31		
1955	28	30	2	
1958	26	32	2	
1961	28	30	1	1
1964	27	30	2	1
1967	27	28	4	1
1970	26	26	5	3
1974	29	29	1	1
1975	27	35	1	1
1977	26	35	2	1
1980	27	31	5	1
1983	30	28	5	1
1984	34	33	8	1
1987	32	34	9	1
1990	32	34	8	2
1993	29	36	9	2
1996	29	37	9	1
1998	29	35	11	1
2001	28	35	11	2

1   Fusion, Liberal, and Nationalists (1910–1922); Nationalist-Country coalition (1925–1928); UAP-Country coalition (1931–1943); Liberal-Country coalition (1946–1974); Liberal-National Country coalition (1975–1980); Liberal-National coalition (1983–2001).

Source: *Odgers' Australian Senate Practice* 2001: 26–27, and the June 2002 Supplement. Figures reflect the composition of the Senate after newly-elected Senators have taken their seats.

Table 3.3 presents the party affiliations of Senators since 1909. What is particularly noteworthy is how evenly the Senate has been divided since 1949 between the Australian Labor Party (ALP) and the major non-Labor party or coalition. There were at least two minor party or Independent Senators in office following each of the 18 Senate elections since 1955. Fifteen of those 18 elections produced Senates in which the number of minor party and Independent Senators equalled or exceeded the difference between the number of ALP Senators and the number of Senators representing its major opposition. And half of the 18 elections resulted in two seats or less separating the two major political forces in the Senate. If Labor or its opponents had been able to amass consistent and consistently large majorities in the Senate, the presence of a relatively small number of Independents or minor party Senators would have mattered much less, and perhaps not very much at all.

It is the combination of PR elections for the Senate and the generally equal balance of forces in Australian national politics that has created opportunities for the Senate to exert influence as an independent force in government.[39] As Farrell and McAllister (1995: 247) put it, 'the history of the Senate has gone through two distinct and contradictory stages: first, when it has been gelded as a result of party control, and, second, when it has been galvanised by party control. The principal defining point of distinction between the two stages has been electoral reform.' The reform to which they refer, of course, was the shift to PR. But as they indicate, there is a second factor that must be added to the equation: the discipline that prevails within parliamentary parties in both houses and especially in the House of Representatives. If the Labor, Liberal and National parties were relatively loose coalitions of factions, and if factions of one party sometimes found common ground with factors of one or more of the other parties, then minor party and Independent Senators would not have the potential leverage that they enjoy when Labor and its opponents confront each other like armies trained to march in lockstep.

---

39 Evans (1997a: 4) also has argued, rather ingeniously, that the shift to PR for Senate elections also has strengthened the hand of each state in the legislative process: 'While thereby producing what might be called an ideological distribution of the legislative majority, proportional representation, paradoxically, has also bolstered the Senate's function of requiring a geographically distributed majority. Because the party numbers are always so close in the Senate, the parties are further discouraged from ignoring the less populous states. *Because every Senate seat is vital, every state is also vital.*' (emphasis added) Of course this is true only because Labor and the Coalition enjoy similar levels of popular support and neither enjoys majority support nationwide.

A system of disciplined parliamentary parties

In Chapters 6 and 7, we will be looking at how Senators have voted on divisions—votes on which the position of each participating Senator is publicly recorded. Analysis of comparable votes in the US Congress is complicated and time-consuming because it involves examining the individual voting decisions of 100 Senators (or, even worse, 435 Representatives). Fortunately for our purposes, analysing divisions in the Commonwealth Parliament is much easier because, in 2000 for instance, there are only eight votes in the Senate to be examined: one vote for each of the five parties represented in the Senate and one vote for each of the three Independents. During 1996–2001, which is the time period we will examine in the later chapters, each of the four parties with two or more Senators can, in most cases, be treated for voting purposes as a single entity, because the members of each party almost always vote together. Such is the strength of party discipline in parliamentary voting that defections by Coalition Senators now are rare and defections by Labor Senators are virtually unknown. Since the Coalition returned to government in 1996, only the Australian Democrats and the Greens (when there have been two of the latter serving together in the Senate) have split their votes from time to time.

Party discipline in Parliament is so strong that many analysts now refer to the Commonwealth as not having a system of responsible government but, instead, a system of responsible *party* government.[40] For Hamer (1991: 41), for instance, 'What we now have is not a responsible government; it is a party government. Australia has gone to the extreme lengths of viewing all legislation as a vote of confidence and any legislation amended by the House of Representatives against the Government's wishes as a vote of no confidence in that Government.' The strength of parties in Canberra reverberates through the political system in many ways and fundamentally affects the relations between the Parliament and the government, and the prospects for enforcing parliamentary responsibility and governmental accountability (Evans 1993a). Here is Elaine Thompson's summary:

---

40 In political science, there are generalizations, not laws. Souter (1988: 470) cites two exceptions to the general proposition that party and not State interests have dominated Senate decision-making. 'Only rarely did senators vote along State rather than party lines, as the federal Conventions had intended they should. In 1952, for example, all ten Senators from Tasmania (five Liberals and five Labor) voted with the Opposition to pass an amendment concerning land tax assessment. In 1958 all South Australian senators voted together for an amendment to the Snowy Mountains Hydro-Electric Power Bill, safeguarding their State's share of the River Murray's water.'

> It is the fight in the party room, not on the floor of the house, that is the heart of our system. It is in the party room, not on the floor of the house, that changes in the leadership occur—that prime ministers are forced to yield, that ministers are forced to resign portfolios. The cabinet is not a committee of parliament but a committee of the governing party or parties. Party discipline in the lower house is possible because of the deals done in the backrooms of the party. Sharing of power occurs not between executive and legislature but between the party and its leaders. (Thompson 1980: 37)

In the conclusion to their bicentenary study of the Commonwealth Parliament, Reid and Forrest (1989: 484) identify a 'trinitarian struggle' as providing 'the constitutional and conceptual framework for examining the Parliament in action ... ' This is puzzling because, for all practical purposes, whatever struggle there may have been between the House of Representatives and the government has been resolved in favour of the latter. The reason lies in the discipline of Australia's parliamentary parties that has transformed, or relegated, the House to a forum for debate where the government is certain to prevail.

In the first Parliament, elected in 1901, 59 of the 75 seats in the House were held by members associated with Free Trade and Protectionist parties; Labor held 14 of the remaining 16 seats. Two years later, after the 1903 election, the House again was divided among the same three groupings, with Labor picking up nine seats at the expense of the Free Trade and Protectionist members who nonetheless held two-thirds of the seats. In 1909, however, as Labor's apparent strength continued to grow, the Free Trade and Protectionist parties joined together in what became known in the 1910 election as 'Fusion,' reflecting their shared opposition to the ALP and its policies.

The combination of single-member constituencies and preferential voting has contributed to (but has not been the sole cause of) the development of a party system that, for purposes of the House of Representatives, comprises two and one-half parties combined into two opposing forces. One side of the political divide has been occupied since the first days of the Commonwealth by the Australian Labor Party. Since the fusion of 1909, the other side of that divide has been dominated by the Liberal Party or its predecessors, the Nationalist and United Australia parties. Representatives of the National Party or its predecessors, the Country and National Country parties, also have won House seats at each election since 1922, though a smaller number than either the ALP or the Liberals. For most of the time since then, the Liberal and National parties in the House have been in a formal or informal coalition—hence the characterization of the House as comprising two and one-half parties but two opposing political forces.[41] In most cases, the two coalition partners have agreed not to field candidates against each other in House elections. More often, however, each party has run its own candidates and encouraged its voters to cast their second preference votes for the candidate of the other party. Thus, the preferential voting system has protected the Liberal and National parties against the danger that they could split the non-ALP votes in certain constituencies, thereby allowing the election of ALP candidates whom they and most voters opposed.

Just as the threat posed by the growing electoral success of the Labor Party stimulated the fusion of those opposing it, the discipline that Labor imposed on its candidates and MPs compelled its opponents to become equally concerned with maintaining internal party cohesion in parliamentary voting. As early as 1900, the Labor Party required its candidates to agree to a pledge:

> I hereby pledge myself not to oppose any selected Labor candidate. I hereby pledge myself if returned to the Commonwealth Parliament to do my utmost to ensure the carrying out of the principles embodied in the Federal Labor Platform, and on all such questions to vote as a majority of the Federal Labor Party may decide at a duly-constituted caucus meeting. (quoted in Jaensch 1992: 243)

Although Labor's opponents, now the Liberal and National parties, never have required a similar pledge, in practice the voting discipline in the House of all three parties now is almost perfect (except for the occasional 'free' votes that the parties sometimes allow on issues of strong personal belief such as abortion, euthanasia, or, in 2002, stem cell research). This is how Dean Jaensch has summarized the situation with regard to the ALP:

> The Australian Labor Party is quite open about its demand that its representatives shall be its delegates, and it enforces discipline over parliamentary members with a formal pledge. Members of the party pledge themselves to be bound by the platform and rules of the party and by the decisions of the executive and conference, not to oppose any endorsed Labor candidate at any election *and to vote according to the majority decision of the caucus of the parliamentary party on all questions in*

---

41 This situation makes references somewhat awkward. I generally refer to the two opposing forces in Parliament as Labor (or the ALP) and the Coalition (of the Liberal and National parties). References to 'the Opposition' should be understood to be references to one or the other of these two forces, as appropriate. By contrast, references to the 'non-government' members of the Senate should be taken to refer to members of the Opposition plus Independent Senators and Senators representing other parties such as the Democratic Labor Party or the Australian Democrats.

parliament. They face expulsion from the party if they break any aspect of the pledge. (Jaensch 1991: 136, emphasis added)

With respect to the Liberal Party, the situation is much the same in practice though not in theory:[42]

> It is a matter of frequent celebration in Liberal Party rhetoric that in contrast to their Labor rivals, Liberal Members of Parliament are free men and women, able to exercise their minds and judgments as they see necessary. This is true only at the margins. The solidarity of the Liberal Party in parliament is hardly less marked than that of the ALP, and for much the same reasons. (Singleton, et al. 2000: 277)

Even the occasional free votes do not necessarily reflect party decisions to *allow* their members freedom of choice. Designating a vote as a 'free', or 'conscience,' vote can be a way for a party to acknowledge intense divisions in its ranks and to avoid the possibility of a revolt inside the party room.[43] When confronted with policy choices on which members' convictions are so profound that some will insist on going their own way, it can be easier for the party to stand back and take no official position. If the party insists on discipline instead, it then may have to face the embarrassment of defections, possibly coupled with the awkwardness of penalising members for their unwillingness to abandon their individual consciences. And even if party discipline prevails, enforcing the party position still may cause lasting resentment on the part of those members who felt compelled to vote for a party position that contradicted their own intensely held views.

There have been two transformative events in the history of the Commonwealth Parliament. The first was the emergence in 1909–1910 of a disciplined party system; the second was the switch to PR for Senate elections beginning in 1949. The effects of the first event were felt immediately; the second did not affect 'the numbers' in the Senate until the 1955 election. To get a feel for how both events changed the Senate, we can take a moment to look at the Senate before fusion and then during the period between fusion and the advent of PR.

---

42 Lucy (1985: 357–359) contests this characterization, pointing to '101 instances of Liberals crossing the floor of the house in a division' when Fraser was Prime Minister in 1975–1983, and arguing that the dissidents were not penalized by being denied their party's reselection for the next election. Such defections no longer occur.

43 These votes are uncommon and tend to be on matters, such as euthanasia and stem cell research, that many members view as raising moral issues. That is why they sometimes are called 'conscience' votes. However, members sometimes are allowed to vote as they choose on other kinds of questions, so 'free' votes is the more inclusive term.

Ian Marsh is our guide to the pre-fusion period. In his *Beyond the Two-Party System* and other writings, Marsh advocates an alternative conception of policy-making in Australia that emphasizes ad hoc coalition building that would escape the constraints of the two-party system with its disciplined party voting in Parliament and its concentration on policy development within ministries and Cabinet. He contrasts (1995: 272–302) the dynamics of contemporary policy-making, and especially the role of Parliament, with the situation that prevailed during the first years of the Federation until 1909, when fusion occurred and the party system coalesced into the Labor Party and a non-Labor bloc. Marsh looks back, with evident wistfulness, on a brief period in which policy-making and coalition-building in Parliament were more fluid than they have been at any time since, even with today's non-government majorities in the Senate:

> Parliament was a substantial arena in the 1901–9 period. This contrasts with the dignified and ritualistic role it has come to play in the two party era. Parliament provided the prism through which cross-cutting aspirations were refracted and refined into programs and measures... . Parties first needed to attract substantial electoral support for their programs. Then governments were created and unmade according to their ability to gather majority support for their measures in parliament. Furthermore, they were required to obtain majorities in two chambers. (Marsh 1995: 283, 292)
> In the first ten years, the Senate used its powers regularly against governments. It functioned as the house of minorities it was intended to be, using its committees to gather information and to build opinion among senators. The committees became the key institutional mechanism for investigating strategic issues. There were frequent disagreements between the houses, particularly on tariff issues. Disputes between the chambers were fierce, but accommodations ultimately were reached. Indeed, these cameo dramas became an occasion for public learning. The site of contention was not party conferences or internal party committee processes, but parliamentary committees and debates within and between the houses. The political drama constituted the setting in which the educative role of political investigation and deliberation was more fully realized. (Marsh 1999: 195)

Marsh offers several specific examples of the Senate's legislative activity before the consolidation of the party system, and its impact on the relations between the two houses in enacting new law. The first case he mentions, the 1902 tariff bill, was discussed in chapter 2. He continues:

> Conflict between the houses also arose in relation to the British Preference bill in October 1906. The Senate majority united in rejecting the H of R's handling of its proposed amendments. The H of R had suggested the

amendments were unconstitutional in form. The Senate also sought provisions postponing operation of the coloured labor clause in relation to shipping. The H of R sought an amendment that had the effect of granting preference to British goods irrespective of the means of transit. The Senate held firm after several exchanges with the H of R. The H of R ultimately had three options: to accept the amendments, to persuade the Senate, or to initiate a double dissolution. It accepted the Senate's proposals. This set the pattern for future relations. (Marsh 1995: 290–291)

I have quoted Marsh at length because he portrays a bicameral legislative process that bears a much greater similarity to the process today than to the process during the four decades between fusion (1909) and PR (1949).

On that period, we have Geoffrey Sawer's 1963 exposition of the policies and politics of each Commonwealth Parliament from 1929 through 1949.[44] For our purposes, what is most striking about Sawer's detailed summaries and analysis is how often the Senate largely disappears from view. Certainly this is not an oversight on the part of the author, who was an influential expert on Australian constitutionalism and especially federalism. Instead, the lack of discussion of the Senate in his book can only reflect the fact that, throughout the period it covers, the method of electing Senators tended to produce Senate majorities that supported governments and their House majorities.

There were a few occasions during this period, however, when the government did not have a working majority in the Senate. Even when the party winning a House election also won a majority of the Senate seats contested at that election, it still might find itself without a Senate majority if it held relatively few of the Senate seats that had not been contested. In such cases, Sawer's picture of the Senate is not unlike that of recent Senates with non-government majorities. An excellent example is the first parliament he portrays, the Twelfth Parliament of 1929–1931, with its ALP majority in the House but not in the Senate. Sawer (1963: 15) points to the calculations that both government and non-government parties had to make then, and since, in such situations: 'the non-Labor parties, and especially the Nationalists, were so strongly entrenched in the Senate, the party battle in the parliament resolved mainly into a question as to how far the government would go in order to meet Senate majority opinion, and how far the Senate majority would go in meeting government desires in order to avoid provoking a double dissolution.'

---

44 A companion volume published in 1956 provides a comparable analysis of the first eleven parliaments.

In some cases, the results of these calculations led to compromise and, in the case of the Conciliation and Arbitration Bill of 1930, one of the two conferences that the two houses ever have convened:

> The Senate, recognizing that the government had a mandate for a general overhaul of the [conciliation and arbitration] system, passed the second reading without division and the main fight was joined in Committee. But the Opposition Senators were divided on a number of major issues, and even at this stage compromise settlements were achieved on many clauses, to the disgust of the more stiff-necked Nationalists.
>
> The Bill returned to the Representatives with thirty amendments; these included many incidental matters to which Labor was strongly opposed ... .
>
> However, the government, to the sorrow of its left-wing supporters, decided to negotiate through managers ... a conference was held at midnight in the last hours of a sitting, and the resulting compromise rushed through two Houses of exhausted members. The Senate insisted on nineteen of its amendments and a further seven were accepted subject to modifications; in detail, it was a Senate victory, but the government gained the substance of its three main principles. (Sawer 1963: 17)

However, the situation prevailing during the Twelfth Parliament was very much the exception during the 40 years between 1909 and 1949, when the hardening of party lines fundamentally transformed the way in which the Parliament usually worked. After the first decade under Federation, parliamentary politics increasingly became bipolar, and almost perfectly so after the emergence of the Liberal-Country/National coalition. For all intents and purposes, there came to be only two political forces in the Parliament—the government and the Opposition—and one or the other controlled the Senate. Party discipline grew stronger, even if it remained somewhat weaker than it now has become. It was the strength of party discipline, when combined with the adoption of PR (a decision we will examine later in this chapter), that created the possibility for today's political dynamic in Parliament.

It probably is fair to say that the leaders of every party would like to have the dependable support of all their parliamentary members. Yet the degree of unity in parliamentary voting that characterizes Australian parties is unusual among modern democracies. How are we to account for it?

The phrase 'party discipline' does not capture the entire relationship between each member of the Commonwealth Parliament and his or her party, at least if that party is the ALP or either member of the Coalition. Party unity in parliamentary voting reflects, in large part, the voluntary cohesion of each party's members. Although there certainly have been, and are, factions and factional battles within each party, intra-party differences usually have paled in comparison with the policy differences between the parties (though now it often is said—as it has been said periodically since the 1970s—that Labor and the Coalition are moving toward the political centre and, consequently, toward each other). Thus, most members of each party would vote with each other most of the time for reasons of personal conviction even if there were no penalties for 'crossing the floor' and voting with the other party instead.

There are at least five other reasons why the levels of party cohesion in parliamentary voting undoubtedly would be very high even it were strictly voluntary. First, a party has a powerful incentive to preserve its own voting cohesion if it anticipates that the other parliamentary parties will vote cohesively. A party puts itself at a terrible disadvantage if it does not actively discourage its members from crossing the floor to vote with the opposition when it knows full well that no opposition members will be allowed to cross the floor in the other direction. One reason for the increased cohesion of the non-Labor parties early in the Twentieth Century was the knowledge that they were facing a highly cohesive Labor Party. Second, parties and their members believe that they will be more successful in presenting themselves to the public as a plausible alternative government if they appear to be united and to speak with one clear voice. A party that seems to be at odds with itself over policy risks appearing to be a party that does not know what it believes, what it is doing as the Opposition, and what it would do as the government. The danger is even greater, of course, for the party that already is in government. And third, the simple psychological effect of peer pressure should not be under-estimated. In a world so full of uncertainties as the world of government and politics, there is great comfort for many legislators in being and remaining a member in good standing of a group with shared interests, concerns, and values.

Fourth, party cohesion can greatly simplify life for Representatives and Senators. The party develops positions for them, saving them the need to study the issues independently, identify and evaluate the various policy options, weigh the likely effects of implementing each alternative policy on their individual electorates as well as the nation, and evaluate how supporting each of the available policy options is likely to affect their own political support and futures. The virtual certainty that members of Parliament will support their parties' positions also largely immunizes them against demands from constituents and others that MPs vote one way or the other. Members of Parliament are free to express their sympathy with those who approach them but they also may explain that they are committed to support a contrary position taken by their parties. In fact, lobbyists in Canberra generally do not concentrate on efforts to persuade backbench MPs because they have concluded that 'to lobby individual MPs is a waste of time, energy, and resources.' (Jaensch 1986: 137)

Finally, Representatives and Senators are fully aware that their prospects for advancement depend on their standing within their parties. In the case of the Coalition, the leader of the Liberal Party—in consultation or negotiation with his National Party counterpart—selects which MPs will join the government and in what capacities. So an ambitious MP has good reason to want to be seen by his or her leaders as a loyal member of the team. In the case of the ALP, it is the parliamentary party that decides which of its members will hold leadership positions; then it is the party leader who allocates these positions among the members chosen in the party room. In either case, an MP with a reputation as a rebel or a maverick or as someone who is out of step with his or her colleagues is less likely to be among those chosen for ministerial (or shadow ministerial) positions than Representatives or Senators of equal competence who always sit with their party colleagues during divisions.

Still, if the incentives for voluntary cohesion are not enough, there are sanctions that party leaders can and do impose to ensure that party unity in House and Senate votes is virtually perfect among ALP members and close to perfect among Coalition members.[45]

Representatives or Senators sometimes oppose their party leaders vociferously in private conversations and behind the closed doors of their parliamentary party rooms. But they may put their careers at risk if they do so publicly and, even more, if they cross the floor to vote against the overwhelming majority of their fellow party members:

> Almost every vote in Parliament—regardless of whether it is on a matter of great national importance, on a confidence motion in the government, or on a simple machinery amendment of a very unimportant Bill—is taken as if the life of the government depends on it.[46] As well, every vote is taken as if

---

45 It should not be assumed, however, that Australian Representatives and Senators routinely seethe with frustration at having to support party positions that they have carefully weighed and found wanting. McKeown and Lundie (2002: 5) observe that 'The party system is so strong that even when a free vote is granted on complex or major issues the outcome of the vote may not change.' They also quote Fred Chaney, who served in both houses, as having concluded that 'the failure of many members to have a view that they were prepared to articulate and argue for within the party forum [that is, behind the closed doors of the party room] was far more of a problem than excessive party discipline.'

46 For this reason, parties, especially those in government, may be somewhat more willing to accept occasional defections in the Senate than in the House; the fate of the government does not rest on the outcome of Senate divisions. The result, according to Reid and Forrest (1989: 41), is that party has dominated proceedings in the Senate, 'but not with the same relentless emphasis on government and

the decision will play a major part in the next election, and that election is only days away. (Jaensch 1986: 44–45)

There have been members, to be sure, who have been openly critical of their party leaders or their party's policies, and still have survived politically. Some even have succeeded in replacing the leaders they have criticized: prime ministers Robert Menzies, Malcolm Fraser, and Paul Keating are examples. They must know, however, that if they fail and remain in the House or Senate, they are very likely to be relegated to the back benches for the foreseeable future. Even worse, they may find their parliamentary careers at an end, because the primary sanction that Australia's parties have to ensure the discipline of their members in parliamentary voting is their influence over the process of selecting candidates for election and re-election to Parliament.

The key fact is that there are no primary elections in Australia, unlike the United States where party members can nominate themselves to become their party's candidate for a House or Senate seat, and where the other party members in that electorate then vote to choose which of those self-nominated hopefuls will receive the official party endorsement.[47] Instead, the 'preselection' process in all of Australia's major parties is controlled by party activists in a process that often is closed to wider participation and even to public view.

In the Labor Party, preselection processes vary from state to state, but in all states the selection of parliamentary candidates is in the hands of some combination of state and local party members, who, in light of their own commitment to the party, naturally value party loyalty in prospective candidates and in their incumbent Representatives and Senators. If ALP incumbents ever think about voting against the party position, notwithstanding the pledge that they have signed, they must assume that they may well be expelled from the party and, even if not, that they are very unlikely to receive another nomination from the party activists who control their future in electoral politics. In the Liberal Party, too, pre-selection is in the hands of active state or local party

---

Opposition that has been the hallmark of the history of the House of Representatives.'

47 Concerning the Liberal Party, Jaensch (1992: 266) found it 'notable that while no uniform pattern has developed across the party, every state has rejected plebiscite preselection, except South Australia. At the time of the reformation of the Liberal Party in 1944, Menzies argued strongly against such rank-and-file preselection, and South Australia abandoned it in the mid-1970s. Menzies had a sound reason: plebiscite preselection encourages parochialism; the candidate who has built up strong local support may not be the 'best' person to represent the party at state or national level.' Of course, as Jaensch recognized, this begs the question as to what qualifies someone as the 'best' person.

members. But 'the combination of a local emphasis in preselection with Burkean independence provides an environment where party rebels can emerge and prosper' (Jaensch 1992: 266), at least in comparison with the Labor Party:

> The Liberal member, tempted for whatever reason to go against the party line, must consider the effects of such behaviour on his chances to retain endorsement. Those Liberals who have been rebels and who have retained their endorsement have usually done so on the basis of their membership of, or support from, the party's power elite at the state or local level.

If so, dissidence may not be deadly if it reflects a disagreement between national and state-local party officials or perhaps between factions within the party. Furthermore, Representatives may be able to establish such strong personal reputations with their electorates that, if their seats are marginal ones, their party may be reluctant to risk control of those seats by denying them reselection as punishment for one or more voting defections. Senators, on the other hand, are considerably less likely to be able to develop such protective cushions of public support when each of them is only one of 12 Senators representing an entire state. So although all electoral politics in Australia are party politics, party probably is even more important in Senate elections than in House elections. Furthermore, the mechanics of voting in Senate elections was changed in 1984 in a way that put the fate of incumbent and prospective Senators even more firmly in the hands of the officials of their parties.

Before 1984, the preferential voting system in Senate elections made it possible, at least in theory, for Senators and Senate candidates to promote their elections by capitalizing on whatever individual popularity they enjoyed, rather than relying entirely on voter support for their parties. Voters had to express a preference ordering among all the Senate candidates on the ballot; most important, even if a voter's first six choices were the six candidates of the same party (in the case of a normal half-Senate election), the voter still could choose—indeed, had to choose—the order in which to vote for each of the six. However, most voters relied on 'how to vote cards' that the parties produced, so each voted in accordance with the preference ordering that his or her party recommended. For this reason, the opportunity for Senators, particularly in the most populous states, to develop a 'personal vote' was much more hypothetical than real.

The need to assign numbers, in order of the voter's preference, to all the candidates on the ballot made for a relatively large number of 'informal' votes—votes that were not counted because voters had not marked their ballot papers completely or correctly. So in 1984, the electoral law was amended to make it possible for voters in Senate elections to cast a single vote for a party (actually, for the party's preferences) instead of for individual candidates. As amended in 1984, the electoral law now provides for each Senate ballot to be divided in half, and voters may cast their votes either 'above the line' or 'below the line' that now divides the ballot. Australians who choose to vote 'below the line' cast their votes in the same way that they did before, numbering all the candidates in order of preference. Alternatively, a voter who casts his or her vote 'above the line' finds on the top half of the ballot only one box for each party, not separate boxes for each individual candidate. If the voter places a '1' in the box of one of the parties, the voter thereby casts his or her votes in accordance with the preference ordering of all candidates that his or her preferred party has published.[48]

Not only does such 'Group Ticket Voting' (GTV) simplify voting, it allows voters to vote for a party, not for individual candidates. The result has been that far fewer ballots are spoiled because most voters now choose to vote 'above the line' in Senate elections—in other words, most votes in these elections now are cast for parties, not individual candidates.

> The effect of the introduction of GTV has been spectacular. Senate informal voting, which averaged 9.4 per cent in the five elections prior to the change, has been just 3.7 per cent in the five elections since. In addition, the overwhelming number of electors [85.7 per cent] voted 'above the line' in the first use, and the proportion of GTV votes has continued to rise until nearly 95 per cent voted in this way in 1996 ... . No doubt this has been very satisfying for party managers, for each vote above the line is a vote in a party-preferred order, and to that extent is a vote controlled by a party. (Bennett 1996: 56)

The party determines the order in which its candidates (as well as all other candidates) are preferred by all the voters who vote for the party 'above the line'. In turn, this means that the fate of each party candidate is every bit as much in the hands of the party's officials as it is in the hands of the voters. A Senator or Senate candidate who is in the good graces of those party officials can hope to be ranked first or second among the party's candidates, whereas a Senator who has fallen out of favour with the same party officials may be relegated to a lower position. The difference is critical. The candidates that each major party or coalition ranks first or second on its list of six for a half-Senate election are almost certain to be elected; those ranked fifth and sixth are

---

48 'Parties may submit a preferred order of voting to the AEC [Australian Electoral Commission], so that an above-the-line vote will be dealt with by polling officials as if the voter had voted in that order.' (Bennett 1996: 26)

almost certain to be defeated. The third-ranked candidate will win if his or her party does well in the election; the fourth-ranked candidate will win only in the event of a landslide victory.

This also was true before 'above the line' voting because voters tended to vote for their party's candidates in the order in which the party chose to have listed on the ballot. In the first PR election, in 1949, seven Senators were elected from each state.[49] In anticipation of that election, the then-Clerk of the Senate, J.E. Edwards (1948: 244), wrote that:

> One of the results of the new system of voting will be that in actual practice the choice of most of the Senators will be made in party pre-selection ballots. With 7 candidates to be elected each of the two major parties seems assured of 3 seats while the remaining seventh seat will be determined by the electors.

Scott Bennett (1996: 88–89) explains that, in contemporary half-Senate elections, with six Senate seats at stake in each state, 'a major party realistically can expect to win a maximum of three of the six Senate seats being contested—to win four would require a highly unlikely party vote of 57.2 per cent.'[50] There is nothing particularly subtle about this. Any Senator who is thinking about voting against the party's position on an issue of consequence certainly is aware of this calculus and how offending his or her state party can affect the Senator's prospects for re-election. Consider the case of the first Aboriginal to be elected to the Senate:

> In 1972 the Liberal Party earned many plaudits for selecting Neville Bonner as a Senate candidate, and Bonner duly became the first Aboriginal member of any parliament in Australia. Early in his term, Bonner was prepared to defend the Coalition policies on Aboriginal matters, but he gradually swung to a more pro-Aboriginal stance, infuriating Queensland Liberals and Nationals, who accused him of being too 'one-sided' in his performance as a Senator. Eventually the Liberal Party dropped him to what was considered an unwinnable position on the party list for the 1983 election. Bonner resigned from the party and stood as an Independent, a tactic that very nearly won him back his seat, for he was the final candidate to be eliminated from the count. (Bennett 1996: 91)

---

49 It was necessary to elect seven Senators per state at the 1949 election in order to bring the Senate up to its new, larger size.

50 '[T]he increase in the number of Senators in 1984 from ten to twelve per State, six elected every three years, and the reduction of the required quota from 16.66 per cent to 14.28 per cent made it virtually impossible for a government to win four quotas or 57.12 per cent of the vote in any State.' (Coonan 1999b: 13–14)

While PR may have weakened the position of the two major
protagonists in the Senate vis-a-vis the minor parties and Independents,
the 1984 'reform' has strengthened the position of each of the two
major parties vis-a-vis their own Senators and Senate candidates.[51]

One question remains: why have Australia's political parties been so
intent on maintaining strict party discipline? One reason is the Labor
Party's historic sense of itself as a movement as much as a party, a
group of like-minded people who come together in support of a
common cause rather than a set of shared policy views or even an
ideology. Its Representatives and Senators are elected to office as
representatives and agents of the movement, so it is appropriate to hold
them to a strict standard of discipline. According to Reid and Forrest:

> In a system in which the assumption of Executive office depended upon
> obtaining and maintaining a majority in the House of Representatives, the
> Labor Party quickly recognized the importance of organisation and
> discipline. These, in fact, were qualities to which, in 1901, many Labor
> members already subscribed, partly as a legacy of the practices and
> traditions of the union movement and partly as a result of the experiences
> of the colonial parliamentary Labor parties. (Reid and Forrest 1989: 14)

For the non-Labor parties, an emphasis on discipline in practice, though
not in principle, has been an essential tactical response to the challenge
of a dependably united Labor Party. In addition, though, Evans has
argued that strict party discipline in Canberra reflects the importation of
a mistaken understanding of party discipline under the 'Westminster
model' which so many Australian politicians and political analysts
claim as their own. According to Evans (1982: 49), the 'Westminster
model'

---

51   One effect should have been to create safe Senate seats for party loyalists because
at each election party selectors are likely to rank them first or second among the
party's Senate candidates. Senators, on the other hand, who have shown more
inclination to rock the party's boat, such as Bonner, may be moved down to a place
on the list that makes their re-election doubtful or effectively impossible. If so, we
confront the ironic implication that the Senators most likely to gain the
parliamentary experience and knowledge of government affairs that comes with
extended tenure are more likely to be those who accept the guidance of their party
leaders and restrict any doubts they may have about party policy to discussions
behind the closed doors of the party room. However, Australian Senators do not
measure their tenure in decades as many American Senators such as Strom
Thurmond and Robert Byrd have done. When one looks down from the gallery of
the Senate in Canberra, one sees few heads of grey hair. The 'father of the Senate'
today—who has served longer than any of his colleagues and who, interestingly, is
an Independent—has been there only since 1975.

is held to demand that a government which is defeated on even the most trivial matter in the lower house immediately resign or call an election. ... This curious belief helps to ensure that party discipline in Australia is so much more intense and rigid than it is in almost any other democratic country, including, of course, Britain. Members of parliament are imbued with a notion that governments must by definition be supported by every vote in the lower house, or a collective resignation or an immediate dissolution will ensue, and they very seldom deny their party their votes, as members of the British House of Commons do, if not with regularity, at least with sufficient frequency apparently to involve complete departure from the 'Westminster System' in the land of its origin.

We do not know what Australian MPs have in mind when they think or speak about the 'Westminster model,' so we cannot judge how their understanding of it may affect their voting behaviour. However, savvy party leaders might very well include references to the model and the behaviour it demands among the arsenal of rhetorical weapons that they deploy to ensure that all their troops head in the right direction when the division bells ring in the House or Senate chamber.

To summarize a complicated story, the use of proportional representation for electing Senators has made it very likely that Australian prime ministers will continue to lack party majorities in the Senate, and the highly disciplined nature of Australia's national parliamentary parties make it very unlikely that the government will be able to cobble together majorities in the Senate by picking off a handful of Senators who are willing to vote against their own party colleagues. The results of Senate votes, therefore, are determined by the collective, unified positions of the major and minor parties, as well as the positions of however many Independent Senators there happen to be at the moment. How the different parties cope with this situation is the primary focus of Chapters 6 and 7. But there is much ground to be covered before that, beginning with the obvious and interesting question: how did the parties and the Senate come to find themselves in this situation?

The shift to proportional representation

During almost all of the first 50 years of experience under the Constitution, the potential for conflicts that are implicit in it were limited by the ability of governments, especially after the party fusion of 1909, to secure majorities in both houses. The import of the data presented earlier on government strength in the House and Senate can easily be summarized: before the 1949 election, the government party or coalition usually, but not always, also held a majority of seats in the Senate; after that election, the government party or coalition usually, but not always, did not. Before 1949, there were only two occasions—in 1913–14 and again in 1929–31—when the Opposition held a majority of Senate seats. Then in 1948, the method of electing Senators was changed in a way that led ultimately to a reversal of this situation, so that contemporary governments usually have faced non-government majorities in the Senate. Solomon (1986: 17) is not alone in having concluded that 'Under the latest electoral system used in the Senate, it would be most unusual for any Government to have a majority in the Senate.'

Clearly, then, the decision made in 1948 to switch to a system of proportional representation for electing Senators has made a difference. We already have noted some of the consequences of this decision; several chapters to follow will elaborate, in one way or another, on other consequences for the role of the Senate and for the relations between the Senate on the one hand and the House of Representatives and the government on the other. It is natural to ask, therefore, why the 1948 decision was made and whether it was intended and expected to lead to significant changes in the dynamics of the Commonwealth's political system.

The conventional, perhaps cynical, explanation is that Ben Chifley's Labor Government was motivated in 1948 primarily by calculations of short-term political advantage. 'Labor knew that it would lose the 1949 election (and probably most of its contested Senate seats) and so devised this change to consolidate its parliamentary power base in the Senate to frustrate the expected Menzies government.' (Uhr 1999b: 1) Going into the 1949 election, Labor enjoyed a 33–3 Senate majority. So by instituting PR, it hoped to ensure that the ALP would come out of those elections still enjoying a Senate majority even if it lost control of the House. Fusaro (1966: 390) explains:

> Because of the staggered system by which senators retire, eighteen members of the upper chamber did not have to stand for re-election in 1949. Fifteen of these were laborites. Due to the increase in the size of the senate from thirty to sixty members in accordance with the Representation act of 1948, forty-two senators were chosen in the 1949 election. Labor, with the buffer of a majority of the non-retiring senators, and with the expectation that proportional representation would result in a near-even split among the new senators, felt assured of keeping its majority in the senate.

And so it came to pass. Labor emerged from the 1949 election with a 34–26 majority in the (now enlarged) Senate, but with only 47 of 121 seats in the House.[52]

Robert Menzies, the Leader of the Opposition, could hardly have been surprised. During the 1948 debate, he said of the Labor Government's plan that 'It is no more subtle than hitting a man over the head and taking his purse while he is unconscious.' But he preferred to find an argument of principle to support his opposition to the bill, arguing that, 'although a formidable case can be presented for altering the method of electing the Senate, and although a very strong case can be made for introducing proportional representation, no case whatever can be made for having one part of a popularly elected legislature elected under one system and the other part of it under another.'[53] This is a particularly interesting assertion because it was the switch to PR for the Senate that created the possibility, and now perhaps the inevitability, of non-government majorities in the Senate. Surely any government frustrated by the Senate would sympathize with Menzies' argument; any advocate of the Senate as a check on the government and the House would disagree just as strenuously.

John Uhr argues that the explanation of short-term political self-interest 'is true as far as it goes,' but that there was more to it than that. He explains, for instance, that there had been long-standing interest in and support for proportional representation, and urges us to think of the 1948 decision not as a new-fangled innovation, but as 'the final stage in a frequently-deferred plan of parliamentary reform that goes back to Federation':

> Even before Federation, many prominent constitutional framers had expected the first Parliament to legislate for proportional representation for the Senate. Sure enough, the Barton government included Senate proportional representation in the original Electoral Act, but this was rejected in the Senate on the plausible ground that it would undermine the established conventions of strong party government. But over time even the

---

52 Also in 1948, as Fusaro mentions, the membership of the House and, therefore, the Senate also had been increased. As discussed in the preceding chapter, this development has implications of its own for the prospects for minor party representation in the Senate. 'Especially notable is the direct relationship between the rise in the number of senators per state (from six at Federation to ten at 1949 to twelve at 1984) and the steady decrease in the number of votes required to obtain a successful quota.' (Uhr (1998: 114) Then and later, increasing the size of the Senate also increases the likelihood of minor parties securing Senate seats.

53 *Commonwealth Parliamentary Debates*, 21 April 1948: 1002.

partisans of strong party government came round to see the merits of the original plan.[54]

Support for PR had been expressed during the constitutional Conventions, during parliamentary consideration of the first electoral law, and thereafter. During consideration of the Electoral Bill 1902, Senator O'Connor, the minister in charge of the bill, endorsed PR for Senate elections:

> If we wish to have our Parliament made a true reflex of the opinion of the people, we must abandon once and for all the system of the block vote, a system which is absolutely uncertain in its operation and its results, and which leads at best to a majority only being represented. ... The effect of this proportional representation will be that we shall be able to secure the representation of the true majority; that a majority will be represented by its true value, and no more. Any minority which is large enough to have a quota will be represented, and, therefore, the Legislature will be a true reflex of opinion outside. (*Commonwealth Parliamentary Debates*, 31 January 1902: 3541–2)

The Parliament ultimately disagreed and rejected PR. Uhr (1998: 112) contends that the decision was based 'chiefly on the correct perception that it would introduce a war of representation into the new federal parliament, probably challenge the conventions of cabinet government ... and increase the potential of the Senate to compete for popular legitimacy with the House.' Reid and Forrest (1989: 103) argue simply 'that, despite their claims to neutrality, the established major parties did not want any new parties entering Parliament to upset the status quo.' In support, they quote Senator John Clemons: 'What we want is not the representation of minorities in each State. I say at once that this Senate is not the place where all these various shades of opinion should find representation.' I see no need to choose between these two explanations; there is nothing politicians like better than finding arguments of principle that just happen to justify decisions that are in their self-interest.

O'Connor's argument foreshadowed the arguments that would be made in support of proportional representation in 1948 and even today. Precisely because of PR, some contemporary observers find in the Senate a forum for the representation and expression of Australia's diversity that the House, with its disciplined *de facto* two-party system, cannot provide. Ward (2000a: 70) aptly refers to 'a credible, if opportunistic, theory of democratic pluralism,' by which 'Pluralists like Brian Galligan, Campbell Sharman, and Harry Evans argue that

---

54 John Uhr, 'Why we chose proportional representation', version at www.aph.gov.au/ Senate/pubs/pops/pop34/c02htm.

dispersing power away from the executive reflects the diversity of modern society and the fragmentation of modern party politics better than does party duopoly in the lower house.' This argument is exemplified by the following rationale for bicameralism in *Odgers' Australian Senate Practice* (2001: 4):

> Bicameralism is in practice necessary to achieve a parliament truly representative of the people. Bicameralism helps to improve and enhance the representative quality of a parliament and to ensure that it is representative in a way in practice not achievable in a unicameral parliament. Modern societies are complex and diverse; no systems of representation are, of themselves, capable of providing a truly representative assembly. Adequate representation of a modern society, with its geographic, social and economic variety, can be realised only by a variety of modes of election. This is best achieved by a bicameral parliament in which each house is constituted by distinctive electoral process. A properly structured bicameral parliament ensures that representation goes beyond winning a simple majority of votes in one election, and encompasses the state of electoral opinion in different phases of development.[55]

This continuity between arguments made at the Conventions and in the first Parliament and those being made today lend support to Uhr's conclusion that 'the 1948 decision is part of an evolution of Australian parliamentary institutions that gives due recognition to a form of political representation long anticipated as an essential component of the Australian constitutional system.' 'Seen in historical perspective,' therefore, 'the 1948 turn to PR was not really a regrettable detour, as some would have it, but more of a homecoming.' (Uhr 1999b: 30, 32; also Uhr 1995a)

In trying to explain why political institutions change, however, it is never a good idea to rely too heavily on arguments of principle. In addition to Chifley's short-term political interests, there was another, practical reason to support some change in the existing system for electing Senators. There are plausible arguments to be made in favour of either plurality or proportional electoral systems. In Australia, however, some of the election results before 1948 had been so lopsided as to discredit plurality elections and to strengthen the argument that the existing electoral system simply was too unfair to retain. In 1948:

> there was a lingering sense of dissatisfaction with the traditional Senate electoral system, which produced huge majorities in turn to whichever

---

55 Exactly why a variety of modes of election is necessary to achieve adequate representation, and precisely why no systems of representation can produce a truly representative assembly, are not explained.

political party built up House of Representatives majorities. This 'block vote' system was included in the original Electoral Act of 1902 and was revised to include preferential voting from 1919. The practical result of this system was the so-called 'windscreen-wiper effect', which delivered almost all contested Senate seats in each state to whatever political party achieved a majority. Senate majorities oscillated wildly between the two major political parties (Labor and successive non-Labor coalitions), both of which could expect to take their turn as the majority party in the Senate. The first two Senate elections after the establishment of the 1902 Electoral Act saw a relatively even 'two third: one third' distribution of Senate seats. But once the political parties became consolidated, the system began to deliver disproportionate victories to whichever party was riding high with the passing electoral majority: Labor won all of the 18 seats on offer at the 1910 election; non-Labor won all on offer at the 1918 and 1925 and 1934 elections; and Labor won all Senate seats at the 1943 election and 15 of the 18 on offer at the 1946 election.' (Uhr 1999b: 3–4)

The electoral system usually benefited the party in government, as we have seen. When it did not, the consequences for the government were severe. Gavin Souter reminds us of the situation that Scullin's Labor Government confronted in 1929 when it took office and found itself face-to-face with an overwhelmingly hostile Senate:

Scullin was taking office with the largest one-party majority ever achieved in the House of Representatives, but in the Senate his Government would still have only seven votes compared to the Nationalist Party's twenty-four and the Country Party's five. Frank Anstey [a leading Labor MP], borrowing aptly from *Julius Caesar*, wrote in his memoirs that on coming to power the Scullin Government found itself 'sitting on the eggs of the serpent'—eggs which, in Brutus's words, should be killed in the shell lest, being hatched, they follow their nature and grow mischievous. The Senate was an egg that could be crushed, in the event of disagreement between the houses, if the Government had sufficient resolve to seek a double dissolution which might give it control of both houses. Anstey himself advocated such a course, but few of his colleagues fancied the idea. After thirteen years in Opposition most of them were looking forward to office, with or without power, and were not in the least anxious to play double or quits. By the same token the Senate majority was in no hurry to meet the people either, and so the main questions of the twelfth Parliament would be how far the Government was prepared to restrain its demands on the hostile Senate, and how much the Senate was prepared to give the Government—a delicate balancing act performed in the mutual interest of avoiding premature election. (Souter 1988: 257; and see also Denning 1946: 53)

The result was that at least fourteen government bills were defeated in the Senate during that Parliament:

The role of executioner sat strangely on a Senate which for more than two-thirds of the Commonwealth's three decades had been controlled by the same political forces as the House of Representatives, and in consequence had usually been far more inclined to meet the wishes of that place than otherwise. Having long since exchanged the role of States' House for that of lower house's rubber stamp, the Senate was sometimes referred to by outsiders as the morgue ... (Souter 1988: 261)

There was a 'feast or famine' quality to Senate elections before the switch to PR beginning with the election of 1949. Throughout most of the period from 1903 to 1946, Australia had a reasonably competitive two (or two and one-half) party system. There were periods when one party was stronger than the other, but the electorate remained fairly evenly divided between them. Yet Senate elections consistently produced extreme and wildly fluctuating results, results that did not always favor the government. On two occasions, in 1913–14 and again in 1929–31, the government party held only seven of 36 Senate seats.

TABLE 3.4: Percentage of seats won by the Australian Labor Party
in Senate elections, 1903–1946

Year of Election	Seats Won by Labor (%)
1903	73.7
1906	22.2
1910	100.0
1913	61.1
1914	86.1
1917	0.0
1919	5.3
1922	55.6
1925	0.0
1928	36.8
1931	16.7
1934	0.0
1937	8.4
1940	15.8
1943	100.0
1946	83.3

Note: all elections were half-Senate elections except for the double dissolution election of 1914 at which all 36 Senators were elected.
Source: adapted from Fusaro (1967: 330)

Table 3.4 shows the percentage of seats won by the ALP at Senate elections from 1903 through 1946, the last non-PR election. That percentage fluctuated as much as it possibly could: twice Labor won every seat that was contested: three times it lost all of them. The percentage of seats that Labor won increased 77.8 per cent from the 1906 to the 1910 election, dropped 86.1 per cent from the 1914 to the 1917 election, and increased 84.2 per cent from the 1940 to the 1943 election. In only one of these elections did the Labor Party win between 40 and 60 per cent of the seats that were contested (55.6 per cent in 1922)—the range of outcomes that we would expect to find most if not all the time in a competitive party system.

The 1934 election had given 33 of the 36 Senate seats to the United Australia and Country parties, leaving only three for Labor.[56] Twelve years later, the 1946 elections produced precisely the opposite result, giving the ALP 33 seats with only two going to the Liberals and one to the Country Party. To be sure, not all the pre-1949 elections had produced such one-sided results. Following 15 of the 18 pre-1949 elections, however, the government held less than 40 per cent or more than 60 per cent of Senate seats. By contrast, 11 of those 18 elections gave the government between 40 and 60 per cent of all House seats. Senate elections had produced considerably more unbalanced and disproportionate results than had House elections, and this was especially the case in 1946, which produced the Parliament that chose to institute PR for future Senate elections. Writing in that year, Denning explains why the results of Senate elections so often were so lopsided:

> As the party trend in voting for the Senate usually follows the trend in the elections for the House of Representatives, each State usually manages to return a bloc of three members of one particular party. That is helped by the preferential system of voting, which gives an almost unassailable advantage to the fellow-candidates of the party-nominee who gets the highest individual score of primary [first preference] votes. His preferences invariably carry number two and number three on the party ticket in with him, though their primaries might be far below the primaries scored by leading candidates of other parties. (Denning 1946: 61)

Characterizing the Senate in 1941, Souter argues that such exaggerated election results had been accompanied by a decline in the quality of representation in the Senate:

> The Senate at this time bore little resemblance to the brave hopes expressed for it at the federal conventions. Political parties had tightened their hold on senators, particularly since the introduction of preferential voting, and it was fair to say that the calibre of senators had deteriorated. 'With a few exceptions', wrote one observer, 'it was a chamber of ageing party hacks and superannuated servicemen from World War I. It had a high proportion of heavy drinkers'. In 1941 the Senate was again functioning as a rubber stamp. ... As Curtin [the Labor Prime Minister] well knew, however, a tame Senate could easily become a hostile one if the lower house came under different management. (Souter 1988: 338)

---

56 On the difficulties this caused the Labor Government, see Souter 1988: 280–285.

'By 1949,' writes Thompson (1999: 42), 'the Senate, while not quite moribund, was largely regarded as a weak institution, irrelevant to the conduct of politics.'

Such concerns were coupled with others about the consequences of enlarging the House, which was a primary interest of Labor. Because of the constitutional 'nexus' between the sizes of the two houses, increasing the membership of the House required a proportional increase in the membership of the Senate. Uhr quotes the then Clerk of the Senate as having argued 'that to continue a system which might result in a Senate of 60 members all belonging to one party would make a farce of Parliamentary government.' (John Edwards, quoted by Uhr 1999b: 16) In support of the *Commonwealth Electoral Act 1949*, therefore, the Attorney-General, Dr. Evatt, argued, according to Souter (1988: 395–396), that:

> proportional representation, a system used in Eire and Tasmania, was fairer than the preferential block majority system currently in use, and more likely to enhance the status of the Senate. The preferential system had the advantage of usually producing a clear-cut majority; but unless there was a nearly equal and opposite swing at successive elections, the majority could be inordinately large and so unrepresentative of the national electorate as to make a mockery of serious debate.

Uhr also points out that by eliminating the wild swings that had characterized Senate elections, PR promised protection to both the ALP and the Coalition against the danger of electoral devastation. Before 1949, each electoral combatant faced the prospect that, when it was in government, it was likely to have a Senate majority much larger than it needed, and that, when it was in Opposition, it was likely to have too few Senate seats to make any difference. Proportional representation, on the other hand, ensured more stable and comparable levels of representation in the Senate for both Labor and its opponents:

> [A] primary intention of the major parties who initiated and supported the change was to secure a guaranteed minimum of Senate representation for the established political forces which alternated in government and opposition. ... The 1949 changes were made by the major parties from a position resembling the 'veil of ignorance' so celebrated by the political philosopher John Rawls, when the most acceptable decisions about rules for the allocation of goods are made in ignorance of a party's post-decision strength or weakness: not knowing whether you are going to be in government or opposition, it is in your interests to devise inclusive rules which share power between both camps. ... In this case, of course, both the major political forces knew that there was a fair chance that they would spend at least as much time in opposition as in government, even if their

hopes were high that the time in opposition would come later rather than
sooner. (Uhr 1998:142)

So Uhr (2001a: 277) can say in summary that PR was recognized in
1948 'as the revival of a long-discussed option to bring party balance to
the Senate that would be in the long-term interests of both major party
blocs, and as a newly discussed option to provide Labor with a short-
term parliamentary power base through the one-off transitional
arrangements to the larger Senate which would benefit Labor given its
existing domination of Senate numbers.'

The question remains, however, whether in focusing on the
likelihood that PR would prevent such gross imbalances as the 1946
election had produced, the government paid insufficient attention to the
possibility of an exactly opposite outcome: that PR could result in the
Senate being so evenly divided between the ALP and its opponents that
the balance of power might well rest in the hands of a small number of
minor party or Independent Senators. Was the switch to PR, as Galligan
(1995: 145) has claimed, 'a Labor initiative that was not well thought
out'?

Campbell Sharman (1999: 151) has addressed this question,
contending that, 'whatever the intent of the Chifley government in
accepting PR for Senate elections from 1949, the creation of a forum
for an active role for minor parties was not one of them.' So, he asks
'whether the effect of PR in enabling the representation of minor parties
in the Senate and in creating the likelihood that they would hold the
balance of power was simply the result of a massive miscalculation. In
other words, was the representation of minor parties a reasonably
foreseeable result of adopting PR for the Senate, and could their pivotal
role in the control of Senate majorities have been predicted?'

If Members and Senators had foreseen in 1948 that the advent of PR
would lead to minor parties being represented in the Senate, the fairly
even balance, then as now, between voters' support for the ALP and for
the Liberal-Country (now National) coalition should have led them to
predict that minor party Senators might well hold the balance of
power—from time to time, if not as a matter of course. But Uhr (1999b:
7) argues that 'The major parties which managed the transition to a PR
system gave little thought to the possible effects in encouraging the
formation of minor parties, even though the historical case against PR
was that it would jeopardize the conventions of strong party
government.'

In defense of the Chifley Government, however, Sharman argues
that it was not as clear then as it is in retrospect that PR would lead to
regular minor party representation in the Senate. He observes that the
percentage of votes that minor parties had received during the two

decades before the 1949 half-Senate election had never reached the
level that was needed to win a Senate seat after PR was instituted in
1948. In other words, if government and parliamentary leaders had
calculated what the quota required to win a Senate seat was likely to be
during the next forthcoming election, they might well have concluded
that, based on past performance, no minor party would receive that
percentage of votes. 'Excepting the Country Party [which was not a
minor party for these purposes] ... the vote for most minor party and
Independent candidates was far less than 10 per cent and highly
variable between elections' when 'the quota required for winning one
of the five seats available at each half-Senate election after 1949 was 17
per cent of the vote in each state.' Furthermore, 'There was no evidence
of a pool of disaffected voters who might use the Senate to vote for any
party other than the established ones.' (Sharman 1999: 152)

In other words, the results of past elections did not indicate that
minor parties were likely to receive enough votes under PR to achieve
Senate representation. '[T]here was reason to believe that the quota for
gaining representation under the PR system adopted for the Senate in
1948 was sufficiently high to exclude minor parties except in the
special case of the Country Party. The experience of the first three
Senate elections with PR in 1949, 1951 and 1953 confirmed this belief.'
So 'In light of the evidence available in 1948, a strong argument can be
made that the representation of minor parties in the Senate other than
the Country Party (now the National Party) could not have been
predicted.' (Sharman 1999: 153, 151). However, the political reasoning
that evidently prevailed in 1948 assumed that the shift to election by
proportional representation would not affect voters' choices—that
voters would continue to vote under PR in the same way they had voted
before PR.

Between the 'fusion' of the Freetraders and Protectionists in 1909
and the introduction of PR at the 1949 election, minor parties had failed
to secure representation in the Senate.[57] Senators had been affiliated
with the ALP or with one of the two non-Labor parties. Although the
introduction of proportional representation made it easier for minor
parties to achieve Senate representation, the effect was not immediate.
In the first three Senate elections under PR—in 1949, 1951, and 1953—
no minor party Senators were elected. Following the 1955 election,
however, the major party Senators found that they had two Democratic
Labor Party (DLP) colleagues, a development that undermined the

---

57 Solomon (1978: 88) reports that, 'Until 1954 only one independent had ever been
elected to the Senate (in 1904).'

argument that Australians who voted for the DLP or any other minor
party were wasting their votes.

> The political event of the split in the ALP created the DLP with sufficient
> support in one state [Victoria] to secure the election of a DLP senator. This
> gave the new party the ability to use the Senate as a forum for publicising
> the party's views, and raised the visibility of both the Senate and the DLP.
> When this was reinforced by the dependence of the government on DLP
> senators for the control of the Senate, the DLP had a powerful lever to keep
> their policy agenda before the public. The conclusion is that, once a minor
> party had been elected to the Senate and had held the balance of power, a
> clarion call was sent to parties and voters that PR in the Senate could be
> used by a minor party with great effect to influence government policy. By
> the mid-1960s, enough voters were persuaded to view their Senate vote in
> this way to ensure that a steady stream of minor party and Independent
> candidates were elected to the Senate. (Sharman 1999: 154)

The DLP continued to win seats in the next five Senate elections
and, although it disappeared from the Senate in the 1970s, the
candidates and supporters of the minor parties that followed it could
point to its example. According to Solomon (1986: 144), the 'principal
aim' of the DLP was 'to keep the Labor Party from winning
government.'[58] By contrast, the Australian Democrats, who succeeded
the now-defunct DLP in the Senate in 1977, 'claimed to be a centre
party aimed explicitly at using their balance of power in the Senate to
moderate the activities of the government.' (Sharman 1999: 155) Since
then, the Democrats have retained seats in the Senate but never have
elected a Member of the Commonwealth House of Representatives.

> This has meant that the Democrats have consistently regarded the
> legislating and scrutinising functions of parliament as their overwhelming
> concern. This has distinguished them from the DLP as well as from the
> major parties. As far as the Democrats are concerned, there is an almost
> perfect match between their partisan interests and the perpetuation of a
> strong Senate free from control by either government or opposition
> majorities. (Sharman 1999: 155)

Sharman concludes that, whatever the intentions and expectations of the
Chifley Government in 1949, 'the effect [of introducing PR for Senate
elections] was to establish a symbiotic relationship between minor
parties and the Senate—the greater the influence of minor parties in the
Senate, the more visible the Senate became to the public and the more
publicity minor parties got for their policies. The DLP had started a

---

58 '[T]he DLP, by persuading a body of traditional Labor voters to give their second
    preferences to non-Labor parties, helped to keep the anti-Labor, Liberal-led
    coalition in power until 1972.' (Knightley 2000: 248)

revolution in the perception of the role of the Senate and the potential of PR for reflecting the views of any minor party which could generate around 10 per cent of the state-wide first preference vote at Senate elections.'

The implication of this line of argument is that, in opting for PR in 1948, the ALP Government of the day failed to anticipate that changing the way in which Senators were elected would eventually affect how at least some Australians made their voting decisions. As a result, the record of prior Senate elections proved to be an imperfect predictor of future election results. This lack of foresight proved particularly ironic and unfortunate for Labor because the first minor party to secure and retain Senate seats had splintered from the ALP and usually, but not always, voted with the Coalition Government.

Australians have become somewhat more inclined to vote for minor party candidates for the Senate. Stone presents data showing that the combined vote in Senate elections of the ALP and the Coalition declined from 95.3 per cent in 1949–1953 to 83.4 per cent in 1977–1996. Although it would be foolhardy to attribute this trend to any single factor, 'it has been suggested … that these [minor] parties are now valued and supported for the contribution they make to the governmental process' (Stone 1998b: 217–218), a contribution that takes place by virtue of their representation in the Senate. In turn, a rising vote for minor party (and Independent) Senate candidates makes it that much more unlikely that either the ALP or the Coalition will succeed in securing a Senate majority in its own right, and so tends to ensure that minor parties will continue to hold a pivotal position of power in the Senate.[59]

---

59 Bean and Wattenberg (1996) offer two reasons why Australian voters may be more likely than American voters to vote for a House candidate of one party and, at the same election, give their first preference votes to Senate candidates of a different party. First, ticket-splitting in the United States requires a voter to vote for candidates of two major parties that are clearly in opposition to each other—to vote at the same time for both a Democrat and a Republican—whereas Australian voters can vote for a major party in the House election (to determine which party will form the government) and then for a minor party (instead of the other major party) to determine which party will control the Senate. It should be easier to convince oneself to vote for an ALP House candidate and Australian Democrat Senate candidates, they argue with plausibility, than to vote at the same election for the Labor House candidate and also for Liberal or National Party Senate candidates. Second, observant Australian voters have reason to believe that the minor parties for which they vote actually might achieve Senate representation—that those who vote for minor parties in Senate elections are not throwing away their votes, which is the most powerful argument against voting for third parties in US national elections.

Moreover, because minor parties derive their influence from their representation in the Senate, they have an incentive to support and strengthen the Senate as an institution, an incentive that is not shared by either the government or the Opposition.

> Minor party and Independent senators who hold the balance of power [in the Senate] are not more virtuous or more public spirited than other senators; it is just that they have an interest in establishing procedures to enhance the long-term effectiveness—and hence political visibility—of the Senate. In this respect, the interests of minor parties and Independents correspond with a broader public interest. The maintenance of a legislative body which has a role to play that is distinct from the partisan struggle to hold or gain government means that a wider range of interests can be involved in the legislative process than those identified with the government or the opposition. (Sharman 1999: 150)

For the Opposition, the Senate is a valued fortress behind the walls of which it can protect itself from being overrun by the numerically superior forces of the government in the House, and from which it can sally forth from time to time to fight the government on a battlefield that reduces or eliminates its numerical disadvantage. So the Opposition also has a short-term interest in making sure that its Senate fortress is solidly constructed and that it is well-armed and well-supplied. However, as I shall argue later in a different context, the Opposition naturally sees itself as the future government that has to rely on the Senate only temporarily while it rebuilds its strength and heals the wounds it suffered at the last election. Its inevitable role, it believes, is as the dominating, conquering army of government. Consequently, its concern with the Senate as an institution is more transitory than that of the minor parties whose influence will be exercised through the Senate for the indefinite future.

4

The crisis of 1974–75

In 1975, Australia experienced the most discussed and most important constitutional crisis in the history of the Commonwealth.[60] In its immediate aftermath, Howard (1976: 5) concluded that the crisis had precipitated 'a fundamental redistribution of power between the two Houses of the national parliament and between Parliament and the executive.' In retrospect, his assessment has proven to be exaggerated. It is doubtless true, however, that the crisis has continued to reverberate through the thinking of Australian politicians ever since. Even more than a quarter of a century later, the events of 1975 continue to evoke strong, sometimes passionate, reactions.[61]

The events of 1974

The December 1972 elections had produced the Labor Party (ALP) Government of Prime Minister Gough Whitlam, which enjoyed a secure though not overwhelming majority in the House of Representatives over the long-standing parliamentary coalition of the

---

60 For contemporaneous accounts, see Kelly (1976) and Oakes (1976); for the recollections and self-justifications of key participants, see Whitlam (1979), Kerr (1978), and Barwick (1983); for a retrospective account, see Kelly (1995). How the events of 1975 could have unfolded as they did has continued to intrigue political observers and scholars alike. In an otherwise captivating book on Australia in the Twentieth Century, for example, Philip Knightley (2000: 269–282) concludes that the CIA was complicit, and perhaps even instrumental, in a conspiracy that led to Whitlam's ouster. But then Kelly (1976: 1) reports that Whitlam himself had raised the spectre of CIA involvement.

61 In 1991, more than 15 years after the events discussed here, a national survey of voters were asked whether the Governor-General had been right or wrong to dismiss the Whitlam Government. Forty-three per cent responded that he had been right; 33.6 per cent that he had been wrong. But those figures are far less interesting than is the fact that less than one-quarter of those interviewed failed to respond or answered that they did not know. Not only did more than 75 per cent of the respondents remember a political event that had occurred years earlier, they were prepared to offer a judgment about it. For the poll, visit http://ssda.anu.edu.au/polls/D0737.html.

Liberal and Country (now National) parties. Such was not the case in the Senate, however, where the ALP held only 26 of the 60 seats. The Liberal-Country alliance, popularly known as the Coalition, had the same number of seats, leaving control of the Senate in the hands of five members of the Democratic Labor Party (DLP) and three Independents. The DLP Senators usually allied themselves with the Coalition, giving the non-Labor parties a 31–26 margin over the ALP. Even if Labor was supported by the three Independents, what was ostensibly Australia's governing party was in the minority in one of the two houses of Parliament.

The early 1970s unquestionably were an unusual, even unique, period in bicameral relations for the Commonwealth. 'Throughout its first seventy-one years of existence the Senate had rejected only sixty-eight government bills; in the next three years, it rejected no fewer than ninety-three Whitlam bills.' (Souter 1988: 549) This is not to suggest that the Senate hamstrung the Labor Government on all fronts. The Senate passed far more bills (a total of 508) than it rejected. Still, the Senate clearly was much more of an obstacle during this Parliament than it ever had been before.

In April of 1974, the political stakes escalated when the Liberal-Country Party Coalition and its allies-of-the-moment in the Senate voted to defer action on supply bills. 'Supply' is a term sometimes used to refer to all spending bills. At the time of these events, 'supply' also was defined more narrowly to refer specifically to bills that were enacted to authorize spending during the early months of a fiscal year, before the annual budget for that fiscal year was approved. In the 1970s, such supply bills were a necessary and predictable part of Parliament's annual agenda. Today, such bills rarely are needed because Australia changed its annual budget timetable.[62]

As we already have seen, Australia's Constitution (in sec. 53) gives the Senate and the House of Representatives almost the same legislative powers, with exceptions that concern these supply bills as well as other spending and tax bills. In Australia as in the United States, all such bills

---

62 'Strictly speaking, supply was the money granted by the Parliament in the supply bills which, before the change in the budget cycle in 1994, were usually passed in April–May of each year, and which appropriated funds for the period between the end of the financial year on 30 June and the passage of the main appropriation bills. The latter appropriate funds for the whole financial year, were formerly passed in October–November and are now passed in June.' *(Odgers' Australian Senate Practice* 2001: 295) Now the annual budget usually is presented in May, allowing time for appropriations to be enacted before the new financial year begins on 1 July and rendering supply bills unnecessary—unless a general election disrupts the normal schedule, in which case supply may be required.

originate in the House, but unlike the situation in the US Congress, the Australian Senate may not amend those bills. So the Australian House of Representatives has enjoyed constitutional primacy over the Senate with respect to these most critical legislative measures. However, the Senate is not powerless to influence tax and spending legislation. First, the Constitution authorizes the Senate to request that the House approve specific amendments to these bills. Second, the Constitution does not require the Senate to pass the bills, nor does it give the House any immediate or convenient legislative recourse if the Senate does not pass them. The Senate may defeat a tax or spending bill, as passed by the House, or it may vote to defer acting on it.

Gareth Evans, who would later become a senior ALP minister, wrote (1975: 11) at the time that the Senate was breaking a convention in denying supply because 'on 139 previous occasions money bills have been passed by a Senate in which the Government of the day lacked a majority, and none has been previously rejected.'[63] (Note that he strengthens his argument by taking tax and spending bills together, as we would expect a good advocate to do.) Yet this is what the Senate, with its non-government majority, threatened to do in 1974, by moving to defer second reading of Appropriation Bill (No. 4). The merits of the bill were not at issue. Instead, the Coalition, then led by B.M. Snedden, sought to use the fate of the bill, enactment of which was needed to continue the operations of government, as leverage to induce Whitlam and his Ministry to request the Governor-General to dissolve the House so that new House elections could take place at the same time, in May 1974, as the anticipated triennial half-Senate election.

When a motion was made in the Senate 'That the resumption of the debate [on second reading of Appropriation Bill (No. 4)] be an order of the day for a later hour of the day,' the Leader of the Opposition offered an amendment that the debate not be resumed 'before the Government agrees to submit itself to the judgment of the people at the same time as the forthcoming Senate election ... ' (*House of Representatives Practice* 2001: 452–453). Before the Senate voted on the motion or the amendment to it, the Leader of the Government in the Senate announced that the government, anticipating defeat in the Senate, already had sought, and the Governor-General had granted, a double

---

63 Historically, Labor had been no friend of the Senate, even though it was the ALP that instituted PR for Senate elections and, it is safe to say, led to the institution's revitalization (vitalization might be a more apt description). It also was Labor that promoted a stronger Senate committee system. But for many years, the ALP had advocated that the Senate be abolished. It was only at the party's 1979 national conference that it repealed this plank in its platform.

dissolution of both houses of Parliament under sec. 57 of the Constitution.

Howard (1976: 7) points out that Whitlam did not challenge the constitutional authority of the Senate to act (or not act) as it had. Instead, the Prime Minister 'accepted the political challenge' and called for a double dissolution which, as we have seen, triggers new elections to fill all seats in both the House and the Senate, and is the only constitutional mechanism for requiring Senators to face the electorate before the expiration of what otherwise are their fixed six-year terms. Thus, the Opposition in the Senate, with the assistance of DLP Senators, had achieved its immediate political objective, so it allowed prompt passage of the contested appropriation bill as well as others that were required to continue necessary government funding until after the ensuing general election.

As a matter of form, this double dissolution, which was only the third in the history of the Commonwealth, was not based on the Senate's failure to pass Appropriation Bill (No. 4). The Senate had not yet rejected that bill even once, and certainly not twice as sec. 57 requires as a prerequisite for a double dissolution. However, there were six other bills that, the government contended, already had fully satisfied the requirements of sec. 57. What is more, the Prime Minister asserted that these bills were important to the government's legislative program.[64]

Be that as it may, it is reasonable to infer that the Senate's action (or inaction) and the government's response were prompted less by the merits of the bills in question than by the parties' calculations as to which of them were most likely to benefit from new elections to one or both houses.[65] The government could have continued to muddle through

---

64 The Prime Minister also argued that the Senate had taken other steps to interfere with enactment of the government's legislative program, 'stating that 21 out of the 254 bills put before Parliament in the first session had been rejected, stood aside or deferred by the Senate.' However, the Governor-General did not rest his decision to grant the double dissolution on this contention. He stated that, 'As it is clear to me that grounds for granting a double dissolution are provided by the Parliamentary history of the six Bills ... it is not necessary for me to reach any judgment on the wider case you have presented that the policies of the Government have been obstructed by the Senate. It seems to me that this is a matter for judgment by the electors.' (*House of Representatives Practice* 2001: 453)

65 Souter (1988: 516) contends that the government deliberately sought to have these other bills satisfy the requirements of sec. 57 'as a warning to Opposition senators that they too could all be made to face election if they dared to block supply. And that kind of warning was itself a license to break convention [i.e., that the Senate should not block supply bills]. If the Senate was no longer a coward's castle, and senators could be made to share the fate which they had the power to force upon the

with the existing political alignment in Parliament, or it could have asked the Governor-General to dissolve the House only. Instead, the Whitlam Government chose a double dissolution, presumably hoping or expecting that the Labor Party would take effective control of the Senate while retaining its majority in the House. In the process, the government also set a precedent for what would happen in the following year (Howard 1976: 7).

The simultaneous elections of May 1974 did not entirely fulfill the ALP's hopes. The Labor Government remained in office because it kept control of the House. Although Labor's margin over the Liberal-Country coalition in the House was even narrower than it had been before the 1974 election, the strength of party discipline in the House assured Labor's effective control. In the Senate, however, Labor and the Coalition again were tied, this time with 29 seats each, with the two remaining seats held by an Independent and a member of the Liberal Movement, which had splintered off from the Liberal Party several years earlier but would rejoin it several years later. At best, therefore, Labor could hope for a tied vote in the Senate.[66] The deadlock that the Whitlam Government had hoped the double dissolution would break remained in place. There was one other change in Canberra, however, that would prove significant: Sir John Kerr was appointed in July as the new Governor-General.

On the first two days after the new Parliament convened, the House passed the six bills for a third time; the Senate again failed to pass any of them. The government then invoked, for the first and only time in the history of the Commonwealth, the remaining provisions of sec. 57, which set a procedure for breaking a deadlock that the elections following a double dissolution have failed to resolve. This procedure, as described earlier, provides for one more attempt, after a double dissolution and simultaneous elections, for the two houses to reach legislative agreement by conventional means. If this effort fails, as it had in the case of these six bills, the Governor-General may convene a joint sitting of the two houses in which each remaining legislative disagreement is decided by 'an absolute majority vote of the total number of the members of the Senate and the House of Representatives'.

---

lower house, then the blocking of supply might not be such a dishonourable action after all.'

66 In case there was any doubt, sec. 23 of the Constitution provides that 'Questions arising in the Senate shall be determined by a majority of votes, and each senator shall have one vote. The President shall in all cases be entitled to a vote; and *when the votes are equal the question shall pass in the negative.*' (emphasis added)

When the joint sitting took place in August 1974,[67] the ALP's majority in the House left little doubt about the outcome. The government was able to prevail by a narrow margin on each of the six bills.[68] Each received the required absolute majority of votes. There were no amendments to any of the bills for the joint sitting to consider.

The events of 1975

So the situation remained until February 1975, when the Labor Government appointed its Attorney-General, Senator Lionel Murphy, to be a Justice of the High Court (Kelly 1976: 102–108). Although the Prime Minister and his Cabinet colleagues obviously knew that this decision would give them one fewer Senate seats than the Liberal-Country coalition, they also surely must have assumed that this situation was only temporary. When a vacancy occurs in the Senate due to death or resignation (known in Australia as a 'casual' vacancy), the parliament of the Senator's state elects a replacement, according to sec.

---

67 Less than a week before the joint sitting, the two houses exercised their authority under sec. 50 of the Constitution and agreed to a set of 18 'Rules for Joint Sittings' (reprinted in *House of Representatives Practice* 2001: 849-851). These joint rules were not adopted in the joint sitting itself. Instead, they were adopted in advance by the two houses acting separately. With regard to the procedures to be followed during the joint session, the rules provided for the standing orders of the Senate to be followed on all questions that the joint rules did not explicitly address. In this context, *Odgers' Australian Senate Practice* (2001: 116) points to 'the parliamentary convention that the procedure of a joint committee of the two Houses follows the procedure of committees of the Senate when such procedure differs from that of the House whether the chair is a member of the House or not.' So it would seem that the two houses agreed to follow the same general principle with respect to the rules they adopted for the joint sitting: that the default authority would be the Senate's standing orders. Parliament also amended the Parliamentary Papers Act and the Evidence Act to bring the joint sitting under the same provisions that applied to sittings of the House and Senate concerning such matters as immunity and admissibility in court of documents presented at the joint sitting. Also, the Parliamentary Proceedings Broadcasting Act was amended to permit the joint sitting to be televised (Zines 1977: 233–235; *House of Representatives Practice* 2001: 465).

68 The High Court later invalidated one of the bills on the ground that the required three-month interval had not elapsed between the first two attempts to pass the bill by conventional means. The government's position was that the clock began to run when the House passed the bill for the first time. The Court rejected this contention and found (as discussed earlier) that the three-month interval begins only when the Senate rejects the bill or has demonstrated conclusively its intent not to pass it. The challenge to the bill had been submitted to the High Court before the joint sitting began, but the Court ruled that the question would not become ripe for adjudication until after the bill's enactment (see Zines 1977: 224–227, and *Odgers' Australian Senate Practice* 2001: 81).

15 of the Constitution. In every such instance since 1949, when Senators first were elected by proportional representation, a Senator who died or resigned had been replaced by someone of the same party.[69] In this case, however, the New South Wales Parliament, with its Liberal Party majority, chose an Independent to replace the resigned ALP Senator.[70] The ALP's situation deteriorated still further when, following the death of a Labor Senator, the Queensland Parliament chose a replacement who was known to oppose the Whitlam Government.

With the Liberal Party's hand strengthened by these two developments, its new leader, Malcolm Fraser, announced that the Senate again would refuse to act on essential budgetary legislation in another effort to compel the government to call new House elections:

> We will use the power vested in us by the Constitution and delay the passage of the Government's money bills through the Senate, until the Parliament goes to the people. In accordance with long established constitutional practice which the Prime Minister has himself acknowledged in the past, the Government must resign. (*Australian*, 16 October 1975: 1)

Instead of agreeing to the second reading of two appropriation bills, the Senate voted that the bills 'be not further proceeded with until the Government agrees to submit itself to the judgment of the people, the Senate being of the opinion that the Prime Minister and his Government no longer have the trust and confidence of the Australian people … ' (quoted in *Odgers' Australian Senate Practice* 2001: 101) The Senate had agreed to a similar resolution one day earlier regarding a third, non-appropriation, bill.[71]

---

69 However, this had not been the uniform practice before 1948. 'In filling a Senate vacancy in April 1931, the South Australian parliament violated a hitherto respected convention that casual vacancies should be filled by nominees from the same party as the deceased. A Labor Senator, Henry Kneebone, replaced a Country Party senator, but the difference he made to the imbalance of power was infinitesimal … ' (Souter 1988: 280)

70 By contrast, when George W. Bush was elected President in 2000 and the US Senate was equally divided between Democrats and Republicans, the President-elect was effectively barred from choosing Republican Senators to fill senior positions in his Administration if those Senators were from states with Democratic governors. The newly-elected President understood that state governors appoint replacements for Senators who have left office for whatever reason, and that they routinely appoint Senators of their own party. Because of the equal party division in the Senate, Bush could not afford to cause even one Republican Senator to resign if that Senator would be replaced by a Democrat. Any contention that a Democratic governor was somehow honor-bound to replace a Republican Senator with another Republican would have been greeted with derision.

71 It was marginally easier for the Opposition to secure Senate majorities for deferring further action on the bills than it would have been to reject what was portrayed as (and what in fact was) essential legislation. Deferral also kept the bills before the

This time Whitlam refused the challenge, perhaps fearing the electoral defeat that Fraser hoped to inflict, but citing constitutional principle:

> I state again the basic rule of our parliamentary system; governments are made and unmade in the House of Representatives—in the people's house. The Senate cannot, does not, and must never determine who the government shall be. (*Australian*, 16 October 1975: 1)

If the Senate motion skated on thin constitutional ice, the government's resolution in the House made an uncompromising claim for the House's primacy. Its resolution read in part:

(1) This House declares that it has full confidence in the Australian Labor Party Government;

(2) This House affirms that the Constitution and the conventions of the Constitution vest in this House the control of the supply of moneys to the elected Government and that the threatened action of the Senate constitutes a gross violation of the roles of the respective Houses of the Parliament in relation to the appropriation of moneys;

(3) This House asserts the basic principle that a Government that continues to have a majority in the House of Representatives has a right to expect that it will be able to govern;

(4) This House condemns the threatened action of the Leader of the Opposition and of the non-government parties in the Senate as being reprehensible and as constituting a grave threat to the principles of responsible government and of Parliamentary democracy in Australia ... (*Votes and Proceedings of the House of Representatives*, 16 October 1975: 987–988)

In describing these developments, *Odgers' Australian Senate Practice* (2001: 101–102), the Senate's authoritative statement of its procedures, argues with apparent indignation that 'Any contention that there is a convention that the Senate should not defer or reject money bills is insupportable.' *Odgers' Australian Senate Practice* proceeds to cite examples in which the Senate had pressed its requests for amendments to money bills and rejected tax bills, as well as instances in which state upper houses had denied supply. There follow several quotations demonstrating, to put it charitably, that Labor's leaders evidently had reconsidered the views they had expressed in 1970 about the proper role of the Senate.

Senate so that when circumstances changed, the Senate could revive and pass them quickly. That is precisely what ultimately happened.

In 1975, the political clash between Labor and the Coalition seems to have merged in Whitlam's mind with the constitutional clash between the House and Senate.[72]

> Whitlam intended to use the crisis triggered by Fraser to defeat the Senate in such a comprehensive manner that no future Senate would contemplate such action, and to ensure that the contradiction within the Constitution since the inauguration of the Commonwealth was finally resolved with the victory of the Representatives over the Senate and of responsible government over federalism. Whitlam would become the last of the founding fathers. He would resolve the contradiction that they had been unable to resolve. (Kelly 1995: 289)

But Whitlam had been Leader of the Opposition in the House when he announced in 1970 that 'our opposition to this Budget is no mere formality. We intend to press our opposition by all available means on all related measures in both Houses. If the motion is defeated, we will vote against the Bills here and in the Senate. Our purpose is to destroy this Budget and to destroy the Government which has sponsored it.'[73] Although the bill in question was a tax bill, Whitlam had announced his party's willingness to vote against appropriation bills as well. Whitlam took this stand about two months after a similar statement had been made by Senator Murphy, then Labor's Leader of the Opposition in the Senate, who happened to be the Senator whose appointment to the High Court early in 1975 was contributing to the problems that Whitlam's Government was having with the Senate:[74]

> The Senate is entitled and expected to exercise resolutely but with discretion its power to refuse its concurrence to any financial measure, including a tax Bill. There are no limitations on the Senate in the use of its constitutional powers, except the limitations imposed by discretion and reason. The Australian Labor Party has acted consistently in accordance with the tradition that we will oppose in the Senate any tax or money bill or other financial measure whenever necessary to carry out our principles and

---

72 That may explain why, when Whitlam gathered his parliamentary lieutenants around him immediately after being dismissed from office, he neglected to include his own Senate leaders (See Kelly 1995: 266).

73 *Commonwealth Parliamentary Debates* (House of Representatives), 25 August 1970: 463.

74 Souter (1988: 489) reports that Murphy listed '168 financial measures which Labor had opposed in the Senate since 1950.' Souter (1988: 472) also quotes Murphy as having used much the same formulation in May 1967 when the Senate defeated a Post and Telegraph Rates Bill. Note that in both instances, what was at stake was a tax bill, not a spending bill. However important those tax bills may have been for the government's program, the Senate's failure to pass them did not jeopardize government operations in the same way that its failure to vote supply could—and did in 1975.

policies. (*Commonwealth Parliamentary Debates* (Senate), 18 June 1970: 2647)

Later in 1970, Whitlam had gone so far as to imply that it would be in accord with parliamentary practice for the Senate to bring down the government: 'We all know that in British parliaments the tradition is that if a money Bill is defeated the government goes to the people to seek their endorsement of its policies.' (quoted in Souter 1988: 489; see also Liberal Party 1975: 540) However convenient this formulation may have been at the time, it is doubtful that Erskine May would have recognized the constitutional right of the upper house to cast a *de facto* vote of no confidence in the government.

In 1975, after the House and Senate staked out their positions, they proceeded to exchange several more rounds of constitutional broadsides, the House contending that the Senate was exceeding the conventions that limited how its formal authority had been understood and exercised, and the Senate responding that no such conventions existed. Just as *Odgers' Australian Senate Practice* seems to find more merit in the Senate's position, not surprisingly *House of Representatives Practice* (2001: 455) gives more emphasis to the arguments that the House made on three separate occasions during the next several weeks—quoting the House, for example, as rejecting what it characterized as a 'blatant attempt by the Senate to violate section 28 of the Constitution for political purposes ... '

When the House passed a similar pair of appropriation bills for a second time, the Senate again deferred acting on them until the government agreed to new elections:

> The Senate affirmed that it had the constitutional right to act as it had and, now that there was a disagreement between the Houses of Parliament and a position might arise where the normal operations of government could not continue, a remedy was available to the government under section 57 of the Constitution to resolve the deadlock. (*Odgers' Australian Senate Practice* 2001: 103)

Whitlam again refused. Several weeks later, and after intense negotiations and a third attempt to enact the appropriation bills, the new Governor-General took the extraordinary and unprecedented step of acting at his own initiative to invoke his power under sec. 62 of the Constitution:

> There shall be a Federal Executive Council [in practice, the Government] to advise the Governor-General in the government of the Commonwealth, and the members of the Council shall be chosen and summoned by the Governor-General and sworn as Executive Councillors, *and shall hold office during his pleasure*. (emphasis added)

Governor-General Kerr dismissed the Whitlam Government, even though it still enjoyed majority support in the House of Representatives to which, by constitutional convention, it was responsible. To replace it, Kerr appointed a caretaker Liberal Government with Fraser as prime minister. In justifying his decision, the Governor-General argued that, in the Australian system, 'the confidence of both Houses on supply is necessary to ensure its provision':

> When ... an Upper House possesses the power to reject a money bill including an appropriation bill, and exercises the power by denying supply, the principle that a government which has been denied supply by the Parliament should resign or go to an election must still apply—it is a necessary consequence of Parliamentary control of appropriation and expenditure and of the expectation that the ordinary and necessary services of Government will continue to be provided. (quoted in *Odgers' Australian Senate Practice* 2001: 104)

In this position the Governor-General was supported by the Chief Justice, who wrote that:[75]

> the Senate has constitutional power to refuse to pass a money bill; it has power to refuse supply to the Government of the day. ... a Prime Minister who cannot ensure supply to the Crown, including funds for carrying on the ordinary services of Government, must either advise a general election (of a kind which the constitutional situation may then allow) or resign. (quoted in *Odgers' Australian Senate Practice* 2001: 105)

Not surprisingly, the two houses reacted very differently. The Senate acted almost instantaneously to pass the stalled appropriation bills. The House agreed to a motion expressing its lack of confidence in the newly-designated prime minister and requesting the Speaker to ask the Governor-General to have Whitlam again form a government. But before the Speaker was allowed to deliver this message, the Governor-General declared, at Fraser's request and by pre-arrangement, a double dissolution of both houses.[76] As Solomon put it:

> In the 1975 double dissolution, the Governor-General had to dismiss a Prime Minister (who controlled a majority in the House of Representatives) and appoint another (who lacked the confidence of that House) to find an advisor who was prepared to recommend to him the course he wished to

---

75 Kerr's decision to seek the advice of Chief Justice Barwick and Barwick's decision to provide the advice sought both were controversial decisions in their own right. Kerr thought he needed to make it clear that he already had decided what to do before he consulted the Chief Justice. See Kerr 1975: 542.

76 Kelly (1995: 271–274) and others have asserted that Kerr deliberately delayed receiving the Speaker until he could argue that it was too late to accede to the House's request because both houses already had been dissolved.

adopt—namely the dissolution of both Houses of Parliament under section 57. (Solomon 1978: 169)

The basis for Kerr's action was not the appropriation bills, which had not satisfied the timetable of sec. 57, but a total of 21 other bills that did qualify and that, perhaps fortuitously for Kerr and Fraser but not for Whitlam, the ALP Government had been 'stockpiling' (*Odgers' Australian Senate Practice* 2001: 100). Indeed, Zines (1977: 238) observes, 'it certainly appears paradoxical and even ironical that the dissolution was brought about against the wishes of the House of Representatives and on the formal advice of the leader of a party that was concerned to obstruct it'—and, we might add, the leader of the party that had caused the repeated defeat in the Senate of the very bills that now provided the constitutional grounds for the double dissolution.

The December 1975 elections gave the Coalition a solid majority in the Senate and the largest majority ever won in the House, confirming the short-term political acumen of Fraser's strategy.

Constitutional contention

The Whitlam years were a period of recurring controversy and continuing commotion. In part this reflected Whitlam's own style and personality. Kelly (1976: 351) quotes him as having said that, 'When you are faced with an impasse you have got to crash through or you've got to crash.' Whitlam had brought the ALP back into government in 1972 after so many years in Opposition that his ministers had to learn what it meant to govern, and not all of them succeeded. The most notorious episode, though not the only one that led to ministerial resignations and sackings, was what became known as the 'loans affair', in which a minister was given wide latitude in using questionable intermediaries to negotiate a massive loan from obscure Middle Eastern sources. Whitlam failed to exercise effective supervision over the activities of some of his most senior ministers and even allowed himself to become more directly involved in an attempt to raise money from Iraq to help the Labor Party fund its 1975 election campaign. Whitlam's brief tenure in office undoubtedly was the most tumultuous time in recent Australian history; there is little question that the policies and practices of his government were the prime cause for the Coalition's confidence that the electorate would welcome an early election to remove Whitlam and Company from office.

Our primary concern, though, is with the four major constitutional questions that the events of 1975 raised:

(1) What are the legislative powers of the Senate with regard to money bills?

(2) How are vacancies in the Senate to be filled?

(3) What is the authority of the Governor-General to dismiss the government of the day, and under what circumstances should that authority be exercised? and

(4) When should the Governor-General dissolve Parliament and compel new House and Senate elections?

In each case, a textual reading of the Constitution provides answers that are satisfactorily clear, if only by implication, but not necessarily satisfying.

First, sec. 53 prohibits the Senate from initiating or amending money bills, but the Constitution does not require the Senate to vote on them, much less to pass them, nor does it give the government and the House a quick and easy recourse if the Senate fails to approve any such bills that the House passes. Although one could argue that the authors of the Constitution *meant to* deny the Senate the ability to frustrate the government's budgetary decisions, or that the Constitution *should have* done so, one could argue just as well that the authors *would have* done so if they had thought it necessary.[77] With the experiences of the United Kingdom and the United States readily at hand, as we shall see, that option did in fact occur to them. So a strict reliance solely on the text of the Constitution leads to the conclusion that the Senate had acted within its formal constitutional powers.

Second, sec. 15 provides for each vacancy in the Senate to be filled by vote of the parliament of the affected state. At the time, the Constitution did not constrain the state parliament's choice in any way, and it certainly did not require that the replacement be of the same party as the Senator he or she was replacing. Although Australia's Constitution originally made no mention at all of political parties, it was written at the same time that the outline of Australia's political party system was becoming visible on the horizon. Although one could argue that the Constitution's authors *may have expected* that vacancies would be filled in ways that preserved the political status quo in the Senate, or that the Constitution *should have* mandated that result, one also could argue that the Constitution's *failure to do so* is telling in view of the growing importance of political parties when the Constitution was

---

77 As evidence that the possibility of the Senate acting as it did in 1975 would not have come as a surprise to the Constitution's authors, W.H. Moore wrote in his 1910 study *The Constitution of the Commonwealth of Australia* (p. 144): 'a check upon the Ministry and the Lower House lies in the fact that the Upper House might in an extreme case refuse to pass the Appropriation Bill, and thereby force a dissolution or a change of Ministry. These are the conditions recognised by the Constitution.' See the discussion in the chapter that follows on the constitutional debates relating to the powers of the Senate.

written. Or one could argue that the introduction of proportional representation for Senate elections should have been accompanied by a constitutional amendment or, failing that, an explicit convention regarding the filling of casual vacancies.[78] In any event, a strict reliance solely on the text of the Constitution leads to the conclusion that the parliaments of New South Wales and Queensland had acted within their formal constitutional powers.

Third, sec. 61 vests the 'executive power of the Commonwealth ... in the Queen and is exercisable by the Governor-General as the Queen's representative.' Under sec. 62, there is to be a 'Federal Executive Council to advise the Governor-General in the government of the Commonwealth.' Further, sec. 64 empowers the Governor-General to 'appoint officers to administer such departments of State of the Commonwealth as the Governor-General in Council [that is, 'the Governor-General acting with the advice of the Federal Executive Council'] may establish.' These officers shall be members of the Council; they must be, or must soon become, members of the House or Senate; and, of particular importance, they 'shall hold office during the pleasure of the Governor-General.' Formally, therefore, all executive power is vested in the Governor-General who sometimes is to act with the advice of a Council comprising members of Parliament whom he appoints and may dismiss whenever he chooses. The proverbial visitor from Mars might not appreciate that these provisions are intended to provide for responsible parliamentary government in which actual executive power rests with the prime minister and Cabinet, neither of which is named in the Constitution at all. Nonetheless, if we rely solely on what the Constitution says, we can conclude that the Governor-General acted within his formal constitutional powers in dismissing the incumbent government, and for whatever reasons he thought sufficient.

Fourth, sec. 57 empowers the Governor-General to dissolve both houses when a legislative deadlock has arisen, without specifying the reasons for which, or the circumstances under which, he may or should do so. And surely one situation in which the Governor-General would be most justified in invoking this power is when a stalemate in Parliament threatens to interfere with effective, even normal, operations of the Commonwealth government and when that stalemate might well be broken by new elections. Since the Constitution was written, however, the role of the Governor-General had diminished in practice, as the bonds tying Australia to the Queen had been reduced to little more than a formality. Although one could argue, then, that the

---

78 The issue in fact was canvassed when the first casual vacancy occurred after the 1949 election; see Sawer 1977: 130–133, 199–202.

Governor-General in 1975 *should not* have exercised a power granted to occupants of his office three-quarters of a century earlier, under considerably different political conditions, one could argue equally well that there had been more than ample time and opportunity to strip the Governor-General of this power if it was not thought advisable to leave it in his hands to be used *in just such circumstances.* So a strict reliance solely on the text of the Constitution leads to the conclusion that the new Governor-General had acted within his formal constitutional powers.

Not surprisingly, however, the four actions—the refusal of the non-government majority in the Senate to act on money bills, the failure of two state parliaments to replace resigned or deceased Labor Senators with persons of the same political persuasion, the double dissolution granted at the request of a newly-installed caretaker government, and especially the Governor-General's decision to dismiss the Whitlam Government when it still enjoyed the confidence of a majority in the House of Representatives—all provoked intense criticism, as well as arguments that textual analyses of what the Constitution does or does not say ultimately were beside the point. Critics argued, often passionately, that essential conventions and understandings that surround and supplement the spare terms of the Constitution are every bit as important, and deserve as much (or more) deference and respect, as the text itself.[79] This is true in any constitutional democracy, or so it was argued, but it is particularly true in Australia, in light of the roots of Australian constitutionalism in Great Britain, where the absence of a written constitution places such conventions at the heart of democratic governance.

While it may be true that the Senate, the two state parliaments, and the Governor-General acted in accordance with the constitutional text, their critics argued that they should not have done so. Just because a constitutional officer or entity *has* a constitutional power does not mean that the power *should* be exercised, or that it should be exercised *at will.* The Senate *should not,* it was claimed, have interfered with the ability of the government and the House to enact legislation that was essential to implementing their program and to funding the daily operations of the Commonwealth government. The state parliaments *should not* have ignored or nullified the will of the people, as expressed in Senate elections, by filling Senate vacancies with supporters of

---

79 For a strong, even extreme, statement of this position, see Archer and Maddox (1976).

parties that the voters had rejected at the polls.[80] And the appointed Governor-General *should not* have interfered with the democratic process by exercising his constitutional authority to dismiss a government that still enjoyed the confidence of the House, nor should he have granted a double dissolution except upon the advice of that government.[81] What is more, all four actions were unprecedented in the post-World War II era, and surely the non-Labor majorities in the Senate and in the two state parliaments acted as they did only for reasons of short-term partisan advantage.

The situation seems to have been reasonably clear. Each of the protagonists—the non-government majority in the Senate, the two state parliaments, and the Governor-General—acted constitutionally, at least according to the text of the document. On the other hand, each acted in an unusual if not unprecedented manner and in violation of established conventions, or so their critics asserted, and all four were charged, though some more than others, with acting for partisan reasons. The text of the Constitution and some of the most important conventions that had developed around it had come into conflict.

As Galligan (1984) argues, disagreements over whether the Senate and the Governor-General acted properly in 1975 turn on whether the Australian Constitution is to be interpreted literally—a dubious proposition in light of the almost unlimited executive power that the Constitution vests in the Governor-General and its failure even to

---

80 This argument would be weaker if Senators were elected by plurality vote. Then one could contend that the voters in a state had elected each individual Senator on his or her own merits, and not necessarily as the representative of a political party. If so, the state parliament should not be obliged to look to party affiliation as a controlling qualification in selecting someone to fill a Senate vacancy. Instead, the election of Senators by proportional representation lends strength to the argument that the voters had chosen a party to represent them in the Senate, more than the specific individuals whom the victorious party had nominated. In filling a Senate vacancy, therefore, the state parliament should be required to respect that choice of party.

81 On the day following the double dissolution, the Speaker wrote to the Queen that 'the failure of the Governor-General to withdraw Mr. Fraser's commission and his decision to delay seeing me as Speaker of the House of Representatives until after the dissolution of the Parliament had been proclaimed were acts contrary to the proper exercise of the Royal prerogative and constituted an act of contempt for the House of Representatives. It is improper that your representative should continue to impose a Prime Minister on Australia in whom the House of Representatives has expressed its lack of confidence and who has not on any substantial resolution been able to command a majority of votes on the floor of the House of Representatives.' The Speaker asked the Queen to restore Whitlam to office. The reply on behalf of the Queen noted that, while she was following events 'with close interest and attention,' it was not for her to intervene (quoted in *House of Representatives Practice* 2001: 458).

mention the prime minister and Cabinet, much less their responsibility to the House—or whether it is to be understood only in light of the fundamental but entirely undefined conventions of responsible government that its authors recognized, supported, and expected to be followed. Whereas US constitutional lawyers might say that the 'black letter' of the Constitution cannot be trumped by conventions that are not even clearly implied by the text, many Australians, drawing on their familiarity and comfort with the very different character of British constitutionalism, are at ease in accepting, in Galligan's words (1984: 152), 'the Australian Constitution for what it is: a hybrid combination of legal and conventional, written and unwritten parts.'

Not surprisingly, there were sharp disagreements in and soon after 1975 as to who was right and who was wrong (e.g., Archer and Maddox 1976 and Howard 1976), and the debate has continued (e.g., Kelly 1996 and Paul 1996).

Compare the following statements from the books on which the House of Representatives and the Senate each rely for authoritative expositions of their procedures:

> [A] rejection of supply by the Senate resulting in the fall of a Government strikes at the root of the concept of responsible government. (*House of Representatives Practice* 1981: 67)

> It is inconceivable that any Senate would deny Supply and force an election except in circumstances when it strongly believed that it was acting in the public interest. The electoral sanction is the safeguard against any irresponsibility. (*Odgers' Australian Senate Practice* 5th ed., 1976: xx)

A Senate majority certainly would justify any decision to deny supply by claiming that it was acting in the public interest. So this formulation really proposes little prior restraint on the Senate's exercise of its constitutional power, leaving it to the electorate to hold the Senate accountable for its exercise of that power, but only after its goal has been achieved or the damage has been done, depending on one's point of view at the time.

Critics of the Senate and the Governor-General have argued that, especially in light of British constitutionalism and the assumption on the part of those who wrote Australia's Constitution that they were embracing the essential elements of British parliamentarism, some conventions were at least as important—and binding—as the text of the Constitution itself. To illustrate, Archer and Maddox (1976: 147–148) contend that, 'despite the fact that a selection of legal rules, embodying traditional British institutions adapted to a federal situation, were collected in one document, there can be no doubt that the Australian constitution framers intended the British conventions to operate within the new system.' They proceed to argue that the Australian Constitution 'is above all a summary of British experience. The written document is certainly the foundation of the Australian constitution, but it is not by any means the whole.' Noting that the written Constitution says nothing about the prime minister, the Cabinet, or political parties, they conclude that 'these institutions depend on *conventions* of the constitution, and they are just as essential a feature of the total Australian constitution as the legal document itself.' (emphasis in original)

The contrary argument is essentially that conventions can only supplement, not supplant, explicit statutory or constitutional provisions.[82] West (1976: 50) argues, for instance, that 'conventions, in British parliamentary practice, exist where statute has not been precise; they do not exist where statute is quite clear, for that would be to defy the authority of parliament and the laws it has passed.' If a law trumps a convention, then so too must a provision of the Constitution. It is tempting to argue, therefore, that because the Constitution gives the Senate almost the same legislative powers as the House, its authors must have intended the Senate to use those powers. This argument would be much more persuasive, however, if it were not for the respects in which it was understood at the time, and has been understood ever since, that the black letter of other constitutional provisions was not to be interpreted and implemented literally—for example, the vesting of executive power in the hands of the Governor-General, with no reference to a prime minister or Cabinet. If everyone accepts that the authors meant for the Constitution to say one thing but mean another with respect to executive power, why should their words be read literally with respect to legislative power?

Solomon aptly summarizes the conventions that were at issue in 1975:

> the convention that the Governor-General acts only on the advice of his ministers, the convention that those ministers must control a majority in the House of Representatives, the convention that the Senate does not reject money bills, the convention that states should replace dead or retired Senators with men selected from the same party as the departed Senator, the convention that the Commonwealth selects the day on which Senate elections are held, the convention that a government which does not have

---

82 Reid (1977: 243–245) went much further than most other commentators in dismissing constitutional conventions as 'a chimera'—'simply political rhetoric'. Underlying this conclusion is his criticism of what he saw as a tendency to 'inanely chant "convention" at every threatened or proposed change of course', when 'Every alleged convention in Australian government (that is, every established practice or method) is explicable in terms other than convention; that is, if we take the trouble to reason "why".'

assured supply will resign, the convention that a Prime Minister defeated on the floor of the House will resign—and so on. (Solomon 1978: 186)

Like West, he goes on to suggest that the strength of, and respect for, conventions—the unwritten rules of the game—needs to be greater in Britain in the absence of written rules of the game—i.e., a written Constitution. In fact, he concludes (1978: 188) that, in Australia, 'a convention is nothing more than an established practice which remains a practice only as long as it suits the practitioners.' One wonders if he would have reached the same judgment if he had been writing before the events of 1975, not some years later.

One way of responding to the crisis was to amend the Constitution in order to entrench the conventions so that they would not be violated again. That was the purpose and effect of the 1977 constitutional amendment[83] which amended sec. 15 to provide that:

> Where a vacancy has at any time occurred in the place of a senator chosen by the people of a State and, at the time when he was so chosen, he was publicly recognized by a particular political party as being an endorsed candidate of that party and publicly represented himself to be such a candidate, a person chosen or appointed under this section in consequence of that vacancy, or in consequence of that vacancy and a subsequent vacancy or vacancies, shall, unless there is no member of that party available to be chosen or appointed, be a member of that party.

The third and fourth issues might have been resolved if the Australian public had approved a 1999 proposed constitutional amendment that would have transformed Australia into a republic and replaced the Governor-General with a President elected by Parliament. At least there would have been an opportunity to debate whether the President should have the same powers as the Governor-General and, if so, perhaps to clarify the circumstances under which those powers should be exercised. However, the amendment failed in a national referendum in November 1999, by a margin of roughly 55 to 45 per cent (Kirby 2001).

It is the first issue, the constitutional powers of the Senate and the way in which it exercises those powers, that is of primary interest here. Twenty years after the fact, Kelly (1996: 114) described the events of 1975 as the detonation of a 'time bomb.' 'A number of the founding fathers knew they had implanted a contradiction at the heart of the Constitution'—'the contradiction ... between responsible government

---

83　The idea for this amendment pre-dated the events of 1974–1975. It had been included as a recommendation in the 1959 final report of a parliamentary joint select committee appointed in 1956 (*House of Representatives Practice* 2001: 31).

and federalism.' Paul (1996: 121) has responded by observing that the Commonwealth Constitution was written before Great Britain approved the Parliament Act of 1911 'which upheld the supremacy of the Commons especially in budgetary policy by denying to the Lords any power over money bills and by substituting a suspensory veto for an absolute veto over almost all other measures.'[84] As we have seen, however, the drafters were well aware of the long-established understanding in London that money bills were the constitutional responsibility of the House of Commons.

Also writing two decades after the crisis, Galligan (1995: 73) has argued that the events of 1975 'did not show that the Senate had power to defeat or remove a government. What it showed was that through wielding its plenary legislative power the Senate could harass a government, deny it supply and create deadlock.' In that instance, 'That stalemate was broken by the vice-regal *coup de grace.*' Kelly (1996: 117) makes a complementary argument—that 'It is one thing to insist that a government obstructed by a Senate motion to deny supply cannot remain in office once funds to provide for the ordinary services of government have expired. It is quite another to insist that a government denied supply by such a Senate motion has therefore lost the confidence of the parliament and, unless it resigns or advises an election, must be dismissed.' In this way, he can conclude that the Governor-General acted precipitately in dismissing the Whitlam Government. Kerr had justified his action by contending that 'A prime minister who cannot obtain supply, including money for carrying on the ordinary services of government, must either advise a general election or resign.' This, Kelly contends, 'was to construct a constitutional theory from a legal power.'

> According to historical precedent, constitutional provision and political theory, the Governor-General should not have treated the deferral of supply by the Senate as a want of 'confidence' in Whitlam and therefore as grounds for a dismissal. He should have treated the situation as a test of the Senate's financial power to obstruct a government which, if persisted in to the point where funds might expire, would require a general election.

The distinctions that Galligan and Kelly draw are fair and useful in theory, but it is not clear whether, for practical purposes, their distinctions make a difference. One wonders whether the Senate's lack of authority 'to defeat or remove a government' offered much solace to former Prime Minister Whitlam. If the Senate can compel the

---

84 Paul (1996: 121–122) notes that the British House of Lords had rejected the Asquith Government's budget in 1909.

government to resign by refusing to provide funding for continuing government activities, is that not compelling evidence that the prevailing constitutional theory of responsible government is at best incomplete and at worst misrepresentative of the true state of affairs? As Jaensch (1997: 86) has put it, the events of 1974 and 1975 demonstrated that 'any Australian elected government is in office, *but not in power*, if it does not control the Senate as well.' (emphasis in original)

The Crisis in Retrospect

I have argued that the Senate had (and still has) the constitutional authority to deny supply. As we shall discuss in more detail in the next chapter, the Constitution's authors understood that this authority existed and contemplated the consequences of its exercise. As the events of 1975 unfolded, many wished that the Constitution did not say what it does say, but wishing does not make it so.

To argue that the Senate exceeded its authority is to argue that the explicit terms of the Constitution must be interpreted in light of fundamentally important constitutional conventions that deserve to be accorded at least equal weight. Not so. As West noted, the conventions that give shape and stability to the British political system effectively substitute for a written constitution; they do not supplement or supplant it. The continuity and vitality of democracy in the UK in the absence of a written constitution that defines, allocates, and limits powers, and in the absence of an independent judiciary to interpret and apply the constitution, are indeed extraordinary—just as they are unique and of limited relevance to Australia, where a different question arises: what happens when a core convention collides directly with the written Constitution? In my judgment, the Constitution must prevail. Otherwise, who is to say, if not those in power, exactly what the conventions are and when they are sufficiently fundamental to supersede a direct constitutional prohibition or grant of authority? No, when there is a written constitution, conventions can help to resolve its ambiguities and to fill its interstices, but they cannot be allowed to control if they contradict the Constitution. Otherwise the Constitution has only as much force as those in power choose to allow it.

The same essential argument applies to the so-called reserve powers of the Constitution. Perhaps the most remarkable thing about the Australian Constitution is the executive power that it vests in the Governor-General and its failure even to mention the prime minister and Cabinet and the basic elements of responsible government. Certainly none of the authors intended for the Governor-General to exercise all of those powers all of the time at his own discretion; some of the authors may not have intended for him ever to exercise any of them except upon the advice of his 'advisors.' The authors created the polite fictions of the Constitution because they thought it unnecessary or too difficult to entrench the actual dynamics of parliamentary government. This decision, however sensible it may or may not have been, has had consequences. And the prime consequence has been to leave critically important powers, such as the power to dismiss a prime minister who continues to enjoy the support of the House, in the hands of the Governor-General to exercise if and when he sees fit. If this now is thought to be inappropriate, the solution is to amend the Constitution, not to pretend that it means something other than what it says.

However, the existence of a power is neither a license to exercise it at will nor a directive to exercise it at all. With respect to the legislative powers of the Senate and its power to reject money bills, the authors of the Constitution devised no foolproof mechanism to prevent the exercise of those powers from creating governmental crises. Instead, they depended on the wisdom, the judgment, and the prudence of those who would be entrusted with acting under the Constitution. The Opposition had the authority and the numbers to deny supply, but it need not and *should not* have done so. The Governor-General had the authority to dismiss the government, but he need not and *should not* have done so when he did.

The accounts of 1974–1975 satisfy me that Prime Minister Fraser and the Coalition deferred supply primarily if not solely to compel an immediate House election that they as well as Labor were convinced they would win. In other words, they took their extraordinary actions for reasons of short-term partisan advantage. The government had demonstrated exceptionally poor judgment, especially regarding the loans affair, but the government's actions could have awaited the verdict of the voters at the next scheduled election. There was no constitutional crisis, other than the one that the Coalition created, that compelled a change of government. Even if all the Coalition's criticisms of Whitlam's Government were well-founded, there was no economic or international crisis that was about to bring Australia to ruin if Labor was allowed to remain in office until closer to the end of its three-year term. There was no imminent risk to Australian democracy, other than whatever risk emanated from the crisis that the Coalition provoked. Surely there was evidence of bungling, ineptness, incompetence, and remarkably unwise decisions (see Oakes (1976) and Kelly (1976, 1995), for instance). But democracies have survived worse—much worse. And there was no evidence that government ministers were enriching themselves, or that they were abusing their powers in ways that threatened the rights and freedoms of Australians.[85]

Although the conventions of responsible government do not trump the Constitution, they are valuable and valued, and are to be violated only in extreme and unusual circumstances. Even giving due weight to all the failings of Whitlam and his ministry, there were no such circumstances in 1974–1975. The controlling circumstance was the Coalition's conviction that if it could force a House election, it would win. The prospect of winning is not reason enough. Fraser and the Coalition acted constitutionally but irresponsibly.[86]

Neither party could claim with a straight face to have been motivated consistently by attachment to constitutional principle. In 1967, Prime Minister Harold Holt had claimed on behalf of the Liberal Party that it had 'long been a cherished principle of Labor policy that the Senate should not frustrate the financial policies of a Government possessing a majority support in the House of Representatives' because 'It is one of the most firmly established principles of British Parliamentary democracy that a House of review should not reject the financial decisions of the popular House.' So when the ALP decided that its Senators could abstain from voting on a money bill but not vote to reject the bill, Holt criticized the stratagem as a 'cynical abandonment of a long-held principle' and a 'blatant exercise of political opportunism' (Sawer 1977: 126–127). In his 1979 memoir of the crisis, Whitlam positions himself as the defender of responsible government, just as he had as the events unfolded and during the subsequent election campaign. Yet it is worth bearing in mind his 1970 statement, as well as that of Senator Murphy, quoted earlier, and especially Whitlam's declaration that his 'purpose is to destroy this Budget and to destroy the Government which has sponsored it.' (quoted by Sawer 1977: 126) It also should be remembered that, when the Coalition was on the verge of blocking supply in 1974, Whitlam had been quick to seek a double dissolution. The prerogatives of the House

85 Ironically, and certainly unintentionally, the Liberal Party came to the same conclusion. In a leaflet defending its position to the public, the Party (1975: 539) asked 'Is there a crisis? What is it all about?' The Party's response? 'It is about whether we should have an election. An election of the House of Representatives will decide whether the Whitlam Government should continue—or whether we should have a Liberal/National Country Party Government headed by Mr. Fraser.'

86 The responsibility does not rest entirely on Fraser personally, though it is doubtful that the Coalition would have refused to pass the appropriation bills in 1975 without his determined leadership. It will be recalled that the Coalition, under different leadership, that of B.M. Snedden, had refused to vote supply in 1974, and Snedden evidently was contemplating doing it again in 1975 before Fraser replaced him (see Kelly 1976: 102).

and the principles of responsible government do not seem to have been his paramount concern then, presumably because he was as confident of winning an election in 1974 as he was fearful of losing one in 1975.[87]

We can never know what Whitlam and Labor would have done in 1975 if they had been in Opposition but in control of the Senate. We do know, however, what Fraser and the Coalition did: they exercised a valid constitutional power but for party political reasons that disregarded the delicate balance that is built into the Commonwealth Constitution. For this they are culpable.

The Governor-General dismissed the government before the crisis came to a head—before supply ran out—and so he acted prematurely. Undoubtedly he believed that he was acting in a timely and responsible manner in order to prevent an approaching crisis from actually exploding through the Australian economy. In doing so, however, he prevented the political process from running its course, and gave up too soon on the prospects of a political resolution. I share Sawer's assessment (1977: 161):

> One might expect so grave a decision, obviously so prejudicial to the elected government in a parliament not yet eighteen months old, and in circumstances imperilling the reputation of the Governor-General's office, should not be taken until it was virtually certain that no change in the Senate's attitude would take place. This was not at all certain on 11 November 1975.

As David Butler wrote in 1979, 'If he [Kerr] had waited another week or two, the problem would either have solved itself or the justification for decisive action would have become more apparent.' (quoted in Mayer 1980: 56; see also Howard and Saunders 1977: 280)

According to Kelly (1995), public opinion was running strongly against the Opposition's decision to defer supply (even if both sides wondered whether those results were related to how votes would be cast in a 1975 general election). At that point, though, both the political and the economic effects of the Opposition's strategy were largely prospective and hypothetical. If money actually had stopped flowing, I think it very likely that there would have been a powerful public outcry and that one side or the other would have broken. I suspect the army to retreat would have been that of the Coalition of whom Labor and the media could and would have said that 'the only reason the people of

---

87   At the time of the 1975 dispute, Gareth Evans acknowledged (1975: 11), referring to the Senate's refusal in the previous year to vote supply, that 'Mr Whitlam did capitulate in similar circumstances in 1974, but only because he judged that he had a good chance of taking the electorate with him—a judgment which subsequent events vindicated.'

Australia are losing their jobs and not receiving their benefits is because the Coalition refuses, for the rankest of partisan purposes, to allow the budget to come to a vote in the Senate.' I believe that the Coalition would have fractured in the face of such pressure (Sampford 1987: 123). And even though there is no guarantee this would have happened, there was time for Kerr to find out before acting. Yes, there would have been some short-term disruption, but no long-term damage unless both sides still refused to budge, in which case the Governor-General still would have had the option to act.

In this respect, the American experience may have something to offer, though only in retrospect. In 1995, the Democratic President and the Republicans in Congress were unable to agree on most of the annual appropriation bills by the time the new fiscal (financial) year began on 1 October. Consequently, much of the federal government shut down for several days in November, when almost 800 000 government employees could not work because they could not be paid, and then again for several weeks that encompassed Christmas and New Year's, when almost 300 000 employees were told not to report to work for the same reason. When the impasse ended in mid-January 1996, it was primarily because the congressional Republicans realized that they were paying a heavy price among voters for their intransigence. Public opinion polls were blaming them by a two-to-one margin for the shutdown.

There were two primary reasons why the blame fell where it did. First, President Clinton was able to communicate his position effectively, both because of his skills and because of the media attention he was able to command. And second, the Republican congressional leadership, especially House Speaker Newt Gingrich, seemed unrepentant, publicly proclaiming that they were content to shut down the government in order to force the President to make policy concessions. It also is instructive that the disruptions caused by the shutdown were short-lived; creative accounting minimized some damage and no one ultimately lost any salary or benefits.

Unless the costs of a short-term shutdown in Australia would have been significantly greater and more immediate than they had been in the US, Kerr exaggerated the risk of delay when he wrote in his 1978 memoirs that:

> If I did not act, very great suffering on a nation-wide scale would follow. I was not prepared to gamble with the future of the Constitution, the economy, and the financial security of very great numbers of people, indeed directly and indirectly the whole nation. ... I was not prepared to delay until after the disaster came to pass in order to get a watertight ground for action based upon visible chaos. (Kerr 1978: 335)

Disaster? Chaos? I doubt it. But was not the Governor-General wise to err on the side of caution? Surely so if all he had to consider was the possible economic disruption caused by a temporary government shutdown. The problem is that he does not seem to have balanced these possible costs against the possible—and, as it turned out, the actual—costs of the political disruption caused by the dismissal.

The temporary government shutdowns in the US carried some cost in money to the Federal budget, to be sure, but the political cost to Republicans was more severe. Although they continued to hold majorities in the House, the momentum behind the so-called 'Republican Revolution' of 1995 had dissipated. The episode also has made another such 'train wreck' much less likely. In fact, budget disagreements in Washington now immediately elicit assurances from both branches and both parties that a settlement will be reached in time to prevent the government from closing again.

It was not until government offices actually closed that American public opinion began to crystallize to the detriment of the Republican Party. Until then, the contest between Democratic President and Republican Congress was merely an 'inside the Beltway' struggle that affected few Americans and to which most Americans paid little attention. Who would benefit and who would suffer politically was something that only became known when all the speeches and votes and vetoes threatened to have actual consequences. And when the political costs and benefits did become clear, Republican intransigence soon melted away.

In 1975, the Governor-General argued that both sides were fixed in their positions, and he was convinced that neither would change. But there is no way he could have known because he dismissed Whitlam at least several weeks before the available funds would have run out. The only things he should have been able to predict with confidence were, first, that only when supply actually was exhausted would it become clear who were the political winners and losers, and, second, that the losers would be under intense pressure to cut their losses. Kerr acted when he did presumably because he had become satisfied that the impasse would not be broken through the normal political process. Perhaps he was right, though I doubt it for reasons I have offered. What is most important, though, is that he did not wait to find out. Even as events were unfolding, there were clear indications that Fraser was having more and more difficulty holding his troops in line. According to Kelly (1995: 235):

> A balanced assessment is that there was at least as much evidence that the Senate would crack as that it would hold. The one certainty is that the immediate future was unpredictable. Kerr's implication that there were no

grounds for a political solution is inconsistent with the volatile mood of the time. Kerr says that because the Senate had denied Supply three times he had to accept this 'as their decision'. Yet many Coalition figures did not accept this as the 'final' decision and expected a backdown.

In sum, 'Fraser told Kerr that the Senate would hold; Whitlam told him that the Senate would crack. Kerr accepted Fraser's judgement and rejected Whitlam's.' (Kelly 1995: 234) However, he need not have accepted either judgment when he did. Governor-General Kerr dismissed the Whitlam Government on November 11, roughly two weeks before its funding actually would have run out. From mid-October, when the Coalition first voted to defer the supply bill until the day Kerr acted, nothing actually had changed. 'It was a political crisis on 16 October and it remained a political crisis on 11 November.' (Kelly 1995: 233) It was not yet an actual crisis with serious effects beyond the confines of Parliament House. We can never know for certain what would have happened if the Governor-General had let another week or more pass. However, Kelly (1995: 240) goes on to quote the Opposition Leader in the Senate to the effect that 'if the crisis had continued beyond 20 November towards 30 November then Opposition Senators "would have melted away like snow in the desert."'[88]

The Governor-General acted prematurely, before he had no choice, before the combatants had drawn anything more than rhetorical blood, and before their positions had publicly recognizable and practical consequences. He did not allow the political process to run its course, and so he erred seriously.

As we saw in the preceding chapter, there was nothing unusual in the government confronting a Senate with a non-government majority dominated by a disciplined Opposition party anxious to replace the government in office. Yet 'The Liberal-National Country Party-controlled Senate demonstrated between 1972 and 1975 that a government must have a majority in the Senate if its very existence were not to be at risk. This had not previously been the case':

---

88 November 11 became a prominent date because it was just about the last date on which it was possible to set the wheels in motion for an election before Christmas. 'Supply would be passed the day Whitlam was dismissed or Fraser cracked or a compromise was struck. The only difference between a solution in mid-November and one in late November is that the former would produce an election before Christmas and the latter an election in the New Year. ... In his determination to secure a pre-Christmas election Kerr was dismissing a government that was still able to meet all its financial obligations.' (Kelly 1995: 233)

Many governments had survived in the face of hostile Senates. Their legislative programs might have been (and often were) subject to harassment, but most proposed laws were passed. While the Senate was aware that it probably had the power to force a government to the polls, this power was rarely discussed and the threat of its use never made. Throughout the life of the Whitlam government, the opposition constantly threatened to use this Senate power and of course in the end did so. (Solomon 1978: 9–10)

From a party political viewpoint, Fraser's strategy in 1975 succeeded admirably. So we might expect that similarly situated Opposition parties could have looked for, and found, similar opportunities in the years that followed. This is evidently what Colin Howard (1976: 6) feared when he concluded that, especially because of Kerr's dismissal of the Whitlam Government, 'at the point where political tactics and constitutional law interact, the rules of Australian national government have changed.' Writing soon after the events of 1975, he found in them a fundamental shift from 'the principle of majority government in the House of Representatives' to the conclusion that 'to be entitled to govern a party must be able to ensure the passage of its money bills through both Houses and not just one.' Therefore, he concluded, 'the way has now been cleared for minorities either to prevent a government elected by a majority from governing at all or to permit it to do so only on terms dictated by the minority.' (1976: 8–9)

Indeed, it has been argued that the events of 1975 actually could have elevated the Senate to a position of political and institutional superiority over the House. The government, with its House majority, can secure a dissolution of the Senate before the expiration of Senators' fixed terms only by satisfying the time-consuming requirements for a double dissolution, and then only if it is willing to put at risk the seats of all Representatives as well as all Senators. By contrast, the groundwork now had been laid for the Senate to have two opportunities annually—there typically are two sets of appropriation bills to be passed each year—to force the government to resign and ask for a dissolution of the House simply by refusing to pass those bills, thereby putting the operations of the government at risk.

Surely Howard was partly correct in that nothing has happened since 1975, as a matter of constitutional amendment or interpretation, to prevent a similarly-positioned Senate from again denying supply in order to force a House election or, if the requirements have been met, a double dissolution.[89] Instead, however, both the Coalition and the ALP

---

89 When a potential deadlock over essential spending legislation appears on the horizon, satisfying the constitutional requirements for a double dissolution on those

have, as matters of party policy, foresworn any interest in using their numbers in the Senate to block essential money bills in order to pressure the government to resign. Both of Australia's major political combatants recognize that they took the Commonwealth to the brink in 1974–1975. I credit them with recognizing that it would damage the constitutional regime if either were to insist on taking the powers of the Senate to their logical extreme. I certainly credit them with calculating that it would not be in their political interests to be held responsible for the consequences.

The Theory of Dual Responsibility

Before dismissing Whitlam, Kerr sought the advice of Sir Garfield Barwick, who then was the Chief Justice of the High Court. In his written advice to Kerr and later in a memoir on the subject, Barwick elaborated a theory that Kerr adopted as his own, a theory that, in Australia, the government of the day is actually responsible to both the House of Representatives and the Senate. On its face, this theory seems to derive from the most hard-headed assessment of the realities of the Constitution. In fact, it is a radical theory, especially coming from the occupants of two of the most traditional roles in the Australian political system, one that makes the Senate potentially the more powerful of the two chambers, and one that ultimately is incompatible with the spirit and intent of the Constitution (Sampford 1987).[90]

To anticipate the discussion in the next chapter, it was no secret to the authors of the Commonwealth Constitution that there was an incompatibility between the operations of a system of responsible government as they had come to know it and a Senate with powers almost the same as those of the House of Representatives. Some thought that the problem was more serious in theory than in practice,

---

bills requires an interval of at least three months. One consequence, then, is that any government confronting a Senate that it does not control has an incentive to ensure that it is in a position to request a double dissolution not only if and when it wants to but also if and when it needs to. To do so, the government must welcome, or even seek to create, legislative deadlocks with the Senate on non-money bills so those bills can serve as double dissolution 'triggers', having satisfied the requirements of sec. 57 of the Constitution before the crisis blossoms.

90 This line of argument does have a pedigree. Robert Garran, who later would become co-author of the seminal *The Annotated Constitution of the Australian Commonwealth,* wrote in 1897: 'that the parliamentary system for federal purposes may develop special characteristics of its own is not unlikely. Thus the familiar rule that a Ministry must retain the confidence of the representative chamber may, in a federation—where both Chambers are representative—develop into a rule that the confidence of both Chambers is required.' (quoted in Solomon 1978: 182–183)

and that the balanced judgment and good sense of Australians steeped in British constitutional traditions would prevent the logical possibilities of the Constitution from being carried to their ultimate, destructive extremes. There were others who were more inclined to agree with Winthrop Hackett that the proposed Constitution created a collision waiting to happen: 'either responsible government will kill federation, or federation ... will kill responsible government.' (*Convention Debates*, 12 March 1891: 280) Some of those who saw an actual danger, not a hypothetical one, in the combination of provisions proposed for the Constitution were prepared to sacrifice responsible government or search for some way of adjusting it so that it would rest more comfortably alongside the Senate in what was admittedly a constitutional marriage of convenience.

There does not appear to have been any determined advocacy at the Conventions for the idea that it was practical and desirable to require the government to retain the support of majorities in both houses in order to remain in office. There was a recognition, of course, that the authors were giving the Senate the power to refuse supply, but no evidence that the authors thought that the denial of supply by the Senate would have the same meaning as the denial of supply by the House—the ultimate way in which the House can enforce the responsibility of the incumbent government to it. Writing ten years after Federation, W. Harrison Moore predicted that the Senate would rarely exercise its acknowledged power to refuse to pass an appropriation bill. He recognized that the Senate 'might in an extreme case refuse to pass the Appropriation Bill, and thereby force a dissolution or a change of Ministry.' However, in carefully modulated terms, he let it be known that doing so could be predicated only on a theory of dual responsibility; and for that, there was no precedent on the continent that recently had become a nation:

> In the balance of power in the Commonwealth, it is a factor not to be neglected that, while the Senate has a recognized power over money bills beyond that of any other second chamber in the British Dominions, it can hardly exercise the extreme power of rejecting the Bill for the 'ordinary annual services of the Government' upon any other ground than that the Ministry owes responsibility to the Upper not less than to the Lower House. That is a position which in the future, the Senate, as the House of the States as well as the Second Chamber, may take up; but it is a position from which even in the history of Parliamentary Government in the Colonies, the strongest supporters of the Upper House have generally shrunk. (Moore 1910: 144–145)

Yet that is essentially the position that Kerr and Barwick took up in 1975 and thereafter. In the statement that the Governor-General issued to explain his reasons for dismissing the Whitlam Government, Kerr asserted that:

> The position in Australia is quite different from the position in the United Kingdom. Here the confidence of both Houses on supply is necessary to ensure its provision. In the United Kingdom the confidence of the House of Commons alone is necessary. But both here and in the United Kingdom the duty of the Prime Minister is the same in a most important respect—if he cannot get supply he must resign or advise an election. ...
>
> When ... an Upper House possesses the power to reject a money bill including an appropriation bill, and exercises the power by denying supply, the principle that a government which has been denied supply by the Parliament should resign or go to an election must still apply—it is a necessary consequence of Parliamentary control of appropriation and expenditure and of the expectation that the ordinary and necessary services of government will continue to be provided. (quoted in Mayer and Nelson 1976: 542–543)

Several years later, in his memoirs, he added (1978: 315) that 'There is a sense in which a Government must retain the 'confidence' of the Senate to be able to continue in government. It must have the confidence of the Senate expressed by the passing of supply by the Senate.'

It is unclear precisely how, or how precisely, Kerr intended to use the word 'confidence.' When we say that, in Great Britain for example, a government would have to resign if it lost in the House of Commons on a vote of no confidence, we mean that the government must resign as a matter of constitutional principle. Is this what Kerr had in mind when he wrote that an Australian government 'must have the confidence of the Senate expressed by the passing of Supply by the Senate': that a Senate vote against providing supply is its way of voting its lack of confidence in the government, and that the two votes are constitutionally equivalent, either requiring the government to resign as a matter of constitutional principle? Or was he making an argument grounded not in constitutional principle, but in the practicalities of political power: that if the Senate (but not the House) blocks supply, the government still has a constitutional right to remain in office, but it is no longer practical for it to exercise that right because it lacks, or soon will lack, the means (i.e., money) to continue functioning as a government must? The latter interpretation can be read into his statement that, when the Senate rejected supply, the government had to resign or there had to be an election because one or the other was 'a necessary consequence of Parliamentary control of appropriation and expenditure and of the expectation that the ordinary and necessary services of Government will continue to be provided.' In the same sentence, though, the Governor-General elevated into a 'principle' the necessity for a government, if denied supply, to resign or submit to an election.

It is all rather confusing, and the Chief Justice's letter of 10 November 1975 to Kerr (reprinted in Kelly 1975: 344) does not offer much help. In that letter, Chief Justice Barwick found 'an analogy between the situation of a Prime Minister [in London] who has lost the confidence of the House of Commons and a Prime Minister [in Canberra] who does not have the confidence of the Parliament, i.e. of the House of Representatives and of the Senate. The duty and responsibility of the Prime Minister to the Crown in each case is the same: if unable to secure supply to the Crown, to resign or to advise an election.' (Reprinted in Kelly 1975: 344) He leaves us with the same questions: in what sense may an Australian prime minister have or not have 'the confidence of the Parliament'? Is the duty to resign or seek an election grounded in constitutional principle or practical necessity?

In his 1983 memoir of the affair, Barwick is more enlightening. First, he establishes, convincingly enough, that the Senate had the constitutional power to act as it did. Second, he argues, reasonably enough, that a government that cannot convince Parliament to pass essential spending legislation cannot remain in office. It may go voluntarily or involuntarily, but go it must, whether its departure brings on a new government from the same Parliament, or a new election for the House only or for the House and part or all of the Senate. But then he turns to the more interesting and difficult question: whether the Senate's action was 'proper', not simply whether it was constitutional.

In turn, this question can be broken in half. First, is it ever proper for the Senate to deny supply, knowing that the inescapable result must be the departure of a government that a majority in the House presumably continues to support? And if so, then second, under what circumstances is it appropriate for the Senate to do so? Implicit in his answers to these questions is a provocative theory of how the Australian Constitution should work.

With respect to the House, Barwick explains that a vote of no confidence is effective both because of the government's acceptance of the conventions of parliamentary government and because of the threat implicit in the House's vote:

> [A] motion of no confidence carried by the House ought to be followed by the resignation of the ministry or by advice to the Governor-General to dissolve the House. The result would be the holding of a general election. The carrying of such a motion is an indication that if the ministry does not take such a course the House in due time will not introduce or carry an appropriation bill for supply. (Barwick 1983: 41–42)

A government leaves office after a vote of no confidence by the House not only because the House thinks it should, but also because the government understands that if it does not, it is the House that will deny supply when the opportunity arises. The constitutional principle is predicated upon this prediction.[91]

Barwick goes on to acknowledge that a government is *not* expected to resign in the face of a Senate vote of no confidence or the Senate's failure to pass 'bills sent up by the House which are considered by the executive government to be essential to its own legislative programmes.'

> In other words, whilst it may be said that the government does not need in general to have the confidence of the Senate in the sense that it must retain the confidence of the House, it must so far have that confidence as to obtain the Senate's concurrence to the annual grant of supply. Thus, the only way the Senate may send a government to the polls is by rejecting or failing to pass an appropriation bill for supply. *Put another way, it can be said that the only way the Senate can secure for the electorate an opportunity to express its attitude to the executive government is by not concurring in the grant of supply.* (Barwick 1983: 42; emphasis added)

Here begin to emerge his answers to our questions about the propriety, not the constitutionality, of the Senate's action. Such an action is justified when there is good cause for the Senate to 'secure for the electorate an opportunity to express its attitude to the executive government.'

> The power to withhold supply in my view should be regarded as a power held in reserve to be used only on some very special occasion calling for its exercise. The Senate should treat itself as holding the power on behalf of

---

91 After making the point that if the House votes no confidence in the government, it must resign immediately, even if it still has funds to continue essential government operations, he derives from it the conclusion that, contrary to my argument, the Governor-General was justified in dismissing the Whitlam Government even while supply remained available. 'Thus, in considering what the Prime Minister ought to have done when the Senate clearly indicated its unwillingness to provide supply— and thus indicating that the Parliament no longer approved the retention of the ministry in government—was not affected by the state of the funds in the Treasury which the ministry could lawfully use in government.' (Barwick 1983: 54) This again indicates the degree to which he considers a Senate vote to deny supply the equivalent of a House vote of no confidence. Sawer, however, disagrees: 'Denial of supply by a *lower* House is one of many ways by which loss of confidence in the government may be expressed, and has always been considered in that context. Denial of supply by an upper House, like any other upper House expression of no confidence in a government with a lower House majority, has ever since the Reform Act of 1832 been regarded as irrelevant to the principles governing responsible government.' (Sawer 1977: 146)

the electorate. It should be used where the Senate forms the view that the interests of the electorate or of some definable part of the electorate requires its use. This presupposes a special occasion when the circumstances, *such as the policies and performance of the executive government of the time*, warrant the use of the power. (Barwick 1983: 46; emphasis added)

The 'special occasion,' Barwick clearly implies, need not involve government actions that are demonstrably criminal or unconstitutional or that put the security or survival of the nation at risk; it is sufficient for a majority in the Senate to conclude that 'the policies and performance of the executive government' warrant the use of a power that compels that government to resign or be dismissed. But is this position not incompatible with the concepts of responsible government and ministerial responsibility? Yes, he argues, and when this incompatibility arises, it is the latter that must give way:

[I]f there were any seeming antipathy between the concept of responsible government and the Senate's legislative power to reject or to fail to pass an appropriation bill for supply ... the operation of the principle of ministerial responsibility must be modified in some fashion to accommodate the exercise of the Senate's powers. (Barwick 1983: 44–45)

The implication of this argument is that a Senate majority should be free to deny supply, and thereby bring down a government, whenever it wishes. The standard that Barwick erects is so weak as to constitute no barrier of principle to deter an Opposition from doing in the future what Fraser did in 1975 because it disagrees with the government's policies, and what is just as important, because it thinks that 'the interests of the electorate' require the Senate to use its power so the electorate can 'throw the bums out.'

And that is precisely what Barwick has in mind. His theory is not one of dual responsibility, in which the government is effectively responsible to both the House and the Senate. Fundamentally, his is a theory of government responsibility to the Senate. The Senate should send the government to face the voters at an election when a majority of Senators believe that the government has lost the voters' support. The Senate has both the right and responsibility to force the government to resign because the House obviously will not do so:

There must be occasions when because of a government's performance or the policies (not electorally endorsed) which it pursues, the electorate should not have to wait the effluxion of a Parliament's term to express its dissatisfaction with the executive government and its antipathy to those policies. ... A government with a majority in the House, disciplined to the point where dissidence is unlikely to surface, could do untold harm to the country if no means existed to bring about a dissolution during the parliamentary term. It could become as absolute an executive as a seventeenth century monarch claimed to be. If the Senate did not have the power to send to the polls a government which, because of its actions, has ceased to have the confidence of the electorate, such a disaster might ensue. (Barwick 1983: 47–48)

Party discipline in Parliament, by this argument, has stood responsible government on its head in two respects. First, it is the House that is the obedient agent of the government, not the converse; and second, it is the Senate that must make the government responsible to it by using its power over supply, because the House will not enforce responsibility in any meaningful sense, no matter how the views of the electorate may have changed since the last election.

In 1975, the Opposition in the Senate argued that Whitlam and his colleagues 'had lost the confidence of the electorate because of the government's own performance in office', so, Barwick finds, 'if the expressed views of the Opposition were genuinely held, then a case for the exercise of this reserve power did exist.' More generally, 'If the majority of the Senate is convinced that the electorate has lost confidence in the government and should be given the opportunity to express itself, the power to fail to provide supply would be properly exercised.' Barwick acknowledges that the Opposition party could benefit politically. However, the Senate's power to deny supply 'should not be a tool in the hands of a political group out to achieve some particular party political objective by means of the pressure of a threat of the exercise of the power. It should not be an instrument to produce instability in government by its capricious or merely party political use.' (Barwick 1983: 48–50)

I have quoted Barwick at length to present what I trust is a fair summary of his argument because he states so clearly why we must reject it as a theory of how the Australian polity should operate. I agree with the Chief Justice that the Senate has the constitutional power to refuse to pass any bill, including an essential money bill, and that the existence of a constitutional power carries with it the perfectly reasonable presumption that there is some circumstance under which it is appropriate for the Senate to exercise that power. Supporters of the government, *any* government, might argue otherwise: that any exercise of the Senate's power to reject any important bill, much less a basic annual money bill, is an unwarranted interference with the government's ability to exercise its electoral mandate (we will take up this argument in Chapter 9). But Barwick would take us much too far in the other direction by endorsing the propriety of a non-government majority in the Senate deciding to deny supply and thereby bring down a government whenever it chooses to argue that the electorate has lost confidence in that government.

Especially in an era of seemingly permanent non-government majorities in the Senate, adopting Barwick's approach would risk producing precisely the kind of government instability that he recognized to be a danger. Kelly, arguing that Barwick and Kerr sought 'to construct a constitutional theory from a legal power', illustrates the 'political absurdities' that could ensue:

> For example, under this constitutional theory the Senate, whose members may have been elected three and six years earlier, by blocking Supply can vote no-confidence in an elected government, force the Representatives to the people without having to face any election itself and, if it dislikes the government formed after the subsequent election, vote no-confidence six months later thereby repeating the process. (Kelly 1995: 293–294)

Furthermore, surely it is naive for Barwick to justify efforts by Opposition-led majority coalitions in the Senate to bring down governments, and then to believe that oppositions will refrain from doing so for 'merely party political use.' Parties, just like the individual politicians comprising them, have a natural capacity for equating what is in their political interests with what they perceive to be in the nation's interests. What the former Chief Justice offers to us, then, is the ultimate supremacy of the public opinion poll. The non-government majority in the Senate would be gauging public opinion even more intensively than it already does, waiting for the government's support to falter and then calculating whether its weakness will persist long enough for a new election to take place. And if there is not a supply bill that can be blocked to compel an immediate election, why would it not be equally legitimate for the Senate majority to block every other bill on the Notice Paper until the government agrees to resign? After all, the goal is for the Senate to force the government to face the electorate. Whether the Senate accomplishes this by denying supply or by creating a governmental crisis in some other way, such as engaging in a legislative work stoppage, would hardly seem to matter.

The government has the option of requesting the Governor-General to dissolve the House well before its three-year term would expire, but at least some lip service is paid to the notion that the Governor-General might not grant such a dissolution if it is sought only to increase the government's majority in the House (see the discussion in Chapter 2 of the double dissolution of 1983). However weak this constraint may be (and it is my view that this is a matter that should be decided by the government and the people, not the Governor-General), there would be none at all limiting when the opposition and its Senate allies could force a House election on the government. The best way the government could protect itself would be by ensuring that at least one bill has qualified under sec. 57 as a double dissolution trigger, so that the non-government majority in the Senate would have to be prepared to put all its seats at risk as well.

No, Barwick's approach to how the Senate should invoke its legislative powers with respect to money bills is entirely too casual. I accept that non-government majorities still retain the right to block supply and, by blunt force, they can try to compel a government to resign when the money runs out. I also accept that they may do so for the same kinds of self-interested reasons that provoked the crisis of 1975. But I cannot join him in inviting them to do so. Since 1975, fortunately, non-government majorities in the Senate either have failed to read his analysis or they have found it unpersuasive as a guide for political action.

5

Original intent and expectations

The discussion thus far raises a collection of related questions about the intent and expectations of those who designed the Commonwealth's Constitution. What role did its authors expect and want the Senate to play? In giving the Senate the legislative powers it received, how did they foresee the relations between the Senate, on the one hand, and the House of Representatives and the government, on the other? And how did they reconcile (or fail to reconcile) their commitment to responsible parliamentary government with their commitment to federalism as manifested in the Senate? These are big and complicated questions about which books can be, and have been, written. The discussion that follows seeks only to highlight some of the salient arguments, explanations, and observations that have been offered.

Writing the Australian Constitution

The Australian Constitution was the eventual product of a pair of Conventions, the second of which met in several locales, and a series of referenda.[92] The first Convention convened in Sydney in 1891. It framed a draft constitution for consideration by the individual colonies, but they failed to act decisively on it. In 1897 a second Convention met in Adelaide. It produced a draft that was submitted to the colonial

---

92 An initial caveat is in order. The records of the meetings of the constitutional Conventions are voluminous. They report the sometimes intense debates over an extended period of time among a group of thoughtful and strong-willed men to whom agreement did not always come quickly or easily. By selective quotation, therefore, it is fairly easy to construct arguments in support of different, even contradictory, understandings of their intent and expectations regarding the more contentious provisions on which they ultimately settled. I have relied largely on the research of others into these records, so much of this chapter is based on my selective use of the material they selected for their own purposes. It also is worth bearing in mind Galligan's (1986: 94) observation that, 'If the Federation Debates have not been well understood, it is partly because many of the delegates, particularly from the small States' side, were not very clear about the issues under discussion.'

parliaments which responded with suggested amendments that the Convention took up when it reconvened in Sydney later in 1897. The Convention began its last meetings in January 1898 in Melbourne and adjourned in mid-March of that year. The proposed constitution that emerged from this process was the subject of referenda in four colonies. Three approved it, but in New South Wales it failed to receive the number of votes that, by prior decision, were required to adopt it. A conference of the colonial premiers then met in Melbourne in January 1899 and agreed to a series of amendments, one of which changed the margin necessary to approve a bill in a joint sitting from a three-fifths majority to an absolute majority of the total membership of both houses. New referenda were held at which five of the six colonies approved the amended draft, with Western Australia adding its concurrence somewhat later. With minor amendment, the Constitution was embodied in a bill approved by the British Parliament in July 1900.[93]

The Constitution was written by men of British background or birth who came from Australian colonies with (in most cases) well-established parliamentary systems. So from the beginning, their deliberations were shaped by a prevailing assumption that they would create a parliamentary government. Yet there also was little question that they would produce a federal constitution that preserved the identities of the colonies when they became states and somehow provided for a division or sharing of powers between the states and the Commonwealth. According to Samuel Griffith, the Premier of Queensland and later the first Chief Justice of the High Court of Australia, federation was possible only on the condition that:

> the separate states are to continue as autonomous bodies, surrendering only so much of their powers as is necessary to the establishment of a general government to do for them collectively what they cannot do individually for themselves, and which they cannot do as a collective body for themselves. (*Convention Debates*, 4 March 1891: 31)

Jaensch (1997: 46) describes the concerns of the states as the federal constitution was being conceived:

> At the time of the moves towards a nation in the 1890s, there were in existence six independent nation-states in the colonies. Each was self-governing, and had its own constitution, system of laws, practices and procedures of government and, most important, its own economic interests, and it was not surprising that each treated with considerable caution any

---

93 These events are well-summarized in Moore 1910: 40–55. The extended narrative history by La Nauze (1972) is essential reading.

suggestion that it should submerge itself within a national, unitary government.

There were, in fact, two pressures. On the one hand, the colonies could understand and support the need for a new national authority to provide for common needs and protection against external threat. In economic terms it made sense to have free trade between the colonies, and a national policy on duties and tariffs for overseas trade. A common defence, the need for a national transport and communication system, coupled with a growing sense of nationalism in at least some of the colonies, were some of the forces towards unity. On the other hand, the colonies, especially the smaller ones such as South Australia, Tasmania, and Western Australia (which had only received its self-government in 1890), feared that they would lose all their independence in a unitary system, and also that they would be dominated by the larger populations and stronger economies in New South Wales and Victoria. Above all, the constitutionalists in the colonial parliaments and economies were determined to protect their, and their colonies' economic interests.

If his characterization is fair, the similarities with corresponding American state concerns more than a century earlier are almost uncanny. No wonder the Australians looked not only to British practices, but also to the American constitutional compromise as they designed their new Commonwealth.

How were the state and Commonwealth governments to be connected? The obvious answer, based on the authors' familiarity with the US Constitution (Hunt 1930) and the governments of their own states,[94] was the Senate.

One constitutional issue over which there was little debate in the Conventions was the provision that the national parliament was to be bicameral. All the experience of the delegates to both gatherings pointed to the institution of a bicameral legislature, as did the oft-cited examples of federal governments, the United States and Canada, and the concept seems to have been accepted automatically. (Bennett 1971: 112)

A key question about the structure of the new Commonwealth Parliament had been answered before the first Convention assembled in 1891, and it was not put in doubt during the second Convention of 1897–1898. The Parliament would be bicameral.

From the perspective of either London or Washington, the product of the Conventions' deliberations can be dismissed as conceptually

---

94 'The Australian colonies all accepted the Westminster model and the necessity for a bicameral system. New South Wales and Queensland opted for upper houses whose members were nominated by the Governor. The other colonies allowed their upper houses to be elected, but with a restricted franchise based on property ownership.' (Jaensch 1997: 135)

incoherent. What they created was a parliamentary federation, a construction that, according to Sharman (1990: 205), is fundamentally and inherently contradictory:

> [T]he institutional components of parliamentary federations are not self-checking elements reflecting a coherent notion of constitutionalism but represent competing views of the role of government. To this extent, parliamentary federations have no constitutional design in the sense of an internally consistent set of governmental structures with a clear philosophical basis for their justification.

The creation of the Commonwealth was a voluntary act on the part of the then-colonies, who chose to federate without being pressured to do so by irresistible military, political, or economic necessity. So there could be no Commonwealth that was not embedded in a federal constitutional structure, and no federal constitutional structure that did not include a Senate having significant constitutional powers. Yet the authors of the Constitution still opted for a parliamentary government that was responsible to the House of Representatives.[95] In doing so, they sought to combine federalism and responsibility in an unprecedented way, even though they had before them a readily available alternative in the form of the US presidential-congressional system.[96]

Galligan (1995: 46) has argued that 'The constitutional founding of the Australian nation was not an occasion either of great patriotic moment or grand institutional innovation. It was a more pragmatic piecing together of established parliamentary practices and available federal institutional arrangements.' How pragmatic were their decisions? If the Commonwealth Constitution entrenched a contradiction between federalism and responsibility, the obvious question to ask is 'Why?' Several possible answers—hypotheses—suggest themselves.

---

95 It was not quite so self-evident to Lord Bryce, writing in 1905, that it was the House, not the Senate, that would dominate under the new Constitution. He (1905: 312) wrote that 'Australians evidently expect that the usage hitherto prevailing in all the Colonies of letting the Ministry be installed or ejected by the larger House will be followed. Nevertheless the relations of the Commonwealth Houses are so novel and peculiar, that the experience of the new Government in working them out will deserve to be watched with the closest attention by all students of politics.'

96 Decades later, when constitutions were being written for the soon-to-be-independent British colonies of sub-Saharan Africa, the power of the British example again came into play, though in a different way. This time, the office of a powerful and directly elected president was grafted onto parliamentary government, resulting in a constitutional system that was equally incoherent conceptually. See, for example, my 1994 paper on 'Parliamentary Reform in Zambia: Constitutional Design and Institutional Capacity,' presented in Berlin at the XVIth World Congress of the International Political Science Association.

The Constitution's authors simply might not have appreciated the potential problem they were creating. While it may not be rocket science—in this case rocket *political* science—to recognize the contradiction today, it is not beyond contemplation that they could have failed to think through all the possible consequences of their choices. For proof that such a thing can happen, we need look no further than the recent ill-conceived and short-lived Israeli innovation of having a directly-elected prime minister preside over a government responsible to a parliament in which his party might not have a working majority and, indeed, with such a low electoral threshold as to almost guarantee a fragmented party system and the need for coalition governments.

Alternatively, the authors might have recognized the contradiction but considered it the price they had to pay or a risk they had to take. One of the challenges of writing the Constitution, as it had been more than a century earlier in the United States, was satisfying the concerns of all the states that their separate identities and powers would be submerged under the weight of the Federation unless strong legislative powers were vested in the Senate. The less populous states were especially insistent that their equal representation in the Senate was essential to protect them against potential domination by the larger states. This equality of representation would mean little, however, if the Senate itself was powerless to prevent whatever legislation the House of Representatives might concoct.

Finally, the authors might have thought that, whatever constitutional powers they gave the Senate, it was unlikely to exercise them in ways that would jeopardize or disrupt the essential relationship between the government and the House of Representatives on which responsible government depends. At the time the Constitution was drafted, after all, the House of Lords in London also retained its historic legislative powers, but it exercized them with such self-restraint that what might be a problem in principle had not (yet) proven to be a serious problem in practice. It was not until a decade after the Commonwealth Constitution was completed that Britain found it necessary to curtail the legislative powers of the House of Lords by enacting the *Parliament Act 1911*.

Galligan (1995: 75) quickly disposes of the possibility that the problem of reconciling federalism and responsibility was lost on those who met to create the Commonwealth. To the contrary, he explains that 'the design of the Senate and its accommodation with responsible government' was the 'single most contentious issue for the Australian founders, and the one that took up the most space in the Convention debates and almost caused the break-up of both the 1891 and 1897–98

Conventions ... ' In broad terms, the parallel with the Philadelphia Convention of 1787 is striking and far from surprising.

Consider the comments of Griffith, whom Souter (1988: 15) calls the 'real leader' of the 1891 National Australasian Convention, and who deserves to be quoted at length:

> We propose, as I understand it, assuming that the house representing the states is to have the authority which I think it must and ought to have [namely, the authority to amend all bills, including financial legislation], to associate with it a system which has never in the history of the world been tried in conjunction with it. We propose to have an executive government having ... seats in Parliament. How shall we guarantee that the machine will work if we insist that these ministers shall hold their offices in form as well as in reality, by the will of one house only? Does not the possibility of a very serious deadlock occur here to every hon. gentleman at once? The majority of one house of the legislature will certainly be made up of the representatives of the larger colonies. Probably two colonies in that house [New South Wales and Victoria] will be able to overshadow all the rest. ... Now, that majority representing the people of these two states in that house would have the making and unmaking of governments. On the other hand, there would be an independent body in the constitution representing the states. Suppose that independent body ... differed from the house of representatives representing two states, there would be certainly a deadlock at once. ... I point out that the experiment we propose to try has never yet been tried. We must take into consideration the existence of those two forces possibly hostile, even probably hostile, before, say fifty or a hundred years are over, and we must frame our constitution in such a way that it will work if that friction does arise. (*Convention Debates*, 4 March 189: 35–36)

Therefore, according to Galligan (1980a: 2), Griffith concluded that:

> it was necessary to determine which part of the system was essential and to modify the other part to fit it. Griffith insisted that the federal principle was supreme and had to be embodied in the legislature since the minimum condition of federation—'the only compromise possible'—was to 'give to the house representing the states as states ... an absolute power of veto upon anything that the majority of the states think ought not to be adopted.'

For Galligan (1986: 96), 'the small States' position rested on *a claim of principle*, that federalism entailed equal State representation in a Senate that had the same legislative powers as the House, and *a claim of practical necessity*, that the security and protection of States' rights and interests required it.' (emphasis added) One also can argue that the strength of their position rested even more on another potent 'claim of practical necessity': the fear that the prospects for federation might collapse if the concerns of the small states were not satisfied.

Griffith's concern was shared by Richard Baker, later to become the first President of the Senate, who thought that responsible government 'is unworkable with two Houses of co-equal powers' (quoted in Bennett 1971: 163). At Sydney in 1897, Baker summarized the problem as he saw it. 'The essence of federation is the existence of two houses, if not of actually co-equal power, at all events of approximately co-equal power. The essence of responsible government is the existence of one chamber of predominant power.' (*Convention Debates*, 17 September 1897: 784) Henry Higgins concurred:

> The hon. gentleman [referring to Baker] says that in a federation you must have a states' house and a people's house; that these two houses must be equal; that if you have responsible government you cannot have that state of thing—that under responsible government you must have one house greater than the other. That is quite true. The two things are inconsistent. They will not mix logically; they are perfectly irreconcilable. (*Convention Debates*, 17 September 1897: 790)

To Deakin, the Convention was creating 'what you may term an irresistible force on the one side, and what may prove to be an immoveable object on the other side, and the problem of what might happen if these two were brought into contact.' (*Convention Debates*, 15 September 1897: 582) Winthrop Hackett, a Western Australian and 'an ardent States' righter' at the 1891 Convention, thought there would be no peaceful resolution: 'either responsible government will kill federation, or federation in the form in which we shall, I hope, be prepared to accept it, will kill responsible government.' (*Convention Debates*, 12 March 1891: 280)

If forced to choose, as he evidently thought he must, Hackett's commitment to federalism was stronger than his adherence to the British model of responsibility. So too for Griffith, who spoke of 'the apparent inconsistency ... of the system of giving equal powers to the states as represented in one house, and of making the executive government depend for its existence upon the other house.' His preference also was to lean in favor of the federal side of the balance; and as we have seen, he was prepared to give the Senate 'an absolute power of veto upon anything that the majority of the States think ought not to be adopted.' Deakin, on the other hand, was not prepared to adulterate responsible government as he understood it, which would be the inescapable result of attempting to combine a responsible ministry with a legislatively empowered Senate:

> The Senate would be in a position to 'defy, for all time, the will of the people of the country.' Therefore, according to Deakin, the Senate had to be modified. That could best be done by modelling it on the House of Lords

rather than the American Senate and giving it only 'those powers that have always belonged, under responsible government, to a second chamber, namely, the power of review, the power of revision, the power of a veto limited in time.' (Galligan 1980a: 3)

Galligan goes on to aptly summarize the options that appeared during that first, 1891, Convention for addressing the problem that Griffith, among others, had identified:

> Three more or less distinct positions were put forward during the 1891 debates. Some like Deakin championed responsible government at the expense of the Senate; others like Baker and Hackett wanted to abandon responsible government in order to protect the Senate's power. The third position was more complex. It acknowledged the theoretical validity of Griffith's dilemma but accepted the practical necessity for having the two inconsistent institutions: responsible government because familiarity and history had sanctified it,[97] and federal bicameralism because the small states demanded it as a condition of federation. The two institutions could be made to function in harmony, it was claimed, by means of the traditional good sense that was part of the British political culture inherited by the Australian colonies.

It was the third position that ultimately prevailed, but not, I would argue, because of a conviction that 'the two institutions' could be harmonized, but with a hope born of necessity that the inconsistency would remain a problem in theory only.[98]

Some early drafts of the Constitution provided for Senators to be selected by the state parliaments. By the 1897 draft, sentiment had shifted in favor of direct popular election (except to fill casual vacancies).[99] In speaking at the Sydney Convention meetings in 1897,

97 A 'hereditary preference', O'Connor called it (Galligan 1980a: 6).

98 It would be a mistake, however, to view the Senate only as a necessary manifestation of federalism and, therefore, a necessary price of federation. At the time the Commonwealth Constitution was written, four of the colonies had elected upper houses. If a contradiction or incoherence was being built into the new federal charter, it was not a new one. 'Since 1975 it has been constantly asserted that in the Commonwealth Constitution responsible government and federalism threaten one another. It has become routine to quote the prescient Hackett who warned that one would kill the other. What is rarely said is that responsible government had been threatened much earlier by the creation of strong elected upper houses in four of the colonies which became the Australian states. A strong upper house (with equal representation of the states) may have been a necessary condition for federation but federalism was not necessary for the creation of strong upper houses in Westminster-type parliaments.' (Rydon 1983: 34)

99 Sawer and Zappala (2001: 1) remind us that the Australian Senate was the first national upper chamber to have its members chosen by direct popular election. Ratification of the Commonwealth Constitution and the first elections of Senators under the Constitution both predated direct election of US Senators.

John Quick, who would co-author with Robert Garran the seminal 1901 *The Annotated Constitution of the Australian Commonwealth*, supported a directly elected Senate. However, Quick also recognized that having two popularly elected houses made it even more important for there to be a procedure to break deadlocks that could arise as the two houses exercised their legislative powers:

> Now, in an ordinary constitution, where we have an upper house not elected by the people, or not elected on the same basis as the lower house, that second chamber would be disposed to yield to the pressure of the lower chamber elected upon a popular basis; but here, where we are creating a senate which will feel the sap of popular election in its veins, that senate will probably feel stronger than a senate or upper chamber which is elected only on a partial franchise, and consequently, we ought to make provision for the adjustment of disputes in great emergencies. (*Convention Debates*, 15 September 1897: 552)

During the interval between the 1891 and 1897–1898 Conventions, Griffith and Baker looked beyond the need for a procedure to resolve specific legislative disagreements, and devised two possible schemes for addressing the larger problem of how to reconcile the requirements of responsible government with the powers of the Senate. According to Galligan (1995: 80):

> One suggestion was that the Senate would approve the ministry at the first sitting of parliament and not be able to withdraw its support subsequently, with the ministry remaining in office as long as it retained the confidence of the lower house. Another suggestion entailed a more radical departure from responsible government; it had the ministry being elected for a fixed term by a joint sitting of both houses of parliament.

Quick and Garran (1901: 706) elaborated on the views of Griffith and others (paraphrasing Hackett in the process) who were convinced that federation and responsibility could not be reconciled, and who were not averse to resolving the contradiction in favor of the Senate.[100] They attributed to Griffith and those who shared his analysis an argument:

> that the same principle of State approval as well as popular approval should apply to Executive action, as well as to legislative action; that the States should not be forced to support Executive policy and Executive acts merely because ministers enjoyed the confidence of the popular Chamber; that the State House would be justified in withdrawing its support from a ministry

---

100 According to Aroney (2002: 284), 'Baker supported an executive responsible to both houses of the legislature as embodying the strengths and avoiding the weaknesses of the American and British systems.'

ORIGINAL INTENT AND EXPECTATIONS

of whose policy and executive acts it disapproved; that the State House could, as effectually as the primary Chamber, enforce its want of confidence by refusing to provide the necessary supplies. ...

On these grounds it is contended that the introduction of the Cabinet system of Responsible Government into a Federation, in which the relations of two branches of the legislature, having equal and co-ordinate authority, are quite different from those existing in a single autonomous State, is repugnant to the spirit and intention of a scheme of Federal Government. In the end it is predicted that either Responsible Government will kill the Federation and change it into a unified State, or the Federation will kill Responsible Government and substitute a new form of Executive more compatible with the Federal theory.

This analysis anticipated the argument that would be made decades later by Governor-General Kerr and Chief Justice Barwick, during and after the crisis of 1975, as well as the primary reason why others thought the argument to be particularly pernicious.

Once it was decided that there was to be a Senate, that it was to be directly elected, and that it was to enjoy substantial legislative powers, there were three primary questions that remained to be resolved. First, just what legislative powers should the Senate have: should its powers equal those of the House of Representatives, or should the House enjoy some legislative primacy? Second, what, if anything, should the Constitution provide in order to resolve the legislative deadlocks that might arise as a result of the two houses exercising their constitutionally-assigned legislative powers? And third, just what role was the Senate expected to play in the new constitutional order; was it to be a house of the states, a house of review, a combination of both, or something else? Let us consider each of these questions in turn.

The Senate's legislative powers

According to Galligan's (1995: 77) reading of the constitutional debates regarding the first question, there was 'broad agreement' that, except respecting money bills, the Senate should have the same legislative powers as the House, and that the House should initiate money bills but the Senate should have the power to reject them. The remaining controversy was over whether the two houses should enjoy equal powers with respect to these bills. In particular, should the Senate be empowered to amend them?[101]

---

101 Or to put it differently, should the Senate have only a veto over each money bill in its entirety, or should it also have a 'veto in detail,' reflecting Griffith's claim for 'the senate representing the States to exercise the power of veto as to any item of expenditure of which they disapproved'? John Downer proposed unsuccessfully in

Frederick Holder, who would become the first Speaker of the House of Representatives, argued at the Adelaide meetings of the second Convention that the Senate's legislative powers should be the same as those of the House, even regarding these most important bills:

> [I]f we are to have called into existence a Senate for no other purpose than to preserve the rights of the separate States as States, we must take care that the Senate shall be able to preserve those rights. ... Equal representation of the States in a manifestly inferior House would be of no value to the smaller States. We might as well have no Senate at all. ... [W]e should provide absolute strength in that House whose business and whose only reason for existence will be the protection of the interests of States one against the other. To set up a Senate which will have no power of the purse will be to set up an absolutely worthless body. (*Convention Debates*, 26 March 1897: 146, 148)

Scott Bennett summarizes the reactions of those from the larger colonies to arguments from small colony representatives such as Holder that the Senate should enjoy equal powers with the House over financial legislation:

> The representatives from the larger colonies viewed this development with alarm, for they could foresee a parliament in which the majority represented in the House could be defeated by a minority represented in the Senate. The example of the House of Lords, which had for some time appeared to have given up any real pretence to financial control, was outlined, as also were the dangers to responsible government that would ensue from having the finances of the government of the day dependent upon the upper house. (Bennett 1971: 127)

But as the argument made by Carruthers of New South Wales made clear, there were practical considerations as well as constitutional principles at stake:

> It is absurd that you should give to a House which may have a majority of representatives from the smaller contributories power to control the finances of the whole Federation. ... It will be intolerable if the 2 ½ million of people living in New South Wales and Victoria find the bulk of the money necessary to support Federation only to see the financial policy of the country governed by a minority of the people who might hold the majority in the Senate. (*Convention Debates*, 25 March 1897: 91–92)

1891 that the Senate 'have the power of rejecting [money bills] in whole or in part.' This, he argued, amounted to something less than the power to amend because it would not empower the Senate to propose alternatives, such as increases or decreases in spending levels, for provisions that a majority of the states opposed (Galligan and Warden 1986: 96–98).

A bar against Senate amendments to tax and spending bills was included in the draft that emerged from the 1891 Convention in Sydney.

If the Senate was to be foreclosed from amending money bills, what options remained? To deny the Senate any part at all in making what are among the most important legislative decisions that any parliament makes each year? Or to allow the Senate the power to say only 'yea' or 'nay' to money bills after the House passed them? Baker, speaking at the 1897 meetings in Sydney, foresaw the problem that might eventually arise if the Senate could reject but could not amend money bills initiated by a government responsible solely to the House. Referring to the powers of some colonial upper houses, Baker feared that a Senate with the power only to reject these bills would be:

> like a fort which has only one big gun, and that gun so powerful and so uncertain in its effect that they hardly dare to let it off, because it may burst and injure those who occupy the fort, and possibly blow it to pieces. This big gun is the power of refusing to grant supplies, and to thus cause the stoppage of all the functions of government. (*Convention Debates*, 17 September 1897: 785)

By this view, the Senate's power to reject a money bill, like any other bill, either would be meaningless because the Senate never would exercise it, or it might be calamitous if the Senate ever were to use it.

Yet that is what the authors ultimately decided: let the Senate defeat an essential money bill but not amend it.[102] The requirement that 'The Senate had to pass all bills including taxation and appropriation bills before they became law, and conversely it had the power to veto all bills. … was accepted very early on in the 1891 Convention and never again seriously questioned.' (Galligan 1980a: 5) As already noted, the contention was not over this question, but over whether the Senate should be empowered to amend money bills or only suggest certain amendments for the House's consideration. However, the right of the Senate to reject a spending bill unavoidably carried with it the right to pass such a bill only if the Senate was satisfied with its content—in other words, only if it was amended, directly by the Senate or indirectly by the House acting at the Senate's request, in whatever ways a majority of the Senate considered essential.

During the 1975 crisis, some argued that the authors of the Constitution surely could not have thought that the Senate they were creating would ever actually fire its 'big gun' and bring the government

---

102 Although contention over this issue almost caused a rupture in the Adelaide meetings of the second Convention (Galligan and Warden 1986: 94).

to a halt by denying it essential funds.[103] Yet consider this statement by Griffith at the first Convention in 1891:

> [I]t must be remembered that it is not proposed to deny the senate the power of veto. Surely if the senate wanted to stop the machinery of government the way to do that would be to throw out the appropriation bill. That would effectively stop the machinery of government. I, for my part, am much inclined to think that the power of absolute rejection is a much more dangerous power than the power of amendment; yet it is a power that must be conceded. We all admit that; and in a federation there is much more likelihood of that power of rejection being used than there is of the power of amendment being used. (*Convention Debates*, 17 March 1891: 429)

Griffith's final prognostication proved mistaken and we cannot know how many others shared his views on this point. What we can say, though, is that the danger that the Senate could and might reject an essential appropriation bill was raised at an early stage in the constitutional debates.

It also is noteworthy that Victoria's Legislative Council, its upper house, had done just that in 1865, then twice again in 1867, and once more in 1877.[104] Furthermore, these events were so dramatic and contentious that they could not possibly have slipped the minds of the Convention representatives from Victoria, or from the other colonies (Hutchison 1976: 41–50).

When the Legislative Council in Melbourne refused to vote supply in 1865, according to Wright (1992: 75), the state premier 'advised all public servants that they could not be paid and that government activities would have to be curtailed. The result was an eruption of meetings, marches, letters, editorials and petitions, overwhelmingly in favor of the Legislative Assembly [the lower house].' After the first refusal of supply in 1867, the ministry resigned, only to be called back to office for just long enough to have another supply bill rejected, and

---

103 Hughes (1980: 45–46) argues that the authors never seriously contemplated the Senate using its power to defeat a supply bill for this purpose. 'Although the Constitutional Conventions paid considerable attention to the Senate's power in respect of money bills, speakers perceived the problem in terms of a misuse of a particular financial measure to accomplish some extraordinary end, with the Senate blocking that measure to defend the rights of one or more of the states. Such reference as was made … to the possible use of the Senate's power against a 'corrupt' lower house was exceptional and not taken further in debate.'

104 My thanks to Ken Coghill of Monash University and former Speaker of the Victorian Legislative Assembly for calling these events to my attention. See Wright 1992: 74–91. These events involved tacking unrelated provisions on appropriations bills, and may have encouraged the authors of the Constitution to insert secs 54 and 55 that bar tacking in the Commonwealth Parliament.

for the Governor then to dissolve Parliament. Although the ensuing election returned the same Assembly majority that the Council had thwarted, the colonial secretary in London nonetheless instructed the Governor that:

> You ought not to again recommend the vote [the Appropriation Bill] to the acceptance of the Legislature, except on a clear understanding that it will be brought before the Legislative Council in a manner which will enable them to exercise their discretion respecting it, without the necessity of throwing the colony into confusion. (quoted in Wright 1992: 79)

In light of this instruction, the former ministry refused to form a new government, even though it held 60 of the 78 Assembly seats. For a brief period, there was, for the first time, a government formed by a member of the Council, a government that lacked a majority in the Assembly, and, therefore, a government entirely at odds with the basic conventions of the Westminster system.

After the Council's action in 1877, 'Exhausted members shouted hysterically of injustice, instability, insurrection.' (Wright 1992: 87) The Assembly then sought to bypass the Council by insisting that the Governor make funds available once they were approved by the Assembly acting alone. The Governor reluctantly complied and, for his efforts, 'was ignominiously transferred to Mauritius.' (Wright 1992: 89) Surely in light of such events, and the public furor surrounding them, the authors of the Commonwealth Constitution understood that the Senate they were creating might, sooner or later, exercise all the powers it was granted, and that those powers would include the right to refuse supply unless the Constitution specifically precluded the Senate from doing so—which it did not, and does not, do.

These circumstances make it more difficult to explain the decision, which was not seriously challenged, to allow the Senate the power to defeat any bill, even the most essential appropriation bill, though Uhr (1989a: 138–139) makes a valiant effort, explaining that 'the argument which won the day' was:

> that there should be a Senate with full veto power over all kinds of legislation, but one which could not initiate, amend or otherwise attempt to mould basic financial measures. To allow the latter powers would be to permit the Senate to interfere with the basic machinery of responsible government. *Outright rejection was different and legitimate*: it would be the strongest possible action of dissent from a government's policy, and the government thus defeated could seek a new House election with the hope of popular endorsement of its policy. It seems that most thought that the Senate would be somehow bound to accept such a mandate won by a government. However, to empower the Senate to amend even basic financial measures would be to tempt the Senate to frustrate the more

mundane matters relating to the machinery of government, creating
uncertainty, and deviating the course of administration away from the
accepted conventions of responsible government in which the lower house
is primary. (emphasis added)

The contemporaneous statement that has been offered in explanation is
one made by Barton in Adelaide during the 1897 meetings. The
perplexing nature of the question warrants quoting Barton at some
length:

If the Second Chamber makes suggestions ... and if the suggestions are not
adopted, that House must face the responsibility of deciding whether it will
veto the Bill or not. If the procedure is to be by way of amendment, and the
amendments are disagreed with by the House of Representatives, and are
still insisted upon by the Second Chamber, then it is upon the House of
Representatives that the responsibility must rest of destroying its own
measure. ... In the first case the responsibility rests where it should, with
those who wish to negative the policy of finance upon which the entire
policy of the Government hangs; because without money you cannot
govern. If the policy of the Ministry according to their desires in the main is
not carried out there must be another Ministry, and those who lead to the
formation of that Ministry should take the responsibility. If the procedure is
by way of suggestion, which is insisted upon, the Senate must take the
responsibility of the veto. (*Convention Debates*, 14 April 1897: 557)

I find these proffered explanations to be somewhat less than clear
and compelling, and wonder whether there is another one that lies in the
difference between the cannon of rejection and the shotgun of
amendment. Perhaps the Constitution's authors thought they could
satisfy those concerned with protecting state interests by giving the
Senate the power to reject any bill, including money bills, because they
were confident that this power would not be used in circumstances that
would jeopardize the functioning of responsible government. That 'big
gun' of which Baker spoke simply was too powerful, too dangerous—
and too likely to backfire. We will encounter an argument that supports
this explanation later in this chapter.

So the view that prevailed at the constitutional Conventions appears
to have been that Australia should enjoy responsible government
conventionally understood, with the government responsible only to the
House and with the Senate unable to amend money bills, but that the
Senate should be empowered to reject all bills, even money bills, in
their entirety. It must have been the widespread assumption that the
Victorian experience had been aberrational and—for whatever reason
or reasons, and maybe (or especially) with that experience in mind—
that the new Commonwealth Senate was very unlikely ever to fire its
'big gun.' And in fact, this assumption proved to be well-founded—

until the 1970s. In his 1946 book on the Parliament, Denning (1946: 64) concluded that 'the House of Representatives controls the raising and expenditure of money, and the Senate cannot interfere except to throw the whole financial machinery into disorder, and precipitate a crisis. So we see that, despite its technical seniority, the Senate occupies a very restricted and inhibited place in the parliamentary order.'

Yet two other points need to be kept in mind. First, the Constitution carefully circumscribed, in secs 54 and 55, what either a spending or taxing bill may contain, so that the House could not take undue advantage of the limits on the Senate's legislative powers. And second, the Senate was allowed to request that the House agree to specific amendments to any money bill.[105] To those with an expansive view of the Senate and its place in Australia's constitutional firmament, the effect of permitting such requests, as we have seen, was to restore the Senate's legislative status to one of essential equality with the House, because a determined Senate majority can refuse to pass any money bill that the House will not amend to the Senate's satisfaction.[106]

Breaking legislative deadlocks

Although the Senate ultimately was given the power only to request, not make, amendments to critical financial legislation, every other bill was vulnerable to the possibility of legislative disagreements between the houses that could not readily be resolved. That possibility was a necessary consequence of the powers that each house enjoyed, and a reflection of the larger problem of combining federalism and responsibility in the same charter of government. As we saw earlier, three options for resolving the underlying problem had emerged clearly as early as 1891: sacrificing federalism to the requirements of

---

105 But I do not rest much weight on that grant of authority because it is something that the Senate surely could have done anyway. Barring an explicit constitutional prohibition, there is no reason why the Senate could not have said to the House, in effect: 'Before we vote on passing or defeating this money bill that we have been debating, we would like to know if the House would be willing to make certain amendments that would make us much more inclined to pass the bill.' While such a communication to the House might have been extra-constitutional, I see nothing that would have made it unconstitutional even if there were no express authority for it in the Constitution. The procedure for requesting amendments evidently had its origins in procedures of the South Australian Parliament (Galligan and Warden 1986: 92).

106 There was no consensus about how much difference it was likely to make in practice that the Senate could not amend money bills directly but could request amendments to them. George Reid said that 'a strong Senate will compel attention to its suggestions; a weak one would not insist on its amendments.' (*Convention Debates*, 7 March 1898: 1998)

responsible government; sacrificing the purity of responsible government to the demands for a national parliament that reflected the federal nature of the Commonwealth; or somehow joining the two together in a marriage that would last. The first two options were rejected because they necessitated emasculating one or the other. That left only the third option, which could be approached in one of two ways, or a combination of both. 'One was to rely on the good sense of those who operated the system to make it work ... ' (Galligan 1980a: 4) '[H]owever we may err in allotting too much or too little power to this or that body,' Barton said, 'we still have the good sense of an English-born race to carry us through ... ' (*Convention Debates*, 17 March 1891: 410)

The other approach, and one that was compatible with the first, was to embed in the Constitution a procedure for resolving legislative deadlocks as they occurred. However, the draft Constitution that emerged from the 1891 Sydney Convention contained no such procedure. When the Australasian Federal Convention first met in Adelaide in 1897, it confirmed the 1891 draft in this respect. At the Sydney meetings of the second Convention, however, this issue was revisited, and at length. Richardson (2001: 298) calculates that the debate over whether to include a procedure for resolving legislative deadlocks and, if so, what that procedure should be, 'lasted six days and accounted for some 400 of the 1100 pages of the official record, making deadlocks easily the most debated single subject in the entire series of Convention debates.' One proposal called for a deadlock to be resolved by a simple majority vote at a national referendum, an approach that would work to the obvious advantage of the most populous states and so was unacceptable to the less populous ones.[107] The alternative was some form of double dissolution procedure, for which there was precedent in a procedure that South Australia had adopted in 1881.

The virtues and vices of both approaches continued to be debated, as were various permutations and combinations of consecutive or simultaneous dissolutions of both houses, sometimes linked to joint sittings or referenda and sometimes not. The issue remained unresolved when the Convention reconvened in Melbourne in January 1898. It was then and there that agreement finally was reached to include the procedures now found in sec. 57, but with the requirement for three-

---

107 'The Convention could find no consensus on the appropriate form of referendum. The conservatives argued for a dual or double referendum requiring a majority of votes and a majority of States while the radicals argued for a single mass referendum requiring only a majority of votes.' (Galligan and Warden 1986: 107)

fifths majorities at joint sittings. Still later, in January 1899, when the six colonial premiers met in Melbourne, they changed this requirement to an absolute majority of the members of both houses. (At that meeting, the premiers also agreed that neither house should be able to prevent a constitutional amendment from being submitted to a referendum.)

The issue was not simply one of deciding what mechanism, or which of the two, would be more efficient or dependable; there were thought to be important political interests at stake. Galligan (1980b: 251) summarizes the choices nicely:

> The usual colonial procedure of a single dissolution of the House of Representatives was available, but was rejected because it would leave the House at the Senate's mercy. Popular plebiscite was also considered and discarded since a popular majority would most likely favour the House. Similarly, a joint sitting of both Houses of Parliament was rejected because the Senators would be out-numbered two to one by members of the House.

In fact, any mechanism for overcoming legislative disagreements could undermine the leverage that the Senate was thought to give to the small states and for which they fought so doggedly during the Conventions.

> The small states feared that any method of resolving deadlocks would undermine the power of the Senate by enabling the large States, through the executive, to manipulate a deadlock and thus ensure *de facto* control of the Senate. They saw a proposed mechanism for resolving conflicts not as a precautionary measure to avoid a parliamentary, and hence a national crisis, but rather as a sinister instrument of coercion. (Galligan and Warden 1986: 106)

From this perspective, Bennett concludes (1971: 131) that, on balance, what became sec. 57 was 'a clear victory on points for the larger colonies', a victory that contributed to the balance of the overall compromise that included equal representation of the states in the Senate. Perhaps the reason for this outcome, Galligan and Warden suggest, is that the small states were even more opposed to the most likely alternative to the double dissolution and joint sitting procedure. That alternative was some form of a national referendum at which the voting strength of the larger states would allow them to prevail (assuming the merits of the bill actually did put the small and large states at odds with each other). For delegates from the smaller states, 'The referendum was ... an instrument far more antagonistic to the spirit of federation and their own States' interests than was the simultaneous dissolution.' (Galligan and Warden 1986: 108)

As Galligan (1995: 85) points out, however, this mechanism was not well-suited to deal with deadlocks over supply, 'being too cumbersome and time-consuming.' No joint sitting can occur until after the two houses have reached deadlock three times over the same bill, and with a double dissolution and new elections intervening between the second and third attempts. If deadlocks were to be anything other than rare, the Constitution's mechanism for resolving them was hardly workable. O'Connor had recognized this when he advised distinguishing between deadlocks over supply, which could bring the operations of the government to a halt, and deadlocks over all other bills, which did not entail the same risk. For the former, he proposed that a deadlock be broken by a vote at a joint sitting, without the need for an intervening double dissolution and the time-consuming process of holding an election.

This proposal was rejected in favor of the sec. 57 procedures that apply equally to all bills and that cannot offer a timely resolution of a deadlock over supply. This brings us to Galligan's conclusion that 'The lack of a fail-safe mechanism for handling supply deadlocks, not the Senate's legislative power over such bills, is the problem in the Constitution.' Why did the authors not address this problem more satisfactorily? Galligan's answer is that they thought it unnecessary to do so because the Senate would not act in a way that would put the essential operations of government at risk:

> It seems that most delegates considered O'Connor's 'dangerous' deadlocks were so serious as to be practically unthinkable. According to Glynn, a deadlock over an appropriation bill would 'open up the way to a revolution' and the fear of such a thing occurring would 'operate as a sanction to prevent it.' ... At Melbourne, McMillan suggested that the blocking of supply would throw the whole finances of the Commonwealth into confusion and 'would mean revolution.' (Galligan 1980a: 9)

'[T]he Australian founders profoundly trusted their rugged sense of British constitutionalism and parliamentary politics,' such that either 'prudential restraint' or the deterrent of giving the Senate only the 'big gun' of rejecting supply would suffice (Galligan 1984: 144–145).

Was this naive? W. Harrison Moore, a respected legal scholar who was not involved in drafting the Constitution, evidently did not think so. In his commentary on the Constitution, published a decade after Federation, he wrote that, especially in view of the bar against Senate amendments to the most critical appropriation bills, deadlock, 'bringing the machinery of government to a standstill—is a contingency so remote as hardly to be within the range of practical politics.' (1910: 154) Recall that it was not until more than a decade later that Britain found it necessary to adopt the *Parliament Act 1911*. And recall also that the US Constitution is entirely silent on mechanisms for breaking deadlocks between the American House and Senate, deadlocks that were likely enough to arise in view of the different modes of electing the members of each. Perhaps the essential difference is that the prospect of new laws being delayed or prevented by deadlocks in Congress probably would not have perturbed many authors of the US Constitution, given their skepticism about an activist, expansionist federal government.

So the most plausible conclusions seem to be that: first, authors of the Australian Constitution recognized that they were giving the Senate powers that could lead to deadlock; second, their mechanism for breaking such deadlocks ultimately favored the House; and, third, this mechanism would not work well, or at all, for spending legislation; but, fourth, they were sufficiently confident that good sense and restraint would prevail that they did not think it necessary to devise a more practical mechanism to expedite resolutions in cases of deadlock.

A House of the States? A House of Review?

As the statements by Holder and Carruthers, quoted above, reveal, the questions we have asked about the powers of the Senate, and its exercise of those powers, are inseparable from questions about the kind of institution the Senate was expected to be, and especially whether it was to be a 'House of the States,' and if so, what that meant.

Souter (1988: 21) estimates that debate concerning 'the composition and powers of the Senate vis-a-vis those of the lower house … occupied more than one-third of the 7053 pages of the federation convention debates in the 1890s.' Much of this debate, and especially about the Senate's powers over financial legislation, turned on the relations between large colonies/states and small ones, and on the relations between a House based on population and a Senate based on representation of the states as such. Opponents of equal powers for the two houses emphasized that the Senate with equal powers could block the House to the detriment of responsible government. Underlying that argument was the assumption that any such Senate action would represent the interests of the states (that is, a majority of the states, and presumably the less populous ones) coming into conflict with the interests of the general public as represented in the House.

Delegates to the constitutional Conventions debated whether there were distinctive state interests that required protection, whether any such differences in interests distinguished the small states from the large ones, whether the powers proposed for the Commonwealth were restricted enough to protect the states' ability to protect their own interests, and, therefore, whether it was necessary to provide for equal representation of the states in the Senate and to empower the Senate to

amend those all-important money bills. Implicit in these debates was
the assumption that Senators would approach issues and evaluate
government proposals from the perspective of the interests of their
respective states. Senators were to be directly elected, but that did not
mean that they would be insensitive to their states' preferences and
needs. There was no question that the smaller states saw in the Senate
their protection against domination by New South Wales and Victoria.
The questions were, first, how much any of the states, as states, needed
the protection that the Senate could provide them, and, second, how
much protection the Senate would be constitutionally empowered to
provide.

Hugh Collins has concluded that the Constitution's authors
approached these questions as questions of practical governance, not
abstract political theory. In Australia:

> [F]ederalism is a product of convenience rather than conviction. Unlike
> Switzerland, or French and British Canada, Australian federalism is not a
> means for preserving the integrity of linguistically distinct communities
> within a single polity. Nor, as in the American case, is it traceable to the
> normative assumption that, even within a relatively homogenous
> community, power should be divided between levels as well as branches of
> government. Rather, the constitutional framework chosen in Australia in
> the 1890s was a practical adjustment to circumstance. Faced with small
> communities separated by great distances but already endowed with
> political institutions, those seeking a limited range of cooperative action in
> matters like defense, trade, and immigration found a federal scheme
> expedient. (Collins 1985: 152)

There are two other matters that deserve mention here. The first is
that a second chamber such as the Australian or American Senate is not
an essential element of a federal system. Federalism is characterized by
more than one level of government and some division of powers among
them. Federal systems differ, for instance, in how powers are
distributed between or among levels of government, where the residual
jurisdiction resides over undistributed powers, and how disagreements
or incompatibilities between national and state (or provincial, etc.)
policies or legislation are to be resolved. Notwithstanding Baker's
claim at the Sydney Convention in 1897 that 'The essence of federation
is the existence of two houses, if not of actually co-equal power, at all
events of approximately co-equal power,' the representation of the
states within the legislative structure of the national government is not
an essential part of the federal arrangement (Sampford 1989: 356–361).
If a constitution assigns certain authority to the national government
and other authority to subnational governments, perhaps with an
independent court to adjudicate boundary disputes, there is no

compelling reason why the subnational units have to be represented as such in the councils of the national government.

When states are given representation in the national Parliament, they typically are given equal representation or at least representation that does not accurately reflect population disparities among the states. The essential reason for such representation is not theoretical, it is political, because the smaller states want disproportionate influence over how the national government exercises its powers within its constitutional jurisdiction and using its own resources. It is understandable why smaller states want such representation; it is in their interests to have it. But it is no more natural or necessary for the states to have a share of the powers of the federal government than for the federal government to have a constitutional share in the governance of each state—for example, by giving the US President a veto power over legislation enacted by each of the 50 states. An 'upper' or 'second' house in which the states are represented equally may be a price that smaller states demand for their agreement to federate, but it is not necessary to the design or operation of federal systems.

It follows that I must disagree with an assertion that Griffith made during the debates and that Galligan (1980b: 251) quotes with evident approval. In support of the proposition that the Senate had to have the same, or very close to the same, legislative powers as the House, Griffith invoked the 'strict federal principle' that 'in a federation the laws—and the laws affecting money as well as others—must be passed by the consent of a majority of the people of the commonwealth and also with the consent of a majority of the states.' To the contrary, I find nothing inherent in federalism which requires, for reasons of theory or 'strict principle', that the states as such should have anything to say about how the federal government allocates the funds that it has received under its own constitutional powers and that it now proposes to spend to fulfill its own constitutional responsibilities. Most of those who spoke during the debates about the Canadian system were less than enamoured with it, primarily because of the dominance of the government in Ottawa and a consequent lack of provincial autonomy. I doubt that any federal system can work, or work well, if the federal and state governments are entirely autonomous within completely separated constitutional jurisdictions. Some sharing, some overlap, some inter-penetration probably is inescapable as well as desirable. But from that starting point, it is a long jump indeed to the conclusion that a 'strict principle' of federalism requires a simple majority of the states to have a veto power over the federal government's budget.

It also follows that the problem for the Constitution was not to reconcile responsible government with federalism but with something that is often and easily thought to be, as Baker suggested, essential for a workable federal system—the Senate. Like others before me, I succumb in these pages to the seductive ease of summarizing the 'problem' or the 'contradiction' as one between federalism and responsibility. Though I admit that this is not quite right, I claim the justification of artistic license. In addressing subjects like these, clear and simple formulations are hard to find and harder to discard.

Second, while many authors of the Constitution undoubtedly thought of the Senate as the House of the states, and even more of them probably spoke of it in those terms for convenience, there is an alternative conception of the Senate which needs to be noted. In his *A Federal Republic* (1995), Brian Galligan has been the most eloquent advocate of an understanding of the Senate which we may summarize by describing both houses of the Commonwealth Parliament as being Houses of the People, both being directly elected, but elected in different ways.

> [T]he Senate is not less democratic or legitimate than the House of Representatives; the two houses are simply constituted according to different principles of representation of the people, one being federal and based on State electoral constituencies, and the other being national and based on local, single-member electorates. The two houses of parliament are both directly elected by the people but on different constituent bases. (Galligan 1995: 74)

Here Galligan takes issue with Quick and Garran (1901: 414), in whose view the authors of the Australian Constitution confronted the same problem as had the framers of the US Constitution: 'how to reconcile the creation of a strong national government with the claims and susceptibilities of separate, and, in their own eyes, *quasi*-sovereign States.' The solution, according to Quick and Garran:

> was found in a Parliament partly national and partly Federal. The national part of the Parliament is the House of Representatives—the organ of the nation. The Federal part of the Parliament is the Senate—the organ of the States, the visible representative of the continuity, independence, and reserved autonomy of the States, linking them together as integral parts of the Federal union.

So the Senate, they conclude, is 'the Council of States in the Federal Parliament'.[108] Galligan rejects this analysis, arguing instead that the

---

108 'The Senate is not merely a branch of a bicameral Parliament; it is not merely a second chamber of revision and review representing the sober second thought of the nation, such as the House of Lords is supposed to be; it is that, but something more than that. It is the chamber in which the States, considered as separate entities, and

Senate is just as much part of the national government as the House, the only difference being in the basis of representation. The essential point to Galligan is that the members of both houses are directly elected, albeit in different ways. Quick and Garran's characterization might well apply to the US Senate before the 17th Amendment and to the German Bundesrat today, but not at any time to the Australian Senate. Precisely because the Senate is directly elected, it does not, he might argue, represent the States as such and so cannot be 'the Council of States in the Federal Parliament'.

Perhaps the core of Galligan's argument is that 'parliamentary responsible government was incorporated into the federal constitution, not vice versa.' (Galligan 1995: 7) Elsewhere, he (1997: 23) has asserted that 'Australia's constitutional system is fundamentally federal and republican rather than parliamentary and monarchic. ... That is not to say that the parliamentary and, to a lesser extent, the monarchic parts are not important but rather that they are subservient to the overarching federal and republican parts.' Putting aside the question of its republican and monarchic elements, Galligan's exposition (and especially his 1995 book) are a valuable corrective to the more frequent assertions that the essential characteristic of Australian government is responsible parliamentary government. However, I should think it suffices to stress the centrality of both elements.

Galligan's key contribution may be in emphasizing that federalism was neither an after-thought nor a secondary concern for the Constitution's authors. They did not construct a system of responsible government and then attach to it, as an ill-fitting appendage, a federal structure and a constitutionally potent Senate. Anyone who has proposed or might propose abolishing the Senate should not view that proposal as a way to clean up or simplify or streamline the structure of Australian governance. Such a proposal would be even more radical in its effects than a proposal to scrap the forms of responsible government in favor of a directly-elected president and an American-style system of separate institutions sharing the powers of the Commonwealth government.

In any event, whether it is accurate to say that the Senate was intended to be the House of the States, observers of the Parliament in practice are virtually unanimous in stressing that whatever the Senate

corporate parts of the Commonwealth, are represented. They are so represented for the purpose of enabling them to maintain and protect their constitutional rights against attempted invasions, and to give them every facility for the advocacy of their peculiar and special interests, as well as for the ventilation and consideration of their grievances.' (Quick and Garran 1901: 414)

may be, a House of the States it is not. Fifty years ago, Partridge (1952: 175) opined that 'the Senate has proved to be a falsely-conceived institution. The chief assumption about the structure of our polity which dictated its design (the assumption that there are distinct and decisive State interests which could be separately represented) has turned out to be false.' Cody reports interviews with small state Senators who:

> characterised equal state Senate representation as a discernible benefit to their states. Their defence of equal representation was largely negative, much like Australians' justification for an upper house. That is, in both cases the Senate prevents undesirable outcomes through reaction to government policies and practices more than it facilitates desirable outcomes through proactive policy initiation of its own. Senators conceded that the Senate's operation does not give small states great power, but they contended that their states would enjoy still less party room leverage if the Senate and its party caucuses were majoritarian like the Representatives. (Cody 1996:105)

Such assertions must be weighed with care in the absence of independent empirical verification because we would hardly expect small state Senators to say anything different. And Cody himself concludes that 'small states derive remarkably limited benefits from equal state representation.' This is about as much as we can say today for the Senate as the House of the States.[109]

The primary reason, of course, is the strength of party discipline and the importance of that discipline for decision-making in the House and, to only a slightly lesser extent, in the Senate as well. As we already have seen, the strength of parliamentary parties in the Commonwealth is no new development; it is largely a product of the emergence of the ALP and the 'fusion' of non-Labor forces in the election of 1910. What made this development so consequential was the strict discipline that the Labor Party imposed on its Representatives and Senators, a discipline that had ripple effects:

---

109 Referring to Canada, Evans (1997a: 4–5) notes 'the extreme alienation of the outlying provinces, particularly the western provinces, caused by the domination of government by the centres of population. ... Such serious alienation has not occurred in Australia, and a primary reason for this is that the federal structure of the legislature, unlike the non-federal structure of the legislature in Canada, has altered the representational system by forcing majorities to be geographically distributed.' This was a more persuasive argument before the crystallization of Australia's party system in 1910. In this context, it probably is fair to observe that the concerns the small states expressed in the Conventions about the prospect of being dominated by the large states was, in most respects, more a fear of domination by the twin population centres of Sydney and Melbourne.

The other looser-knit groups organised around free trade and protection, which had dominated colonial politics through the federation period and in the early Commonwealth parliaments, were forced to realign into a Liberal 'fusion' and adopt comparable disciplined practices. Disciplined party politics reinforced the logic of parliamentary responsible government and was in turn reinforced by it. The Senate became a party house and played second string to the House of Representatives where the government did battle with the Opposition. (Galligan 1995:8)

Senators could not be loyal and disciplined members of their party and, at the same time, be willing to give first priority to the interests of their states. According to Souter (1988: 67), politics in the Senate 'were a mixture of State and party politics from the very beginning.' Regarding the first Senate, which pre-dated the emergence of two disciplined party blocs, he concludes that:

The Senate on this maiden voyage had nailed its colours to the mast. It had insisted upon its right to press requests; had tried unsuccessfully to establish the right of ministers to address either house, an innovation which would have been quite at variance with British parliamentary tradition; and in the last weeks of parliament declined to concur in resolutions of the 'other place' that a conference be held between the two houses to consider the selection of the permanent seat of government. At such a conference, Senator Simon Fraser ... reminded his colleagues, representatives would outnumber senators two to one. (Souter 1988: 80)

The first Senate also asserted its standing with respect to bills making appropriations. According to Moore (and *Odgers' Australian Senate Practice* 2001: 292–293), the Senate immediately made clear its dissatisfaction with the House's apparent claims to primacy that were reflected in how the first supply bill in 1901 was drafted:

As soon as the Bill reached the Senate, objection was taken that no estimates formed part of the Bill, and that it contained nothing upon which the Senate could exercise its judgment in the exercise of its constitutional powers. In this view the Government acquiesced, and on their suggestion the Senate made the first exercise of its power under sec. 53 by returning the Bill to the House with a request that the House would so amend the Bill that it might show the items of expenditure comprised in the sums which the Bill purported to grant. The House accepted the position, the Bill was laid aside, and a new Bill introduced. (Moore 1910: 145–146)

That bill also asserted that the appropriation was being 'made by' the House of Representatives. When the Senate objected to this formulation, the House amended the bill to state instead that the appropriation 'originated in' the House.

Yet as early as 1905, one observer, H.G. Turner, felt justified in calling the Senate 'merely an appendage, necessary to give statutory force to the decisions of the party which dominated the other House' (quoted in Souter 1988: 125). Souter concludes that 'the party system had come to dominate the intended "States" House as well as the House of Representatives.' By 1909, he reports (1988: 117), 'the "States' House" had lost some of its former zeal for States' rights,' and a constitutional amendment concerning Commonwealth grants to the States was 'passed by the upper house pretty much on party lines,' even though 'its provisions involved a substantial transfer of power from States to the Commonwealth.' 'In practice,' Hutchison (1983: 145) finds, 'the Australian Senate has since 1901 rarely been seen as *a*, let alone *the* forum, for the promotion and protection of state interests.' She continues:

> Bodies such as the Premiers' Conferences and the Loan Council, and direct negotiations between federal and state ministers and public servants, are the real medium of federal-state interaction. There are only about 20 occasions on which one can document a purely states'rights, rather than partisan, reaction to legislation.

Since strong disciplined parties emerged so soon after the Constitution took effect, are we to conclude that its authors simply failed to anticipate this development? Certainly not all of them (Irving 1999: 74). It was J.M. Macrossan of Queensland at the 1891 Convention who predicted that the strength of party would overcome the interests of the states in the Senate:

> We have been arguing all through as if party government were to cease immediately we adopt the new constitution. ... The influence of party will remain much the same as it is now, and instead of members of the senate voting, as has been suggested, as states, they will vote as members of parties to which they will belong. I think, therefore, that the idea of the larger states being overpowered by the voting of the [smaller] states might very well be abandoned; the system has not been found to have that effect in other federal constitutions. Parties have always existed, and will continue to exist where free men give free expression to their opinions. (*Convention Debates*, 17 March 1891: 434)

Isaacs concurred, arguing in 1897 that 'men do not vote according to the size of their States,' and Higgins found evidence for this position in Lord Bryce's observation that, in the United States, 'There has never been, in fact, any division of interest or consequent contest between the great States and the small ones.' (*Convention Debates*, 26 March 1897: 173–174; 25 March 1897: 100)

Deakin took much the same view at Sydney in 1897:

> I have always contended that we shall never find in the future federation certain states ranked against certain other states, or that party lines will be

drawn between certain states which happen to be more populous and those which do not happen to be so populous. ... What is absolutely certain is that, as soon as this federation is formed, parties will begin to declare themselves in every state. Every state will be divided. ... There exists in each colony a party that can be considered liberal, and also a party that can be considered conservative. Is it not, then, inevitable, that so soon as the federation is formed, the liberal parties in the different colonies will coalesce and throw in their lot with each other; and that the conservative parties in the different colonies will do the same, irrespective of state boundaries ... . There will not be any question of large or small states, but a question of liberal or conservative. (*Convention Debates*, 10 September 1897: 335)

So, Deakin concluded:

The contest will not be, never has been, and cannot be, between states and states. ... it is certain that once this constitution is framed, it will be followed by the creation of two great national parties. Every state, every district, and every municipality, will sooner or later be divided on the great ground of principle, when principles emerge.

In this event, 'Contests between the two houses will only arise when one party is in possession of a majority in the one chamber, and the other in the possession of a majority in the other chamber.' (*Convention Debates*, 15 September 1897: 584)[110]

We cannot know for certain how widespread their views were. La Nauze (1972: 119), however, refers to the 'unrepresentative character' of the arguments that both Macrossan and Deakin had made. When confronted with these arguments, 'the delegates were unconvinced. They remained fixed on the idea that the principal political divisions in the Commonwealth would be based on the states ... ' (Reid and Forrest 1989: 12) And it should be remembered that, as the debates took place, the ALP was still very much in the process of development, leading Galligan (1986: 101) to conclude that:

Deakin and his colleagues failed to follow through their insight ... and so did not anticipate the acute problems that might arise if the federal bicameral legislature were controlled by opposing parties. If Deakin and his colleagues anticipated parties, it was not the disciplined parties that were to dominate Australian politics after 1910 and force the constitutional crisis of 1975.

---

110 During the Adelaide debates earlier in the year, he had said that, 'From the first day that the Federation is consummated ... the people will divide themselves into two parties ... . [W]hichever way parties may move, one thing is certain, namely, that their division into the more populous States on the one side, and the less populous States on the other side, is the last possible eventuality of a thousand eventualities which are more likely to occur.' (*Convention Debates*, 30 March 1897: 297)

Here is a plausible basis for explaining why the authors of the Constitution fought so doggedly over whether the Senate should be allowed to amend money bills but had few if any qualms about empowering the Senate to veto each and every one of those same bills (and all others). In an earlier analysis of the events of 1975, Galligan (1980b: 252) argued that 'Those who framed the Constitution did not envisage a deadlock over supply since they were unfamiliar with disciplined political parties.' They could understand why a particular provision in an appropriation bill might be opposed by a single Senator, or by all the Senators from the same state, or even by all the Senators from a group of (small) states. But if they did not envision the Senate being dominated by intense competition between two disciplined party blocs, it is not surprising that they thought it unlikely that Senators or the Senate would want to defeat, in its entirety, a bill for the essential purpose of keeping the existing wheels of Government turning. Galligan (1980b: 255) elaborates:

> The Australian Constitution which was the mature fruit of nineteenth-century practices and beliefs was not designed to cope with the bipartisan [i.e., two-party] politics that polarised the nation along class lines immediately after federation. The legislative system took for granted a liberal consensus and faction or pluralist politics. It presupposed the parliamentary practices of the day in which majorities were formed from loose coalitions of relatively autonomous members. The founders took for granted a system in which personalities and issues dominated, and debate and compromise determined outcomes ... . The rapid rise of the Labor Party to national prominence after federation partly undermined the ideological consensus that the Constitution presupposed and made its working problematical ... . When the two houses of a bicameral legislature are controlled by opposing and disciplined parties, the system is prone to deadlock.

This argument makes untestable assumptions about how the authors envisioned the future shape of parliamentary politics. However, it has the compelling advantage of allowing us to explain their decision by reference to calculations that they could make as experienced political animals, instead of or in addition to relying on more ethereal arguments on the same point such as the one, quoted earlier in this chapter, that Barton made.

Did the perhaps-not-widely-enough-anticipated and all-too-soon-to-be-realized growth of strong parties preclude the Senate from serving as a House of Review, if not the House of the States? That question is more difficult to answer because the notion of the Senate as a House of Review has proven to be so amorphous. Both in the contemporaneous debates and the contemporary literature, there is a frustrating imprecision in discussions of what a House of Review is to review, and to what end (e.g., Wright 2001). Some discussions imply that a House of Review is concerned less with the wisdom and workability of proposed legislation than with the implementation of legislation already enacted; to use American terms, that a House of Review focuses on oversight at the expense of its legislative powers. Other discussions, however, at least imply that characterizing the Senate as a House of Review is a way of describing how the Senate should exercise its legislative powers. This alternative sense suggests that the Senate acts as a House of Review if and when it assesses how well government legislation is designed and drafted to achieve the government's own objectives, not whether those objectives are desirable and whether enactment of the legislation, in the judgment of Senators, would be good for Australia. If so, then it would be appropriate for the Senate to make polite suggestions for what, by the government's own criteria, would be improvements in its legislation, but certainly not to try to defeat or unduly delay that legislation.

Let me illustrate the problem with applying this concept to the Senate by referring to two often-cited scholarly efforts that take on the subject directly: Fusaro's 1966 article on 'The Australian Senate as a House of Review: Another Look,' and Mulgan's 1996 article on 'The Australian Senate as a "House of Review".' What does each author mean by a House of Review; how can we tell if that is what the Senate is and what the Senate does? What does or would or should the Senate review? And what is or would be or should be the purpose and product of this review: to clarify, to elucidate, to publicize, to evaluate, to modify, or even to reject?

In other words, assuming that whatever the Senate reviews is something the government supports, is it appropriate for the Senate as a House of Review to interfere with or even prevent the government from doing what it wants to do or continuing with what it already has begun to do? Or should the Senate accept that the government has the right, if not the unquestioned power, to determine the general lines of policy, and that the appropriate role for a House of Review is to illuminate the implications and consequences of government policy and perhaps to suggest changes that will enable the government to achieve its policy goals more efficiently, effectively, parsimoniously, or fairly? It should be obvious that different answers to these questions can produce quite different concepts of what it actually does or should mean for the Senate to be that House of Review.

In the earlier of these articles, Fusaro adopts a concept of review that encompasses both legislative proposals and executive actions. He makes clear that his primary focus is on cases 'in which the senate has

changed or attempted to change legislation sent to it from the lower
house,' but also asserts that the Senate's 'power to review the acts of
the executive' is another 'aspect of review' (Fusaro 1966: 384). So
'review' can refer to the exercise of the Senate's legislative powers and
also to the activities of the Senate in monitoring and sometimes
attempting to influence, restrain or control the government's executive
actions. 'Review' is both prospective and retrospective: it applies both
to government proposals and to government actions. (For the
retrospective aspect of review, I will use the American term,
'oversight.')

With regard to prospective, legislative review, how is the Senate as
a House of Review to be distinguished from the Senate as a House of
Lawmaking? Fusaro's answer is that 'review' of proposed legislation is
'legitimately constructive,' not 'politically obstructive' (385). In
looking at the Senate in relation to the first double dissolution in 1914,
he asks whether the Senate's record was 'one of legitimate review, or
one of political obstruction.' How are we to distinguish one from the
other? Fusaro uses both quantitative and qualitative criteria. The
percentages of House bills that the Senate amended or rejected were not
large enough to constitute a record of obstruction (386). Evidently more
important, though, is the fact that the double dissolution made possible
by what qualifies as the Senate's 'review' of legislation (because it was
not 'politically obstructive') led to the defeat of the government:

> When a party succeeds in winning support for itself, as labor [controlling
> the Senate] did in 1914, democratic practice has the effect of bestowing
> upon it the cloak of righteousness. While the senate's behaviour might thus
> have been obstructive in the eyes of the Cook government its actions can
> hardly be called anything but legitimate, either constitutionally or in its
> representation of the popular will. (Fusaro 1966: 386)

By clear implication, then, legislative review is to be distinguished
from legislative obstruction not (1) on the basis of how many bills the
Senate failed to pass in the form the government had proposed them,
nor (2) on the basis of how much impact on the government's program
the Senate had in amending or rejecting government bills, but instead
(3) on the basis of whether or not the public's verdict at the subsequent
election favoured the party controlling the government and the House
or the party controlling the Senate.

Fusaro also looks at the experience of the Scullin Labor
Government following the 1929 election, when he also confronted a
non-ALP Senate. After presenting the same kind of data on the numbers
of bills that the Senate amended or rejected, he goes on to observe that
'The varied tactics used by the senate, although at times the obvious
results of party hostilities, were nevertheless constitutionally in line

with the chamber's reviewing power.' Those tactics included, in the case of the Central Reserve Bank Bill of 1930, referring the bill to a committee and then agreeing to a motion in the chamber that the bill be read 'this day six months'—'a parliamentary tactic which, in effect, killed the measure' (see the discussion of this motion in Chapter 7). So, it would seem, the Senate was acting as a House of Review when it first delayed and then killed what would seem to have been a bill of some consequence.

Fusaro discusses other bills that the Senate rejected on party votes, but finds those actions to be compatible with the Senate acting as a House of Review. After recognizing the inescapable influence of parties in Parliament, he judges that 'There is, nevertheless, a function of review which takes place when one party, which represents a sizable portion of the electorate, succeeds in influencing the legislative proposals of another party. ... Thus, the senate controlled by the opponents of the Scullin government was in fact acting as a house of review.' (388) Fusaro also finds this conclusion confirmed by the fact that the percentage of government bills that the Senate rejected 'does not in itself seem overbearing,' and, more important, by the fact that the Scullin Government was defeated at the next election, just as the Cook Government had been in 1914.

> [W]hile the vote did not mean that the people approved of all of the activities of the senate, the support given to the general policies of the party which had controlled that body since 1929 was certainly not a repudiation of the party's use of the senate's constitutional power of review *to try to implement its program.* (389; emphasis added)

Therefore, legislative 'review' in the Senate encompasses rejection of government bills on a party basis and as a way (perhaps the only available way) for the party controlling the Senate to try to promote its own legislative program. Can the Senate know at the time it is acting whether it is acting within Fusaro's conception of it as a House of Review? Not if the primary basis for answering that question is: 'Was the upper house following a publicly approved policy?' (392) Whether Senate action qualifies as appropriate prospective 'review' can only be answered retrospectively—after the next election.

Later in his analysis, Fusaro suggests other dimensions of prospective legislative 'review': that 'a proper function of the house of review' may be 'to educate the public on current issues before the parliament, and to delay controversial measures until the public has had ample time to form and express an opinion,' and perhaps also to amend or defeat legislation 'to safeguard the principles of the constitution' (394). And he concludes that 'much of the criticism [of the Senate] om the fact that the concept of review may be too narrowly defined.' (398) That is not a problem if we accept the definition, or definitions, that emerge from his analysis. Instead, we have three other problems. First, Fusaro offers us no way to distinguish, at the time the Senate is acting, between the Senate as a House of Lawmaking and the Senate as a House of Review. Second, the distinction he does make can be drawn only after the fact. And third, this distinction is based on inferences about public support for the Senate's actions that derive from the results of the next election. His distinction ultimately does not rest on the quantity or even the quality of the Senate's actions themselves. Consequently, we emerge from Fusaro's analysis with a muddier understanding of the concept of a House of Review than when we entered it.

If Fusaro demonstrates how imprecise the concept can be within a single paper, Mulgan's more recent and more careful analysis reveals how much variability there is to be found in the way different analysts define the concept, even if the definition that each uses is satisfactorily explicit, clear, and limited. Mulgan notes the different ways in which different analysts have used the phrase:

> A number of detailed studies of the Senate's effectiveness as a house of review have concentrated on the Senate's legislative record and in particular on the extent to which it has amended legislation received from the House of Representatives [Fusaro's article being one example]. Others, however, have a wider view of review, understanding it to cover general scrutiny of the executive.... Such scrutiny includes not only the Senate's legislative function of reviewing government bills but also the detailed examination of government decisions and administration ...
>
> There is also disagreement about how far the Senate's role as a house of review allows it to go in confronting the government. Given a connection of review with the principles of Westminster-style responsible government and with the archetype of the House of Lords, it is commonly assumed that the Senate will not press its powers, whether of legislative revision or executive scrutiny, beyond a certain point. Thus Souter ... defines review as 'exercising its power in order to monitor and restrain the government of the day, but not to expel it from office'. Those who identify review with the revision of legislative detail clearly imply that review does not seriously challenge the government's authority or its major policies. On the other hand, effective review may not be possible without some degree of confrontation and frustration of the government of the day .... A distinction has been drawn between a 'strong' and a 'weak' sense of review, though the boundaries between the two may be hard to define and the distinction may collapse ... (Mulgan 1196: 192–193)

One thing the various conceptions of 'review' have in common is 'an ancillary role for the Senate as a "second" chamber, a role which cedes initiative, if not power, to the lower house. In this respect, describing the Senate as a house of review can make it compatible with one of the defining assumptions of Westminster-style responsible government ... that executive government is effectively in the hands of ministers supported by a majority in the lower house ... ' (Mulgan 1996: 192) Prime ministers, government leaders in the House, minor party Senators, as well as editorial writers among others, all have distinguished between the Senate as a House of Review and the House of Representatives as the House of Government or the house in which governments are made and in which the government governs. Mulgan (1996: 196) concludes that 'All sides ... appear to recognise that the Senate's review function involves scrutiny of the government within limits set by respect for the government's mandate and its right to govern based on its majority in the lower house.'[111]

Beyond this, however, ambiguities and uncertainties abound. Returning to his attempt to summarize different conceptions of the Senate as a House of Review, we are left (as he fully appreciates) with more questions than answers. What is that 'certain point' beyond which the Senate should not press its powers? Who defines it and how do we know when the Senate approaches or passes it? If it is not appropriate for the Senate as a House of Review to expel the government from office, is it in order for the Senate to do anything short of that in 'exercising its power in order to monitor and restrain the government of the day?' What does or does not constitute a serious challenge to 'the government's authority or its major policies'? How confrontational can the Senate be and how much frustration can it cause the government without overstepping its bounds as a House of Review? Most generally, what is the goal and purpose of the Senate as a House of Review in 'reviewing government bills' or engaging in 'detailed examination of government decisions and administration ... '? How forceful should a House of Review be? Is the Senate functioning well as a House of Review if governments consistently ignore the results of its review of government bills, decisions, and administration?

Mulgan makes a compelling case that, as a concept, House of Review remains unspecified, and that the only defensible answer to whether the Senate is a House of Review is 'yes, no, or maybe,' depending on what definition each analyst has in mind:[112]

---

111 He continues: 'Disagreement arises, however, on the issue of where these limits are to be set.'

112 Mulgan complicates the picture even more, and perhaps necessarily so, by linking the imprecision of 'house of review' as a concept with the equally fuzzy concept of electoral mandates, which is discussed in Chapter 9.

The term 'house of review' thus allows for a wide variation of Senate activism. On the one hand, it may be used to try to restrict the power of the Senate to override the government supported by the lower house; on the other hand, it may be used to assert the right of the Senate to scrutinise such a government effectively. ... [The concept enjoys] an inevitable flexibility ... which forms part of the ideological battleground between governments and their political opponents. Both subservience and resistance to government can count as the exercise of review ... (Mulgan 1996: 197–198)

However the boundaries around the concept of a House of Review are drawn, for Mulgan (unlike Fusaro) they are crossed when the purpose and effect of 'review' is to force changes in government plans and policies. 'Review' 'involves holding government accountable to Parliament and the electorate and implies an adversarial relationship between those scrutinised (the government) and those scrutinising (those outside the government), *with the government retaining ultimate responsibility for decisions, whatever pressure it may have been subjected to through the process of scrutiny.*' (Mulgan 1996: 198; emphasis added) So he distinguishes between 'two contrasting models of the Senate's role vis-a-vis the government of the day: one as an agent of accountability and review, the other as a partner in policy making.' 'Review' does not 'cover the part that the opposition parties and independents in the Senate play in negotiating with governments over policy and sharing in responsibility for decisions.' (Mulgan 1996: 202)

Yet as he recognizes, the distinction between review and policy-making is not easy to maintain because 'Subjecting governments to the process of scrutiny may lead to a change of policy outcome ... (Mulgan 1996: 199) Indeed, if that were not the case, if the process scrutiny of legislation or administration did not change policy outcom. from time to time, it would serve no serious governmental function. It would continue to serve an educational function with a presumed electoral payoff for the scrutinizing parties, but that hardly seems a satisfying *raison d'etre* for the Senate. Furthermore, that function might be performed equally as well by the media with its modern penchant for investigating and its greater ability to disseminate and publicize its findings.

Let us now, finally, return to the question with which all this began: if the development of a strongly disciplined party system in the Commonwealth Parliament effectively ended whatever hopes or possibilities there may have been for the Senate to function effectively as a 'House of the States,' did that same development also prevent the Senate from becoming an effective 'House of Review'?

One answer that reasonably flows from this discussion is that 'it all depends.' It all depends on what we have in mind when we talk about a House of Review. However, we can go further than that. Whether we think of prospective or retrospective review, or whether we have in mind 'strong' review or 'weak' review, we can conclude that the development of disciplined parliamentary parties made effectual review unlikely, so long as the party of government also had a majority in the Senate. Underlying this conclusion is the argument that no government party has any real incentive to have its programs and policies, actions and decisions, subjected to critical scrutiny. If there is to be such scrutiny, let it be behind the closed doors of the government, the Cabinet room, or the party room but not in the light of day, where it can only cause the government political embarrassment and electoral damage.

So I would wager that the inexorable transformation of the Senate into another House of Parties undercut the prospects for the Senate acting as an effective House of Review almost as much as it destroyed expectations that the Senate would be where the less populous states could protect themselves from threatened depredations from the New South Welsh and Victorian hordes. We saw the reason in Table 3.1, which showed that there were only two brief periods between the 'fusion' of the anti-Labor parties and the implementation of proportional representation for Senate elections when the government lacked a majority in the Senate as well as in the House. And with only three exceptions, all the elections between 1910 and 1946 (the last election before the switch to PR), governments controlled the Senate by wider margins than the House. Under these circumstances, it was entirely unrealistic to expect the government's disciplined Senate majority to allow the Senate to be used more than sporadically as a forum for critical reviews of its own legislation or performance.

On the other hand, and on the basis of exactly the same kind of calculations, a Senate with a non-government majority is much more likely to develop the institutional capacity to review government legislation and administration. It surely is no coincidence, for example, that the Senate strengthened its committee system after the pattern of non-government Senate majorities had emerged. Now that control of the Senate rests in the hands of non-government majorities, the current challenge, and one that Mulgan attempts to meet, is to determine how much review is enough, how searching and challenging and demanding it should be, and when prospective and retrospective review by the Senate begins to intrude on the rightful powers and prerogatives of government.

When the issue is defined in this way, it becomes clear why the concept of the Senate as a House of Review has remained so unclear. This concept cannot be specified without also specifying the appropriate place of the Senate in the Australian constitutional and political systems. In a sense, the Senate as a House of Review is useful as a residual notion—as a conceptual container that can hold a variety of contents. If the Senate is not a House of the States and if it should not try to act as a House of Lawmaking, much less a House of Government, it surely must be (or must be suitable to act as) a House of Something. The idea of 'review' has enough elasticity ('flexibility' is the word Mulgan prefers) to allow analysts of disparate opinions to agree that 'review' is what the Senate does or should do, without necessarily engaging in the messy task of trying to reach agreement on what they mean.

6

Coalitions in the Chamber

By this point, there should be no doubt that there are two dominating facts of parliamentary life in Canberra: first, the government controls the House, always in numbers and invariably in votes; and second, the government rarely controls the Senate in either sense. In turn, there are two primary reasons for the second of these facts: first, both the ALP and the Coalition enjoy roughly comparable levels of public support, but neither enjoys majority support in the electorate; and second, the system of proportional representation for electing Senators ensures a fairly accurate translation of votes into seats, so that neither an ALP government nor a Coalition government can expect to have a dependable voting majority in the Senate. Complementing these reasons is a third. The staggered election of Senators, by which half the Senate is elected every three years (except following double dissolutions) means that even if a landslide election should bring a new government into office, that government may have to wait another three years before it can even hope to translate its public support into a solid Senate majority, assuming its public support survives that long, and it can win a second, successive landslide victory.

The need for Senate coalitions

The key implication of this situation is that the Commonwealth legislative process is not simply a process of translating the government's policies into laws, as would be the case in a true 'Westminster' system in which (1) the government can depend on majority support in the lower house, as it can in Canberra, but (2) the government also controls the upper house, or the upper house can do no more than delay enactment of the government's program, which is not the case in Canberra. In the Commonwealth Parliament, as we have seen, a non-government majority can block enactment of the government's program by refusing to pass any bill, even, in extremis, the most essential money bills, as the events of 1974 and 1975 demonstrated. Consequently, the legislative process in Canberra inescapably is a process of coalition-building.[113] The government can depend on its disciplined party majority to pass its legislation in the House, but it must construct a coalition that extends beyond, even if not far beyond, its own party members to ensure that the same legislation also passes the Senate.

As of the end of 2002, the Coalition Government held 35 of 76 Senate seats, with 39 constituting an absolute majority. Therefore, the government needed to find at least four votes from outside its party ranks to pass each bill (and take most other actions in the Senate), though it needed only 38 votes to defeat any motion or block any other action that it opposed.[114] The 41 non-government Senators were distributed among the ALP Opposition (28), the Australian Democrats (7), the Greens (2), Pauline Hanson's One Nation (1), and 3 Independents. From the government's perspective, this situation had remained fundamentally unchanged since the Liberal-National Government under Prime Minister Howard took office in 1996. During those six years, two Senators had left Labor to become Independents and one Australian Democrat had done the same, developments which, as we shall see, made a difference. Otherwise, the Howard Government faced the same challenge in the Senate throughout the six-year period. In years to come, the numbers may change, and it is possible that some minor parties may come and go (as I write, the future of the Australian Democrats is a subject of frequent speculation), but the essential fact—

---

113 We need to establish a clear stylistic convention before proceeding any further. The subject of this chapter is coalition-building among parties in the Senate, and two of those parties (the Liberal and National parties) have, for many years, formed a solid coalition that is commonly known as the Coalition. To minimize confusion, I capitalize 'Coalition' when, and only when, I am referring to the standing partnership of the Liberal and National parties in both houses of the Parliament.

114 My focus in this chapter is on the ability of the government (and, in the concluding section, the Opposition) to achieve its affirmative legislative goals. This requires the government to secure approval for its proposals by majority vote—that is, at least 39 of 76 votes, assuming all Senators vote. I appreciate, however, that in the Senate the government also has to play defence by defeating amendments and other proposals made by non-government Senators. For that purpose, a negative or blocking majority requires only 38 votes, because if there is a tie vote in the Senate on a proposition, the proposition is rejected. This analysis assumes that the required majority always is 39 votes. To do otherwise would require examining each proposition that was the subject of a division to ascertain whether the government supported or opposed it in order to determine the majority the government required for that division, which would greatly complicate both the analysis and the presentation of findings. In any event, what ultimately matters is whether the government won or lost on a division, and that information is included with the division lists on which the data presented in this and the next chapter are based.

the government's need to find support on each vote from non-government Senators—is very unlikely to change.

Voting in the Senate

This and the following chapter provide glimpses into how the government has tried to cope with this challenge and how successful it has been. To explore these questions, we shall look at the record of votes that have taken place in the Senate chamber. But to understand which of those votes we shall examine, a brief summary of how Senators vote is in order.

The Senate's voting procedures are summarised in *Odgers' Australian Senate Practice* (2001: 244–245):

> Every sitting day the Senate determines a very large number of questions, most of which are determined by votes on the voices, that is, votes which are taken by the President calling for the ayes and noes and declaring the result without a record of how each senator voted. Most questions are determined in this way because they are uncontested, but it is not unusual for contested questions to be so determined when senators know and accept the way in which the majority is voting. ...
>
> After a question is put and senators have called aye or no, the President declares whether the ayes or noes are in the majority. Unless the President's determination is contested by the senators declared by the President to be in the minority, the determination of the President is recorded as the result of the vote. Only senators determined by the President to be in the minority may contest that determination and require a formal recorded vote, that is, a division, to be taken. ...
>
> A division is held only if two or more senators call for the division ...

Several points are noteworthy. First, most questions are decided 'on the voices' and without a formal record of how any party group or individual Senator voted.[115] Second, however, it takes *only two Senators*

---

115 There is an interesting difference in this respect between American and Australian (at least Australian Senate) practice. When there is a vote on the voices in either house of the US Congress, the member presiding announces the outcome on the basis of what he or she heard—whether there was a louder chorus of 'ayes' or 'noes'—while giving the benefit of the doubt whenever possible to the majority party (of which he or she always is a member). In the Australian Senate, by contrast, 'The chair would not call the result on the basis of the number of Senators in the chamber on each side at the time, but on the basis of the party numbers those Senators present represented. While the major parties have a chamber duty roster that ensures at least two Senators are present at all times (a Whip and a minister or shadow minister—and sometimes a backbencher as well), the minor party and Independent Senators often are absent altogether. In these cases, the chair might call the result on the basis of what had been said in debate by the now-absent party groups.' Personal communication to the author from an officer of the Senate.

to call a division, which is just about as minimal a requirement as the Senate in its standing orders could impose. And third, even controversial questions may be decided without a division, often because Senators on the losing side of a voice vote[116] conclude that nothing would be accomplished by insisting on a division, except perhaps to inconvenience and annoy their colleagues.

In this chapter and the next, we shall be concerned only with votes taken by *division*.[117] In doing so, we are looking at only a small fraction of the votes that take place in the Senate each year. In 1997, the Senate passed a total of 224 bills and decided 280 questions by division.[118] Three years later, the number of Senate divisions (115) was substantially less than the number of bills the Senate passed (181). It also is fair to say that questions decided by division are unrepresentative of the whole in that, in the great majority of cases, they are questions that are important and often contentious or controversial, at least to the Senators calling each division. However, it would be unwise to assume the opposite: that questions decided on the voices are, for that reason, clearly not important, contentious or controversial; nor would it be correct to assume that the government is happy with the outcomes of all votes on the voices. As suggested in the preceding paragraph, for instance, when a government defeat is a foregone conclusion, its leaders in the Senate chamber may decide that it would not serve their purposes to have their defeat documented by a time-consuming division.

Still, there are two compelling reasons for looking at divisions in the Senate. First, and notwithstanding the arguments above, the most important and divisive questions are the ones most likely to be decided by divisions. And second, not incidentally, we have absolutely no way of knowing for sure who voted on which side of any question that was

---

116 This is the American, not the Australian phrase, which I use for simplicity of exposition.

117 All the data presented in this and the next chapter are derived from descriptive lists of Senate divisions that were compiled by the Statistics Unit of the Senate Table Office. These lists are taken to be complete and accurate. I am grateful to Scott Bennett of the Parliamentary Library's Information and Research Services (IRS) for calling my attention to them, and to Rob Lundie of IRS and Kathleen Griffiths, Statistics Officer in the Senate Table Office, for making them available to me. Senators' votes on all divisions are published, of course, in the Senate's *Hansard* and *Journals*, but in a form not intended and, therefore, far less convenient for analytical purposes.

118 This amounts to slightly more than one division per bill on average. However, this average has little meaning because the total of 280 includes all divisions, including those that were not directly linked to specific bills.

decided on the voices. Not only are divisions the best choice for analysis, they are the only available choice.

Winning and losing

If we now turn to what the Senate actually has done, an obvious, and ultimately the most important, question to ask is how often the government has won and lost when it has come time for the Senate to vote. The first rows of Table 6.1 offer answers with respect to divisions in the Senate during 1996–2001.

TABLE 6.1: Divisions won by government coalitions, 1996–2001

	1996	1997	1998	1999	2000	2001
Number of divisions[1]	197	280	216	224	115	66
Number of winning government coalitions	130	165	152	164	88	51
Percentage of divisions won by government coalitions	68.4	58.9	70.4	73.2	76.5	77.3
Number of *minimum* winning government coalitions	124	137	143	143	81	44
Percentage of winning coalitions that were *minimal*	95.4	83.0	94.1	87.2	92.0	86.3
Percentage of all *minimum* winning government coalitions comprising:						
Government and Opposition	18.5	40.1	32.2	44.7	70.4	77.3
Government and Australian Democrats	37.9	26.3	7.0	37.1	29.6	22.7
Government and Independents	43.6	33.6	60.8	18.2	0.0	0.0

1   Excluded are one free vote in 1996 and nine in 1997, all of which pertained to the Euthanasia Laws Bill 1996.

As we see, the number of divisions has varied considerably from year to year, from as many as 280 in 1997 to as few as 66 in 2001, which was an election year. What has not varied nearly as much, however, has been the government's record of successes and failures on these votes. The government was on the winning side on percentages of divisions that varied from a low of 58.9 per cent in 1997 to a high of 77.3 per cent in 2001. And if we set aside 1997, the government's winning percentage varied within only a nine point range. If we were concerned with genetic differences among types of fruit flies, these year-to-year differences would be considered great. For a large, complex, and human institution like the Senate, what is striking is the relative consistency of the government's success rate.

If we were examining the outcomes of divisions in the House, these data would be evidence of disastrous failure by the government. It bears emphasizing, though, that the present government has been winning between roughly three-fifths and three-quarters of all divisions in the Senate even though it lacks a Senate majority. In all these cases, the government has found sufficient numbers of allies from outside its own ranks. These data tell us nothing, however, about how successful the government has been in winning the divisions that mattered most to it and to the other parties in the Senate. This is a typical limitation of such quantitative analysis. Also (and this is a point to which we will return), we cannot assume that the government's record of success is entirely attributable to the soundness of its policies or the abilities and persuasiveness of its Senate leaders. An unknowable number of government victories undoubtedly were passive or accidental.

Nonetheless, these reservations should not mask the story that the top of Table 6.1 tells: that this government has won in the Senate, far more often than not, even though non-government Senators could have combined to defeat it on each and every division. All of these government victories have required coalitions of support extending beyond the party rooms of the Liberal and National parties.[119] How far have these coalitions extended, and how often have the other parties in the Senate participated in them? Before turning to these questions, we need to consider the government's options for constructing winning coalitions.

---

119 Throughout this chapter and the next, the Liberal and National parties are treated as if they were one party, not two parties in permanent coalition with each other. In light of the behavior of the two parties, this is a perfectly sensible thing to do. Yet there have been instances in which the two Coalition partners have marched off in different directions. Solomon (1978: 74) identifies one such case when the Liberals and Nationals were in Opposition:

[A]t the end of 1973 the [Liberal-Country] opposition was steadfastly refusing to pass the Whitlam government's legislation to establish an Australian Schools Commission which would make grants to government and private schools throughout Australia. Eventually the Country Party opened negotiations with the acting Minister for Education, Lionel Bowen, for some concessions, having decided that it could not afford to reject the legislation outright given the electoral popularity of the measure. The Liberal Party remained opposed to it, despite the Country Party action, but Labor needed only Country Party support to ensure passage of the legislation through the Senate.

The government's coalition options

As I recounted at the beginning of this chapter, the party distribution in the Senate at the end of 2002 was as follows:

Government (Liberal and National parties)	35
Opposition (Australian Labor Party)	28
Australian Democrats	7
Australian Greens	2
One Nation	1
Independents	3

There are a total of 76 Senators, so 39 of them constitute a majority that is sufficient to win. Therefore, the government needed to find at least four votes from outside its party ranks in the Senate to pass each bill and take most other actions. If we put aside for the moment the One Nation Senator and the three Independents, the government had several coalition options: it could construct a large coalition with the Opposition (making 63 votes) or a smaller but sufficient coalition with the Australian Democrats (42 votes). Coalitions with both the ALP and the Democrats also were possible, of course, but the government could win without one or the other. The Australian Greens also could join a government coalition with Labor, the Democrats, or both, but the support of the Greens could not be decisive. In 2002, the Greens were too few to make a majority with the government, and they were not necessary to make a majority if the government had the support of either of the other parties in the Senate.

The government had two more options. First, it could win with the support of the Greens and at least two of the other four Senators who were independent decision-makers—the One Nation Senator and the three Independents. Or second, the government could win without the support of any other multi-member party if it secured the support of all four of the other Senators. In earlier years, as we shall see, the government won a notable number of divisions by relying on the votes of Independents and, since the 1998 election, the sole Senator representing Pauline Hanson's One Nation (whom I shall treat from this point on as if he were an Independent, rather than treating him as if he constituted a party group all by himself). My interest is primarily in coalition arrangements among party groups in the Senate, so in what follows, the Independent Senators sometimes tend to disappear from the analysis, except to the extent that they have made it possible for the government to win without any of the other party groups voting with it. This approach greatly simplifies the presentation, and I do not believe that incorporating the Independents more fully in the analysis would significantly change the essential arguments or findings. However, I do not intend in any way to dismiss the importance of Independent Senators. Instead, think of what follows as a discussion primarily of coalition-building among parties in the Senate.

Table 6.2 presents data on party representation in the Senate since 1996, and documents both continuity and change in the government's options for forming winning voting coalitions. Over the years, the size of each of the Coalition, Labor, and Democrat groups varied by no more than two; but in a closely divided Senate, even such variations can make a difference. Throughout the period, the government could form winning coalitions with either Labor or with the Democrats; and for roughly three years between mid-1996 and mid-1999, when Coalition strength peaked at 37, adding the votes of the two Green Senators could produce the smallest minimum winning coalition possible. During this period, however, there actually were two Green parties, each with one member in the Senate. As a close observer of the Senate has explained:[120]

> The two Green senators were in fact from different Green parties, the Western Australian Greens (Dee Margetts) and the Australian Greens (Bob Brown). My observation is that this partnership was much less cohesive and productive than the earlier partnership between the two Western Australian Greens (Margetts and Christabel Chamarette) and the current Australian Greens duo (Brown and Kerry Nettle), although I doubt that disagreements will be obvious from the records of the Senate. It was not uncommon for Brown and Margetts to put forward their own amendments to the same bill … although they would of course vote for each other's amendments.

Of course, coalitions between the government and either or both of the other parties also would produce winning majorities; in any such case, the support of the Greens would be superfluous, at least numerically. During some periods, the government also could win divisions without any of the multi-party groups, but solely with the support of Independent Senators. As the table reveals, that option was

---

120 'The Western Australian Greens had worked very constructively with the (Labor) Government from mid-1993 till Labor lost office (effectively the end of the 1995 sitting year) allowing the formation of a minimum winning coalition with Labor (29), the Australian Democrats (7) and in 1995 an ALP Senator turned Independent (Devereux). … My impression is that, between mid-1996 and mid-1999, the same level of legislative results was not apparent from the Margetts/Brown partnership, given that, on the numbers alone (forgetting ideology), they could have provided the new Liberal-National Government with the two votes necessary to support the government's measures.' Personal communication to the author from an officer of the Senate.

available during the period from September 1996 through June 1999, and then again during August to December 2002. Earlier in 1996 and between July 1999 and July 2002, a voting combination of the government and however many Independent Senators there were fell short of the magic number of 39.[121] During much of the time, however, the votes of Independents were enough to give the Coalition the numbers it needed for a minimum blocking coalition: a majority of 38 that would suffice to defeat any proposal put forth by one or more of the other parties.

TABLE 6.2: Party representation in the Senate, 1996–2002

	Coalition	Labor	Australian Democrats	Greens	One Nation	Indep-endents
Jan 1996–Jun 1996	36	30	7	2	–	1
Jul 1996[1]–Aug 1996	37	29	7	2	–	1
Sep 1996[2]–Jun 1999	37	28	7	2	–	2
Jul 1999[3]–Sep 2001	35	29	9	1	1	1
Oct 2001[4]–Jun 2002	35	28	9	1	1	2
Jul 2002[5]	35	28	8	2	1	2
Aug 2002[6]–Dec 2002	35	28	7	2	1	3

1   On 1 July 1996, the Senators elected at the half-Senate election of 2 March 1996 took their seats.
2   On 20 August 1996, Senator Mal Colston left the ALP and became an Independent.
3   On 1 July 1999, the Senators elected at the half-Senate election of 3 October 1998 took their seats.
4   On 2 October 2001, Senator Shayne Murphy left the ALP and became an Independent.
5   On 1 July 2002, the Senators elected at the half-Senate election of 10 November 2001 took their seats.
6   On 26 July 2002, Senator Meg Lees left the Australian Democrats and became an Independent.

The likelihood of the various possible party coalitions actually being created in practice depends, naturally enough, on the policies or ideology of each party group (and that of each Independent) as well as its numbers in the Senate. On some bills, the government and Opposition can find themselves voting the same way, by pre-agreement or otherwise, because those bills do not address matters that separate the parties, nor are they bills on which the Opposition thinks that it can gain some political advantage by opposing the government. On other

121 I offer a reminder that, for this analysis, Senator Harris of Pauline Hanson's One Nation party is treated here as if he were an Independent.

bills, however, the prospects for the Coalition and the ALP reaching agreement (forming 'grand coalitions,' if you will) are slight because of sincere policy differences, calculations of political advantage, or both. With regard to the Australian Greens, their positions on the issues that the Parliament addresses would lead us to expect that they should join with either Labor or the Democrats, or both, much more often than with the Coalition government. As we shall see, however, this has not been uniformly true.

The Australian Democrats present what are perhaps the best opportunities and the greatest uncertainties for the government. There has been a tension among Democrat Senators, reflected in recent leadership challenges and departures from the party, between those who envision their party as a force for moderation and sensible compromise between the more extreme positions of both the Coalition and the ALP, and those who stress the need for their party to respond to the preferences and discontents of those on the political left as well as to the danger that, if the Democrats fail to do so, their Senate representation may shrink in favour of the Greens. Because of these philosophical and strategic differences, the Democrats should be more likely to join a voting coalition with the government on some issues, but with the Labor Opposition on others. Unlike the other three parties, as we shall see, the Democrats even have been known to split their votes, some voting with the government and others voting against it. According to Sugita (1997: 157), 'A study of the Senate divisions between August 1981 and December 1996 reveals that there were only eighty divisions during this period when the Democrat Senators did not vote as a bloc.' In comparison with the voting patterns of ALP, Liberal, and National Senators, however, 'only eighty' is almost infinitely large.

This last observation also raises another question: whether we can think of each party group as a single, unitary player. Critics of the House of Representatives as a legislative body sometimes describe it as a place where the government writes bills and its party members vote for them. Reality, however, becomes more complicated if the government finds that its preferred version of a bill faces determined opposition, perhaps led by members of one of its parliamentary party committees, behind the closed doors of its party room. While this would be unusual in Parliament House today, if such a situation were to arise, the government might well have to accept changes in its bill either before the bill is introduced or at some later stage of the process. It may not be helpful to think of the government having to build a coalition among its own party members. Nonetheless, in the process of trying to build a winning coalition in the Senate, the government (and, to a lesser extent, the Opposition) still may want to glance over its collective shoulder from time to time to gauge reactions within its own ranks to whatever concessions it is in the process of making to prospective coalition partners.

Similarly, it is tempting to assume that if either the government or the Opposition reaches a coalition agreement with another party group (or with each other, in the case of a potential grand coalition between government and Opposition), that the negotiator for that party can commit all the other members of his or her party group. In most cases, this is a reasonable assumption because of the strength of party discipline in the parliamentary parties. The Democrats are the only party that has split its votes on divisions during 1996–2001 (except on the handful of free, or 'conscience', votes). However, the strict party discipline on which the other parties insist when it comes time to vote is not enforced with equal rigor at other times and in other venues. In other words, intra-party differences can arise after two or more parties have reached a tentative coalition agreement, with the result that one or more of them then finds that opposition within its own party ranks requires the negotiations to be reopened.

All of this makes the analysis of Senate divisions more interesting than in many other national assemblies, but also much more manageable, methodologically and analytically, than in the US Congress. In most parliamentary chambers with significant powers—that is, in most lower chambers—there is little point in analyzing voting patterns. Unless there is a minority government or one that rests on a shaky majority foundation, the government can be expected to win all (or almost all) contested votes, whatever the procedural equivalent of divisions may be. How non-government parties vote usually does not affect the outcome, nor do occasional defections from the government's ranks matter very much unless they are sufficient in number to cause the government to lose a key vote. Those are the votes worth examining—the rare votes that the government loses—because any one of them could bring about the government's demise.

In the US House of Representatives and Senate, on the other hand, voting cohesion among Democrats and Republicans is quite high—and considerably higher than the most common perception abroad—but still, the outcome of many votes is determined by how large a minority of Democrats vote with the majority of Republicans and how large a minority of Republicans vote with the majority of Democrats. Most Representatives and Senators do not cross the aisle very often but almost all of them do so on occasion, some much more frequently than others. When neither party holds a large majority of seats, the numbers moving (figuratively) across the aisle in each direction is critical to determining the outcome of each vote. This means that the analysis of voting patterns is important and it is a complex undertaking because the unit of analysis is each of the 435 Representatives or each of the 100 Senators.

By contrast, the unit of analysis for Senate divisions in Canberra is, for most purposes, the party. There are 76 Senators, to be sure, but the outcomes of most divisions are determined by how each of the four multi-member parties vote as a bloc. Only if these four 'votes' do not produce a conclusive outcome do the votes of Independents become determinative.

Minimum winning coalitions

With this prologue, we can ask a question that has interested political scientists studying coalition formation in a variety of settings in which groups of participants decide questions by voting. When a winning coalition is formed, what is the likelihood that it will be a minimum winning coalition—in other words, a coalition that is no larger than necessary to win?

We might expect to find minimum winning coalitions whenever the person or party trying to construct the coalition must pay a price of some kind to attract each new member to it. That price may take the form of a compromise. In a legislative setting, for example, the compromise may require the coalition-builder to accept a weaker proposal than he or she personally prefers because that compromise is the strongest proposal that is acceptable to a prospective coalition partner whose support is necessary if the coalition is to be large enough to win. Alternatively, the price may take the form of a side-payment. The coalition-builder may be able to secure a prospective partner's support for the coalition-builder's preferred position if the latter agrees in turn to support the prospective partner's position on a later decision about which the partner cares more intensely. Assuming that a coalition-builder does not want to pay a higher price for victory than is absolutely necessary, he or she will have an obvious preference for a minimum winning coalition. If the group is going to decide the question by majority vote, a coalition comprising 51 per cent of the participants is sufficient to win. Constructing a larger coalition requires paying prices, in compromises or side-payments or both, for votes that are not needed to achieve the coalition-builder's purpose: winning.

Constructing a minimum winning coalition that includes only as many votes from outside the government's party ranks as it needs to win is a parsimonious strategy in two senses. Not only does this strategy minimize the compromises, concessions, or side-payments that have to be made, it also minimizes the time and effort that have to be expended in building the coalition. In an active legislative body, the time, energy, and attention of members are limited, and they are even more limited for party leaders with multiple responsibilities. If coalition-builders are satisfied to construct minimum winning coalitions, they can invest their remaining personal resources (time, energy, attention) in building more such coalitions. Negotiating to secure superfluous additional votes for one bill may come at the expense of being able to secure essential votes for one or more other bills.

On the other hand, there are at least three general reasons why some coalitions are larger than minimal. One reason is uncertainty. A coalition-builder who constructs a minimum winning coalition must be absolutely sure that every member of that coalition will vote as the coalition-builder expects and wants. There is no margin for error. Defeat will result if even one anticipated member of the coalition reneges on his or her commitment or fails to participate in the vote. If anything significant is at stake, this can be too much of a risk to take. So coalition-builders often want some cushion to support their majority. A coalition of 55 per cent may suffice, for instance, depending on how much confidence the coalition-builder has in his or her information about the voting intentions of each of the other expected coalition partners, how much trust he or she has in each of those partners, and how much is at risk. This inevitably involves finding the best balance between costs and confidence. A coalition-builder can be absolutely confident of victory if every participant is incorporated in his or her coalition, but the cost of constructing a universal coalition probably will be much too high, and unnecessarily high, even assuming that it is possible. Perhaps a five per cent cushion is enough, or perhaps ten per cent or more. It all depends on the circumstances.

Second, the results of votes are not always the results of coalition-building efforts. Theories of political coalitions sometimes start from the mistaken assumption, and often an implicit one, that voting outcomes necessarily reflect the successes and failures of attempts by protagonists to build winning coalitions, minimum or otherwise. Yet that is not necessarily the case. In legislative settings, some proposals are assumed, and assumed correctly, to enjoy such widespread support that those responsible for ensuring their adoption need do nothing more than let nature take its course—let the participants vote as they choose, knowing that their free choices will yield the requisite majority. In other cases, there may be legitimate doubt about what the outcome of a forthcoming vote will be, but neither side invests much time and effort to ensuring that its position will prevail. Instead, both sides again allow the vote to take place without having engaged in deliberate coalition-building activities. They may be preoccupied with or distracted by other matters, or they may not care enough about the outcome to make it worth their while to try very hard, if at all, to affect it. The result may be a loss, a narrow victory, or a comfortable or overwhelming one. Those assembled on each side of the question still can be called winning and losing coalitions, but not coalitions that were the product of calculation or effort.

The first of these reasons is not generally applicable to divisions in the Australian Senate because of the strength of party discipline in voting. Except on the few free or 'conscience' votes, Liberal, National, Labor, and Green Senators stand united with their party colleagues on divisions. The Democrats are the only party in recent years to split their votes, and then only rarely. Uncertainties about Senators' voting intentions generally should arise only with respect to Independents, and any such uncertainties should matter only when the votes of Independents are likely to be decisive—that is, when the government has failed to form a winning coalition with one or more other party groups. On the other hand, the second reason for larger-than-minimum coalitions certainly does apply to the Senate. Close observers warn that it is a mistake to look behind the outcome of each division for evidence of the calculations and efforts by party leaders that must be there. Sometimes those leaders can only wait to learn the outcome of a division, perhaps because, with other matters demanding their time and attention, they had done little or nothing to try to determine the outcome. On each vote there is a winning coalition, but the voting record itself reveals nothing about how actively involved anyone was in trying to construct that coalition. Inescapably, I fear, the discussion that follows may imply that more effort was devoted to coalition-building than we would find if it were possible in each case to learn who did what, and with what effect. This is a caveat that deserves to be kept in mind.

The third reason for larger-than-minimum winning coalitions is that winning may not be the only goal that coalition-builders have in mind. There may be other purposes to which the vote can contribute, and those purposes may provide incentives to assemble more than a bare 51 per cent majority. Imagine, for example, that a labor union is about to vote to strike unless management agrees to a ten per cent wage increase. Those supporting the proposal want to win, of course; that is their first and essential goal. But they probably want to do more. They want the vote to contribute to preserving or increasing solidarity in the union's ranks so as many members as possible remain firmly committed to the same goal and the same course of action. At the same time, they want to weaken management's resolve by sending a clear and strong signal that the union is united and determined to achieve its objective. In this situation, winning by a 51 per cent majority is the next best thing to losing. An overwhelming majority is not a luxury that is not worth paying for; it is a necessity.

In the Senate, the government may be willing to make additional concessions in return for additional support when, for example, it wants to demonstrate that it does not stand alone, or when it wishes to leave no doubt that the government—and people—of Australia are united in the face of a common challenge or danger—terrorism, for example. Or the government may be willing to pay a high price for support for a bill by another party, especially the Opposition, in order to immunize itself against partisan attacks for having brought the bill forward. Or the government may find that additional legislative compromises are the price it must pay to move its bill quickly through the stages of the legislative process. The government may be able to win without making those compromises, but only after a more elaborate and time-consuming process than it is willing to endure. The government may face a deadline that is externally imposed—for example, the beginning of the new financial (fiscal) year or the opening of some new international conference or negotiation—or one that is internally imposed—for example, the time pressure that the government's other legislation imposes on the parliamentary schedule or the date the government has chosen for the next election. Under such circumstances, the content of the legislative agreement that gives rise to a larger-than-necessary winning coalition may be less important than the size (even the unanimity) of the coalition and how quickly it can be assembled.

So for any of these reasons, or others, a minimum winning coalition is not always either the desired outcome of a Senate division or the outcome that should be predicted.

Before examining the composition of winning government coalitions, we need to clarify that, in the Senate, a minimum winning coalition is unlikely to be one that is composed of only 39, or 51 per cent, of the 76 Senators. In the context of voting in the Senate, a minimum winning coalition is one that involves the minimum number of coalition partners, not the minimum number of Senators. The only time when the government could form a multi-party coalition of exactly 39 votes was between July 1996 and June 1999 when there were exactly that number of government and Green Senators combined. At all other times, a winning coalition that included the minimum number of parties necessarily included a larger-than-necessary number of Senators: at the extreme, a grand coalition of the government and the Opposition during the first half of 1996 included 66 of the 76 Senators.

Still, we should think of this as a minimum winning coalition because forming it required the agreement of only two participants, even though in this case they were the two largest collective participants in the Senate.

Returning to Table 6.1 with this understanding in mind, we find data on the number and percentage of winning government coalitions that were minimum winning coalitions, and these data are striking indeed. During each of the six years, no fewer than 83 per cent and as many as 95.4 per cent of all the divisions on which the government was on the winning side produced coalitions that were minimum winning coalitions. We cannot know how many of these coalitions were the product of conscious effort—in other words, how often the government worked to secure the support it needed to win, but only that much support and no more—and how often these coalitions were the product of each party following its own inclinations without the government having made much or any effort to ensure that it would prevail. However, if no less than 83 per cent of all the government's winning coalitions were minimal, that means that the percentages of larger-than-minimum coalitions were strikingly low.

It should be emphasized once more, however, that this table tells us about the frequency of minimum winning coalitions only on votes that were decided by divisions, not on all the votes that took place in the Senate. Relatively few divisions were what in Washington sometimes are called 'hurrah' votes, with almost everyone voting on the same side,[122] but it is perfectly reasonable to assume that divisions were less likely to occur on propositions that enjoyed more widespread support. Perhaps what the data are telling us is that when the government had more than minimum winning coalitions on its side, any parties (or Independents) who were not part of those coalitions were less inclined than otherwise to call divisions.

The second half of Table 6.1 addresses the composition of minimum winning government coalitions. How often did the government win by securing the support only of the Opposition, or the Democrats, or Independents? Notice first that the government frequently relied only on the votes of Independents when it was possible to do so and win (which it could not do in 2000 or 2001). In 1996 and 1998, the government won in partnership with only the Independents more often than with only the ALP or only the Democrats. More than half the time the government won divisions in 1998, it did so without the support of

---

122 A division is completed only if there are at least two Senators voting on each side, which precludes any division from producing a unanimous vote on one side or the other.

either of the parties with which it could form winning coalitions. However, that was not the pattern in either 1997 or 1999. Depending on what we make of the data for 1998, we can see a quite stable pattern in the frequency with which the government won in minimum winning coalitions with the Democrats, and a decline in the government's reliance on the support of Independents only.

But perhaps most interesting are the data on 'grand coalitions' between the great putative parliamentary antagonists, the government and the Opposition. In 1999, Senator Helen Coonan, a Liberal minister, wrote (1999b: 14) that, 'With the election of the Coalition in March 1996 the attitude of the Opposition and the minor parties in the Senate could be fairly described as a "culture of confrontation", where the Senate routinely opposes most of the Government's policy agenda.' However true that observation may have been in 1996, Table 6.1 documents how much that situation changed in the years that followed. In four of the six years beginning in 1996, when the government was part of a minimum winning coalition, its coalition partner was the Opposition more than 40 per cent of the time. And most remarkably, whenever the Coalition government won a division in 2000 or 2001 with the support of one other party, more than seven times out of ten that party was the ALP.

During these two years, there were not enough Independents to give the government all the additional votes it needed, so the government could build a minimum winning coalition with either Labor or the Democrats. When a minimum winning coalition was the result, the coalition partnership that emerged far more often than not was between the Coalition and its historic rival and enemy, the ALP—not, as we might have expected, the Democrats. This is one of several indications we shall encounter that the popular image of parliamentary and political warfare defining the relationship between the government and the Opposition, between the Coalition and the ALP, needs to be tempered.

Government coalitions on divisions

Tables 6.3, 6.4, and 6.5 all document in different ways the coalitions that were formed between the government and other parties on divisions during 1996–2001. The first of them, Table 6.3, presents the percentage and number of times each year that the government voted with each of the other parties singly or in various combinations *on all divisions*. The first six rows of this table all represent winning coalitions, except for one 2001 division when the support of Democrat Senators was not enough for a government victory because the Democrats split their votes, some voting with the Opposition. Only in

1997 did the Liberal-National Government and the Greens combine to win more than one division.

In each of the years between 1996 and 1999, the most common voting pattern on divisions was for the government to be opposed by all three of the other multi-member parties. The government voted alone in divisions more than half the time in 1996, 1997, and 1998. This pattern was roughly three times as common as any other in 1997 and 1998. In 2000 and 2001, on the other hand, the government and Opposition voted together against the Democrats and Greens roughly half the time and more than twice as often as the government Senators voted without the support of any other party. However, two points need to be emphasized about divisions in which none of the other parties voted with the government. First, these are not necessarily instances in which the government found no support outside its own party room because this table does not take into account how Independents voted. Second, and precisely because of the Independents' votes, the government won significant numbers of divisions even when it lacked support from other parties. This will become evident when we turn to Tables 6.4 and 6.5.

Table 6.3 also provides several other interesting insights into Senate voting patterns. In each of the six years except the first (1996), for instance, the government voted only with the Opposition more often than it voted only with the Democrats; in 2000 and 2002, government-Opposition coalitions were more than twice as frequent as government-Democrat coalitions. These data are consistent with those in Table 6.1, and they are inconsistent with the characterization of the Democrats as the small centrist party, akin to the FDP in Germany, which is closer ideologically to each of its major rivals than they are to each other. It is hard to think of the Democrats as holding the 'balance of power' in the Senate when they have voted either with the government or the Opposition less often than the government and the Opposition have voted with each other.[123] Second, there were few divisions, almost none in four of the six years, in which the government, Opposition, and Democrats voted together, leaving the Greens isolated in opposition to the other three parties. This may say something about the Greens' bark and their bite; it also suggests that the Greens have not looked for opportunities to force divisions that would clearly differentiate them from the other parties.

---

123 An important caveat is that the Australian Democrats sometimes have demanded divisions, knowing that the government and Opposition would vote together, in order to differentiate their position from those of the major parties. Personal communication to the author from an officer of the Senate.

TABLE 6.3: Voting patterns in Senate divisions, 1996–2001

	1996	1997	1998	1999	2000	2001
Government, Opposition, Democrats and Greens	1 (0.5%)	0	0	0	1 (0.9%)	0
Government, Opposition and Democrats	2 (1.0%)	13 (4.6%)	2 (0.9%)	13 (5.8%)	1 (0.9%)	1 (1.5%)
Government, Opposition and Greens	0	1 (0.4%)	1 (0.5%)	2 (1.2%)	1 (0.9%)	0
Government, Democrats and Greens	3 (1.5%)	6 (2.1%)	6 (2.8%)	4 (1.9%)	4 (3.5%)	6 (9.1%)
Government and Opposition	23 (11.7%)	55 (19.6%)	46 (21.3%)	64 (28.6%)	57[1] (49.6%)	34 (51.5%)
Government and Democrats	47[2] (23.9%)	36 (12.9%)	10 (4.6%)	53 (23.7%)	24 (20.9%)	11[3] (16.7%)
Government and Greens	0	8 (2.9%)	0	3[4] (1.3%)	0	1[5] (1.5%)
Government alone	121 (61.4%)	161 (57.5%)	151 (69.9%)	84 (37.5%)	27 (23.5%)	13 (19.7%)

1 Includes all 15 divisions on the Defence Legislation Amendment (Aid to Civilian Authorities) Bill 2000.
2 Includes 38 of 41 divisions on the Workplace Relations and Other Legislation Amendment Bill 1996.
3 On one division, the Democrats' vote split and the government did not win.
4 The government did not win two of the three votes.
5 The government did not win the vote.

Note: This table does not reflect the votes of Independent Senators. For purposes of this table, the single Senator representing Pauline Hanson's One Nation is treated as if he were an Independent. The Greens are counted as having voted with the government in cases in which *either* the Australian Greens or the Greens (WA) did so. The Australian Democrats are counted in the same way in cases in which they split the votes.

What is perhaps most striking about the data in Table 6.3, though, are the apparent trends in the frequency with which the government has voted alone and the frequency with which it has voted with the Opposition. Admittedly, with data for only six years we cannot distinguish with certainty between ephemeral phenomena and long-term patterns. Nonetheless, it is interesting, to say the least, that there has been an increase each year in the frequency with which the government and Opposition have voted together. In 1996, the government and Opposition voted together and against the two smaller parties only 11.7 per cent of the time. During 1997–1999, the comparable percentages climbed toward 30 per cent but then jumped to roughly 50 per cent in 2000 and 2001. For those who perceive the two parties to be moving toward the policy centre and narrowing the differences between them, here is supporting evidence that is dramatic if only indicative.

An alternative explanation is that what we are witnessing here is evidence of the process of adjustment on the part of a new party (actually, coalition) in government and a new party in Opposition. Since 1996 was the first year in office for the Howard Government, it may not have been particularly anxious to find areas of agreement with the Labor Opposition. What is perhaps more likely is that the ALP, now adjusting to being in Opposition, may have been particularly reluctant to support the government that had just driven it from office. Perhaps with time, one or both sides became more willing to look toward the other as a coalition partner. None of these possible explanations are mutually exclusive, and it would be in the nature of complex human behaviour if there were some degree of truth in all of them. At the same time, as Table 6.3 reveals, there were fewer occasions on which the government found itself opposed by all the other parties. There is a hiccup in the percentage for 1998; otherwise, the frequency with which all three other parties voted against the government declined from more than 60 per cent in 1996 to less than 20 per cent in 2001.

Tables 6.4 and 6.5 focus on divisions that the government won. The first of these tables presents data on how often the government won in each of three ways: (1) with the support of the Opposition, without regard to how the other two parties voted; (2) with the support of one or both of the minor parties, but not the Opposition; and (3) without the support of any of the other three multi-member parties. The last possibility deserves a word of explanation. If we refer back to Table 6.3 and add together for each year all the times the government won by voting with one or more of the other parties, we find that, in 1996–1999, that total does not account for all the government's victories (from Table 6.1 or 6.4). On the remaining occasions, therefore, the government won with the support of a sufficient number of the remaining Senators: the Independents and the sole Senator affiliated with Pauline Hanson's One Nation.

When we examine Table 6.4, we find, as Table 6.3 would have led us to expect, a growth in the frequency with which the government and Opposition voted together, with or without one or both of the other parties. The Opposition was part of the government's winning coalitions more than half the time in 2000 and 2001, compared with less than a quarter of the time in 1997 and 1998, and even less often in 1996. Although the trend line is not perfect, it is so clear that it would be remarkable if the pattern of these data was accidental. The table also documents a fairly stable percentage of government victories attributable to the support it received from (or gave to) one or both of the multi-member minor parties: the Democrats and the Greens. In five of the six years, the percentage of divisions that the government won with the support of one or both of these parties, but not the Opposition, varied between 17.9 and 25.9, which is a reasonably consistent record, as such things go. The exception was 1998, when the frequency of such victories fell to only 7.4 per cent.

TABLE 6.4: Results of Senate divisions, 1996–2001

	1996	1997	1998	1999	2000	2001
Number of divisions[1]	197	280	216	224	115	66
Divisions that the government won	130 (68.4%)	165 58.9%)	152 (70.4%)	164 (73.2%)	88 (76.5%)	51 (77.3%)
Divisions on which the government and the Opposition voted together	26 (13.2%)	69 (24.6%)	49 (22.7%)	80 (35.7%)	60 (52.2%)	35 (53.0%)
Divisions that the government won with the support of one or both minor parties, but not the Opposition	50 (25.4%)	50 (17.9%)	16 (7.4%)	58 (25.9%)	28 (24.3%)	16 (24.2%)
Divisions that the government won with the votes of Independents only[2]	54[3] (27.4%)	46 (17.7%)	87[4] (40.3%)	26 (11.6%)	0	0

1   Excluded are one free vote in 1996 and nine in 1997, all of which pertained to the Euthanasia Laws Bill 1996.
2   'Independents' include the One Nation Senator.
3   Includes 11 divisions on the Telstra (Dilution of Public Ownership) Bill 1996 and eight divisions on the Higher Education Legislation Amendment Bill 1996.
4   Includes 12 divisions on the Telstra (Transition to Full Private Ownership) Bill 1998 and 16 divisions on procedural matters on the same or preceding days.

It is the bottom two rows of the table that are most striking. These present the number and percentage of government victories that cannot be explained by support the government received from other multi-member parties, and so are attributable to support by the Independent and One Nation Senators. We saw in the previous table that the government voted without the support of any of the other three parties almost 70 per cent of the time in 1998. Perhaps it is no coincidence that this was an election year, so all the non-government parties may have been more inclined than usual to oppose the government, and to demand divisions showing that the government lacked the support of any other party. We see in Table 6.4 that the dip in government-minor party winning coalitions in 1998 was offset by the remarkable spurt during that year of instances in which the government did not rely on any multi-member party for its victories. The frequency of such winning coalitions jumped by more than twenty percentage points, to reach 40 per cent of all successful government coalitions, before dropping back by almost 30 percentage points in the following year. Winning coalitions of government and Independent Senators then disappeared entirely in 2000 and 2001 for a simple and sufficient reason that emerges from an inspection of Table 6.2. In those years, even if the government had the support of both Independents and the One Nation Senator, that brought it only 38 votes, leaving it one crucial vote short of a majority. We will return to this point below.

TABLE 6.5: Winning government coalitions in
Senate divisions, 1996–2001

	1996	1997	1998	1999	2000	2001
Winning government coalitions including the Opposition	26 (20.0%)	69 (41.8%)	49 (32.2%)	80 (48.8%)	60 (68.2%)	35 (68.6%)
Winning government coalitions including one or both minor parties, but not the Opposition	50 (38.5%)	50 (30.3%)	16 (10.5%)	58 (35.4%)	28 (31.8%)	16 (31.4%)
Winning government coalitions including Independents only	54 (41.5%)	46 (27.9%)	87 (57.2%)	26 (15.9%)	0	0

Table 6.5 highlights some of the developments we have noted by presenting the number and percentage of winning coalitions that the government formed that included (1) the Opposition, regardless of whether they also included either or both minor parties; (2) one or both minor parties, but not the Opposition; and (3) Independents only (again, treating Senator Harris of One Nation as if he were an Independent). The table reveals an increasing frequency of winning government coalitions with the Opposition and a steady rate of winning government coalitions with minor parties; however, 1998 was the expected exception to both patterns. More generally, all these tables show a government and an Opposition that frequently voted together. These data are at odds with the simplistic notion that the role and responsibility of the Opposition is to oppose. What is more important for Australian politics, however, is that the way in which the Coalition and the ALP vote in the Senate chamber is quite different from the way in which the two parties portray themselves and each other to the electorate.[124] But what happens on those occasions when the Opposition

---

124 In what apparently is a reference to the House, not the Senate, Jaensch (1986: 83) claims that, 'even when the opposition states that it does not oppose a certain Bill,

not only opposes the government, but tries to construct winning coalitions of its own?

The Opposition's winning coalitions

All of the discussion thus far in this chapter has proceeded from the perspective of the government. The primary burden for forming winning coalitions falls on the government because it is the government, not any of the non-government parties, that has the responsibility to initiate legislation and that also is expected to pass most of it. Any government that failed to do so, bemoaning the fact that it lacked 'the numbers' in the Senate, would not remain the government for long. It is also the government that exercises almost total control over the legislative agenda in the Senate as well as in the House of Representatives, and so it is the government that has the incentive to engage in successful coalition-building because it is the government's own legislation and legislative record that depends on it.

There is another side to the story, however. The non-government parties in the Senate, and especially the Opposition, have their own incentives to construct winning coalitions in order to improve (from their point of view) the government's legislation or, alternatively, to block that legislation or secure passage of motions that are critical of the government, and thereby thwart, embarrass, and discredit it. So this analysis would be incomplete if we failed to look at Senate voting coalitions from the perspective of the non-government side of the chamber. In practice, this means examining the Opposition's options and record because it is sensible to assume that it is the Opposition, not the far smaller minor parties, that will take the lead most often in bringing other parties into coalition with it on individual bills and votes. Certainly the Senate Democrats or Greens must approach the Opposition to solicit its support for their motions and amendments, but I am prepared to assume that it is usually the Opposition that acts as prime mover in attempts to build winning coalitions against the government.

Because of its smaller numbers, the Opposition's prospects for creating such winning coalitions have been more constrained than the government's. The essential facts for the Opposition in the Senate throughout the six-year period, as a review of Table 6.2 reveals, is that it could not win *without* the votes of the Australian Democrats and it could not win *with only* the votes of the Australian Democrats. In fact,

the list of [Opposition] speakers is no less long, and the criticisms of the government party no less vehement.'

during the 84 months of 1996–2002, there were only 33 months when the ALP, Democrats, and Greens together could form a majority, and then without a single vote to spare. These numbers drive home how important it is that, in recent decades, there always has been a *non-government* majority in the Senate, but not an *Opposition* majority.

The first row of Table 6.6 presents data on the number and percentage of divisions that the government lost each year. These data cannot be compared on a year-by-year basis with the total numbers of Labor, Democrat, and Green Senators because, as Table 6.2 demonstrates, that number sometimes changed in mid-year when newly-elected Senators were sworn in or when sitting Senators left the parties to which they had belonged. But Table 6.2 also indicates that the only times during 1996–1999 when the three parties together held 39 seats (they never held more than that) were during January–June 1996 and during July 1999–September 2001. If we examine Table 6.6 with this fact in mind, it is striking that the Opposition was not most successful when its representation, combined with that of the Democrats and Greens, was greatest.

The government had its worst losing percentage in 1997 when the three non-government parties held a total of 37 seats and could win only with the support of both Independent Senators. And in 1999–2001, when there were a total of 39 Labor, Democrats, and Green Senators during most of that time, the three parties combined to defeat the government on less than one-quarter of all divisions. Table 6.6 also shows that, except for 1997, there was a steady decline each year in the percentage of divisions that the government lost, though the percentage changes from year to year are too small to ask this apparent trend line to carry too much analytical weight. In hindsight, it may become clear that what these data really are showing is a fairly consistent record of government losses, varying from 22.7 per cent to 31.6 per cent, which is a fairly narrow range for such phenomena, with 1997 being the obvious exception.

We can gain some purchase on these phenomena by referring to the second half of Table 6.6, which shows the frequency with which the Opposition joined with neither, one, or both of the two minor parties to oppose the government on divisions. These data are the same data that are presented in Table 6.3, but from the reverse perspective. Table 6.3 shows, for instance, that on 61.4 per cent of the divisions in 1996, the government voted alone—that is, without the support of the Opposition or the Australian Democrats, or the Greens. This can only mean that on that same percentage of divisions, the Opposition, Democrats, and Greens voted together. Similarly, when the government, Democrats and

Greens voted together (see Table 6.3), the Opposition voted without the support of any other party (see Table 6.6).

TABLE 6.6: Opposition coalitions on divisions, 1996–2001

	1996	1997	1998	1999	2000	2001
Divisions that the government lost	67 (31.6%)	115 (41.1%)	64 (29.6%)	60 (26.8%)	27 (23.5%)	15 (22.7%)
Opposition voting coalitions against the government:						
Opposition, Democrats and Greens	121 (61.4%)	161 (57.5%)	151 (69.9%)	84 (37.5%)	27 (23.5%)	13 (19.7%)
Opposition and Democrats	0	8 (2.9%)	0	3 (1.3%)	0	1 (1.5%)
Opposition and Greens	47 (23.9%)	36 (12.9%)	10 (4.6%)	53 (23.7%)	24 (20.9%)	11 (16.7%)
Opposition alone	3 (1.5%)	6 (2.1%)	6 (2.8%)	4 (1.9%)	4 (3.5%)	6 (9.1%)
Opposition voting with the government	26 (13.2%)	69 (24.6%)	49 (22.7%)	80 (35.7%)	60 (52.3%)	35 (53.0%)

We see from the last row of Table 6.6 an almost unbroken pattern of increases in the frequency with which the Opposition voted with the government to form winning grand coalitions (which may or may not also have had the support of other parties or Independents). We also find that the frequency of government-Opposition coalitions was considerably higher in 1999 than in 1998 and then much higher in 2000 and 2001, even though the Opposition could defeat the government during most of 1999–2001 by joining with the Democrats and the Greens, something that was not possible in 1997 and 1998. In other words, it was when the Opposition seemingly had the best chances to form winning coalitions *against* the government that it was voting more often *with* the government.

Why? Data cannot provide a conclusive answer to the question, but they do suggest several possibilities or subsidiary questions. Note, for instance, how infrequently the Labor Opposition voted with the Democrats but not also with either the Greens or the government. In itself, this is not surprising because a vote on which the Opposition voted only with the Democrats (among the multi-member parties) is, by definition, also a vote on which the government voted only with the Greens, a strange bedfellows combination under most circumstances. The frequency of Opposition-Democrat pairings was consistently low, while the frequency of Opposition-Green pairings was considerably higher and fairly stable, ranging from almost 13 to almost 24 per cent, with 1998 being the clear exception. So there are no marked changes over time in the frequency of either pairing, and there certainly is no marked direction of change in either case.

But now consider the frequency of three-party anti-government coalitions. In 1996–1998, these coalitions formed on more than half of all divisions, though in the latter two years, even the three parties voting together did not form majorities without the support of one or more Independent Senators. Then from 1998 to 1999, the frequency with which the three non-government parties voted together dropped abruptly from 69.9 per cent to 37.5 per cent and continued to fall in the next two years to 23.5 and then to only 19.7 per cent. These data suggest, though they certainly cannot prove, that the Labor Opposition has encountered a frustrating dilemma. At precisely the time that the support of both the Democrats and the Greens could give Labor the numbers for victory, it was becoming harder and harder to bring all three parties together in support of the same positions, even if those positions were nothing more than an agreement to vote against the government's positions. One interpretation that fits the data is that Labor was caught between a pull toward the left from the Greens and a pull toward the center from the Democrats. Whatever policy changes made it easier for the Labor Opposition to reach agreement with one of the minor parties made it more difficult to reach agreement with the other.[125]

The data in Table 6.6, when viewed in light of what we know from Table 6.2 about party representation in the Senate, also point unquestionably to the important, even pivotal, role that Independents (including Senator Harris of One Nation) have played in determining the outcomes of Senate votes in recent years. From mid-1996 through mid-1999 and then again from October 2001 to the present, the votes of one or more of these Senators have been required to win divisions that the government opposed. From the government's perspective, its larger numbers always have enabled it to form majority coalitions without any Independent votes. It also is noteworthy, though, that from September 1996 to June 1999, the government could win without any of the other parties if it had the support of both Independents, Senators Colston and Harradine. Much the same situation has prevailed after August 2002, when the government could reach the magic number of 39 whenever it

---

125 Bear in mind, however, that we only have the vantage point that divisions give us. It may well be that the government did not bother calling divisions when it knew that it would be defeated by an Opposition-led winning coalition.

could combine its 35 votes with the votes of Senators Harradine, Lees, and Murphy (Independents) and Senator Harris (One Nation). Such things are much easier said than done, however, and especially so in light of the fact that two of the Independents (Harradine and Murphy) had been members of the ALP—though Harradine ceased being a member of the Labor Party before his election to the Senate—and the third (Lees) had been the Australian Democrats' leader in the Senate. The numbers make coalitions possible; skill and good fortune are required to make them happen, and even the most adept coalition builder cannot build a coalition that bridges unbridgeable policy and philosophical differences.

Minor parties and the balance of power

There are two conventional understandings about the political situation in the Senate, as it has been in recent years and as most observers expect that it will continue to be. First, there is a non-government majority in the Senate; and second, the minor parties and Independents, or some combination of them, hold the balance of power in the Senate. The first assertion is unquestionably true. The second is not as obviously and completely true as it might seem at first blush and deserves some final words here, although this matter of the balance of power will arise again in the next chapter.

One non-trivial implication of our analysis of Senate coalitions is that the minor parties —individually or jointly, and with or without the votes of Independent Senators—only hold the balance of power in the Senate when the government and the Opposition oppose each other (Young 1997). As we have seen, they have not always done so. In fact, the government and the Opposition have voted together quite often, and when they have done so, the votes cast by the Democrats, the Greens, and the Independents have mattered not at all, at least for the purpose of determining the outcomes.[126] So in this important respect, the leverage of the minor parties in the Senate is more limited than it might seem if we were simply to look at the numbers in Table 6.2 and assume that the government will try to govern and the Opposition will oppose.

There is another respect, though, in which a minor party in the Senate can be constrained in how and when it uses the leverage that its voting power in the Senate gives it. This can be a self-imposed restraint reflecting that party's view of what role is constitutionally appropriate

---

126 Some observers have commented that one or more Independents sometimes have voted against the government when it already was clear that their votes would not be decisive.

for it to play and what role is politically advantageous for it to play. In the case of the Democratic Labor Party during the 1950s–1970s, its Senators probably lost little sleep over these matters. They usually (but not invariably) voted with the Coalition and had little interest in somehow maintaining a balance between the Coalition's influence over policy and that of the ALP from which the DLP had split. In the case of the Greens, its Senators have been too few and its voting leverage in the Senate too limited for its views on these matters to be very consequential—at least not yet.

The Australian Democrats are another matter, however. In some ways, they have been the quintessential minor party: ideologically moderate, positioned in policy terms between the two political behemoths, particularly interested in issues of process as well as policy, and sometimes able to determine outcomes by their choice of which of the major parties to support as well as by their own amendments to government bills.[127] Although the recent fissures within the ranks of the Democrats' Party group have called this characterization into question and even raised questions about the party's political viability, it still is worth examining how the Democrats as a party have conceived of their place in the Senate and in the constitutional order.

In calculating how to take advantage of a position of strength in the Senate, a minor party must weigh its natural desire to use its 'balance of power' leverage to promote its own policy agenda while also demonstrating the public value of the Senate seats it holds against two offsetting considerations: first, its acceptance of the principle that the responsible government elements of the Constitution ultimately do give the government a strong claim to establish the parameters of national policy, if not all its fine details; and second, the minor party's concern that, should it fail to give such deference to the government, the voters could penalize it for exceeding what they think, in however inchoate a fashion, are the legitimate uses of its power. The Democrats' recognition of the balance involved was encapsulated in a statement by Senator Cheryl Kernot, then Leader of the Democrats in the Senate, concerning a 1993 tax bill:

---

127 Some prominent Democrats have conceived of their party's role in the Senate in essentially reactive terms: 'strictly "keeping the bastards honest", that is to make government true to its election promises and accountable to the parliament', whereas others have been more prepared 'to use the party's strategic position in the Senate so that their values and policies could be incorporated into legislation by amending or rejecting it.' (Sugita 1997: 161–162) Under the first conception but not the second, we would not expect Democrat Senators to offer many amendments intended to change bills to bring them closer to the Democrats' own vision of optimal public policy.

These [tax increases] are not our priorities; they are this government's priorities within the parameters of a straightjacket of its own making. Nevertheless, the final shape of the budget is its prerogative, and it will live with the consequence. The Democrats derive some satisfaction from being able to inject fairness into the original budget proposals, and I think it shows that minor parties can make a significant contribution and can achieve significant change.

Beyond that, we respect the government's right to govern and to make the tough decisions on how the budget shapes up. If it were up to us, we would have done it differently. (*Commonwealth Parliamentary Debates* (Senate), 7 October 1993: 1818)

As this statement suggests, the Democrats then felt that they were constrained by what they perceived to be the appropriate constitutional rules of the game. These rules, as they understood them, limited what uses and how much use they could legitimately make of their leverage in the Senate and were rooted in the premise that, notwithstanding the powers that the Constitution gives to the Senate, ultimately the exercise of those powers must not undermine the relationship of responsibility between the government and the House and, through the House, between the government and the electorate.[128] Young (1997) analyzes the changes in the 1993 budget that Keating's ALP Government made in order to secure the votes it needed from the Democrats and the Greens because of an essential strategic fact: the understanding of all parties that the Coalition was committed to opposing the government's tax proposals. This fact obviously strengthened the hands of both the Democrats and the Greens. The Greens pushed somewhat harder and further than the Democrats, and extracted more concessions from the government. However, neither pushed as hard or as far as it might have, given how important it was to the government to have the Senate pass bills that were an essential part of its budgetary scheme.

Young (1997: 70) identified reasons of principle and political prudence for self-restraint by the Australian Democrats:

Put simply, when it came to wielding the balance of power on policy issues, the Democrats were extremely cautious in their approach as they sought to

---

128 The Democrats claim to have imposed another constraint on themselves in the form of what Kernot (1997: 33) described as 'a self-imposed etiquette based around three principles: (1) agreeing not to block supply (i.e. refusing to take the whole process of government hostage in order to achieve an outcome); (2) refusing to cross-trade on issues (i.e. refusing to trade-off a good outcome in one area for a bad outcome in another completely unrelated area); and (3) transparency in policy making (i.e. ensuring public reasons are given for all decisions, with the process as open as practicable).' The first and third of these principles are unexceptionable; the second seems to me to be based on a misguided concept of political purity.

ensure that their actions could not be interpreted as undermining governability. Had the Democrats been seen as obstructing the Budget, or forcing the government to a double dissolution election, the negative fall out could have been significant and potentially undermined their position as balance of power holders. The experience of the Democrats in the Senate had sensitised them to this possibility and thus they sought to accommodate their need to be viewed as playing an active role within the Senate without opening up the party to claims of obstructionism.

With memories of the events of 1975 still so vivid in so many minds, the fact that it was budget-related bills that were at stake both increased the Democrats' leverage and made them particularly wary about using it too forcefully. In her statement quoted above, Kernot emphasized a motive of principle; in her analysis, Young emphasized the Democrats' worry about how the public would perceive and accept their actions. Both concerns undoubtedly were real, and they combined to impose limits on the negotiating leverage of the Democrats (and the Greens), limits that would not have existed if the only things to be calculated were who had 'the numbers' in the Senate and who needed them the most.

Goot (2002: 42) shows that the average major party vote in Senate elections has declined steadily, decade by decade, since the 1940s: from 95.3 per cent to 92.0 per cent to 88.3 per cent to 86.7 per cent to 84.4 per cent to 80.5 per cent. As investment counselors remind us, past performance is no guarantee of future results. If this trend continues, however, the number of minor party or Independent Senators, or both, will almost have to increase, as might the number of different minor parties that secure representation in the Senate. The difficulty, though, is in predicting just what the consequences of this development would be for governments and Oppositions engaged in the task of trying to win Senate votes. On the one hand, a greater fragmentation of party representation in the Senate would complicate the task of coalition-building because there would be more party groups or Independents with whom to consult and perhaps negotiate. At present, coalition-building in the Senate is largely an exercise in wholesale politics; successful negotiations produce Senate votes in bulk. A decline of two-party representation in the Senate (always for our purposes treating the Liberal and National parties as one) would require more retail politics, negotiating compromises or securing support, one vote or a handful of votes at a time.

On the other hand, that same fragmentation could well create a greater array of majority coalition options. There have been times during the years covered by this study when it was difficult, if not practically impossible, for the government to win in the Senate without the support of either the Opposition or the Democrats. And at all times, it was mathematically impossible for the Opposition to win a Senate division unless the Democrats were allied with them. If, let us imagine, the Australian Democrats decline as a force in the Senate, as some have speculated they are likely to do, their voters would have several options: supporting one of the major parties; supporting another, existing minor party—i.e., the Greens; supporting one or more new minor parties to emerge from the ashes the Democrats leave behind; supporting independent Senate candidates; or, what is most likely, some complex combination of the above.

Which tendency is strongest could have a significant effect on the dynamics of decision-making in the Senate. If the Democrats' vote fragments among Independents or new minor parties or both, both the government and the Opposition, depending on their numbers, of course, might be able to piece together winning majorities from among a larger number of smaller political forces in the Senate. Perhaps ironically, the greater the fragmentation in the Senate, the easier it might be for governments and Oppositions to build majorities because of the greater number of potential coalition partners, albeit small ones, among whom to choose to negotiate. The task certainly would be difficult and frustrating, however, if it required either major party to satisfy *all* or almost all of the Senate's minor parties and Independents.

If the Greens were to be the primary beneficiary of a decline or disappearance of the Democrats in the Senate, that would likely have a differential effect on the two major parties, whichever is in government. In light of the Greens' expressed policy views and their expressed opposition to what US analysts call logrolling—offering their support to another party on one issue or vote in exchange for an implicit or explicit assurance of that party's support on another issue or vote—we could expect that alliances between the Greens and the Liberal-National Coalition would be more difficult to form and less frequent than alliances between the Greens and Labor. Depending as always on the numbers, this situation could leave a Liberal-National government dependent on the support of Independents and whatever other Senate votes remain to be found. At the same time, it could make it somewhat easier for the ALP, whether in government or in Opposition, to join with the Greens to form majorities on Senate votes, but only at the expense of being pulled to the political left. (This assumes that it is fair to place the Greens to the left of the ALP and both of them to the left of the Liberals and Nationals on the proverbial unidimensional left-right spectrum.) To put it bluntly, a Labor government might find itself hostage to the Greens, whereas a Liberal-National government might become hostage either to the ALP Opposition or to everyone else in the

Senate except the Greens. In the Senate, the number of seats not held by the major parties is critically important, but so too is who sits in those seats.

7

Dividing the Senate

We know relatively little, and certainly less than we should, about the attitudes of Australians toward their Senate, and their perceptions of what things it does and how well it does them (Young 1997: 9–10).[129] So I am speculating when I suppose that relatively few Australians have an image in their minds of the Senate at work that differs very much from their mental picture of the House of Representatives. I suspect that the public's perception of the Senate probably is shaped by its perception of the House, and the image of the House that most Australians receive from the media is of a highly partisan and contentious body in which each party is able to find in almost any noteworthy development further compelling evidence that the other party (or parties) is, if not corrupt or dishonest, then at least bereft of able leadership, new ideas, sound judgment, and a sympathetic understanding of the needs, interests, and preferences of the Australian people. Depending on the circumstances, either that other party deserves to be kept from winning office or it needs to be removed from office at the earliest possible opportunity.

This is the message that party leaders and spokesmen often are at pains to communicate in media interviews, just as it is the impression they convey during Question Time, which is the only slice of parliamentary proceedings that average citizens are likely to see. Perhaps the fact of non-government Senate majorities has become widely-enough known so that most Australians now differentiate between the two houses and associate the Senate more with concepts such as deliberation and compromise. But perhaps not. The proceedings of the Senate can make the same impressions as those of the House,

---

129 Goot (1999a) has summarized the available data—for example, on public attitudes toward non-government majorities in the Senate and the frequency with which voters have voted for one party in the House and another in the Senate (as many as 17 per cent)—and Bean (1988: 51–52) has reported that a slim majority in a national survey wanted the Senate retained as is and only 11 per cent wanted it abolished. These findings are informative, but they tell us much less than we should want to know about Australians' understanding of what the Senate does and what it should do.

particularly during its Question Time and during debates at which the reputation or core policies of a party or the government are at issue— as, for example, during the debate on the 2002 report of the select committee established to report on the 'children overboard' incident. Yet I believe that the sometimes raucous debates in the Senate, though usually more decorous than those in the House, disguise a little secret that is well-known to those who serve in and work for the Senate but that may come as a surprise to most Australians. The secret? That the work of the Senate often is characterized by cooperation, conciliation, and legislative agreement.

This is particularly true of Senate committees. Take as prime examples the Committee on Regulations and Ordinances and the Committee for the Scrutiny of Bills (see, e.g., Reid 1982). The former was established in 1932 to examine proposed new delegated legislation to ensure, as provided by Standing Order 23:

(a) that it is in accordance with the statute;
(b) that it does not trespass unduly on personal rights and liberties;
(c) that it does not unduly make the rights and liberties of citizens dependent upon administrative decisions which are not subject to review of their merits by a judicial or other independent tribunal; and
(d) that it does not contain matter more appropriate for parliamentary enactment.

Almost 50 years later, the Senate used this committee as the model for a new Committee for the Scrutiny of Bills, which Standing Order 24 charges with examining all bills to determine whether they:

(a) trespass unduly on personal rights and liberties;
(b) make rights, liberties or obligations unduly dependent upon insufficiently defined administrative powers;
(c) make rights, liberties or obligations unduly dependent upon non-reviewable decisions;
(d) inappropriately delegate legislative powers; or
(e) insufficiently subject the exercise of legislative power to parliamentary scrutiny.

It is easy to imagine how non-government Senators could try to turn the work of these committees to partisan advantage. Just consider the opportunities for accusing the government, rightly or wrongly, of issuing regulations that are inconsistent with the law, of proposing ordinances or bills that trespass on personal rights and liberties, and of supporting statutory or delegated legislation that puts the interests of Aussie battlers in the hands of unelected and unaccountable bureaucrats hidden away in their artificial enclave of Canberra. What aggressive party publicists would not salivate at the prospect of using these committees to launch regular attacks on their parliamentary opponents? Yet ask parliamentary observers and you will be told that both committees conduct their business in a measured non-partisan way and almost always manage to reach conclusions in which all their members join, regardless of party.

In similar fashion, if to a lesser extent, the Senate's other standing committees conduct much of their business in a manner that is not nearly as overtly partisan and adversarial as are some of the Senate's proceedings in the chamber. In general, it is fair to say that proceedings in the chamber typically are considerably more decorous and thoughtful than during Question Time, and that proceedings in committee often are more decorous and thoughtful than they are in the chamber.

If so, what accounts for the difference in tenor and tone? In a body as large and diverse as the Senate, no single explanation can suffice. It is reasonable to suppose, though, that some Senators who might prefer a 'come, let us reason together' style recognize, and accommodate themselves to the fact that a primary purpose of some chamber proceedings, especially Question Time, is to provide a setting for gladiatorial combat in which MPs demonstrate their skill to their allies and inflict rhetorical wounds on their partisan opponents.

In committees, on the other hand, the very lack of close media attention allows Senators to concentrate on working together to make good national policy, rather than being preoccupied with the need to claim credit for a monopoly on public wisdom and to take positions designed to influence the outcome of the next elections. More than a century ago, Woodrow Wilson, a future US president who was then a young and all too self-confident political scientist, described (1885 [1956]: 69) the floor proceedings of the House and Senate as 'Congress on public exhibition whilst Congress in its committee-rooms is Congress at work.' In quite a different context, perhaps it can be said that Wilson's first assertion is true of the Australian Senate, and that many Senators wish that his second assertion were even more true than it already has become in the past several decades.

Again, all of this is speculation; it is only a series of hypotheses, if you will, based on my observations and what others, far better informed than I, have told me. However, these speculations do suggest fertile ground for research by Australian political scientists. How do Australians perceive the House of Representatives and the Senate? How and to what extent do they differentiate between the two—in the constitutional functions of the two houses, in their political arrangements, and in their activities and operational styles? What are

the attitudes among Senators themselves toward the institution in which
they serve—including, for example, the adversarial style of the Senate
on public exhibition—and is this the style of policy making and
scrutiny they would prefer? There is much work to be done on such
questions from which students, scholars, and political practitioners alike
would benefit.

Opposing government legislation

Early in his classic study, *Legislatures*, Kenneth Wheare comments on
the relationships between the nature of parliamentary politics and the
size and shape of parliamentary chambers. He argues (1963: 12) that 'A
semi-circular chamber would undermine the two-party system. You
must be either for the government or against it; you must be on one side
of the chamber or on the other. An oblong chamber not only assists
you, but compels you to take sides.' In making this argument, Wheare
was taking sides with Churchill who, during a debate on how the House
of Commons chamber should be rebuilt after sustaining damage during
World War II, contended that:

> Its shape should be oblong and not semicircular. Here is a very potent
> factor in our political life. The semi-circular assembly enables every
> individual or group to move around the centre adopting various shades of
> pink according as the weather changes. I am a convinced supporter of the
> Party System in preference to the Group System. The Party System is much
> favoured by the oblong form of chamber. It is easy for an individual to
> move through those insensible gradations from left to right, but the act of
> crossing the floor is one that requires serious consideration. (quoted in
> Coghill and Baggage 1991: 17)

Interestingly, Wheare pointed to the Australian Parliament as one
that had not adopted the Westminster chamber design. In this he was
correct, whether he had in mind the old Parliament House or the new
one, which also has members' seats directly opposite the Speaker's and
President's chairs, seats that are neither on the government nor the
Opposition side. Yet if we compare the design of any of the Canberra
chambers—House or Senate, old or new—with the designs of the
chambers in London and Washington, they resemble the British
chambers much more closely than the wide semi-circular chambers of
the US Congress. In Canberra as in London, the government ministers
and the Shadow Cabinet sit facing each other on the front benches with
most of their respective supporters arrayed behind them. Members of
the US House and Senate sit together in their chambers with all the

other members of their respective parties, but they face their presiding officer, not each other.[130] Also, they can vote from any place in their respective chambers, but members of the Australian Parliament vote in divisions by moving to sit on one side of their chamber or the other. There is no disguising when one of them is crossing the floor to vote with the Opposition, or there would be no disguising it if it ever happened among ALP or Coalition Representatives or Senators. Both the design of the Senate chamber (soon to be discussed) and the method of voting convey a sense of Government *versus* Opposition—the sense, to repeat Wheare's observation, that 'You must be either for the government or against it; you must be on one side of the chamber or on the other.'

Not surprisingly, several Nineteenth Century British parliamentary leaders have been credited with the assertion that 'the role of the opposition is to oppose,' or words to that effect.[131] Is this a fair and accurate characterization of the posture of the Opposition in the Australian Senate? Of the other, smaller non-government parties? One way of approaching this subject is to look, as we already have begun to do, at the record of divisions in the Senate, when each party takes a public position on whatever question the Senate is considering. In the previous chapter, we examined all the divisions that occurred during 1996–2001 for what they revealed about the attempts of both the government and the Opposition to form winning coalitions in the Senate—the two major protagonists joining forces with each other or

---

130 An Australian expert on the subject has observed that, in the Old and New Parliament Houses, seats facing the Speaker or President were not installed in order to approximate the semi-circular patterns found in Washington and elsewhere. Instead, once a decision was made that the Australian chambers should be able to accommodate all members (which is not the case in London), it also was decided that having some seats facing the Speaker or President was preferable to the alternative of extending the government and Opposition benches to the point that the chambers would become too long and narrow to be practical. Personal communication to the author.

131 The sentiment has been attributed to Disraeli, but several compendia of political quotations credit Edward Stanley, the 14th Earl of Derby and sometime Prime Minister during the 1850s and 1860s. Of course, any Opposition leader is much more likely to echo the public sentiments of George Reid, the first Leader of the Opposition in the Commonwealth Parliament in 1901:

> Our object should be, when Bills framed on sound principles are introduced, to help the Government as far as we can to make them as perfect as they can be made, and to reserve our opposition for matters of a serious character. I hope that this Opposition and those who succeed them will always avoid one serious evil in the working of our parliamentary institutions; and that is an attitude of obstructing measures, the principles of which are not objectionable.
> (*Commonwealth Parliamentary Debates*, 21 May 1901: 105)

combining with one or both minor parties or Independent Senators. And we found that the facts are not fully consistent with the notion that the Opposition always opposes and, for that matter, with the commonplace observation that the minor parties in the Senate hold the balance of power. But not all divisions are the same, of course. Some are more important than others, and some have more direct consequences than others for the content or the fate of legislation. In this chapter, we will look more closely at several of the most consequential kinds of divisions.

The Senate's consideration of a bill is divided into stages that are marked by the first, second, and third reading of that bill. At each stage, the question before the Senate is whether the bill shall be read a first (or second, or third) time. The Senate must vote on that question and decide it affirmatively if the bill is to proceed to the next stage of the process. Defeat of a motion for the second or third reading of a bill does not necessarily mean the defeat of the bill; the Senate can vote again on the same motion after having rejected it. Until the Senate agrees to the first and then the second reading of a bill, however, a motion cannot be made to read it for the third time, and thereby pass it.

The motion for the first reading of a bill normally is made at the time it is introduced, and it is agreed to immediately. 'The Senate has the opportunity to reject a bill at the first reading stage, but in practice the first reading is normally passed without objection and is regarded as a purely formal stage.' (*Odgers' Australian Senate Practice* 2001: 258) The motions for the second and third reading of the bill are equally essential but they also are far more consequential.

The motion for the second reading sets off a debate on the general principles and merits of the bill. By voting for this motion at the end of the debate, the Senate expresses its support for the concept of the bill. 'Passage by the Senate of the motion for the second reading indicates that the Senate has accepted the bill in principle, or at least has allowed the bill to proceed to a consideration of its details, and the bill then proceeds to that detailed consideration and a consideration of any amendments which senators wish to propose.' (*Odgers' Australian Senate Practice* 2001: 259) After the Senate acts on any such amendments (a subject to which we shall return), it then votes on a motion for the bill to be read for the third time. This is the Senate's final vote on a bill; there is no separate vote on passing the bill after third reading. 'When a bill has been read a third time, proceedings on it are completed and it has passed the Senate.' (*Odgers' Australian Senate Practice* 2001: 273)

So there are three hurdles that each bill must jump if it is to pass the Senate. The first is so low as to be virtually unnoticeable. However, the motions for the second reading and for the third reading are the primary opportunities for a majority of the Senate to reject a bill.[132] There are other ways in which bills can effectively be defeated (see below), but the votes on the second and third reading motions are essential moments of choice.

We might expect, therefore, that if 'the role of the opposition is to oppose,' it is at these stages that Opposition Senators assert themselves and that non-government majorities in the Senate halt government legislation in its tracks. If much of the government's legislation is as ill-conceived and as potentially injurious to the Australian national interest as non-government parties often allege, they can prevent it from becoming law by standing together, like Horatio at the proverbial bridge, against motions that the legislation be read a second or third time. Yet readers may have anticipated by now that this is not exactly what happens in practice.

Table 7.1 brings together data on Senate divisions on second and third reading motions since 1996 and the beginning of the Howard Liberal-National Party Coalition Government. Note first that these are data on *divisions* only. For this reason, three points made in the preceding chapter merit reiteration here. First, most questions are decided not by division but 'on the voices' and without a formal record of how any party group or individual Senator voted. Second, however, it takes *only two Senators* to call a division, which is just about as minimal a requirement as the Senate in its standing orders could impose. And third, even controversial questions may be decided without a division, often because Senators on the losing side of a vote on the voices conclude that nothing useful would be accomplished by insisting on a division.

Turning now to Table 7.1, we find that the number of divisions on second and third reading motions combined has never exceeded a total of 21 in any of the six years between 1996 and 2001, even though the total numbers of bills that the Senate passed during these years ranged from a low of 85 to a high of 224. (The table also presents data

---

132 As already noted, a bill can survive even if a motion for its second reading is defeated. 'The motion for the second reading is that this bill be *now* read a second time. The rejection of that motion is an indication that the Senate does not wish the bill to proceed at that particular time. Procedurally, therefore, the rejection of that motion is not an absolute rejection of the bill and does not prevent the Senate being asked subsequently to grant the bill a second reading. ... In practice, [however,] the Senate often indicates its disagreement with a bill by rejecting the motion for the second reading, and that action is taken to be an absolute rejection of the bill.' (*Odgers' Australian Senate Practice* 2001: 259; emphasis in original)

TABLE 7.1: Senate divisions on reading motions, 1996–2001

	1996	1997	1998	1999	2000	2001
Total number of bills passed	85	224	139	206	181	171
Second and third reading motions:						
Number of divisions	14	21	15	16	9[1]	10
Number of divisions as percentage of all bills passed	16.5	9.4	10.8	7.8	5.0	5.8
Number of divisions that the government lost	0	4	2	2	5	5
Percentage of divisions that the government lost	0	19.0	13.3	13.0	55.6	50.0
Number of motions that the Opposition opposed	8	13	10	11	7	8
Percentage of motions that the Opposition opposed	57.1	61.9	66.7	68.8	77.8	80.0
Percentage of all bills passed that the Opposition opposed on second or third reading divisions[2]	5.9	4.9	5.0	4.9	2.8	4.1
Number of motions that the Democrats opposed	8	13	14	9	6[3]	7[4]
Percentage of motions that the Democrats opposed	57.1	61.9	93.3	56.3	66.7	70.0
Number of motions that the Greens opposed	13	20	15	14	7	7[5]
Percentage of motions that the Greens opposed	92.9	95.2	100.0	87.5	77.8	70.0
Second reading motions:						
Number of divisions	8	10	9	9	5	9
Number of divisions as percentage of all bills passed	9.4	4.5	6.5	4.4	2.8	5.3
Number of divisions that the government lost	0	1	2	2	4	5
Percentage of divisions that the government lost	0	10.0	22.2	22.2	80.0	55.6
Number of motions that the Opposition opposed	5	5	7	7	5	7
Percentage of motions that the Opposition opposed	62.5	50.0	77.8	77.8	100.0	77.8
Percentage of all bills passed that the Opposition opposed on second reading divisions	5.9	2.2	4.3	3.4	2.8	4.1
Number of motions that the Democrats opposed	3	6	9	5[5]	4	7
Percentage of motions that the Democrats opposed	37.5	60.0	10.0	55.6	80.0	77.8
Number of motions that the Greens opposed	8	10	9	9	4	7[5]
Percentage of motions that the Greens opposed	100.0	100.0	100.0	100.0	80.0	77.8
Third reading motions:						
Number of divisions	6	11[6]	6	7	4	1
Number of divisions as percentage of all bills passed	7.1	5.0	4.3	3.4	2.2	0.6
Number of divisions that the government lost	0	3	0	0	1	0
Percentage of divisions that the government lost	0	27.3	0	0	25.0	0
Number of motions that the Opposition opposed	3	8	3	4	2	1
Percentage of motions that the Opposition opposed	50.0	72.7	50.0	57.1	50.0	100.0
Percentage of all bills passed that the Opposition opposed on third reading divisions	3.5	3.1	2.2	1.9	0.6	0.6
Number of motions that the Democrats opposed	5	7	5	4[7]	2[8]	0[9]
Percentage of motions that the Democrats opposed	83.3	63.6	83.3	57.1	50.0	0
Number of motions that the Greens opposed	5[10]	10	6	5[10]	3	0
Percentage of motions that the Greens opposed	83.3	90.9	100.0	71.4	75.0	0

1   Excludes two motions that the government opposed.
2   These percentages take account of instances in which there was more than one division on the same bill.
3   Split on two divisions.
4   Split on one division.
5   Not recorded on one division.
6   Excludes one free vote.
7   Split on one division.
8   Split on two divisions.
9   Split on the only division.
10 Not recorded on one division.

separately on second reading motions and third reading motions.) On average, there was one division on a second or third reading motion for every six bills that the Senate passed in 1996, and one such vote for every 20 bills passed in 2000. To make the same point somewhat differently, consider 1999 when the Senate passed 206 bills with only 16 divisions on reading motions. These 206 bills each gave rise to a second reading motion and a third reading motion, making a total of 412 opportunities for as few as two Senators to call divisions. They did so, however, on only 16 occasions, less than four per cent of the time.

Because all of the bills passed were government bills, we know that the government won every vote on reading motions that were decided on the voices.[133] So in every instance in which non-government Senators did not challenge a vote 'on the voices' that the President decided in the government's favor, they were acquiescing in a government victory. In the overwhelming majority of instances, they did just that; both the official Opposition and the other non-government parties did not force divisions, even though any two Senators always can do so.

There are several plausible explanations, all of which undoubtedly contain part of the truth, for the dearth of divisions on reading motions. First, one or more of the non-government parties may support the government's bill, and a division can be called only by Senators on the losing side of the voice vote. Second, the non-government parties may know beyond a doubt that one or more of them does support the government's bill, so there is little point in having a division because the certainty of strict party discipline ensures that the outcome of a division would be the same as the vote on the voices. (But even when the outcome of a division is a foregone conclusion, one party or another still may want a division in order to create a public record of each party's position on the bill.) And third, some bills simply are so inconsequential or non-contentious that a division is not worth the bother; even if not all of the parties support the bill, the bill's opponents may not care about enough about defeating it to try to mobilize their forces and prevail in a division.

The prevalence of the second and third motives is exceedingly difficult and probably impossible to measure. We can gain some purchase on the first argument, though, by looking at the outcomes and voting patterns on the divisions on reading motions that have taken place. Returning to Table 7.1, in none of the six years examined did the

---

133 Unless there were instances in which the government chose not to try to prevent one or more of its own bills from being defeated, at least at that moment, by declining to require a division when a second or third reading motion, taken on the voices, was decided against it.

government lose more than a total of five divisions on such motions. In percentage terms, however, the frequency of government defeats jumped from less than 20 per cent on both second and third reading motions during 1996–1999 to more than half of the divisions on the same motions during 2000 and 2001. The numbers involved are so small that this development (which is attributable largely to the results of divisions at second reading) must be approached with great caution. Perhaps, an observer has suggested to me, the 2000–2001 data reflect the fact that the government already had been in office for four years. In its fifth and sixth years, its legislative agenda may have included a disproportionate number of bills that it knew would face stiff opposition but that it still thought worth trying to pass.

During the Howard Ministry from 1996 to 2001, the government prevailed on almost 80 per cent (67 of 85) divisions on second and third reading motions. How often did any of the non-government parties contest these outcomes? We have seen that (1) there have been relatively few divisions to decide these motions; (2) in absolute terms, the government has failed to win few such motions, however they were decided; but (3) the government has a more checkered record when we look at the percentages of divisions on reading motions that the government has won and lost. What can we say about the positions that the non-government parties have taken on these divisions?[134]

Not surprisingly, each of the three non-government parties (the Green Senators are treated as one party) usually have opposed a majority of these divisions, with one exception: the Democrats opposed only three of the eight second reading motions decided in 1996. (Also, neither the Democrats nor the Greens opposed the one third reading motion that was decided by division in 2001.) The most consistent opposition has come from the Greens; taking second and third reading motions together, the Greens opposed as few as 70 per cent of them in 2001 and as many as 100 per cent of them in 1998. Never during these years did the Democrats vote against a higher percentage of reading motions than the Greens, whether we look at second and third reading motions separately or together. The rate of Democrats' opposition to both motions combined ranged from slightly more than one-half (56.3 per cent) in 1999 to 93.3 per cent in the preceding year. Again, the numbers of motions are so small that the exact percentages are of questionable significance. The two findings that do stand out are, first, that the Democrats have been less likely to oppose government reading motions than the Greens, and, second, that the Greens have a strong

---

134 As before, the one Senator representing One Nation is treated here as if he were an Independent.

record of opposition, always exceeding 75 per cent on divisions on second reading motions.

These findings are consistent with the difference that some observers have noted in the respective stances of the Democrats and the Greens toward the Senate and the government, with the Democrats proclaiming more deference than have the Greens to the right of the government, in light of its electoral mandate,[135] to determine the general directions of government policy—and so by implication, the right to have its legislation proceed through the stages of consideration in the Senate, barring truly compelling reasons to oppose its movement from one reading to the next. From this perspective, it may be surprising that the Democrats have opposed second and third reading motions as frequently as they have.

These findings also may tell us something about the extent of the policy disagreements of each minor party with the Coalition Government. It is considerably more difficult to position the Australian Democrats than the Greens on a unidimensional left-right spectrum; recent disunity among Democrat Senators makes that clear. However, most observers probably would agree that the Greens have differed philosophically with the Coalition Government more consistently than have the Democrats, so we would expect the Greens to have opposed this government more often on reading motions. If there were a Labor Government instead, the pattern we observe might very well be reversed.

What of the official Opposition, which always must bear in mind that, if it succeeds in defeating a reading motion, it also may be giving the government a double dissolution trigger? When there have been divisions on reading motions, how consistently has the Opposition opposed? Although the data are mixed, what we can say is that the level of Opposition opposition to these motions has been no higher than that of the two much smaller parties. During 1996–1998, in fact, the Labor Opposition usually supported the government on second and third reading divisions as often or more often than did the Democrats or the Greens. Only in 2000 and 2001 did the Opposition vote against second and third reading motions on divisions at least as often as the other two parties.

The best indicator in Table 7.1 of the frequency with which the Opposition has attempted to defeat government bills at second or third reading is the percentage of all bills passed that the Opposition opposed on either a second reading division, a third reading division, or both. By

---

135 We will explore the matter of mandates in Chapter 9.

this measure, Opposition opposition was exceptional, not routine. During these six years, the Opposition never voted, on divisions on second or third reading motions, against as many as six per cent (in 1996) of the bills that the Senate passed. In 2000, the frequency of its opposition was cut in half, to less than three per cent.

Any Opposition always faces a choice. It can work with the government to improve its legislation by persuasion or amendment or both, and support government bills when those bills have merit and when there is no compelling reason not to support them. In this way, the Opposition can take satisfaction in playing a constructive role in lawmaking even when it is not in power. In the process, it also can demonstrate to the national electorate that it is a responsible Opposition that can be trusted to be made the government.

Alternatively, the Opposition can oppose, using whatever procedural leverage it has to impede enactment of government legislation, by blocking it when possible or, if not that, by delaying it to the point of obstruction. In this way, the Opposition can sharpen public perceptions of its policy differences with the government and try to convince voters that the government's inability to move its legislative program through the Parliament, or its difficulty in doing so, is proof positive that it does not deserve to be returned to office at the next election. In the long run, from this point of view, the Opposition and the nation are ill-served by an Opposition that is willing to support government bills if the government first accepts some Opposition amendments. First, the result is legislation that is only less bad than it might otherwise have been; and second, this approach allows the government to claim credit for enacting its bills—bills that the Opposition cannot effectively criticize because it voted for them.

The data presented in Table 7.1 offer only one glimpse into legislative strategies and decisions in the Senate. It always is dangerous to rely too heavily on such data, especially when the number of data points is so small, to reach conclusions about the workings of collectivities as complicated as parliaments and their party groups. Yet what stand out so dramatically in this table are, first, the dearth of divisions that any of the non-government parties has called on second and third reading motions, and second, the even smaller number of reading motions on which the Opposition has used divisions in attempts to prevent government bills from advancing to the next stage of the legislative process. These data certainly do not portray a Labor Opposition that has defined its role as trying to defeat government legislation whenever the opportunity arises.

It is possible, of course, that the Opposition only called divisions on reading motions when it thought that it had some possibility, even if no assurance, of winning. This may well have been true in some cases. However, I find three other inferences to be at least as plausible: first, that much of the legislation on which Parliament acts is not significant enough to provoke determined opposition; second, that the policy differences between government and Opposition are not as pervasive or as great in practice as their spokesmen often advertise them to be for electoral purposes; and third, that the Opposition has deliberately chosen not to fight the government to the bitter end on every bill that it cannot support. None of these inferences strikes me as particularly implausible or difficult to accept. It is not surprising that most of the legislation that Parliament considers does not separate the parties. Much of the work of government is routine and non-controversial; so is the legislation that makes it possible. By the same token, it is predictable enough that elected politicians will succumb to the temptation to exaggerate their policy differences with their partisan opponents in order to give the electorate compelling reasons to vote for them.

It also is not surprising that the Opposition has not chosen to try to block the second or third reading of all the bills it opposes. It is in the Opposition's interest to project an image of responsibility—to emphasize what it favours as much as what it opposes. If an Opposition is best known to the public for trying to defeat bill after bill after bill, voters would naturally have difficulty visualizing that Opposition as the government. Also, it can be costly for the Opposition to try to assemble majorities to defeat second or third reading motions. To construct a majority on such a motion, the Opposition, like the government, has to find support from other parties. If this support arises voluntarily, well and good. But if not, the Opposition has to pay a price for that support, perhaps by agreeing to support one or more minor parties on other issues or other motions. But there is a third reason that may be more compelling than the others. Members of the Opposition, as responsible public officials, often must believe that blocking legislation would not contribute to dealing with problems that members of both major parties recognize as real, serious, and requiring legislative action. Simply saying 'no' to government bills often is not the best sound for the Opposition to make, on either policy or partisan grounds.

What we may see in Table 7.1 is evidence of the Opposition as the Government-in-Waiting. As I shall have occasion to argue again, the parliamentary Opposition must see itself as being in Opposition only until after the next House election or, in the worst case, the election after that. Otherwise, its members may lapse into despondency. Especially in eras when the alternation of parties in government occurs often enough so that neither party is labelled a permanent Opposition,[136] the Opposition of the day must always be asking itself whether the tactics that it employs today (or worse, the permanent institutional reforms that it supports) may come back to haunt it when it once again holds the positions of power that it so richly deserves. As a result, the Labor Opposition during our recent six-year period, as the once and (it assumed) future government, may have chosen not to oppose the Coalition government on reading motions, or to call divisions on those motions, unless powerful policy differences compelled it to do so, out of a calculation that if it made determined and consistent efforts to block the progress of Coalition legislation through the Senate, the Coalition would have every reason to do the same when their positions are reversed.

Instead, the Opposition as well as the other non-government parties may concentrate not on blocking a government bill but on making it better—making it more palatable or at least less objectionable. Especially if the non-government parties want to avoid being accused of preventing the Commonwealth from addressing a widely recognized need, or if they believe that there are no realistic prospects for blocking a bill by defeating a reading motion, the non-government parties may focus their energies not on preventing the bill from passing but on amending the bill before it does pass. To take our inquiry further, therefore, we need to look beyond divisions on second and third reading motions, however important they are, to the amendments that are proposed in the Senate chamber.

Three opportunities to amend

Senators have three primary opportunities to offer amendments in the chamber in relation to each bill that the Senate eventually passes. During the debate on the motion that the bill now be read a second time, Senators can propose amendments to that motion. Then, if and when the Senate agrees to the motion, it proceeds to consider the bill's text in the committee of the whole, a process that can (but usually does not) involve considering each clause of the bill in sequence, and during which Senators can offer amendments to make changes in the text of the bill. (The committee of the whole is a committee on which all Senators serve and that meets in the Senate chamber. It is a parliamentary device that permits a process of debating and amending a

---

136 As the Republicans in the US House of Representatives were labelled the 'permanent minority' after losing control of the House in the 1954 election and not regaining it until the 1994 election.

bill that is more flexible and that gives more Senators more chances to participate than if the Senate were acting under its normal rules of procedure.) Finally, when the motion is made that a bill now be read a third time, Senators can move amendments to that motion. At each of these stages, Senators can offer amendments in relation to the bill it is considering,[137] but only amendments in committee of the whole, to which I shall refer as committee amendments, can actually change the text of a bill and, therefore, have the possibility of becoming law.

When the Senate is debating the motion for second reading, Senators can propose amendments *to the motion*, but not to the bill, because at that moment the Senate is considering only the motion; it is not yet considering the bill itself. That can happen only after the Senate passes the second reading motion. So each second reading amendment can propose only to make some change in the text of the motion, and that motion simply proposes that the bill be now read for a second time. Under these circumstances, most second reading amendments are devices for Opposition and other non-government Senators to express their opinion of the bill and to give their reasons, often with rhetorical bravado, why the bill should be opposed or how it will need to be amended when the opportunity for doing so arises in committee of the whole. Similarly, when the Senate is considering the motion for third reading, the text of the bill is no longer before the Senate for amendment. The Senate already has agreed to the bill in principle and already has disposed of all amendments to it, so an amendment to a third reading motion is unusual and is likely to deal only with questions such as when the third reading is to take place (see below).

Second reading amendments take two primary forms. One form proposes to add something—usually a statement of opinion—at the end of the motion. (We shall look at the other form in a few paragraphs.) The reason why these amendments sometimes are called 'pious amendments' may become clear if we look at a reasonably typical second reading amendment that was proposed to a tax bill. As always, the motion before the Senate was that the bill be now read a second time, and a Senator moved that the motion be amended by adding to it the following:

---

137 There is at least one other opportunity that can be used to offer amendments affecting a bill. After the Senate completes its consideration of a bill in committee of the whole, an amendment can be offered to the motion that the report of the committee be adopted. When offered, such amendments often propose that bills be referred to committee, but not that they be prevented from proceeding further through the remaining stages of the legislative process.

but, in respect of the Taxation Laws Amendment Bill (No. 3) 1986, the Senate condemns the Government for—

    (a) its failure to control Government spending to the point where it has broken its 'Trilogy' commitment to hold taxation to no more than 25 per cent of gross domestic product and proceeded to tax Australians to the highest point in our history;

    (b) its contempt for ordinary taxpayers, illustrated by its decision to charge a $200 fee for appeals against the Tax Commissioner's rulings regardless of the size or complexity of the claim;

    (c) its incompetent handling of the withholding tax issue, whereby the Government changed the tax rules, caused a run on the dollar, and retreated 27 days later; and

    (d) its disgraceful treatment of the Defence Forces Reserves, by withdrawing the tax free status of reservists' pay, thereby causing a grave rundown of reserve forces and damage to their morale and effectiveness, and belatedly restoring the concession. (*Journals of the Senate*, 23 October 1986: 1354)

It is hard to imagine that a group of men and women capable of doing so many deplorable things in a single bill would be allowed within the city limits of Canberra, much less have the government of the Commonwealth placed in their hands. Yet such often is the tenor of second reading amendments, which propose, for instance, that the Senate 'notes with concern … ' or 'condemns the government for … ' or 'deplores the Government's decision to … ' or 'expresses its concern at … ', or all of the above, and so on.

The rhetorical flourishes aside, the key points are two. First, such an amendment does not actually propose to change the text of the bill in question, nor could it do so at this stage of the proceedings. And second, such an amendment does not even oppose the second reading of the bill; the amendment would amend the motion to state that the bill shall now be read a second time but, by the way, the government's policy embodied in the bill is misguided and offers proof positive of its lack of fitness to continue governing. Less often, this form of second reading amendment can be used to try to postpone the next stage of a bill's consideration until, for instance, a certain date arrives, or until a minister makes a certain document available or something else happens. But even in these instances, the purpose and effect of the amendment, if it wins, is not to stop the bill indefinitely by preventing it from being read for the second time.

By contrast, committee amendments are very different parliamentary creatures. Like most second reading amendments, they may be offered with political motives in mind; but unlike all second reading amendments, committee amendments propose to amend the text of the bill and, if passed, could well become part of the laws of Australia. In general, second reading amendments are part of the political-electoral process; committee amendments are much more part of the law-making process. Our interest, therefore, is almost exclusively in committee amendments and not second reading amendments (or rare third reading amendments), but not entirely so because there are some second and third reading amendments that, if passed, would have real parliamentary effects on the fate of bills, if not their content.

For example, there is a charmingly arcane device which, to the regret of those who appreciate parliamentary nuance, now rarely is used. The Senate can amend the motion that a bill be now read a second time or a third time by replacing 'now' with 'this day six months' (in other words, six months from the date of the vote). In fact, this is the only amendment that can be moved to a motion for the third reading of a bill. On its face, the amendment would seem to do nothing more than defer the date of the second or third reading and so might not do irreparable damage to the bill's prospects for enactment. But not so. 'If this amendment is carried the bill is disposed of with an indication of finality greater than if the motion for the [second or] third reading is simply rejected.' (*Odgers' Australian Senate Practice* 2001: 259–260, 272) This, then, is an example of a reading amendment with teeth; it proposes to kill a bill.[138]

The other form of a second reading amendment also can affect the progress or even the fate of a bill, not just express an opinion about it or about the government that is advocating its enactment. The difference between the two forms of second reading amendments derives, first, from how they are drafted. Instead of proposing to add something to the motion, which already provides for the bill to be read a second time, a second reading amendment can propose to replace the text of the motion. If such an amendment wins, therefore, the amended motion no longer provides for second reading. So if the Senate approves the motion, it will have an entirely different effect on the bill and its fate. A second reading amendment in this second form proposes to prevent the bill from being read for the second time and, therefore, halts its legislative progress unless and until the Senate considers and adopts another second reading motion for that same bill.[139]

---

138 In 1996, Senator Brown of the Australian Greens offered such an amendment to the third reading motion for the Euthanasia Laws Bill 1996; and Senator Harris of Pauline Hanson's One Nation moved the same kind of amendment to the Defence Legislation Amendment (Aid to the Civilian Authorities) Bill 2000.

139 It also is possible, though much less common, for a second reading amendment in the first form to have procedural consequences. My thanks to Cleaver Elliott, Clerk Assistant for the Senate Procedure Office, and Rosemary Laing, Clerk Assistant for the Senate Table Office, for alerting me to these possibilities, and to Kerry West of

I cannot report exactly how often Senators have offered second reading amendments in recent years that proposed to affect the progress of bills in significant ways, not just express opinions about them and the government. Since 1975, however, there have been at least 165 second reading amendments moved that proposed to strike from the motion the words that authorized second reading and to replace those words with different provisions that proposed to affect the bill adversely. Not surprisingly, each and every one of these motions was moved by a non-government Senator.

The Senate agreed to 21 (or 12.7 per cent) of these motions and thereby derailed at least that many bills, some temporarily and others permanently. Of the 21, one had the effect of defeating a bill[140] and two others called for bills to be withdrawn and redrafted in ways that the motions specified. The remaining 18 successful motions affected bills in ways that inflicted less direct and lasting damage: eight referred bills to committee, seven precluded further consideration of bills until certain events had taken place, and the other three delayed further consideration until specific dates. With one exception, therefore, these winning motions did not actually cause the defeat of legislation. In principle at least, each of them left open the possibility of the bill in question receiving a second reading at some later time—for example, after having been rewritten in the ways specified by the amendment—if the government was willing to pay the Senate's price.

Perhaps the most famous, or infamous, of such amendments in recent memory were those offered in October and November 1975, amendments that were soon to lead to the dismissal of the Whitlam Government. With regard to each of several bills, including the essential appropriation bills, there was a motion before the Senate stating 'that this Bill be now read a second time.' In each case, an Opposition Senator moved to 'Leave out all words after 'That', insert 'this Bill be not further proceeded with until the Government agrees to

the Procedure Office for her assistance in identifying the kinds of second reading amendments discussed here.

140 On 26 February 1985, an amendment was made to replace the text of a motion for second reading. When considering such an amendment, the Senate first voted on whether to leave out the words already in the motion. Then, when that question was resolved in the affirmative, the Senate next voted on whether to insert the words that had been proposed to replace the words it had just voted to omit. In this case, the Senate agreed to leave out the words of the motion but then rejected two versions of the words proposed in their place. The *Journals* reports that 'The President drew attention to the fact that all that was left of Senator Chipp's motion was the word 'That' which, by itself, was not acceptable as a motion.' (*Journals of the Senate*, 26 February 1985: 57) The standing orders have since been amended to preclude this absurdity.

submit itself to the judgment of the people, the Senate being of the opinion that the Prime Minister and his Government no longer have the trust and confidence of the Australian people' for reasons each amendment proceeded to enumerate. In each case also, the Senate agreed to the motion as amended, which no longer authorized second reading. After Whitlam's dismissal, however, the bills that were necessary to ensure the availability of supply during the coming election period were quickly revived and passed the Senate.

Amendments in committee of the whole

The best opportunity for Senators to affect the content of new laws arises when bills are subject to amendment during the process of considering them in committee of the whole.[141] Table 7.2 presents a general picture of how often Senators have availed themselves of this opportunity in recent years, and with what success.[142]

As we observed earlier, the number of bills that the Senate passed has varied from year to year and, not surprisingly, so too has the number of bills to which amendments were moved as well as the number of bills to which amendments were agreed. On the other hand, what is striking about the data in Table 7.2 is the stability of the percentages of bills passed that were subject to one or more amendments. During five of the six years between 1996 and 2001, Senators proposed at least one change in no fewer than 43.5 per cent and no more than 45 per cent of the bills that the Senate ultimately approved. In the world of social science, and especially political

141 This discussion treats amendments and Senate requests for amendments as if they were the same, and references in the text to amendments should be understood to encompass requests as well. Constitutionally, amendments and requests are not the same, as advocates of the primacy of the House would be quick to point out. My reasons for taking them together are threefold. First, amendments and requests for amendments are not alternatives; depending on the nature of the bill being considered, each is the only means available to the Senate if it wants to change the text of that bill. Second, advocates of the Senate's powers argue that the difference between amendments and requests is essentially one of form and procedure, not a difference of kind. If the Senate is determined to have the text of a money bill changed, the House must take account of the Senate's request for that change just as it must take account of a Senate amendment to some other bill, because a money bill cannot be enacted so long as the Senate request remains unresolved. And third, not irrelevantly, taking amendments and requests together greatly simplifies both the analysis and the presentation.
142 Previous inquiries into this subject have been few and far between. Helpful exceptions are O'Keeffe (1996) and Elliott (1997), both officials of the Senate, and Lovell (1994) and Uhr (1997, 1998). Annual reports of the Department of the Senate include statistics.

science, and legislative research even more so, greater variability is the norm. Fortunately, the dip to 35.3 per cent in 1998 provides an exception to what otherwise would be a disconcerting regularity.

Whatever changes may have been taking place in Parliament or in Australian politics more generally, in most years Senators sought to amend (directly or by request) more than 40 per cent of the bills they passed. Nor are we finding a scattering of amendments that amounted, on average, to just about one for every two bills. The total number of amendments that Senators proposed also varied from year to year, but resulted in an average of no less than 7.5 amendments that were moved per bill, and more than 10 per bill in three of the six years. This calculation includes all the bills that Senators did not attempt to amend at all. If we ask instead how many amendments Senators offered, on average, to those bills that were subject to any such attempts, we find that the average number of amendments exceeded 20 per bill during 1996–99 before declining to 16 per bill in 2000 and 2001.[143]

These data by themselves would seem to put paid to any thought that Senators (or, more aptly, parties in the Senate) do not perceive the Senate chamber as a forum in which to at least attempt to legislate, or perhaps to use amendments as a procedural device for formulating and publicizing important policy differences among the parties. By their nature, however, averages can disguise as much as they reveal, and that certainly is true in this instance. In fact, amendment activity in the committee of the whole was quite concentrated. For each of the six years, ten bills accounted for more than 60 per cent of all the amendments moved and voted on, and more than 70 per cent in 1999 and 80 per cent in 1996. If we were to eliminate these bills from the calculations, the average numbers of amendments in Table 7.2 would drop precipitously. The averages in the table certainly would be a poor basis for predicting the number of amendments moved during consideration of any individual bill.

What we need to ask next, of course, is how often efforts to amend bills have succeeded. Turning again to Table 7.2, we find that, over the entire period, the Senate agreed to at least one amendment or request to more than one-third of the bills it passed. The annual percentages again are quite consistent, varying from roughly 33 per cent to roughly 39 per

---

143   This analysis is unable to take account of motions to amend bills simply by striking provisions from them. When such a motion is made, the Senate does not vote on whether to remove the provision in question from the bill. Instead, the Senate votes on whether the provision should 'stand as printed.' Therefore, a majority of at least 39 votes is required to preserve the provision. If the outcome is a tie vote instead, the provision has failed to receive majority support and so it is stricken from the bill.

TABLE 7.2: Frequency of winning amendments moved in
committee of the whole, 1996–2001[1]

	1996	1997	1998	1999	2000	2001
Number of bills passed by the Senate	85	224	139	206	181	171
Number of bills to which amendments were moved	37	101	49	90	80	77
Percentage of bills passed to which amendments were moved	43.5	45.0	35.3	43.7	44.2	45.0
Number of bills to which amendments were agreed	31	81	46	80	71	50
Percentage of bills passed to which amendments were agreed	36.5	36.2	33.1	38.8	39.2	29.2
Total number of amendments moved	879	2151	1454	2136	1383	1288
Total number of amendments agreed	390	1337	780	1605	866	1013
Percentage of amendments agreed	44.4	62.2	53.6	75.1	62.6	78.6
Average number of amendments moved per bill passed	10.3	9.6	10.5	10.4	7.6	7.5
Average number of amendments agreed per bill passed	4.6	6.0	5.6	7.8	4.8	5.9

Source: *Business of the Senate*, editions for 1996–2001, produced by the Senate Table Office.
1.   Includes requests for amendments; excludes amendments on which free votes were permitted, and amendments to amendments and amendments moved but then withdrawn or left pending; excludes divisions on whether matter in a bill, proposed to be stricken or replaced, should stand as printed; treats two or more amendments considered together as one amendment.

cent. Only in 2001, the last year covered by this study, did this percentage slip to just below 30 per cent. Over the entire six-year period, the Senate agreed to an average of slightly less than six amendments to every bill that it passed, the annual rate varying from a low of 4.6 in 1996 to a high of 7.8 in 1999. (Again, however, the same caveat about these averages applies.) Furthermore, the Senate approved considerably more than half of the amendments that Senators proposed. Only in 1996 did the percentage of amendments agreed to fall below the 50 per cent level (44.4 per cent in 1996). In 1997 and 2000, the Senate agreed to more than three of every five amendments; and in 1999 and 2001, the success rate of amendments exceeded 75 per cent. In quantitative terms, the Senate chamber has been a hotbed of policy change: more than a thousand amendments were offered in most years; in some years, more than a thousand were approved; almost half of the bills passed were subject to amendment; more than a third of those bills were amended; and on average, the Senate approved more than half of the amendments that Senators proposed, and more than six amendments for each bill that the Senate passed.

This is only part of the story, however, because not all amendments are the same. For one thing, some are of greater significance than others, just as some bills are more significant than others. In fact, it can be argued that, as a general though not invariable rule, the most significant bills are the ones that Senators are likely to be most interested in amending. If so, the number of amendments proposed to different bills can be taken as a measure, albeit an imprecise one, of the relative importance of those bills or at least the controversy they inspired. At a minimum, we need to be cautious about averages, such as the average numbers of amendments moved or approved per bill, because such averages conceal considerable variation. While Table 7.2 shows that Senators proposed at least one amendment to almost half the bills they passed, the other side of that coin is that a majority of bills was passed without any formal procedural effort being made to change them.

A smaller number of bills were subjected to large numbers of amendments that the Senate approved. To choose just one example from each year, the Senate agreed to 167 amendments[144] in the committee of the whole to the Workplace Relations and Other Legislation Amendment Bill 1996; 277 to the Telecommunications Bill 1996 that the Senate passed in 1997; 198 to the Native Title Amendment Bill 1997 [No. 2], passed in 1998; 173 to the Aboriginal and Torres Strait Islander Heritage Protection Bill 1998, passed in 1999; a mere 59 to the Family and Community Services and Veterans' Affairs Legislation Amendment (Debt Recovery) Bill 2000; and 176 to the Financial Services Reform Bill 2001. If these and a handful of other bills were excluded from the calculations, that average of more than six amendments approved for each bill the Senate passed would be much, much lower.

Equally important, there are different reasons for Senators to propose amendments and for the Senate to agree to them. If we apply a dichotomy familiar to students of Congress, we can suppose that Senators will propose some amendments with the hope or even expectation of changing the bill and thereby affecting public policy; but we also can expect that Senators will offer other amendments for purposes of position-taking—to clearly differentiate the positions of

---

144 These numbers exclude amendments to amendments and amendments that were withdrawn.

their party from the other parties on the subjects those amendments address—even though they do not expect the amendments to prevail. Furthermore, of course, the consideration of amendments, like almost everything else in Parliament House, takes place in a partisan context. Senators, except the handful of Independents, normally do not propose amendments solely at their own initiative; they act on behalf of their parties. So it is essential to distinguish between amendments that are offered by non-government Senators to change or challenge government policy from those that are offered by government Senators to improve or correct government bills or to embody the policy compromises to which the government has agreed in order to construct its winning majority coalition.

In 1948, a spirited 'case for the defence' of the Senate was published by J.R. Odgers, later to become the Clerk of the Senate and the original author of *Australian Senate Practice* (later named in his honour). In his article, Odgers (1948: 91–92) sought to show that the Senate had been successful as 'a House of review' (a concept, as I have argued, of recurring and profound fuzziness) by pointing out that, between 1937 and 1948, the Senate had made 173 amendments or requests for amendments that became law to 47 bills from the House. However, Odgers acknowledged a possibility that Fusaro later confirmed:

> A check of the Senate debates, however, reveals that of the amendments and requests Odgers writes about, some were made by Opposition-controlled Senates, and the great majority were sponsored by the Government itself and usually introduced by a Minister or other Government representative in the chamber. Thus, Odgers' 'defence' may show a certain usefulness on the part of the Senate in that it affords a Government a second chance to perfect its own legislation; but it does not demonstrate any tendency for the Senate to act independently, save when the Government has controlled only the lower house. (Fusaro 1967: 333)

In fact, the one Senate amendment to which Odgers specifically referred was one that the government evidently proposed to correct 'an important flaw' in the measure that was discovered during the Senate's consideration of the bill.

The moral is that the sheer numbers of Senate amendments tell us something, but not nearly as much as we would like to know. By looking a little more closely at the six bills that the Senate amended in so many respects, we can glimpse some of the different patterns and dynamics that can underlie the numbers. In some instances, the amendment process is dominated by the government for its own purposes. In the case of the 1996 workplace relations bill and the 1997 telecommunications bill, 98 per cent of the winning amendments to each bill were government amendments, as were 89 per cent of successful amendments to the 2001 financial services bill.[145] However, the Opposition offered almost as many winning amendments as did the government to the 1998 native title bill; amendments to the family and community services bill of 2000 also were just as likely to come from the Opposition as from the government. By contrast, the Opposition and the Democrats joined together to propose all but one of the 173 amendments that the Senate approved to the Aboriginal and Torres Strait Islander Heritage Protection Bill passed by the Senate in 1999; only one government amendment to the bill prevailed.

Even when presented with such stark differences in outcomes, we have to be careful about the inferences we draw. Government amendments may win in the face of opposition from some non-government parties; however, such amendments also may be technical amendments that fail to embody policy differences that divide the parties, or they may constitute compromises that the government has negotiated with non-government parties—or all of the above, depending on the amendment. Similarly, when the government and the Opposition share amendment victories evenly, that could reflect a very closely divided Senate in which the minor parties and Independents support the government on one amendment and then vote with the Opposition on the next. On the other hand, it could reflect a harmonious situation in which government and Opposition have worked out their differences and, perhaps for purposes of public presentation, have agreed to share credit for offering the amendments that implement their agreement. The same might even be true when the Opposition offers most of the winning amendments; it may do so with the acquiescence of the government; such an understanding even might be an element of the agreement that the government and Opposition reached with each other.[146]

One way to differentiate among such possibilities is to look not only at which parties offered the winning amendments, but which of them

---

145 Few things in parliaments are as simple as they may seem. A helpful reader kindly pointed out in a personal communication that the telecommunications bill had been examined in detail by one of the Senate's legislative committees. 'The majority report [of the committee] made 64 broad recommendations for amendments. Non-government senators also made additional recommendations in minority reports but, given the shortcomings found by the committee (which had a government majority), the government would have been foolish to ignore them. *All the government amendments are attributable to the committee's report.*' (emphasis added)

146 Some amendments are circulated and offered jointly, as the notes accompanying some of the tables in this chapter indicate.

offered amendments that did not win—amendments that were negatived, in the unfortunate parlance of the Senate. The Senate did not reject any amendments to either the 2000 family and community services bill or the 2001 financial services bill. On the other hand, there were 239 losing non-government amendments (204 from the Opposition) to the 1996 workplace relations bill, compared with 167 amendments (164 from the government) that won; and the 1997 telecommunications bill, to which 271 government amendments were made, also was subject to six winning and 76 losing non-government amendments. In the case of the 1998 native title bill, which saw 89 government amendments and 86 Opposition amendments passed, 262 non-government amendments (but only seven Opposition) amendments were defeated, compared with only five government amendments.

We can infer with confidence that there are serious party differences over bills to which many amendments are offered and negatived. However, we need to be somewhat more cautious about our inferences regarding bills that were subject to few losing amendments or none at all. That record could reflect consensus in the Senate. However, it also could reflect a deliberate decision by one or more non-government parties simply to oppose the government's legislation, not to try to ameliorate its evils by amendment or to offer their own policy alternatives (which would involve having to formulate them with precision and defend them in the chamber). Or consider the Aboriginal and Torres Strait Islander bill that the Senate passed in 1999. The ALP and the Democrats jointly proposed 172 amendments to the bill that the Senate approved; by contrast, the government offered only one winning amendment and two losing amendments. Perhaps the government, recognizing that it lacked 'the numbers' on this bill at that time, saw no useful purpose in offering more amendments that it knew would be defeated, especially since the government always knows that it will have a second bite at the proverbial apple when the House either amends any Senate amendments that the government cannot accept without change, or when the House simply rejects those amendments, returning them to the Senate in either case for renewed consideration.

The legislative process in any truly democratic assembly is a complicated business; there often may be more than one reason why something does or does not happen, which is precisely what makes studying it both interesting and challenging. By itself, knowing which parties have won and which parties have lost on amendments in the Senate chamber, and how often, tells us part of an interesting story. To understand the full story, we would need to know why each amendment was moved and how important or controversial, how good or bad, each party thought it to be. Even worse, we would need to know what other amendments might have been offered but were not. That kind of rich and textured understanding cannot be achieved by any kind of quantitative analysis; each important bill has its own story, which is why case studies of 'how a bill becomes a law' can be so valuable. However, the fact that quantitative analysis has limits does not make it pointless, both because of the questions it can answer and the others which it can identify and specify.

So we turn next to the record of each party group in the Senate in proposing amendments (which, again, includes requests for amendments) in the committee of the whole. Table 7.3 presents data on the amendments moved on behalf of each party; Table 7.4 addresses the frequencies with which those amendments won and lost.

The clearest message of Table 7.3 is one we already have heard: that the opportunity to move amendments to bills in the committee of the whole is an opportunity for the government as well as for non-government parties. In fact, the government's own drafting procedures recognize that amendments to a bill may need to be drafted while the Senate is considering it, and without a chance to subject them to the normal vetting process. The normal process, as described in the *Legislation Handbook*, by which the government prepares, reviews, and approves bills and amendments is impressively elaborate. In general, the same process that applies to bills also applies to amendments that the government contemplates proposing or accepting. However, the authors of the *Handbook* acknowledge that:

> In the Senate, there will be situations where government amendments are negotiated and agreed during debate on a bill, or prepared in anticipation of their likely need during debate to ensure passage, and there will not be time for the formal approvals to be sought. In such situations, it is up to the relevant minister to clear any amendments with the Prime Minister, other ministers, and the relevant government members' policy committee, as appropriate and as time permits.[147]

In 1999 and again in 2001, the government accounted for more than half of the committee amendments on which the Senate voted. In the latter year, government Senators, almost always ministers, offered more than 3.5 times as many amendments as did Opposition Senators. In the other four years, the Opposition did move more amendments than the government but not by particularly wide margins, and in only one of the six years (1997) did the Opposition account for as much as 40 per cent of all the amendments moved. In part, this may reflect a difficulty that

---

147 *Legislation Handbook*, Department of the Prime Minister and Cabinet, 2000: 53. [www.dpmc.gov.au/pdfs/LegislationHandbookMayoo/pdf]

the ALP had in adjusting to being in Opposition after 13 years in government. It also may be that Labor sometimes made deliberate decisions not to worry about 'fixing' government bills; if there were problems in government bills that were going to pass, they were problems for the government to identify and solve. In addition, one close observer has suggested an additional reason:

> Organisationally, the ALP in opposition has given firm authority over portfolio issues to its shadow ministers, most of whom are in the House of Representatives. They therefore do not understand how a legislative chamber works and do not appreciate how the Senate can be used. They also are electorally very sensitive, which sometimes has led them to decide that no action is better than action that could make the electorate nervous.[148]

If we sum together the amendments moved by all 'other' Senators—all the non-government and non-Opposition Senators—they accounted for a majority of the amendments offered in 1998 but only one of every eight in the following year. It is fair to say that in three of the six years, one group of Senators dominated the amending process by offering most of the amendments—the minor party and Independent Senators in 1998 and the government in 1999 and in 2001—but not in the other three years in which the initiative in proposing amendments was more evenly distributed.[149]

It would seem, then, that the stage of detailed consideration of bills in the committee of the whole which, it should be emphasized, takes place in the chamber on public view, is not a forum dominated by an Opposition party that is ready with amendment after amendment designed either to improve government legislation or pick it apart, clause by clause. As often as not, the other non-government parties and Independents have offered more amendments than the Opposition, notwithstanding their smaller numbers and more limited resources for developing amendments.[150] By and large, the Democrats have proposed more amendments than the Greens (putting aside the amendments they offered jointly), which is consistent with the notion that the Democrats are more likely than the Greens to find something worth trying to salvage in bills brought forth by a Liberal-National government.

---

148 Personal communication to the author from an officer of the Senate.
149 It also should be noted that these data are subject to sudden jolts that do not recur. Note particularly the 165 amendments that Senator Harris of the One Nation party moved in 2000 (108 of them to the Gene Technology Bill 2000), compared with seven in the preceding year and 19 in the following year.
150 In addition to needing resources to develop the policies expressed in amendments, non-government parties also need to have their amendments drafted. The government has its Office of Parliamentary Counsel; the Department of the Senate provides a drafting service for non-government Senators.

TABLE 7.3: Party activity in moving amendments in
committee of the whole, 1996–2001[1]

	1996	1997	1998	1999	2000	2001
Total number of amendments moved	879	2151	1454	2136	1383	1288
Amendments moved by:						
Government[2]	282 (32.1%)	685 (31.8%)	355 (24.4%)	1243 (58.2%)	375 (27.1%)	709 55.0%
Opposition[2]	312 (35.5%)	897 (41.7%)	356 (24.5%)	629 (29.4%)	489 (35.4%)	193 (14.9%)
Australian Democrats	126 (14.3%)	411 (19.1%)	436 (30.0%)	155 (7.3%)	206 (14.9%)	321 (24.9%)
Greens[3]	150 (17.1%)	99 (4.6%)	135 (9.3%)	100 (4.7%)	142 (10.3%)	41 (3.2%)
National Party	0	0	1 (0.1%)	0	0	0
Australian Democrats and Greens jointly	0	33 (1.5%)	151 (10.4%)	0	0	0
One Nation	0	0	0	7 (0.3%)	165 (11.9%)	19 (1.5%)
Independents	9 (1.0%)	26 (1.2%)	20 (1.4%)	2 (0.1%)	6 (0.4%)	5 (0.4%)

Source: *Business of the Senate*, editions for 1996–2001, produced by the Senate Table Office.
1. Includes requests for amendments; excludes amendments on which free votes were permitted, and amendments to amendments and amendments moved but then withdrawn or left pending; excludes divisions on whether matter in a bill, proposed to be stricken or replaced, should stand as printed; treats two or more amendments considered together as one amendment.
2   Includes amendments moved jointly with one or more other parties.
3   Combines Australian Greens and the Greens (WA).

The data in Table 7.3 are frustrating in that they do not reveal obvious patterns or trends. What we can say is that, for each of the three groups of Senators (government, Opposition, and 'other'), the percentage of amendments that each offered ranged roughly between the mid-20s and the mid-30s in four of the six years. However, the percentage of government amendments twice jumped to more than one-half; the percentage of Opposition amendments fell below 15 per cent and rose above 40 percent; and the percentage of amendments from the minor parties and Independents hit an even higher high and an even lower low. Furthermore, the exceptional years for each group fit no evident temporal pattern, nor are there any apparent relationships between the percentages of amendments that the government, Opposition, and minor parties offered and any changes that occurred in the partisan composition of the Senate (see Table 6.2). Between July 1999 and September 2001, for example, the number of government (Liberal and National) Senators held constant at 35, while the percentage of government amendments fell from 58.2 per cent in 1999 to 27.1 per cent in 2000 before rising again to 55.0 per cent in 2001.

The Opposition always has needed the support of the Democrats to win in the chamber, as we have seen. So we might expect the Opposition alone, or those two parties together, to offer the largest share of amendments when they needed the fewest additional votes for victory. But if that is what we expected, we would be mistaken. Throughout 2000, the ALP and the Democrats together held 38 Senate seats compared with 35 for the government, and the two parties proposed 50.3 per cent of all committee amendments. Throughout all of 1997 and 1998, however, only 35 Senators belonged to the two largest non-government parties, and those parties moved 60.8 per cent of the amendments in 1997 and 54.5 per cent in the following year. The variations that Table 7.3 reveals are not associated, in any way that these data reveal, with changes in the ever-important and all-important 'numbers' in the Senate.

Ultimately, the numbers or percentages of amendments that each party has offered are far less important, especially in light of the diverse reasons why amendments may be offered, than how often its amendments have won or lost, either on the voices or by divisions, which is the subject of Table 7.4. The table speaks to two related questions. First, what are the sources of winning amendments? Of all the amendments to which the Senate agreed during 1996–2001, what share of them were offered on behalf of each party? And second, how successful was each party in having its amendments approved? Of all the amendments offered on behalf of each party, what share of those amendments did the Senate agree to?

With respect to the first question, the table shows that the government accounted for far more of the winning amendments than did the Opposition, even though it always must be remembered that neither the government nor the Opposition had a majority in the Senate. Throughout this period, the government held between six and nine more seats than the Opposition and, for this reason, the government had a wider array of possible winning coalitions that it could form. The government, for example, always could win just by joining forces with the Democrats while, for the Opposition, having the voting support of the Democrats never was enough. So perhaps we should expect to find that the government was the source of somewhat more winning amendments than the Opposition, but the magnitude of the differences is interesting.

TABLE 7.4: Success rates of amendments and requests moved in
committee of the whole, by party, 1996–2001[1]

	1996	1997[2]	1998[3]	1999	2000	2001
Percentage of all amendments agreed to that were moved by:[4]						
Government	72.1	50.5	44.9	77.0	43.2	69.9
Opposition	6.9	29.9	35.3	19.6	45.3	12.4
Australian Democrats	8.5	16.0	12.8	2.4	10.5	16.9
Greens	10.8	1.6	2.9	0.7	0.8	0.9
Independents	1.8	1.6	1.9	0.1	0	0
Frequency with which amendments were agreed to when moved by:[5]						
Government	99.6	98.5	98.6	99.4	99.7	99.9
Opposition	8.7	44.6	77.2	50.1	80.2	65.3
Australian Democrats	26.2	52.1	22.9	25.2	44.2	53.3
Greens	28.0	22.2	17.0	16.2	4.9	19.5
Independents	77.8	80.8	75.0	100.0	0	0

1. Includes requests for amendments; excludes amendments on which free votes were permitted, and amendments to amendments and amendments moved but then withdrawn or left pending; excludes divisions on whether matter in a bill, proposed to be stricken or replaced, should stand as printed; treats two or more amendments considered together as one amendment.
2 Percentages do not sum to 100 per cent because five successful amendments were moved jointly by the Australian Democrats and the Greens.
3 Percentages do not sum to 100 per cent because 16 successful amendments were moved jointly by the Australian Democrats and the Greens, and one moved by the National Party (but not for the Coalition government).
4 The number of all amendments and requests that were moved by each group of Senators and agreed to by the Senate as a percentage of all the amendments and requests *to which the Senate agreed.*
5 The number of all amendments and requests that were moved by each group of Senators and agreed to by the Senate as a percentage of all the amendments and requests *that group of Senators* moved.

In three of the six years, the government was the source of about 70 per cent of the amendments that the Senate approved, and never less than 40 per cent. The Opposition, by contrast, offered less than seven per cent of the winning amendments in one year (1996), and only once was the source of more than 40 per cent of those amendments. The exceptional year was 2000, when the Opposition accounted for a slightly greater percentage of winning amendments than the government, and in 1998 the figures for the government and Opposition are reasonably close. In 1996, however, the ratio of winning amendments moved by the government to those moved by the

Opposition was more than ten to one, and five years later, it was more than five to one.

Another way of approaching the same question is to compare the percentage of winning amendments that were moved by each party with the percentage of all amendments on which the Senate acted that were moved by each party; in other words, to compare the record of the government and Opposition from this table with their record from the preceding table. Consider 1996, which offers the most dramatic contrast. In that year, 32.1 per cent of all committee amendments were offered on behalf of the government, but 72.1 per cent of all the committee amendments that won were government amendments. In comparison, in the same year the Opposition proposed slightly more amendments, 35.5 per cent of the total, but originated less than seven per cent of the winning amendments. In all six years, the government offered a higher percentage of winning amendments than all amendments; in four of the six years, the opposite was true for the Opposition. The government was not the source of larger shares of the winning amendments simply because it offered larger proportions of all amendments.

When we look at the record of the two minor parties, we find that, after 1996, the Democrats accounted for a larger share of winning amendments each year than did the Greens, but the Democrats also offered higher percentages of all committee amendments than did the Greens. What is more interesting is to compare the Opposition with the two minor parties together as sources of winning amendments. In 1996 and 2001, the Democrats and Greens combined to propose a larger percentage of winning amendments than the Opposition. In four of the six years, however, considerably more of the amendments the Senate approved were moved by the Opposition than by the other two non-government parties combined.

With respect to the second question that Table 7.4 addresses, there is no question of the government's success in having the Senate agree to its amendments in the committee of the whole. When no less than 98.5 per cent of the government's amendments won each year, nothing more on the subject needs to be said. The track record of the non-government parties is far more varied and interesting. The Opposition's success rate ranged about as widely as possible, from 8.7 per cent in 1996 to 80.2 per cent in 2000. But the Opposition's dismal record in 1996 should not disguise the fact that, in the other five years, more than 40 per cent of its amendments won, with at least half of its amendments winning in three of those years. After 1996, the Democrats consistently enjoyed more success with their amendments than did the Greens, which may reflect the much greater experience that the Democrats have had in the

Senate. The same data also may tell us something about where each of the two minor parties usually has been situated, in policy terms, in relation to the governing Coalition and the Labor Opposition. By no means are the two possible explanations mutually exclusive.

In general, the government has been active and successful in using its opportunities to offer amendments to its own bills in the committee of the whole. It sometimes has accounted for a majority of all the amendments moved, although usually for something more like one-quarter or one-third of those amendments. More important, in four of the six years, it was the source of a greater percentage of the winning amendments than all the other parties combined, and in only one year did Opposition Senators move a larger share of the winning amendments. Most impressive of all, the government's amendments rarely have lost, even though it never has had its own numerical majority in the Senate.

How to account for these findings? There are two general reasons why the government would want to propose amendments to its own bills: either it wants to, or it needs to. The government may offer amendments to make improvements in its bills (as in the case to which Odgers referred in his 1948 article). The desirability of making certain improvements may come to the government's attention after its bill has been drafted and introduced in the House; or the wisdom of making those improvements may emerge while the House is acting on the bill, but the government may not have time to make them at that stage of the legislative process or it may prefer to make them in the Senate. By deferring its amendments until a bill has had its second reading in the Senate, the government gains time to assess its possible amendments and perfect the ones it decides to make. And by moving those amendments in the Senate instead of the House, the government is able to avoid any suggestion that it has had to make any compromises or concessions in the chamber where it enjoys unquestioned control. In the House, according to David Solomon:

> Tight control over the government party or parties is maintained irrespective of the importance of the particular issue. The most trivial matter is deemed important to the prestige of the political parties. Even if an opposition discovers a patent error in a bill, an amendment in the House will not succeed unless the minister in charge of the bill decides to accept the amendment. Most ministers, faced with that situation, prefer to correct their errors by introducing their own amendments, generally when the bill reaches the Senate. They argue with backbench supporters who want to vote for an opposition improvement to a bill that the government and the Parliamentary Draftsman will need to look at the matter to see whether other clauses might also be affected. But the basic emotional argument, which so completely pervades Parliament House in Canberra that it rarely

has to be voiced, is that the government will somehow suffer damage if a vote goes against it—irrespective of the issue on which the vote is taken. (Solomon 1978: 39)

Alternatively, of course, the government may propose amendments in the Senate to its own bills because those amendments are the price it has to pay for the extra votes it always needs to win (which takes us back to the emphasis in the last chapter on successful coalition-building). So some 'government amendments' could equally well have been proposed by the other party with which they were negotiated. Unfortunately, Tables 7.3 and 7.4 do not enable us to determine how often the government has moved amendments out of choice and how often it has acted out of necessity. The fact that the government's amendments almost always win is consistent with both generic explanations.

Many, perhaps most, of the government's amendments probably are to make improvements in its bills in the form of minor adjustments or corrections of inadvertent errors and oversights—changes that none of the other parties has any reason to oppose. Consequently, those amendments always win. The remaining government amendments almost certainly are coalition-creating amendments. If there is an understanding with one or more non-government parties (or Independents) that they will join the government in supporting the amendments they have negotiated with the government, and that they then will support the bill as amended, those amendments also will win, except in the unlikely event of a misunderstanding or a collapse of the coalition agreement.

The tables also show that, taken together, the non-government parties usually, but not always, have offered more amendments in the committee of the whole than the government. Also in general, the Opposition usually, but not always, has offered more amendments than the Democrats and Greens combined. We can think of the government and Opposition as alternative cores of potentially winning coalitions, each trying to attract the additional votes it needs at the expense of the other (although we found in the last chapter that often this is not the case, and that the Opposition often has voted with the government on divisions). In such cases, both the government and the Opposition have incentives to move amendments that will attract the winning margin of additional votes or implement winning coalition agreements that already have been made. Unlike the government, though, the non-government parties do not have to propose amendments to make minor improvements or technical corrections in bills. Only if we could identify and set aside the government amendments offered for the latter purposes could we begin to make a true comparison of how often the two major players in the Senate have used the amendment process for coalition-building purposes.

The government accounts for a large share of all winning amendments and almost all government amendments win because some of its amendments, the minor and technical ones as well as the negotiated ones, are certain to win. The Opposition accounts for a smaller percentage of winning amendments and its winning percentage is consistently lower than the government's because some of its amendments are almost as certain to lose. Like the government, the Opposition has more than one general reason for moving amendments. It may propose amendments that it thinks or at least hopes will win. Perhaps the government may not oppose them with the hope that the Opposition then will be satisfied with the amended bill and so will support it. Or perhaps the Opposition amendments will attract the support of the minor parties and so will defeat the government. There also are occasions, however, when the Opposition offers amendments, even knowing they will lose, because those amendments enable it to define and publicize its policy disagreements with the government (see, e.g., Young 1997: 97–99). As I already have observed, any Opposition has to balance its desire to win a vote today against its desire to win an election tomorrow. The Opposition sometimes will have a choice between moving an amendment that represents less than its optimal policy but that is likely to unite all (or a sufficient number of) non-government Senators against the government, and offering an amendment that presents its policy clearly though in a way that will not bring it the allies it needs to win. In those instances, sometimes it will choose one and sometimes the other, depending on the policy and electoral consequences it envisions.

There are other possibilities we have not considered and other implications of the data that we have not explored. But there is only so much that can be gleaned, and so much that can be inferred with any confidence, from data on the successes and failures of amendments when we lack information about which parties supported them and which opposed them. The data in Tables 7.2–7.4 encompass all the amendments in committee of the whole on which the Senate voted, including amendments decided on the voices as well as those decided by divisions. Only when there is the record on an amendment that a division provides can we delve further into why it won or lost. So just as we looked at all divisions in the last chapter and divisions on reading motions earlier in this chapter, we now turn to an examination of divisions on amendments moved in the committee of the whole.

Divisions on committee amendments

By focusing on committee amendments that the Senate decided by divisions, we can gain more purchase on the extent to which non-government parties have tried to use the process of considering legislation in committee of the whole for their own purposes and how successful they have been, and we can examine how often non-government parties have (or have not) joined with each other, or with the government, to pass or defeat amendments. Before doing so, however, three preliminary matters need to be addressed briefly.

First, and as I have emphasized before: not all amendments are the same. When we looked in the preceding chapter at all Senate divisions between 1996 and 2001, we were not mixing apples and oranges; we were mixing grapes and watermelons. Some of the issues those divisions settled obviously were far more important than others. The justification for examining them all together is that, in each case, one party or another saw some reason for insisting that question be decided by a division.[151] Now when we look at all committee amendments on which the Senate voted during the same period, we confront the same fact and the same analytical problem it creates. Some of the amendments were much more important than others, but there is no manageable and ultimately satisfactory way to know which are which. For example, we supposed earlier in this chapter that some government amendments were of a minor or technical nature while others embodied important policy changes that the government needed to make in order to secure passage of its bills. Without examining each amendment, we can only guess at how many government amendments fell into each category. By looking at committee amendments that gave rise to divisions, not only do we gain access to more interesting information about each of them, we also can invoke a reasonable hope that we are looking at amendments that, more often than not but not always, were more important than the amendments that the Senate accepted or rejected on the voices.

---

151 In some cases, the reason for calling a division may have had nothing to do with the importance of the question to be decided. For example, the losers on the voices may refrain from calling a division, even though the question being decided is an important one. The losers may prefer not to document the composition of the winning coalition that defeated them, or they may want to save time and demonstrate a cooperative attitude. In other instances, a non-government party may call a division, which consumes valuable government time, when it wants to send a message to the government that it is angry or frustrated about something else that the government has or has not done.

Second, not all amendments are offered for the same reason. Earlier I offered a distinction that is familiar in American political science between policy-making and position-taking. The calculations of victory or defeat in the Senate are relatively simple; it suffices to be able to predict with confidence the voting intentions of a small number of disciplined party groups and a smaller number of Independents. So when a truly important amendment comes to a vote, party leaders who have done their homework often should know already whether they are about to win or lose. And, as we shall see, in some years, the winning percentages of some parties have been so high or so low that party leaders still could make informed guesses about the outcomes of votes on committee amendments even when they had only imperfect information about others' voting intentions.

So we have to assume that divisions were called on different amendments for different reasons. In some instances, divisions undoubtedly were called with the expectation of changing the outcomes of votes on amendments. If, for instance, the result of the first vote on an amendment, a vote taken by the voices, was not indicative of the known positions of the parties on that amendment, bringing in all Senators to participate in a division reasonably could be expected to produce a different result. In other instances, divisions probably were called because the fate of amendments truly was in doubt, and proponents or opponents who had been declared the losers when the votes were taken on the voices saw nothing to be lost and something possibly to be gained by calling divisions on the same amendments. But in still other instances, divisions certainly were called without any hope or expectation of winning, but for the purpose of position-taking: putting each party on the public record as favouring or opposing the policy position that an amendment embodied. In these cases, the divisions were less elements of the legislative process than they were elements of the ongoing electoral process, with each party using votes in Parliament to position itself favourably vis-a-vis the others.

And third, the undeniable facts that some amendments are more important than others and that some are offered for different reasons than others both can be adduced to sustain an argument that the kind of quantitative analysis in which we are engaged really is not very important or useful. It is quality not quantity that matters. The argument is easy to make: 'I, as a party leader, really don't care if I lose divisions on nine out of ten amendments so long as I win the tenth, because that tenth amendment is ten times more important to me and my party than all the others combined.' This may be absolutely true. In my judgment, though, what it implies is not that quantitative analysis is uninformative but that it only can tell part of the story. The work of legislatures is too complex to be reduced satisfactorily to statistics. If that were not so, they would not be very interesting at all. But numbers and statistics can enable us to identify patterns and trends, help us to speculate about the reasons for them, and encourage us to seek answers for questions that otherwise might not have occurred to us.

TABLE 7.5: Amendments moved in committee of the whole, 1996–2001[1]

	1996	1997	1998	1999	2000	2001
Total number of bills passed by the Senate	85	224	139	206	181	171
Total number of committee amendments	879	2151	1454	2136	1383	1288
Number of committee amendments decided by divisions	84	111	63	88	40	11
Percentage of committee amendments decided by divisions	9.6	5.2	4.3	4.1	2.9	0.9
Number of committee amendments decided by divisions, per bill passed	1.0	0.5	0.4	0.4	0.2	0.1
Total number of winning committee amendments	390	1337	780	1605	866	1013
Number of winning committee amendments decided by divisions	8	22	6	14	3	3
Percentage of committee amendments decided by divisions that won	9.5	19.8	9.5	15.9	7.5	27.3
Number of winning committee amendments decided by divisions, per bill passed	0.09	0.10	0.04	0.07	0.02	0.02

1   Includes requests for amendments; excludes amendments on which free votes were permitted, and amendments to amendments and amendments moved but then withdrawn or left pending; excludes divisions on whether matter in a bill, proposed to be stricken or replaced, should stand as printed; treats two or more amendments considered together as one amendment.

Now, finally, with these preliminaries having been addressed, let us turn to Table 7.5, which presents the 'big picture' on divisions on amendments that were moved in the committee of the whole. As in some of the other tables we already have examined, the ratios and percentages here are more interesting than the absolute numbers. Consider, for instance, how frequently Senators called divisions on amendments. In not one of the six years did even ten per cent of the committee amendments provoke divisions. What is more, the percentage of committee amendments that were decided by divisions declined steadily from the high-water mark of almost ten per cent to, remarkably enough, slightly less than one per cent. In 2001, the Senate acted on 1,288 committee amendments, but resorted to divisions only 11 times. If we ask how many divisions on committee amendments there were, on average, on each bill the Senate passed, we find that the question is hardly worth answering because the answers range only from 0.1 to 1.0.

The most plausible conclusion to draw is that Senators usually saw no useful purpose served by calling divisions (which are not exactly costless because they do consume time and disrupt the activities of Senators engaged in activities outside the chamber).[152] In the overwhelming majority of cases, the outcomes that divisions would have produced were foregone conclusions, so calling divisions would have been pointless except to put the positions of all parties formally on the public record. And the first half of Table 7.5 suggests that divisions on committee amendments are not very often thought to be useful for purposes of clarifying party differences on important policy questions—that is, position-taking.

There are at least three reasons why this might be so. First, the House passes most bills before they reach the Senate, and the Senate then engages in second reading debates on them before the opportunity arises to debate and vote on substantive amendments, so by then party positions usually have been fully elucidated. Second, there are other more visible and even theatrical opportunities, especially Question Time and media interviews, to define, loudly if not precisely, whatever party differences may not yet be well known. And third, there is only limited value in forcing each Senator to cast his or her individual vote on the public record because, at least for government and Opposition Senators, there is no suspense as to how each of them will vote. This is in marked contrast to the situation in the US Congress, where each Representative and Senator, by his or her votes, constructs a unique voting record that he or she has to defend at the next election.

Finally, and as a cautionary note, these data require us to bear in mind that, in the remainder of this chapter, we will be concerned with numbers that are quite small. As a result, any ratios or percentages derived from them, or trends or patterns apparent in them, must be treated gingerly.

---

152 Elliott (1997: 43) quotes a government Senator responsible for moving a tax bill through the committee of the whole in 1990 as observing that, because the legislative process is 'an uncertain and time consuming process … the government has decided in the interests of getting legislation passed that will achieve its primary purpose, but not all of its purposes, and will not be in its preferred form but will be in a workable form, it will accept the amendments moved.' Perhaps if the government had been willing to invest the time and effort, it could have defeated the amendments or amended them to make them more acceptable, but perhaps it would have had to resort to divisions to do either. Sometimes, when time is short and much work remains to be done, a legislative half-loaf is satisfying enough.

The second half of the table addresses only committee amendments that won. Of greatest interest are the numbers of committee amendments that won by divisions as percentages of all the committee amendments that were decided by divisions. In other words, when there were divisions on amendments, how frequently did those amendments win? There is no obvious trend line over time in these percentages, but the key point is that in only one of the six years did more than one in five of the divisions on amendments produce a winner. Compare these data in Table 7.5 with the percentages, found in Table 7.2, of all committee amendments (including requests) to which the Senate agreed. As we have seen, over the entire period and in every year except 1996, the Senate agreed to most amendments, and to more than three-quarters of them in 1999 and 2001. The winning percentages of those committee amendments that were decided by divisions were far, far smaller. If the fate of an amendment could be decided by a vote on the voices, it stood a good chance of winning. But if an amendment could not win on the voices, a division was unlikely to rescue it from defeat.

This points to an implication to which I shall return in the conclusion to this chapter. An amendment from a non-government party is most likely to prevail after successful negotiations that result in it being approved on the voices. In such cases, a division on the amendment is unlikely, either because the government has agreed to accept it or because the government understands that there is a certain non-government majority in support of the amendment and chooses not to document that fact by a division. The poor success rates for amendments that were decided by divisions suggest that many of these divisions were called even though their outcomes were predictable. If inter-party negotiations fail to produce agreement on an amendment, the party proposing it still may decide that a division is worthwhile, either to create a public record of everyone's positions on the proposal even though it is doomed to defeat (that is, for position-taking purposes) or with the hope that a majority in support of the amendment somehow may appear when the division takes place. These are speculations, of course; the data tell us nothing about the reasons why divisions were called on amendments that then were defeated. What we can say is that the data certainly are consistent with the idea that requiring a division on a committee amendment sometimes is a last resort for a party when prior negotiations on one of its amendments have been unsuccessful. Most last resorts fail to produce the desired result, and these divisions have been no exception to that rule.

As we have done before, let us now differentiate among these divisions on the basis of party generally and the government and

Opposition more specifically. The next table, Table 7.6, distinguishes among divisions on committee amendments moved by the government,

TABLE 7.6: Senate divisions on committee amendments, 1996–2001[1]

	1996	1997	1998	1999	2000	2001
Government amendments moved on which there were divisions	7	4	3	6	2	1
as a percentage of all amendments moved	8.3	3.6	4.8	6.8	5.0	9.1
Opposition amendments moved on which there were divisions	42	60	22	35	9	5
as a percentage of all amendments moved	50.0	54.1	34.9	39.8	22.5	45.5
Others' amendments moved on which there were divisions	35	47	38	47	29	5
as a percentage of all amendments moved	41.7	42.3	60.3	53.4	72.5	45.5
Amendments moved on which there were divisions, per bill passed						
Government	0.08	0.02	0.02	0.03	0.01	0.01
Opposition	0.49	0.27	0.16	0.17	0.05	0.03
Others'	0.41	0.21	0.27	0.23	0.16	0.03
Winning amendments opposed by the government in divisions	7	21	6	14	3	2
per bill passed	0.08	0.09	0.04	0.07	0.02	0.01
Success rate[2] in divisions on						
Government amendments	85.7	100.0	100.0	100.0	100.0	100.0
Opposition amendments	7.1	26.7	13.6	34.3	33.3	40.0
Others' amendments	11.4	10.6	7.9	4.2	0	0

1 Includes requests for amendments; excludes amendments on which free votes were permitted, and amendments to amendments and amendments moved but then withdrawn or left pending; excludes divisions on whether matter in a bill, proposed to be stricken or replaced, should stand as printed; treats two or more amendments considered together as one amendment. Amendments moved by the government or the Opposition jointly with one of the minor parties are treated as government or Opposition amendments.
2 The percentage of all government (or Opposition or others') amendments decided by divisions to which the Committee agreed.

those moved by the Opposition, and those moved by 'others'—the two minor parties, the Independent Senators, and the sole Senator representing One Nation. The numbers presented in this table are the numbers of amendments in each category *on which there were divisions*. So, for instance, the 'number of government amendments moved' for each year is the number of all government amendments that were decided by divisions, and the accompanying percentage is the percentage of government amendments moved on which there were divisions as a percentage of all amendments moved on which there were divisions.

Notice how few divisions there have been on government amendments. In absolute terms, it never required all ten fingers to count those government amendments on which divisions occurred. In percentage terms, divisions on the government's committee amendments never constituted as much as ten per cent of all such divisions. On the other hand, the government enjoyed an almost perfect success rate in the exceptional instances when its committee amendments were subject to divisions. And what of divisions on non-government committee amendments? The most striking finding is that most of the divisions on non-government amendments were not on committee amendments proposed by the Opposition. All told, there were fewer divisions (173 versus 201) on Opposition amendments than on those moved by other non-government Senators. In three of the six years, the Opposition was responsible for markedly smaller percentages of all divisions on committee amendments than were the minor party and Independent Senators.[153] In 2000, the Opposition moved less than one-quarter of the committee amendments on which divisions took place, and it never accounted for much more than half of those amendments. In absolute though not in percentage terms, we can discern a fairly steady decline in the frequency of such Opposition amendments, if we are prepared to pass over the exceptional year of 1997, but it is harder to see any trends in the numbers or percentages of divisions on amendments by other non-government Senators.

The last rows of the table tell what are perhaps more interesting stories. We observe here a steady decline in the rate at which the Senate agreed to committee amendments offered by minor party and Independent Senators when those amendments were decided by division. In fact, the Table Office lists of divisions fail to show even one such amendment in either 2000 or 2001. In each of the six years, these Senators moved no less than 40 per cent of the committee amendments on which divisions were held, but with low and decreasing rates of success. In 2000, the Democrat, Green and Independent Senators accounted for almost 75 per cent of the committee amendments on which there were divisions; yet not one of their amendments won.

By contrast, the success rate of the Opposition was much higher, though never approaching 50 per cent and far, far below the almost perfect record of victory that the government enjoyed. This is a classic

---

153 As before, the One Nation Senator is grouped here with the Independents because he also accounts for a single vote in the chamber.

question of whether the proverbial glass is half-full or half-empty. The rate at which Opposition committee amendments won on divisions increased from seven per cent in 1996 to 40 per cent five years later; even so, when push came to shove, its amendments still lost more often than they won. Now compare the Opposition's track record when committee amendments were decided by divisions with its track record on all committee amendments—that is, the data in Table 7.4 on the frequency with which the Senate agreed to all the amendments (and requests) that the Opposition moved. The Opposition's winning percentage on all committee amendments, including those decided by divisions, was, except in 1996, far higher than its winning percentage when divisions took place. When the Senate held divisions on the Opposition's committee amendments, it never won more than 40 per cent of the time; from 1997 through 2001, in comparison, the Opposition never won less than 40 per cent of the time, and in one year won at twice that rate, when we add into the mix the far greater number of committee amendments decided on the voices.

The first thing to be said is that these data support the supposition offered earlier that the relatively low rates at which committee amendments won when they were decided by divisions are attributable primarily to defeats of amendments moved by non-government Senators. But of course, there is more to be said than that.

The success rate of Opposition amendments was consistently so much lower than that of the government because of the strong likelihood that most Opposition amendments on which there were divisions were amendments that the government actively opposed. It is perfectly reasonable to suppose that a considerable number of Opposition amendments were not actively opposed by the government because it saw no need to oppose them; the amendments either were constructive or insignificant. In other cases, the government must have supported Opposition amendments, either overtly or tacitly, because those amendments embodied compromises or concessions that the government had agreed to make, either in return for explicit assurances of Opposition support or with the hope that the amendments would suffice to elicit Opposition support. When it is evident that the government supports an Opposition amendment, any other party would have no reason other than position-taking to require a division on it. So we can expect that when there were divisions on Opposition committee amendments, it was because the government was on one side of the question and the Opposition was on the other. In those cases, the government was much more likely to prevail—more likely, in terms of the preceding chapter, to succeed in building winning coalitions.

There is an even more dramatic contrast between all votes on all committee amendments and division votes for those amendments moved by the Democrat, Green, and Independent Senators (again comparing Tables 7.4 and 7.6). On their committee amendments decided by divisions, their collective success rate was never more than 11 per cent and fell to zero in 2000 and 2001. On the other hand, the rates at which the Senate agreed to all of their committee amendments were, to understate the case seriously, consistently and significantly higher. When we look at the fate of all their committee amendments, the Greens' record only once fell below that 11 per cent high for amendments decided by divisions; the Democrats' record always was at least twice that high; and the success rates for Independents on all their committee amendments was astronomically higher, before collapsing to nothing in 2000.

The same argument adduced in the preceding paragraph with regard to Opposition amendments should apply with even greater force to divisions on Democrat, Green, and Independent amendments that the government is very likely to have opposed. Furthermore, the inference that Opposition amendments were more likely to prevail over government opposition than amendments of minor party and Independent Senators is consistent with the expectation that, psychologically at least, it is considerably easier (though still challenging) for the Opposition to build winning coalitions than for other non-government Senators to do so because the Opposition needs a much smaller additional increment of votes to win. Ultimately, though, it may be less important to know how often non-government parties (and Independents) won than to know how often the government lost. That number never exceed 21 per year and only two or three in the two most recent years. Even in 1997, when the government opposed 21 amendments that won on divisions, that number constituted roughly one per cent of the more than 2100 committee amendments offered that year, and about 1.5 per cent of those committee amendments that won.

We have returned, then, to the need to construct majority coalitions in the Senate where no party has a natural electoral majority. From the success rate that the government has enjoyed when its committee amendments have been subject to divisions, we can infer that it has had little difficulty in finding the few extra votes it has needed to build one of the possible winning coalitions that we explored in the previous chapter. As we also have seen, the non-government parties have been far less successful in assembling majorities to support their committee amendments on divisions. Table 7.7 helps us to understand why.

Because party representation in the Senate has not been constant during 1996–2001 (see Table 6.2), there is no single formula that

identifies the essential elements of any majority coalitions that the
Opposition ALP or the Democrats or Greens could hope to build.[154]
During some parts of the period, for example, the Opposition absolutely

TABLE 7.7: Party support for committee amendments moved by non-government
parties and opposed by the government in the Senate, 1996–2001

	1996	1997[1]	1998[2]	1999	2000	2001
Percentage of Opposition amendments supported by[3]:						
Australian Democrats only	0	3.3	0	0	11.1	0
Greens only	57.1	26.2	31.8	51.4	66.7	40.0
Both parties	42.9	63.9	68.2	48.6	22.2	40.0
Neither party	0	6.6	0	0	0	20.0
Percentage of Australian Democrat amendments supported by:						
Opposition only	0	4.0	0	0	0	0
Greens only	20.0	44.0	47.6	87.5	100.0	100.0
Both parties	80.0	52.0	52.4	4.2	0	0
Neither party	0	0	0	8.3	0	0
Percentage of Greens' amendments supported by:						
Opposition only	30.4	5.9	0	14.3	0	0
Australian Democrats only	21.7	29.4	60.0	47.6	100.0	100.0
Both parties	43.5	47.1	40.0	4.8	0	0
Neither party	4.3	17.6	0	33.3	0	0

1   One amendment was offered jointly by the Australian Democrats and the Greens and
    opposed by the Opposition.
2   Six amendments were offered jointly by the Australian Democrats and the Greens; the
    Opposition supported four and opposed two of them.
3   If an amendment is listed as having been offered jointly by the Opposition and one of
    the minor parties, it is treated here as an Opposition amendment.

needed the Greens' one or two votes; at other times, the Opposition
could prevail without those votes if it had the support of the
Independent Senator Harradine, or all Independents, or perhaps Senator
Harris of the One Nation party as well. What we can say, however, is
that Labor could never prevail over the government without the support
of the Australian Democrats; the Democrats' support was always
necessary though never sufficient. So it is interesting to discover from

---

154 The number of votes required to win also depends on the number of votes actually
    cast. When Senators are absent from a division without being paired (to prevent
    their absence from affecting the outcome), the number of votes required to win that
    division changes accordingly.

the first section of Table 7.7 that the Opposition has had a checkered record in attracting the Australian Democrats to support its committee amendments on divisions. In only two of the six years (1997 and 1998) did the Democrats support Opposition amendments (either alone or with the Greens) so much as half the time; in 2000, the Opposition lost its essential coalition ally on two of every three divisions on committee amendments.

On the other hand, the Opposition had a wonderfully constant ally in the much smaller and, therefore, less pivotal Green delegation. During 1996–1999, the Greens (or the sole Green) voted with the Opposition (either alone or with the Democrats) on the latter's amendments more than 90 per cent of the time each year, and still 80 per cent or more of the time during 2000–2001. The Table Office records do not show a single division on an Opposition committee amendment in 1996, 1998, or 1999 on which the Opposition lacked the support of the one or two Green Senators. The ALP's problem was that its far more steadfast ally was its far less (numerically) valuable one. And here we reach the limits of what our data reveal, because we cannot infer from them how often the Opposition resolutely tried but failed to reach coalition agreements on its amendments with the Democrats, or how often it sat back, hoped for the best, and found, when the votes were cast, that its proposals were consistently more appealing to the Greens than to the Democrats. For that matter, the data cannot tell us how often the Democrats voted against the Opposition and with the government not so much because of alliances that the Opposition failed to strike with it, but because of the alliances with the Democrats that the government had succeeded in consummating.

The Democrats and Greens obviously face a steeper uphill climb in securing the adoption of their committee amendments on divisions. Without the support of the Opposition, the fate of their amendments is sealed unless they can reach agreement with the government. If the goal of the Democrats and Greens in moving a committee amendment is to win, notwithstanding the government's opposition—in other words, policy-making, not position-taking—then their first and overriding concern must be attracting the Opposition into coalition with them on that vote. Interestingly, then, the second and third parts of Table 7.7 indicate that neither of the minor parties has been particularly successful in this regard, and that their rates of success have declined.

When we look at some of the numbers, we see that the Opposition (in alliance with the Greens) supported Democrats' committee amendments on divisions 80 per cent of the time in 1996, but that rate dropped to less than 60 per cent during the next two years, and evaporated thereafter. The corresponding rates at which the Greens had the support of the Opposition (again, either alone or with the Democrats) started at a slightly lower level, remained at or above 40 per cent for the next two years, and then remained on the radar screen in 1999 before crashing in the two most recent years. Both the Democrats and the Greens have demonstrated increasing and impressive rates of success in attracting the support of each other as their sole ally, but to what end? Again we are left with questions that the data cannot answer. Do these data reflect a change in strategy on the part of the minor parties? Have they become less interested in making what may be relatively marginal changes in legislation by devising amendments that are acceptable to the Opposition as well as to each other, and more interested in staking out positions that clearly distinguish them from the Opposition as well as the government? Or has the Opposition moved away from them, and increasingly spurned their efforts to form winning coalitions? We saw, especially in Table 6.3, how often the government and the Opposition came to vote together during 2000 and 2001. Perhaps it is the ALP that has been repositioning itself, vis-a-vis all the other parties, with the result that it has become easier for it to find common ground with the government than with the other non-government parties.

In brief conclusion

In reviewing the work of political scientists on the American Congress, I sometimes have thought that if the data they present contradict what my judgment and experience tell me is true, then I am prepared to believe that something is wrong with the data.

The data presented in this chapter and the last would seem to call into question two of the most commonplace assertions about the Australian political system. One is that the essential dynamic of Australian politics is the competition between the government and the Opposition. That competition is inherent in the structure of a parliamentary system, and reinforced in Australia by the historic differences between the Labor Party on the one hand and the primary non-Labor party or parties (now the Liberal-National Coalition) on the other. Geoffrey Brennan, for example, has observed that:

> Liberal-Labor animosity has become one of the habits of Australian political discourse, and an explicit Liberal-Labor compromise on a matter of policy would be implausible (and perhaps electorally costly to both sides) except in circumstances that were widely regarded as 'exceptional'.
>
> The patterns of relationship in the lower house are more or less replicated in the upper ... . [E]xplicit Coalition/Labor Party negotiations over detailed aspects of proposed legislation are difficult to imagine: the

two major parties in the Senate are more or less locked into their assigned lower house roles. (Brennan 1998–99: 7)

Yet upon examining the voting record of the parties in the Senate, we have found, in this chapter and the last, that the Opposition has not been opposing the government very regularly or very aggressively, that the Opposition has frequently been voting with the government, and that the Opposition has had less than a stellar record of success in reaching agreement on committee amendments with the other non-government Senators whose support it needs to prevail over the government.

The second assertion, and one that we considered in the last chapter, is that the balance of power in the Senate is held by the minor parties and Independents. Yet in recent years, those cross-bench Senators have not had much success in securing the government's support on divisions for their committee amendments. And by the same token, the data do not present an impressive track record of accomplishment for either the Democrats or the Greens in securing the support of the Opposition for their amendments that the government has opposed. Among the most striking disparities we have found in our data are the large percentages of committee amendments (decided by divisions) moved by minor party and Independent Senators and the minimal levels of success their amendments have enjoyed.[155]

The lesson to be drawn, I would argue, is not that either or both assertions is wrong, but that both need to be specified and clarified.

The data suggest that the competition between the government and the Opposition has manifested itself in recent years in intense disagreements over a select set of issues and bills (and, of course, a readiness to take advantage of any unexpected opportunity that comes along). These data are consistent with a conception of politics in Canberra operating on two tracks simultaneously. On one track, the government and the Opposition hammer away at each other for all each is worth, looking to exploit whatever chinks in each other's armour they can find. This is the track that, not surprisingly, attracts media coverage and, therefore, is most visible to the Australian public. At the same time, however, and on a second track, a much more cooperative process of governance is taking place, with the two parties managing to find common ground on the preponderance of legislative business. Australia

---

155 However, a caveat from the previous chapter needs to be reiterated here. The minor parties sometimes have called divisions, knowing that both the government and the Opposition were going to oppose them, precisely in order to differentiate themselves from the major parties.

would be well served if the public heard as much about this second track as it does about the first.

Referring to the period from mid-1996, the beginning of the Howard Ministry, through mid-1998, Senator Meg Lees (2000: 32), then Leader of the Australian Democrats, documented both the quantitative and qualitative side of the argument about the relations between the government, the Opposition, and the Senate: '[O]f 427 bills [the House passed], only two remain negatived—the Workplace Relations Amendment Bill and the Telstra Privatisation Bill. ... That is, 99.54 per cent of bills have been passed.' Yet those two bills and the Senate's failure to pass them may have received more public and media attention than most of the other bills combined, and may have mattered more to the government than most of the other bills combined.

If our findings here seem inconsistent on their face with popular perceptions of the Senate, and especially government criticisms of the Senate, it is at least partly because of, first, the Opposition's natural inclination to look for ways to portray itself as an alternative to the government; second, the government's equally natural inclination to look for opportunities to berate the Opposition for opposing it, especially on matters near and dear to the government's collective heart; and third, the seemingly irresistible impulse of the media to concentrate its reporting on instances of conflict, not cooperation. All three participants (for surely in this regard, the media are participants) have mutually reinforcing tendencies that do not always serve the Australian public well.

Hugh Collins has offered the interesting, though counter-intuitive, argument that the intensity of public conflict between the parties reflects not how wide the gap is that separates their policy positions, but how narrow that gap has become. Writing in 1985 about the lack of substantive knowledge and opinion underlying voters' party preferences, he argued (1985:154) that:

> partisanship can be habitual because there is so little to understand: the competitors are offering only slightly different brews of the same ideological ingredients. Because the basic values are so similar, the party competition characteristically focuses upon tactics and motives rather than upon strategies and goals. Since in practical operation the parties are so alike, the rhetoric used by each side typically strains to present the rival in the image of its most extreme and impotent faction.

By this logic, the degree of policy agreement, in quantitative terms, that we have seen reflected in Senate divisions actually gives the parties an added incentive to highlight and even exaggerate whatever policy disagreements do exist between them, if they are to be able to differentiate one from the other in the public mind.

With respect to the successes and failures of those holding the balance of power in the Senate, I think the data point to the Senate chamber as a venue of last resort for the minor parties. When decisions on their proposals are made by divisions, the preferred processes of collegial discussion and quiet negotiation evidently have failed, and so, as we have seen, their amendments are quite likely to fail. It would be a mistake, however, to measure their influence solely by this yardstick. First, the likely defeat of the minor parties' (and Independents') own amendments still leaves them with the power to decide the fate of amendments moved by both the government and the Opposition. To this extent, the influence of the minor parties is reflected not so much in the divisions on their own amendments, but in the divisions that determine the fate of amendments from the major parties. And second, the record of divisions on amendments cannot in any way capture the influence of the minor parties in securing adoption of other amendments without the need for divisions.

Senator Kernot, then Leader of the Democrats, illustrated this second point in proclaiming the influence that her party was able to have on the content of a workplace relations bill once it became clear to the Coalition government that the bill would not pass without Democrat support:

> The Minister for Industrial Relations quickly made it clear he was prepared to negotiate, and 70 hours of face to face meetings between Senator Murray and myself for the Democrats and the minister ensued over the next two months. ... The culmination of those negotiations was an agreed position ... . [The agreement reached] was formalised in a detailed 60 page ... document, which outlined some 170 amendments to be made to the Bill. (Kernot 1997: 34)

The government and the Democrats jointly moved 164 amendments of which only five provoked divisions. This compares with 33 divisions on Opposition or Green amendments to the same bill.

In other words, this was precisely the kind of legislative negotiation and compromise to which non-government control of the Senate can give rise. As is the case in every democratic capital, there is more to the legislative process in Canberra than meets the public eye. In this sense, the data presented here on the successes and failures of the minor parties on divisions are like the tip of the iceberg. They are important in their own right, because of what we see when we look at them. But they also are important because of what they tell us is there but we cannot see. They encourage us to look beneath the surface, at what is not recorded in *Hansard* or reported in tomorrow's newspaper, if we want to develop a more complete understanding of the legislative process in the Senate.

8

The Senate and
the House of Representatives

Readers may recall from the Introduction that Arend Lijphart has identified 'strong' bicameral systems as ones in which the two houses are symmetrical—their powers are comparable or nearly comparable—and incongruent—their members are elected in significantly different ways. But there may be another way to identify, though not define, strong bicameral systems without resorting to an analysis of constitutional powers or electoral laws. If the two houses enjoy dependably harmonious relations, that is a strong indication of weak bicameralism. Strong bicameralism, on the other hand, is likely to be accompanied by, and reflected in, recurring competition and tension between the two houses. By this measure, the Australian Parliament unquestionably is characterized by strong bicameralism.

The primary sources of strain are constitutional, political, and institutional. From time to time other, more idiosyncratic and transitory strains appear, but the essential tensions between the House of Representatives and the Senate are more or less built into the structure of Australia's federal polity. In an important respect, relations between the two houses in Canberra are more complicated and difficult than they are between the two houses of the US Congress in Washington. In Washington, it often makes sense to speak about the relations between the House of Representatives and the Senate and then to change the subject in order to discuss the relations between the Congress and the President. In Canberra, in many respects, both subjects are conveniently discussed at the same time.

In many daily matters, the House and Senate interact with each other without regard to the government—for instance, in the transmission of legislative papers between the two houses.[156] In other

---

156 To every generalization there is an exception. To anticipate a later section of this chapter, the House's standing orders (specifically, SO 248) provide that, if the House of Representatives disagrees to a Senate amendment, it is to return the amendment to the Senate with a statement of the reasons for the House's decision. The Clerk of the Senate, Harry Evans, recalls instances in which these statements indicated why 'the government' disagreed to an amendment, not the House. He took this to mean that the decision to disagree had been made in a ministry office,

and more politically important respects, though, it can be difficult to distinguish relations between the Senate and the government from relations between the Senate and the House of Representatives. Disputes between the former often manifest themselves in the form of disputes between the latter. *Odgers' Australian Senate Practice* (2001: 75) goes so far as to say that:

> In practice, under the system of government as it has developed in Australia, relations between the two Houses are relations between the Senate and the executive government, as the latter, through its control of a disciplined party majority, controls the House of Representatives. ... There is value, however, in treating the matter [the Senate's relations with the House] on the basis of the constitutional assumption of dealings between two representative assemblies, as this pattern may in certain circumstances, for example, a government in a minority in the House, reassert itself.

The reputation of the House

So much of the discussion in the previous chapters has focused on the Senate that it is fitting that we precede any further discussion of relations, procedural or otherwise, between the two houses with a brief digression into the reputation of the House. This digression will provide necessary context for our discussion of bicameral relations in this chapter and also for our examination of the role and value of the Senate in the next chapters.

Almost invariably, questions about bicameralism and bicameral parliaments quickly become transformed into questions about 'second' or 'upper' chambers—about 'senates.' Why is a bicameral parliament preferable to a unicameral one? What does a unicameral parliament lack that a bicameral parliament offers? In practice, such questions become translated into others. What is the value of the senate? What added value does the senate provide that justifies the additional complications, delays, costs, and duplication of effort that it entails? If the senate is elected in the same way as the lower house (for convenience, let us call it the assembly), why bother having it? If it is elected on a different basis—for example, if each state or province is guaranteed equal representation or representation that is not proportional to its population, then the senate's democratic legitimacy often is questioned. (Needless to say, these questions echo much more largely if the senate is not elected at all, as in Canada or Britain.) 'Why bicameralism?' usually means 'Why a senate?'

---

that the statement had been written by ministry officials, and that, through an oversight, it had not been revised to attribute the statement to the House.

We will address questions of this nature in the two concluding chapters. Here, let us take the opposite tack and ask, 'Why the House of Representatives?', or, more accurately, 'What is the House of Representatives?' The answer to this question is essential for understanding and assessing the Senate. We can examine the Senate in isolation from the House if we limit ourselves to asking how the Senate works and what it does. But if we also want to ask whether the Senate is a valuable institution, or whether there is anything that the Senate should do that it is not doing or something that it should do better, those kinds of questions can be answered only in relation to the House. Before we can evaluate what contributions the Senate has made to democratic governance in Australia, and whether the Senate should be abolished, strengthened, weakened, or left alone, we need to ask what is it that the House does and how well does it do those things. We cannot really know why (or even if) we need the Senate unless we know what we would have if there were no Senate.

When we turn our attention to the side of Parliament House where the House of Representatives lives, we immediately encounter a surprising problem. In all conventional accounts, the House is the more important of the two chambers because that is where, in principle, governments are made and can be destroyed. Yet, outside of textbooks, the House of Representatives has evoked far less interest than the Senate among political scientists and other analysts. The reason that immediately comes to mind is that they may not think the House is a very interesting place.

Much of what has been written about the House in recent years—except for what the House has written about itself—has been terse, critical, even dismissive, and sometimes downright impolite. Whatever questions there may be about the democratic legitimacy of the Senate, about whether it unduly interferes with the government's ability to govern, and so on, at least the Senate is an interesting place, and arguments about it have generated a significant body of literature, much of it thoughtful. As for the House, however—well, here is a small sample of what has been said about it by people who otherwise seem to be temperate in their judgments:

> The lower House in the Commonwealth Parliament is well and truly under the thumb of the government. By political usage governments consider themselves responsible to it and, as at Westminster, the parrot-cry 'responsibility' has made constructive parliamentary reform impossible. (Reid 1964: 93)

> The House of Representatives has become an empty shell of a legislature. (Jaensch 1986: 90)

[The House] is totally useless as a legislature, merely acting as t stamp for the bills produced by the governing party. As an example oɪ ɪ performance, during the twelve years between 1976 and 1987, under two different governments, not a single Opposition amendment was accepted to any of the 2,000 bills passed (except for two bills which were handled by an experimental procedure which was soon stopped by the Government). Bills were contemptuously bulldozed through under a guillotine—for example, ten bills being allowed a total of five minutes for all stages of consideration. (Hamer 1996: 66)

An unwillingness to compromise, especially with the opposition, is an unfortunate side effect of the parliamentary process in the House of Representatives. There, the brutal fact of having the numbers encourages the government to have an arrogant disregard for the views of the opposition. This is reciprocated by an opposition that sees no reason to compromise when its major goal is simply to embarrass the government and keep its powder dry for the next election. (Sharman 1998: 8)

[D]espite the House's privileged constitutional position in financial legislation, it has conceded to the Senate the primary legislative role even in this area. It is not unreasonable to describe the House as a rubber stamp for the financial and all other legislation proposed by the government, and the Senate as the only part of the parliament which acts as an independent check on the government. (Solomon 2000: 9) In short, the House has become 'the government's lap-dog under our present system'. (Solomon 2000: 19)

Even a major study of Parliament that Parliament itself commissioned to mark Australia's bicentenary paints a dismaying portrait of a House that is dominated by the government by virtue of party discipline:

The effects … have left their mark on the House in a number of different ways: by the record of comparatively few sitting days; by the limited opportunities for non-ministerial members to scrutinise legislation; by the constraints imposed upon members in initiating proposed laws or amendments to the proposed laws initiated by ministers; by the strong disposition of the House to stage discussions or permit statements without decisions rather than parliamentary debates; by 'the gag', 'the guillotine', and time limits on speeches; by a weak rather than a strong system of parliamentary questions seeking information from ministers; by the reluctance of the House to declare its privileges; and by its preference for a Speaker—its chief executive and presiding officer—who has strong ties to the majority party. (Reid and Forrest 1989: 470)

These quotations easily could be multiplied. I would happily have balanced them against an equivalent array of complimentary and optimistic assessments of the House—had I encountered them. The almost universal conclusion of outside observers is that the House is ineffectual as a legislative body because of government dominance made possible by virtually perfect party unity on votes.

Furthermore, there are no realistic prospects for changing this condition; no government would allow significant change because every government is content with a quiescent House. Assessments of the House as a forum for scrutiny and oversight are not much more positive. Critics acknowledge that the Opposition has opportunities to make speeches and ask questions critical of government policies, but there are no comparable opportunities for it to use the potential resources of the House actually to evaluate and compel improvements in those policies.[157] Many critiques of the House convey almost a sense of anger at its failure to fulfill what are thought to be its constitutional responsibilities, and a profound sense of dismay combined with resignation at the stranglehold on the House that the government enjoys.

Neal Blewett, a former minister as well as member of the House of Representatives, offers a particularly lucid exposition of the political logic of government–House relations:

> If a government only exists and can only survive if it controls the representative chamber, then the key political imperative is to ensure effective and continuing executive control of that chamber. The rise of the disciplined political party, a necessary phenomenon in mass electorates, has provided the instrument by which a party leadership through democratic elections gains control of the chamber, maintains that control, and seeks to use that control in that forum to continue in office through further electoral success. ... [T]he consequence of the rise of the party has been the diminution of the individual MP and the subordination of the Parliament to the dictates of the Executive. This is a universal characteristic, not a peculiarly Australian phenomenon.
>
> Party solidarity within the Parliament and without therefore becomes a governing virtue because it is essential to the survival of government. Apart from this instrumental value, party solidarity is seen as a virtue in itself for it becomes, with media encouragement, one of the key criteria for determining fitness to govern. The consequence of this is that the critical parliamentary decisions are not made in the Parliament but in the party caucuses, and debates in the Parliament, at least in the House of Representatives, have little to do with legislative decisions and everything to do with election decisions. They are mostly predictable set-piece confrontations in which each side seeks to inflict as much electoral damage on the other as possible. (Blewett 1993: 3–4)

---

157 An illustrative critique of the House is offered by David Hamer (1996), who served in the House for eight years and in the Senate for twelve more.

As a complement, Reid and Forrest (1989: 62) develop the logic behind what we might think of as a syndrome that directs the Opposition's attention away from the House chamber and from attempts to influence national policy from its side of the floor. Opposition leaders, they contend, 'have ... accepted the virtual inevitability of Executive control of the House in a party-dominated Parliament.'

> In consequence the parties in Opposition have accepted the unlikelihood of defeating the Government on a division, and their activities as an Opposition, within the House, are openly directed towards the electorate. In seeking this audience the Opposition needs to enlist the assistance of the media which ... have become increasingly reluctant to cover the details of parliamentary affairs. With party leaders available to project their differences, media attention is unlikely to be attracted by the House's passage of legislation, the inquiries of its committees or its consideration of the estimates. In consequence the Opposition has made few objections when procedural and other opportunities in these areas have been denied to it. The routine of parliamentary business affords few opportunities for headlines or colourful exposure, and thus it has been neglected by members of the Opposition conscious of more 'profitable' ways of spending time to foster their re-election and the government's defeat.

So, Solomon (1998: 73) concludes, 'The energies of the opposition in parliament are directed primarily to the negative end of trying to destroy the government. The stars of the opposition are usually its best head-kickers.'[158]

Although Solomon was speaking about the House, these assessments of Opposition strategy in the House may shed some light on our findings in Chapter 7 about the frequency and successes of Opposition amendments in the Senate. It would be surprising, to say the least, for the Opposition to adopt the posture just described in the House, but then to focus its energies in the Senate on amending or even defeating government bills. By this reasoning, the Opposition has little incentive to try to defeat government bills whenever it possibly can on second or third reading motions because its primary goal is not to block government legislation but to convince the electorate that that legislation is ill-conceived and detrimental to the average Australian. True, defeats can make the government look inept, but the costs in time and effort of arranging to block government bills is great when weighed

---

158 Not surprisingly in sports-crazed Australia, Anne Lynch, the Deputy Clerk of the Senate, has spoken of 'the tendency, in the House, to play politics like a rugby game, with two hard-playing front rows lined up against one another, forever trying to score.' (*Evening Post* (Wellington, NZ), 4 July 1994: 7)

against the pay-off that any successes produce for the Opposition. Unless the bill is a particularly important one, Opposition victories on divisions are more than likely to make no public impression worth measuring, especially in comparison with the mileage that the Opposition can hope to get from a press conference or a public event staged to press home the argument that whatever legislation the government is forcing through the Parliament is doing grave damage to the nation.

The same logic helps to explain the relative dearth of Opposition amendments in the Senate's committee of the whole, and its unimpressive track record in finding the Senate allies it needs to have those amendments pass. Solomon presumably would say that the process of negotiating agreements with the minor parties over the wording of Opposition amendments is what Americans would call 'inside baseball'—matters of obscure parliamentary manoeuvring that are assumed to be of no interest to the Australian public and, in any case, are virtually invisible to the public because the media usually fails to cover them and explain their significance. Motions and amendments and divisions in the Senate may not be unimportant but, according to this way of thinking, they have little impact on the outcome of the all-important next election. This argument smacks of hard-headed realism. And yet it is the Senate which is supposed to be the venue in which government legislation can be subjected to serious scrutiny and in which serious legislative business can be conducted. If that rarely happens in the Senate because the interest and attention of the Opposition is directed elsewhere, the Senate is weakened as a place where the government is held accountable.

But I digress. Returning to the House, Reid and Forrest (1989: 24) also argue that the government typically can ignore the Opposition in the House with impunity: '[A] government's strategy will be directed almost wholly towards its own side. If it can remain solid, and hence retain its majority in the House, then there is little need for concern with the other members. The acid test of responsibility is the ability to continue in office, and this will be determined not by the House as a whole but by the government members in it.' And so the concept of responsibility becomes perverted beyond recognition.

Taking these critiques together, it is small wonder that the House so often receives such low marks for autonomy and influence. Yet some of those inside the House respond that the critical assessments of their professional home fail to appreciate recent changes in the House and some of the subtleties and nuances of House activities that allow it to make more of a difference than is apparent to the naked eye. In truth, the House of Representatives sometimes is dismissed too quickly as being only an 'electoral college' that chooses the government from among its members (and those of the Senate), and then subsides into quiescence, approving the government's legislative program without challenge or change. The government must remain attentive to the preferences and priorities of its parliamentary party; its members may give it a great deal of latitude, but even that latitude has limits.[159] The prime minister often may be able to announce government policy and assume, correctly, that his party in the Parliament will fall into line behind that policy. And he may be able to do that again and again. But if those policies are failing, or if they inflame public opposition, or if they take the party where many of its members really do not want it to go, the members of the governing party retain what might be thought of as a kind of 'reserve power' to change their own leadership. Still, it is in the nature of reserve powers that they rarely if ever are exercised, and only when a serious institutional failure makes recourse to them necessary.

Less drastically, a government sometimes does need to adjust its legislation in response to demands, pleas, and even the expert advice of its own backbenchers in the House. Before his apparently terminal disillusionment (see Chapter 9), Solomon (1986: 76–89) stressed the valuable role that party committees in the Parliament can play, in giving Members a forum in which to develop and express their expertise and in encouraging a government to take another hard look at its draft legislation before sending it through the formal stages of the legislative process. Government policy also can be affected by the debates that take place in the government's party room.[160] Furthermore, government bills do not always emerge unscathed from the House Chamber. While we would not expect an Australian government to lose a division in the House on an amendment, governments do accept the gist of some Opposition amendments in the House, or they may respond to Opposition arguments by offering corrective amendments in the Senate.

---

159 On the role of the Labor Party caucus during Whitlam's ministry, see Kelly (1976: 203–216).

160 What goes on inside the party room takes place behind closed doors and is revealed only in rumors and unattributed reports, so we cannot know for certain how often the government's backbenchers persuade their leaders to make changes in legislation, nor can we know how significant those changes are. For the same reason, these internal party debates do not contribute to the public understanding of government policies that is essential for preserving public support for democratic institutions. Furthermore, debates within the parliamentary parties are not activities of the Parliament as such; these internal party discussions could take place at party headquarters or in a hotel meeting room if it were not simply more convenient to hold them at Parliament House (Jaensch 1986: 43–44).

Even so, it is asking too much to think of the House of Representatives as a law-making place. But perhaps the problem is not with the House, but with our expectations. A perfectly reasonable argument can be made that the House and Senate are not to be judged by the same standards because they differ in the functions they are able to perform. Referring to Westminster, Griffith and Ryle (1989: 6) argue that 'It is … as a debating forum … not as a governing body, that Parliament should be assessed.' The same argument can be made with equal weight about the Australian House of Representatives.[161] It is neither fair nor reasonable to evaluate either lower house on the basis of how much, how often, and how well it contributes to shaping the content of new legislation. Because of the strength of party discipline, which is a more powerful force in Canberra than in London, the House of Representatives is deprived of any realistic opportunity to have much of an independent effect on legislation. So the House must be evaluated against more realistic criteria. For example, how well do its legislative debates clarify the arguments for and against alternative policies, and how well do its other deliberations hold the government to account for its actions and decisions?

Because of the predictable presence of non-government majorities in the Senate, on the other hand, it can engage in serious legislative work, in the sense of participating actively and constructively in writing new laws for the nation. Government control of the House means that non-government Senators rarely can hope to see their own legislation enacted, but they can defeat government legislation when necessary or, more often, make passage of that legislation contingent on government acceptance of amendments to its original proposals. Just because the Senate can legislate, however, does not necessarily mean that it should legislate or that it should be evaluated as a legislative body. As we shall find in the next chapter, those who support the notion that the government, by virtue of its majority in the House, has an electoral 'mandate' to enact its legislative program, are not sympathetic to a Senate that actively asserts its legislative powers.

I should be explicit, therefore, in stating my position: because the constitutional and electoral systems combine to give the Senate the power and incentive to play an active part in the legislative process, it

---

161 Ward (2000a: 69–70) quotes Blewett as having written in 1993, for example, that 'It may be … that instead of paying attention to reform of the House of Representatives we should accept that chamber as essentially a debating forum between two party teams, and particularly their leaders, designed to clarify choices for a mass electorate, and concentrate on perfecting the Senate as a House of legislative review and as the body for effective scrutiny of the Executive.'

should do so, and it is fair and right to evaluate the Senate on the basis of how well it does so, though not only on that basis. My view is that democratic governance benefits from a legislative process that involves more than parliamentary argument over, and then ratification of, government proposals, even if (actually, especially because) that process compels the government to make compromises that take into account different opinions and a wider array of interests. As a practical matter, the House cannot legislate so it should not be asked to do so. For equally practical reasons, the Senate can legislate; and since it can, it should. I state this clearly because those who do not agree with this position can be forewarned that there may be much in what follows, especially in the concluding chapter, with which they also will disagree.

At the risk of some oversimplification, the ironic problem for the Parliament is that the House of Representatives is criticized, loudly and often, for what it does not do (that is, legislate), while the Senate is criticized, equally loudly and equally often, for sometimes doing what the House does not. What the Senate sometimes does is what some critics of the House wish it would or could do. What the House does best (that is, debate) is just about all that some critics of the Senate think it should do.

So we have a situation in which neither house of the Parliament (at the risk of anthropomorphizing them) thinks that its virtues and value are sufficiently appreciated, certainly not by the other house or by ostensibly sophisticated observers, and, what is worse, not by the Australian people. Members of the House, and especially backbench Members, who spent any amount of time reading the House's reviews in the press might well wonder why they bother getting out of bed in the morning, much less running for re-election. The institution in which they work and with which they are identified is 'contemptuously bulldozed' so often that it is 'totally useless.' It is derided as 'an empty shell' and 'a rubber stamp,' and as being so much 'under the thumb of the government' as to be nothing more than 'the government's lap-dog.' And these are the evaluations of scholars with a professional commitment to, and appreciation of, national legislatures!

On the other side of Parliament House sit Senators whose institution has been criticised regularly as an inconvenient and potentially dangerous growth on the Australian body politic. Having never fulfilled its intended role as the House of the States, it makes its presence felt only when it interferes with the government's ability to fulfil its electoral mandate and satisfy the will of the people. A prime minister (Paul Keating) described Senators as 'unrepresentative swill' and for many years, one of the nation's two major political parties (the ALP) made the call for its abolition a regular part of its election manifesto. If the House is dismissed as ineffectual, the Senate often is rejected as having become too effective in hampering the proper operation of parliamentary government.

Under these circumstances, is it any wonder that bicameral relations in Canberra sometimes are less than harmonious?

Aspects of bicameral relations

Putting aside for the moment the relations between each house and the government, there are aspects of House-Senate relations in Canberra that both resemble and differ from the relations between the two houses of the American Congress. In Washington, the members of the House of Representatives and the Senate are elected from different constituencies and for different terms of office. That is true in Canberra as well, but the differences in Canberra are greater because Australian Representatives and Senators, unlike their US counterparts, also are chosen by different modes of election. In Washington, the same political party may not control both houses. That is true in Canberra, but in Washington it is a sporadic, though familiar, phenomenon; in Canberra, careful students of Australian politics believe it will remain a permanent condition unless and until Commonwealth election laws are amended.

In Washington, members of the two houses often have different ambitions. Many Representatives hope to become Senators or perhaps state governors; many Senators hope to become President and some believe that is their destiny. In Canberra too, members of the two houses often have different ambitions, but Representatives hope to become ministers, not Senators, and some easily can envision themselves as prime minister. Australian Senators also seek ministerial appointments, but fewer of these positions are available for Senators, so Senators may seek election to the House in their quest for political advancement. Only once has a Senator been chosen as prime minister and he quickly sought election to the House.[162] So in Washington, the movement within Congress is from the House to the Senate; in Canberra, not surprisingly, it is the reverse. A US Senator has not voluntarily relinquished his seat to run for a seat in the House since well before the American Civil War. An Australian Senator's prospects for advancement to ministerial ranks may be better today than it was decades ago, but there still is some truth to Denning's (1946: 55) observation, made more than a half-century ago, that:

---

162 Though the Constitution is silent on the matter, traditionally the prime minister is a member of the House of Representatives.

If it should appear that a young Senator has the makings of a future Prime Minister, from the viewpoint of his party's interest in seeking eventual successors to the leaders of the day, it is much more likely that he would resign his Senate seat at an opportune moment and find a seat in the House of Representatives, than that he would at some time attempt to lead a ministry from the Senate.

In their legislative activities, each house exercises its constitutional authority to devise its own procedures, primarily in the form of written standing orders. In their essentials, the procedures of both houses, like the general design of the two chambers, are similar because they both reflect Australia's British parliamentary inheritance. Yet there are some significant differences. Some are attributable to the fact that the House, by constitutional requirement, has twice as many members as the Senate. Others reflect differences in the standing of the government in the two houses—enjoying unquestioned control in the House but confronting a non-government majority in the Senate. Not surprisingly, therefore, the procedures of the House are somewhat more protective of the government's political interests and accommodating to the needs of its legislative program.[163]

Some observers also claim to have discerned a stylistic difference in the two houses that reflects the government's continuing lack of working majorities in the Senate and, consequently, the requirement for majority coalitions composed of Senators from more than any one party. For example, Fred Chaney (1988: 170), who served in both houses, found that 'there is a degree of enforced reasonableness in the Senate, which provides some contrast with the more confrontational, gladiatorial mood which characterizes most if not all Australian Lower Houses. There is a sanction on unreasonable behaviour—at least as far as governments are concerned, and official oppositions which will one day be in government.' (Chaney 1988: 170) More than a decade later, Sharman (1999: 157) came to much the same conclusion:

> [T]he polarisation between government and opposition that characterises most debate in the lower house is moderated in the Senate. This, in turn, can lead to a consensus style of politics in which compromise and the accommodation of different points of view are regarded as the normal way of doing business. This is both effective policy-making and good politics. The abrasive style of lower house politics has done much to bring

---

163 In the Senate, for example, a minister has only four minutes in which to reply to a question. In the House, a minister can respond at length. So the effect of the Senate's standing orders is to provide time for more questions to be asked. In neither house, however, is the minister's reply required to directly address the question that was asked.

parliamentary politics into disrepute. The Senate can do much to restore faith in the process of representative democracy.

Reid and Forrest (1989: 467) surely go too far when they say that the Senate is 'a chamber totally different in character from the House of Representatives.' There is no question, though, that the requirements for decision-making in an organization can affect the tenor of its proceedings. Close observers of the US Congress certainly appreciate the truth of this observation. The style of debate in Washington's House of Representatives also tends to be more combative than in the Senate, and undoubtedly this is due in part to the House's procedures which allow its agenda and decisions to be controlled by simple majority vote—that is, by vote of the majority party when it remains sufficiently united. The style of debate and decision-making in the US Senate, by contrast, tends to be more accommodative, partly because the Senate's rules empower the minority party (or even smaller groups of Senators) to delay votes and even kill bills by preventing the Senate from voting to pass them.

As organizations, the two houses in Washington, like the two houses in Canberra, operate autonomously in many respects. Each house, for example, has its own collection of highly-skilled officials, including those who staff its committees. However, there is a somewhat wider array of joint services and shared facilities in Canberra than in Washington. In part, this reflects differences in scale of operations. In Canberra, the House of Representatives and the Senate live together in the same building, and both houses share their building with the government—the offices of the prime minister and other government ministers (though the overwhelming majority of public servants are located elsewhere, of course). This situation creates incentives for joint arrangements; duplication can be inconvenient and costly, but triplification is many times worse. In Washington, on the other hand, the President and the entire executive branch are located 'downtown,' not on 'the Hill' (even if 'downtown,' in some cases, is just a few blocks away). House and Senate plenary sessions take place in the same building, but all personal offices and most committee offices and meeting rooms are located in separate office buildings occupied exclusively by one house or the other. The situation in Washington, therefore, makes it both more feasible and more natural for each house to manage its own facilities (and divide responsibility for managing the Capitol building itself).

The steady pressures for economy and the increasing requirements of security are causing the two houses in both cities to consider—sometimes happily, sometimes not—new forms of cooperation, coordination, or even consolidation in providing non-legislative services. When possible, however, autonomy is preferred. *House of Representatives Practice* (2001: 34–35) describes the relations between the House and Senate in Canberra in terms that would apply without significant change to bicameral relations in Washington:

> Each House functions as a distinct and independent unit within the framework of the Parliament. …
>
> The complete autonomy of each House, within the constitutional and statutory framework existing at any given time, is recognized in regard to:
>
> - its own procedure;
> - questions of privilege and contempt; and
> - control of finance, staffing, accommodation and services.
>
> This principle of independence characterises the formal nature of inter-House communication. Communication between the Houses may be by message, by conference, or by committees conferring with each other. The two Houses may also agree to appoint a joint committee operating as a single body and composed of members of each House.

As in Washington, each house accepts the principle that one house should not intrude into the exclusively internal affairs of the other. 'As an expression of the principle of independence of the Houses, the Speaker took the view in 1970 that it would be parliamentarily and constitutionally improper for a Senate estimates committee to seek to examine the financial needs or commitments of the House of Representatives. In similar manner the House of Representatives estimates committees, when they operated, did not examine the proposed appropriations of the Senate.' (*House of Representatives Practice* 2001: 35)

The primary sources of inter-cameral strain derive from conditions that we already have discussed at length. The first is their sharing of legislative powers under the Constitution, and the recurring disagreements about what powers the Senate actually has; when, if, and how it actually should exercise its legislative powers; and, most fundamentally, whether the two houses are and should be essentially equals or whether the Constitution ordains the primacy of the House of Representatives. Not surprisingly, each house has its eloquent and determined advocates. The second source of strain reflects the seemingly permanent state of divided government in Canberra, with a government majority in the House and a non-government majority in the Senate. There is no need here for another round of extended discussions of either subject. Suffice it to say that they combine in Parliament House today to ensure that there almost always is some underlying degree of tension between the houses as institutions, and that the tension is intensified by the intensely adversarial nature of the public relations between the major parties.

In Washington, a leader in the House of Representatives reputedly once communicated his opinion of a colleague within the more florid standards of parliamentary discourse then in vogue by saying that he held the other Member in minimal high regard. Perhaps that is an apt way in which to think about how Australian Representatives and Senators sometimes think about each other.

> [T]he rivalry between the two chambers ... permeates every level of this building ... . This House chauvinism is manifest in many ways. The House considers that senators are the second XI, frustrating smooth government. The view from the Senate is that the House is full of rowdies dropping artillery shells of personal abuse on each other. The truth is that the rather childish mutual recrimination prevents a more rational solution of problems. (Childs 1992: 43)

Recall that the most famous inter-cameral slur of the modern era was contributed in 1992 by Labor Prime Minister Paul Keating who, in the course of House debate, referred to the Senate as 'unrepresentative swill'.[164] Needless to say, the phrase has continued to reverberate through the halls of Parliament House. But the House has not been immune from barbed comments originating in the Senate. The Clerk of the Senate, Harry Evans, substitutes a pointed pen for a sharp tongue; for example:

> [U]nder cabinet government [in Australia] members of parliament are not legislators or scrutineers of the executive, but occupants of or pretenders to executive office. In effect, there is no legislature. (Evans 1984: 275)
>
> We have thus embraced the very situation which our founding philosophers warned us against as the very epitome of tyranny: the concentration of legislative and executive powers in the same hands. Indeed, we have come to permanent submission to what they saw as the disease of elected government: rule by faction. (Evans 1992a: 2)
>
> The founders did not envisage a situation whereby the leaders of the group which controls 51 per cent of the faction which controls 51 per cent of the parliamentary party which receives 40-odd per cent of the electorate's votes have absolute power to control the country. ... [This situation] has resulted in prime ministers who behave like emperors, even bullying speakers of the House of Representatives in public in sittings of the House, without people being aware that representative and parliamentary government as such has been repudiated. (Evans 1997a: 5)

---

164 *Commonwealth Parliamentary Debates* (House of Representatives), 4 November 1992: 2540. Keating continued 'There will be no House of Representatives Minister appearing before a Senate committee of any kind while ever I am Prime Minister ... '

Bicameral unhappiness manifests itself in many ways, large and small. Two examples, one early and one more recent, will illustrate some of its less consequential manifestations. Souter (1988: 58) explains that, when the newly-created Commonwealth Parliament first began to meet in Melbourne, its *Parliamentary Debates* (commonly known as *Hansard*) was published 'at weekly intervals ... and was also published cumulatively in bound volumes.'

> In both forms the Senate appeared before the lower house, just as it was named first in the Constitution, presumably on some analogy with the House of Lords and its propinquity to the Sovereign. As the Senate did not share that privilege, the vertical dimension of 'upper' and 'lower' houses rang rather false in a federal legislature. In Volume 1 of *Parliamentary Debates* the index for the House of Representatives appeared before that of the Senate. But tradition prevailed, and from then on the States' House somewhat irrationally took precedence over the more numerous house on all occasions.

Although *Hansard* continues to be published, technology moves on and Parliament tries to decide how, and how closely behind, to follow. Whereas *Hansard* is an essential form of communication within Parliament House, each house has become increasingly concerned with how well the Australian public understands what it does and appreciates how well it does those things. In this respect, the House of Representatives and the Senate compete for the attention of the public and the media.[165]

Paul Bongiorno (1999) has argued that the Senate's 1990 decision to permit its floor proceedings to be televised put intense pressure on the House to do likewise, just as many Washington observers believed that

---

165 Each house has an informative website that provides online access to its records and to information about its members, procedures, activities, and history. Each house also has its own publications program (and many of those publications also are accessible online). The House of Representatives recently has been concentrating on communications with the general public through a glossy magazine, a collection of easily digestible factsheets, and a series of other publications written at different levels of detail and sophistication. The Senate has its own factsheets and brochures, but the Senate has been putting more emphasis on communicating with a more elite audience through seminars for public servants, a program of public lectures, and published essays of scholarly tone. The cornerstone publication about the Senate, though not officially endorsed by it, is *Odgers' Australian Senate Practice*, which has been cited and quoted frequently in these pages and which is now in its tenth edition. I understand that the decision by the House of Representatives to produce *House of Representatives Practice*, now in its fourth edition and often quoted here, was provoked in no small part by the evident value and visibility of the Senate's volume. (See the bibliography for information on some of these publications.)

the House of Representatives' 1979 decision to televise led some Senators to fear that the House was coming to dominate public perceptions of Congress (an outcome that naturally was intolerable to Senators). Seven years later, the Senate followed the example of the House. In the same paper (p. 165), Michelle Grattan observed that 'a powerful Senate in which control is not in a government's hands is obviously one of the media's favourite places', in part because of 'the large amount of horse-trading and compromise that can occur,' which in turn 'exposes the political process to more public scrutiny ... ' Question time may receive better coverage in the House than in the Senate because of the formal responsibility of government to the House and because the tenor of the exchanges there is even more combative than in the Senate; however, Grattan contends, policy debates may be covered better in the Senate because they are more likely to matter.[166]

Several other manifestations of inter-cameral strain deserve our brief attention because of their significance for governance. Two only will be mentioned here because we will discuss them at some length in the next chapter. One is the practice of having Senators serve as ministers and the question of whether it would be advisable, from the Senate's perspective, to discontinue this practice. Each modern government draws some of its ministers, usually about one-third of them, from among its party ranks in the Senate. In addition to his or her own ministerial responsibilities, each Senate minister represents one or more House ministers and responds to questions in the Senate about matters for which those House ministers are responsible. It might seem that having Senators as ministers can only enhance the Senate's powers. Yet, as we shall see, a thoughtful argument can be made that the Senate really needs to set itself apart from the government if it is to be as effective as it might be in holding the ministry accountable for its execution of the laws.

A second related issue is the established understanding, or convention if you prefer, that Senators are accountable only to the Senate, not to the House, and, more to the point, that Representatives are accountable only to the House, not to the Senate. It is for this reason that neither house has provisions in its standing orders to permit ministers who are members of one house to appear in the chamber of the other to respond directly to questions relating to their portfolios. In

---

166 Grattan also opined that 'The minor players are accustomed to relying on publicity as part of their limited political tool box. Open government is actually something that governments almost never really believe in. This is not to say that minor party and independent senators who hold the balance of power are more virtuous or more public spirited than other senators, but just that they have different interests.'

some parliamentary systems, there is no requirement that ministers must be members of the parliament. Consequently, those parliaments typically allow ministers some rights to participate in parliamentary proceedings—perhaps only to respond to questions, but perhaps also to participate actively in debates to explain and advocate legislation affecting their portfolios.[167] In Canberra, however, Senators cannot pose questions directly to a minister who is a member of the House; and if they want to hear that minister's explanation of some government policy, they must listen to the debates in the House or, more likely, the minister's statements to the media. Proposals have been made from time to time for a less rigid policy, but such a change obviously would make life less convenient and comfortable for the government, even if it also would promote the accountability of that government to the Parliament.[168]

This convention also extends to meetings of Senate committees which are expected to refrain from trying to secure testimony from any minister who is a Representative (including, therefore, the prime minister). That minister may appear voluntarily, though he or she is unlikely to do so, but it would be considered an affront to the House if a Senate committee were to invoke its powers in an attempt to order a House of Representatives minister to appear before it. The result is that a principle that is based in bicameral comity—affecting how each house treats members of the other—has been extended to protect ministers against being held accountable in the Senate for their actions and decisions as ministers because of their standing as Representatives. We will return to this issue as well in the next chapter, where we shall review several proposals for 'reform' that would affect the Senate.

A third issue arose in the Senate on the very day that I began writing these words. On 5 February 2003, Senator Faulkner, Leader of the Opposition, moved that the Senate censure the government because of its purported policies and intentions regarding military intervention in Iraq, and that the Senate also 'declare that it has no confidence in the

---

167 Executive branch officials in Washington are constitutionally barred from also serving in the Congress, but there is nothing that would prevent one or both houses from allowing Cabinet secretaries from appearing in the House or Senate chamber to defend Administration policies and actions. Proposals have been made to institute a question time in Washington, but they have not received serious consideration.

168 Not surprisingly, therefore, the House's Standing Committee on Procedure advocated in 1986 that all ministers should be members of the House and that, 'as far as the accountability of Ministers at question time was concerned, Ministers who were Members of the House should be responsible to the Parliament and the people through the House of Representatives only.' (*House of Representatives Practice* 2001: 115)

Prime Minister's handling of this grave matter for the nation.' (*Journals of the Senate*, 5 February 2003: 1448) Such motions have been moved in the past, but they serve primarily as an outlet for Senators' disagreement or anger with government policy. When the Senate agrees to such a motion, there is no serious expectation that the censured minister must resign, as he or she almost certainly would do if censured by the House of Representatives. This is one point on which the two houses agree:

> The Senate has on several occasions passed motions of censure of Ministers (both Senate and House Ministers). In none of these cases did the Minister concerned feel compelled to resign as a result. These instances would seem to reinforce the principle inherent in the system of responsible government that Ministers collectively and individually (unless they are Senators) are responsible to the lower House. (*House of Representatives Practice* 2001: 49)
>
> Although a resolution of the Senate censuring the government or a minister can have no direct constitutional or legal consequences, as an expression of the Senate's disapproval of the actions or politics of particular ministers, or of the government as a whole, censure resolutions may have a significant political impact and for this reason they have frequently been moved and carried in the Senate. ... Almost all such motions have been expressed in terms of censuring either individual ministers or the government. There have been no motions proposing want of confidence in the government and very few expressing want of confidence in particular ministers, none of which was successful. No motion of want of confidence in a minister has been proposed since 1979 and the practice now is to frame such motions in terms of censure. (*Odgers' Australian Senate Practice* 2001: 475–476)[169]

Censure motions in the Senate are not necessarily empty gestures. No government wants to see a formal vote to disapprove one of its members or one of its policies. The government finds itself on the defensive at a time and place that is not of its choosing. Also, the debate in the Senate is likely to attract media attention precisely because of the seeming importance of the motion and the dramatic appeal of the event. So Elaine Thompson has concluded that:

> 'The Senate, through the use of its power of censure, has developed an important role in holding ministers answerable. It will censure a minister if

---

169 There is a clear difference in the tone of these two statements. Furthermore, *Odgers' Australian Senate Practice* (2001: 476) goes on to offer the judgment that 'ministers are held accountable in the Senate but not in the House of Representatives to which the ministry is supposed to be responsible.' The fact that a publication so closely associated with the Senate would comment critically on the House is, in itself, indicative of the strains that persist between the two houses.

it believes a minister has not acted with propriety, has failed to declare an interest in a matter, has refused to produce documents in compliance with a Senate order, has misled or lied to the Senate.

The power of censure is taken very seriously by the Senate *and* by the government because a Senate censure can have, and has had, repercussions on the credibility of the government as a whole. (Thompson 1999:47)

Still, it needs to be emphasized that the effect of a censure motion in the Senate is based on its political impact; the effect of a comparable motion in the House has a constitutional force, at least as the Constitution is supplemented by the conventions of ministerial responsibility to the House of Representatives.

A fourth and final issue of interest in the context of bicameral relations is of more direct legislative significance and one that has raised the collective hackles of the government and the House. For years the Senate would complain that masses of legislation, including important bills, were arriving from the House at the last minute. So, Senators argued, they were denied adequate time to review and respond intelligently to those bills and, consequently, to fulfill their constitutional responsibilities as legislators. Governments, in turn, would respond that they were doing the best they could to move their legislative program through the House and on to the Senate as promptly as the complexity and importance of the bills permitted. Finally, in the 1980s, the Senate changed its own procedures in a way that virtually compelled a change in the practices of the House, a development that the Prime Minister at the time, Paul Keating is reported to have dismissed in typically diplomatic fashion as a 'constitutional impertinence' (quoted in Margetts 1999: 2).

John Uhr explains what the Senate did and why:

[I]n the mid-1980s … Australian Democrats Senator Michael Macklin successfully moved what became known as the 'Macklin motion', a resolution declaring that the Senate would defer until the next period of sittings consideration of any bills received after a specified deadline. The purpose was to counteract the trend in which government legislation was forced through in the last few weeks of a ten to twelve-week sitting. The budget sittings are typical: in 1972 some 40 per cent of bills were passed in the final fortnight; by 1987 that figure had risen to nearly 68.8 per cent. (Uhr 1998: 146)[170]

Notice that the 'Macklin motion' as originally adopted was concerned only with when the Senate received a bill from the House. It

170 In modern practice, Parliament has three sitting periods each year, each of which is, in the case of the Senate, defined as 'a period during which the Senate adjourns for not more than 20 days.' (*Odgers' Australian Senate Practice* 2001: 255)

did not propose to affect the legislative process in the House except to impose a consequence if the House failed to complete that process in a timely fashion. As Uhr goes on to explain, this restrained approach had unanticipated consequences, as reforms so often do. 'Unfortunately, the effect of this resolution was that the government began to comply with the Senate cut-off date but at the cost of reducing the initial time available for consideration of the bills in the House of Representatives, with a dramatic increase in the use of the guillotine.' In reaction, the Greens successfully proposed a revision of the 'Macklin motion' in 1993 to include a 'double deadline'. In its current form, what is now the Macklin rule provides that:

> A bill introduced by a minister or received from the House of Representatives is deferred to the next period of sittings unless it was first introduced in a previous period of sittings and is received by the Senate in the first two-thirds of the current period (SO (Standing Order) 111).[171] At the Government's request, the Senate may exempt individual bills from these deadlines and it frequently does so, but it does not grant these exemptions automatically and 'the onus is on the government to convince the Senate to lift the ban on a case-by-case basis. (Uhr 1998: 147)

This is an excellent example of the adjustments and accommodations that bicameralism can require.[172] That the Senate would think that it had some ability to affect the government's legislative timetable, and that it would have the temerity to adopt and enforce this Standing Order, is evidence of a Senate that has become more self-confident and self-assertive and that, through its non-government majority, is somewhat less inclined to think of itself as subservient to the government's preferences and convenience.

---

171 The reaction of the House deserves to be shared in full. On 19 August 1993, the House sent to the Senate a message asserting that:
> (a) the Senate order is a completely unwarranted interference by the Senate in the business of this House; (b) the Senate is a house of review and has no place dictating to this House, the house of government, on the conduct of its business; (c) the order of the Senate is a gross discourtesy by the Senate to the people of Australia in that the order demonstrates a presumptuous desire not to allow the house of the people to have its proper control over the management of its business; and (d) the public interest is not served by the effect of the Senate order, which is to curtail proper debate on legislation in this House by forcing the Government to progress legislation rapidly through the House in order to meet a Senate imposed deadline ... ' (*Votes and Proceedings of the House of Representatives*, 19 August 1993: 174)

172 For a discussion of how the houses of the US Congress have coped with a problem in their bicameral relations, see my 1982 article on 'Germaneness Rules and Bicameral Relations in the US Congress,' in *Legislative Studies Quarterly*, v. 7, n. 3.

Resolving legislative disagreements

Enactment of a law requires that both houses of Parliament pass it in exactly the same form.[173] As we have seen, most bills originate in the House of Representatives (and money bills must originate there), but the Senate often has amended them (or requested amendments to money bills). As we also have seen, the authors of the Constitution recognized that the Senate's legislative powers could give rise to legislative disagreements, which is why they included sec. 57, with its procedures for double dissolutions and joint sittings, as the ultimate mechanism to resolve such disagreements. However, the standing orders of both houses contain elaborate procedures by which they can, and often do, try to prevent their legislative disagreements from reaching the stage of deadlock. It can easily be argued, in fact, that there is greater need for such procedures in Canberra than in Washington because parliamentary deadlock over legislation potentially has more severe consequences in Australia than in the United States. In Washington, it is only the fate of the legislation in question that is at stake; in Canberra, as former Prime Minister Whitlam can attest, it can be the life of the government itself.

Procedures for resolving legislative disagreements are necessary when one house of the Parliament considers a bill from the other house and passes that bill with one or more amendments. Such procedures are equally necessary to govern how the House and Senate address Senate requests that the House agree to certain amendments to money bills that the Senate cannot amend directly. The House cannot simply ignore these Senate requests or dismiss them out of hand in part because the Senate makes its requests before completing the process of bicameral

---

173 Constitutional amendments, however, can be proposed by either house acting alone. Whereas a bill requires only a simple majority vote for passage (that is, a majority of those present and voting, assuming they constitute a quorum), a constitutional amendment requires the support of an absolute majority (that is, a majority of all those eligible to vote). But whereas a bill must be passed by both houses, subject to the double dissolution and joint sitting procedures of sec. 57 of the Constitution, sec. 128 provides that if the two houses deadlock twice over a proposed constitutional amendment (just as they must do over legislation in order for that bill to trigger a double dissolution), the Governor-General may submit the amendment for ratification by popular referendum in the form it was passed by the house that first proposed it, 'with or without any amendments subsequently agreed to by both Houses …' even though both houses have not passed it in the same form. Note that the Governor-General *may* submit the amendment to a referendum; he is not required to do so. In the normal course of events, therefore, we would expect him to take this action only at the behest of the government of the day. Consequently, he is very unlikely to submit an amendment that the Senate passed twice and the House rejected on both occasions.

passage which is a prerequisite for enactment. Therefore, as we saw in
Chapter 2, advocates of Senate power find little difference between the
Senate's right to amend and its right to request amendments when it
cannot amend.[174]

Procedures of the House and Senate

In brief, the procedures the two houses have adopted for resolving their
legislative disagreements, short of deadlocks, double dissolutions, and
joint sittings, and which are quite similar in the House and Senate,
provide for exchanges of messages, positions, and amendments
between the two houses with the hope that these exchanges will
produce an agreement acceptable to a majority in each house.[175]

Odgers' Australian Senate Practice (2001: 252) encapsulates the
procedures of both houses:

> Bills originating in one House of the Parliament are forwarded to the other
> House for concurrence. If they are amended by the other House, they are
> returned to the originating House with a request for agreement to the
> amendments. If there is disagreement over amendments, bills may be
> moved between the two Houses a number of times until the Houses finally
> agree to them in the same form or they are abandoned. Bills which have
> been agreed to by both Houses are forwarded by the originating House to
> the Governor-General for assent.

Readers who are familiar with the US Congress will have noticed
immediately that if we replace the concluding reference to assent by the
Governor-General with signature or veto by the President, this brief
description would aptly summarize Congress' procedures as well, but
with one glaring omission: note that this summary makes no reference
at all to conference committees. We will consider the implications of
this toward the end of this chapter.

These procedures are complex, and not a subject for the faint-
hearted. What follows is only a bare summary of some of their key

---

174 '[T]hese requests are effectively the same as amendments, particularly as the Senate
    usually makes sure that it does not give the third reading to a Bill to which it is
    requesting changes, until it has had a positive response to its request.' (Solomon
    1986: 103)

175 As in Congress, the two houses communicate formally with each other through
    exchanges of written messages by which, for example, the House transmits its bills
    to the Senate for its concurrence and the Senate returns House bills to that body
    with amendments that the Senate has adopted. There is no requirement in the
    Senate's standing orders that it must consider messages from the House, even
    messages conveying government legislation. In practice, however, the Senate does
    so, even when the Senate has a non-government majority.

elements.[176] Since most bills originate in the House, let us begin with a bill that the House has passed and sent to the Senate and that the Senate has passed with amendments. Under Senate SO 131, the Senate returns the bill to the House after third reading with a request that the House concur in the Senate's amendments which are annexed as a schedule 'containing reference to the page and line of the bill where the words are to be inserted or omitted, and describing the amendments proposed ... ' At a time decided by the government, the House then considers the Senate amendments individually, or it may consider some of them in groups if the same motion is to be made to dispose of each amendment in a group.

As the House acts on the Senate amendments, according to House SO 245, it has five key options.[177] First, it may agree to the Senate amendments, in which case there are no disagreements and the bill can be presented for assent. Second, the House may agree to the Senate amendments with relevant amendments of its own, in which case the House returns the bill to the Senate with a schedule of the House's amendments (House SO 247 and 249). Third, the House may simply disagree to the Senate amendments, and so inform the Senate by a message that explains the reasons for the House's disagreement[178] and requests that the Senate reconsider the bill with respect to its amendments (House SO 247). Fourth, the House may postpone consideration of the Senate amendments.[179] And fifth, the House may order that the bill be laid aside. It is the second and third options that interest us here because they create the need to resolve the legislative disagreement arising from the Senate amendments and the House's initial action in response to them.

---

176 The procedures summarized here are discussed in ample detail in chapters 12 and 13 of *House of Representatives Practice* (2001: 423–468) and in chapters 3, 12, and 13 of *Odgers' Australian Senate Practice* (2001: 75–80, 273–279, 320–328). Any reader who thinks the abbreviated explanation presented here is unnecessarily complicated is invited to consult these chapters and the related House and Senate standing orders.

177 Actually more; for example: 'A Senate amendment may be agreed to with or without amendment, agreed to with a consequential amendment, agreed to in part with a consequential amendment, agreed to with a modification, agreed to with a modification and a consequential amendment, disagreed to, or disagreed to but an amendment made in its place.' (*House of Representatives Practice* 2001: 425)

178 'When the House disagrees to any amendments of the Senate to a bill, the Member who moved the motion—That the amendment(s) be disagreed to—shall present to the House written reasons for the House not agreeing to the amendments proposed by the Senate. A message returning the bill to the Senate shall contain any such reasons.' (House SO 248)

179 Of course, the House may take different actions with respect to different Senate amendments.

If the House simply disagrees to the Senate's amendments (option 3 above), the Senate may, under Senate SO 132, reconsider its amendments and decide not to insist on them, in which case the bicameral disagreement is resolved and the bill can be presented for assent. Alternatively, though, the Senate may insist on the amendments to which the House has disagreed, or the Senate may adopt different amendments in place of them. In either case, the disagreement continues because the Senate has chosen not to agree to the House's preference that, in congressional parlance, the Senate recede from its amendments.

If the Senate has proposed new amendments instead of those to which the House previously had disagreed, the House has the same options with respect to those amendments as it had with respect to the Senate's original amendments. If, instead, the Senate has insisted on its original amendments, the House now may agree to those amendments (under House SO 250), thereby resolving the disagreement, or the House may insist on its disagreement to the Senate amendments, or it now may amend the Senate amendments to which it previously had disagreed. In response, the Senate may continue to insist on its amendments to which the House has continued to disagree, or the Senate again can adopt different amendments in their place. If, instead, the House has amended the Senate amendments, the Senate can accept the House amendments or amend them or insist on its original amendments to the House bill (SO 250).

If the House amends the original Senate amendments (option 2 above), the Senate has several options under its SO 132, among which are to accept those amendments, which avoids any further legislative disagreement, or to amend the House amendments, or to insist on its original amendments to the House bill, or to disagree to the House amendments to those original Senate amendments. In the latter case, the Senate includes in its message to the House a statement of its reasons for doing so.[180] In turn, House SO 250 gives the House an equally complex set of options by which it can respond to the most recent Senate action. If the Senate has disagreed to House amendments to the Senate's amendments, for example, the House may withdraw its amendments, or insist on them, or adopt different House amendments instead. Or if the Senate has amended the House's amendments, the House may agree to those new Senate amendments, or amend them, or disagree to them and insist on its original amendments.

---

180 'The reasons shall be drawn up by a committee appointed for that purpose when the Senate adopts the report of the committee of the whole disagreeing to the amendments, or may be adopted by motion at that time.' (Senate SO 133)

Fortunately for Members and Senators this process cannot continue indefinitely.[181] Under House SO 250, if whatever action the House takes at the stage just discussed does not inspire the Senate to agree, the House may no longer propose new amendments.[182] Instead, at this stage, the House 'may return the bill to the Senate, or order the bill to be laid aside, or request a conference.' And 'If the bill be again returned by the Senate with any of the requirements of the House still disagreed to [in other words, if the Senate still refuses to agree to the House's most recent position] the House shall fix a time for the consideration of the message and, on its consideration, shall order the bill to be laid aside or request a conference.'

There is an equally complicated and roughly comparable set of stages and options that are triggered when a bill originates in the Senate and the House then amends that bill in ways that are not immediately acceptable to the Senate. Because relatively few bills begin life in the Senate, and out of consideration for the reader, I will refrain from reviewing all the various possibilities in detail.[183] Instead, I point only to a provision of Senate SO 127. That rule lays out the Senate's options after the House has amended a Senate bill, the Senate has refused to accept those House amendments (at least in the form the House proposed them), and the Senate has made one more proposal to resolve the disagreement. In that circumstance, Senate SO 127 states, that, if the House rejects that proposal and the bill is 'again returned by the House of Representatives with any of the requirements of the Senate still disagreed to, the Senate shall order the bill to be laid aside, or request a conference.'

---

181 According to Jaensch (1997: 107), 'This process will continue until either a consensus (or compromise) has been achieved, or until the government decides it is unable to proceed because of intransigence in the Senate, at which point the latter either rejects the Bill, or it lapses.' This comment suggests that the process rarely continues through all the stages for which the standing orders provide. Furthermore, the House has been known to suspend SO 250 so that the process could continue beyond what the standing orders allow.

182 However, Senate SO 127 and House SO 250 permit amendments between the two houses that go one step beyond the congressional principle that each house has one opportunity to amend the amendments of the other house (in addition to the initial right of one house to amend the bill itself that originated in the other house).

183 *Odgers' Australian Senate Practice* (2001: 274) points out that 'Amendments made by the House to Senate bills usually have the effect of reversing amendments which the Senate has made to government bills in the Senate and to which the government has disagreed.' In other words, if the government is unsuccessful in opposing a Senate amendment to one of its bills that it introduced in the Senate, it can try to reverse that outcome through a later House amendment to the Senate bill. On House amendments to Senate bills generally, see *Odgers' Australian Senate Practice* (2001: 274–277) and *House of Representatives Practice* (2001: 440–441).

To illustrate these procedures in action, let us look very briefly at the actions that the House of Representatives and the Senate took during the last sitting day of 2002 on one of the most important bills they considered during that year. On 24 September, and in response to the terrorist bombing in Bali that killed many Australians and shocked the nation, the House passed the Australian Security Intelligence Organisation Legislation Amendment (Terrorism) Bill 2002. The Senate received the bill on 15 October. After receiving a report from its Legal and Constitutional Legislation Committee, the Senate passed the bill on 12 December, which was supposed to be the last sitting day of the year. Before passing the bill, the Senate made 58 amendments to it, of which 19 were proposed by the Government, 38 by the Opposition, and one by the Australian Democrats.

When the House completed its initial consideration of the Senate's amendments in the early morning hours of 13 December, it had agreed to 15 of the amendments, disagreed to 35 others, and made 14 new government amendments to the bill instead of the remaining eight Senate amendments. The Senate responded by insisting on all of the 43 amendments to which the House had not agreed. In turn, the House agreed to only three of those 43 amendments. It insisted on disagreeing to the remaining 40 Senate amendments and also insisted on five of the 14 replacement amendments to which it had agreed a short time earlier. The Senate, however, was adamant, and once again insisted on all 40 of its original amendments to which the House had insisted on disagreeing.[184] The Senate was saying to the House, in effect, that it would prefer having no bill at all to a bill that did not include those 40 amendments or compromise provisions that were acceptable to both houses. Confronted with this stark choice, and with little reason to think that the Senate would change its mind in the next few hours, the House laid the bill aside. This action marked the government's decision to abandon the bill. However, there is little that is final about the legislative process. The government introduced another bill on the same subject early in 2003, and a heavily-amended version passed both houses in June of that year.

Special procedures for Senate requests

When the Senate cannot amend a bill directly, it can request that the House make certain amendments instead. The Senate votes on what amendments, if any, it wants to request and it then returns the bill to the House before the third reading stage in the Senate. Consequently, the

---

184 This information is taken from the 2002 edition of *Business of the Senate*.

Senate and House must agree on how to dispose of the Senate's requests before the Senate completes its initial legislative action on the bill. If the Senate does decide to request amendments, it returns the bill to the House with the requested amendments attached as a schedule, in the same way that the Senate attaches as schedules the amendments it makes to other bills.[185] The House then 'may make the amendments requested, not make them, or make them in modified form.'[186] After making its decisions, the House returns the bill to the Senate with a message specifying what it has decided with respect to each requested amendment. 'However, if completely unwilling to comply with a Senate request, instead of responding the House may simply lay the bill aside' (*House Guide* 1999: 75), but doing so would kill the bill.

Assuming the House returns the bill to the Senate, the Senate then may pass it with the amendments that the House has made at the Senate's request and without the requested amendments that the House has refused to make. Alternatively, the Senate may refuse to pass the bill. The Senate's third alternative is to insist on the amendments that were unacceptable to the House by pressing its request that the House make those amendments.

As we saw in Chapter 2, the House accepts this practice but, in language reminiscent of the American Senate's posture toward the 'Origination Clause' of the US Constitution,[187] tries to preserve its constitutional position that the Senate has no right to press requested amendments. A publication of the House explains to the general public that:

185 Sometimes the Senate acts on a bill by making some amendments and requesting others. In such a case, 'The message forwarding the requests ... also sets out the amendments which the Senate has made to the bill. The rationale of this procedure is that the House should know of all the amendments required by the Senate before it deals with the Senate's requests. The House cannot actually deal with the Senate's amendments, however, until the requests have been disposed of and the Senate has passed the bill.' (*Odgers' Australian Senate Practice* 2001: 321; see also *House of Representatives Practice* 2001: 427–428)

186 Notice that the House does not amend a Senate request in the same way it would amend a Senate amendment to an amendable bill; instead, the House agrees to a modification of the Senate's request. However, the House may decide to amend a bill directly rather than agreeing to a Senate request for an amendment to the bill. If the House chooses to agree to a Senate request for an appropriation amendment, it may first have to receive a message from the Governor-General recommending the appropriation. In practice, however, this is a formality.

187 In Article I, clause 1 of section 7 states that 'All Bills for raising Revenue shall originate in the House of Representatives, but the Senate may propose or concur with Amendments as on other Bills.'

The House has never recognized the power of the Senate to insist on or
press a request and may decline to consider a Senate message purporting to
do so. However, the House has on most occasions taken the Senate's
message into consideration [i.e., acted on it] after passing a preliminary
resolution refraining from determining its constitutional rights. In recent
years, when a message has been received from the Senate purporting to
press requests for amendments, it has been the practice of successive
Speakers to make a statement referring to the principles involved and which
the House has endorsed, whether declining to consider the message or not.
(*House Guide* 1999: 76)

Odgers' Australian Senate Practice (2001: 326–327) acknowledges the
House's position and offers its own litany of arguments to support the
Senate's right to press requests.

Between 1901 and 2000, a total of 155 bills gave rise to Senate
requests for one or more amendments (*Odgers' Australian Senate
Practice* 2001: 625–661). When we break down the data by decade, we
find that almost half (actually 45.2 per cent) of these incidents occurred
during 1991–2000. That is considerably more than three times as many
as during the previous decade (19 during 1981–1990), and more than
five times more than in any of the other eight decades. In only 19
instances did the Senate press one or more of its requests, doing so
eight times during the last two decades of the century. Interestingly, the
decade in which there were most pressed requests (though only five)
was during the first decade of Federation, 1901–1910, when the Senate
was concerned to establish the reach of its constitutional powers
relating to money bills. In 12 of the 19 instances, the Senate was at least
partially successful in that the House ultimately accepted some or all of
the Senate's pressed requests or accommodated them in the texts of
alternative amendments or replacement bills (*House of Representatives
Practice* 2001: 435–436).

A different but related issue arises when the House thinks that a
Senate amendment should have taken the form of a request (*House of
Representatives Practice* 2001: 428–432). This conflict is particularly
likely to arise because of ambiguity about precisely what qualifies as a
prohibited Senate amendment that would 'increase any proposed charge
or burden on the people' under sec. 53 of the Constitution. In such a
case, the House has several options. First, it may consider the
amendment anyway, but perhaps only after asserting its interpretation
of sec. 53 and implying, if not directly asserting, that the Senate has
exceeded its constitutional authority. Second, the House may refuse to
consider the amendment and inform the Senate that the House will
consider instead a request for the amendment. Third, the House may
disagree to the amendment and, after receiving a new message from the

Governor-General if it considers that necessary, make a similar or identical House amendment and request the Senate to concur in it.[188]

The committee that isn't there

The procedural stages and options that we have been discussing correspond, in broad outline and in many details, to those governing the process by which the US House of Representatives and Senate attempt to resolve their legislative differences. But there is one difference that is most striking. In Washington, the House and Senate may decide, at any point after they have disagreed with each other's position on a bill, that it makes sense to hand the bill over to a conference committee comprising interested Representatives and Senators who meet together to develop a settlement of all the bicameral differences. A conference committee is a temporary joint committee that is set up to write the final version of a particular bill. The committee is composed primarily, and usually only, of members of the House and Senate committees that had been responsible for developing the versions of the bill that each house debated, amended, passed, and then sent to conference. After this committee reaches agreement and submits its report, each house votes to accept or reject the report as a package.

Conference committees are not used for all bills. In fact, at least three-quarters of all bills that become law, and sometimes as many as 90 per cent of them, complete the legislative process in the Congress through an exchange of messages, positions, and amendments between the houses, and without resort to negotiations in a conference committee. On the other hand, conference committees are established to negotiate the final terms of all the most important and controversial bills, except when the imminent arrival of a deadline, such as the end of the two-year constitutional term of a Congress, leaves insufficient time. Furthermore, the House and Senate in Washington essentially never wait to create a conference committee as a last resort, after having exhausted the possibility of reaching agreement through the exchange of messages, positions, and amendments. Instead, the two houses of the US Congress typically agree to create a conference committee on a major bill as soon as each house has passed its own version of the bill.

By contrast, the standing orders of the Australian House and Senate relegate conferences to an option of last resort.[189] The standing orders of the House mention the possibility of a conference as an option only at

---

188 In this complex process, these do not exhaust the House's options. For example, it always has the problematic option of laying the bill aside and letting it die.

189 The Parliament may create conferences, but it does not create conference *committees*.

the last stage of the process of trying to resolve bicameral differences regarding a House bill that the Senate has amended. And the standing orders of the Senate first raise the possibility of a conference on a Senate bill that the House has amended only after the opportunities for exchanging amendments have been exhausted. For the Senate, a conference is only possible 'when agreement cannot be achieved, by an exchange of messages, with respect to amendments to Senate bills' (*Odgers' Australian Senate Practice* 2001: 77). The effect of the two houses' standing orders (Senate SO 127 and House SO 250) is that only the Senate may request a conference on a Senate bill that the House has amended and, conversely, only the House may request a conference on a House bill that the Senate has amended. Since most legislation, and certainly almost all of the most important legislation, originates in the House, the decision to request a conference rests in practice with the House, not the Senate. Other standing orders in each house govern, in almost identical terms, how conferences are to be requested, arranged, and convened (House SO 373–384 and Senate SO 156–162).[190]

Yet what is much more noteworthy than what these standing orders provide is the fact that they never are invoked. In *Odgers' Australian Senate Practice* (2001: 77), the reasons for creating conferences are laid out in terms that sound very familiar to the American ear: 'Conferences between the two Houses provide a means of seeking agreement on a bill or other matter when the procedure of exchanging messages fails or is otherwise inadequate to promote a full understanding and agreement on the issues involved.' However, only two such conferences have been formally created since the founding of the Commonwealth to negotiate the resolution of legislative differences.[191]

In 1930, the House requested a conference after the Senate had insisted on its amendments to the Commonwealth Conciliation and Arbitration Bill 1930. Each house appointed five managers and the conference met in the Senate Committee Room. The managers

---

190 For example, both sets of standing orders require that there be an equal number of members from each house on a conference. House standing orders contain an interesting provision that the Senate standing orders do not. House SO 383 imposes this duty on its managers: 'It shall be the endeavour of the managers for the House to obtain either a withdrawal, by the managers of the Senate, of the point in dispute between the Houses, or a settlement of the same by way of modification or further amendment; but, in the case of bills, no amendment (not being a consequential amendment) shall be suggested by them to any words of a bill to which both Houses have so far agreed, unless these be immediately affected by the disagreement in question.' This prohibition against proposing to amend something to which both houses already have agreed has its counterpart in US congressional rules and precedents.

191 See *House of Representatives Practice* 2001: 444–445.

proposed that the House should agree to some of the Senate amendments, that it should not agree to others, and that the House should agree to still other Senate amendments with modifications. The Senate evidently acted first on the conference recommendations,[192] and both houses agreed to those recommendations. In the following year, a conference on the Northern Territory (Administration) Bill 1931 was arranged and held in the same way (*Odgers' Australian Senate Practice* 2001: 78; *House of Representatives Practice* 2001: 444–445). During the more than 70 years that followed, no other conferences have been held.

There was a third instance in which the Senate requested a conference on a Senate bill, the Social Services Consolidation Bill 1950. The House had amended the bill and insisted on its amendment, and the Senate had insisted on its disagreement to the amendment. However, the House did not agree to the conference. Instead, the House 'desired the reconsideration of the bill by the Senate' and the Senate ultimately agreed to the House amendment.[193] The House's own explanation of its procedures acknowledges (in *House Guide* 1999: 75) that, 'in practice the conference procedure is not used, and if it is recognized that further negotiation by message would be pointless it is usual for the House to order the bill to be 'laid aside'—that is, abandoned and removed from the Notice Paper.'

One reason for the lack of conferences—or perhaps one indication that conferences have been expected to be rare—is Senate SO 158, stating that 'During a conference the sitting of the Senate shall be suspended,' and the corresponding House SO 376.[194] Another lies in the difference between the effect of adopting conference reports in Washington and Canberra. In Washington, the two houses must vote on the managers' recommendations without change; the conference report cannot be amended in either house. And if both houses agree to that report, the effect is to complete the legislative process because all legislative disagreements with respect to that bill have been resolved. In

---

192 This is consistent with the congressional practice that the house which agrees to the request from the other house to establish a conference committee normally acts first on the committee's report.

193 *House of Representatives Practice* (2001: 445) records that, on one occasion in 1921, three members of each house met informally to discuss an amendment that the Senate had requested to an appropriation bill. The Prime Minister reported the recommendation that these members had reached and both houses endorsed it. Consequently, the Senate did not press its request for the amendment.

194 In 1930 and again in 1931, the House waived this standing order (*House of Representatives Practice* 2001: 444). At least in 1931, the Senate did not (*Odgers' Australian Senate Practice* 2001: 78).

Canberra, by contrast, the report of a conference committee, even after it has been adopted, only constitutes a set of recommendations that are subject to further legislative action. 'The adoption of the report of a conference *does not necessarily bind the Senate to the proposals of the conference*, which, with reference to amendments in the bill, come up for consideration in committee of the whole.' (*Odgers' Australian Senate Practice* 2001: 79; emphasis added)

Why? The Australian Senate advertises itself as the second-most powerful upper chamber in the world, with the US Senate obviously being first. So if both Australia and the US have bicameral national assemblies with legislatively-powerful upper chambers, why have conference committees developed as an essential mechanism for resolving legislative disagreements in one of them, but not the other? For the explanation we have to look beyond the standing orders of Canberra's House and Senate. To be sure, these rules do reduce the value and practicality of conferences—by prohibiting plenary sessions when conferences are meeting, and by allowing the adoption of a conference report to leave legislative disagreements still unresolved. However, these and any other rules could be changed if majorities in both houses concluded that those rules were standing in the way of a useful organizational and procedural innovation. No, it is much more plausible to conclude that conferences have not flourished in Canberra because they are not well-suited to the political context of the Commonwealth Parliament, notwithstanding its similarities as a bicameral assembly with the US Congress.

It is always difficult to account for a non-event, for something that has not happened. In this case, though, I think the place to start is with what is perhaps the first questions that arise in thinking about the process of resolving legislative differences in bicameral assemblies. Just how many players are involved, and who are they? When the House of Representatives and Senate in Washington create a conference committee, the members of that committee from each house are supposed to advocate and defend the legislative positions that their house already has taken. At least that is the theory. In practice, it is universally understood that all members of the conference committee have their own interests, preferences, and priorities, as well as those of their political parties, that will have at least as much, and usually more, effect on their negotiating strategies and behaviour than the position of the House or Senate that they ostensibly were appointed to support. In this sense, there are many more players than just the House and the Senate. Neither house's delegation to a conference is at all monolithic, so it is not much of an exaggeration to say that, in any conference committee negotiation in Washington, there are as many players as there are negotiators.

In Washington too, it also is universally understood that what formally are bicameral negotiations between the House and Senate—or to put it better, between members of the House and Senate—actually involve three parties: not just the two houses of Congress, as a reading of the Constitution and of House and Senate rules would suggest, but the President as well. After all, what point is there in the House and Senate reaching agreement between themselves without knowing, or trying to learn, whether the President will accept their handiwork or whether he will veto it? The two houses may not allow the President's preferences to control their decisions. Sometimes, in fact, and especially in times of divided government, a congressional conference committee may deliberately craft a bill that the President almost certainly will not sign into law, preferring what the majority party's members on the conference committee hope will be an effective campaign issue to half-a-loaf legislation. But even in such circumstances, the members of the conference committee, and all interested Representatives and Senators for that matter, surely have a powerful interest in understanding what the President's preferences are before they start drafting the final version of their bill.

The same question arises in Canberra, but in a different form. On Australia's Capital Hill, the question is not whether the government needs to be recognized as a third party in the negotiations between the House and Senate. Instead, the question is whether the final text of Australian legislation actually is the product of bicameral negotiations at all, or whether it is more the handiwork of negotiations between the government and the Senate (actually, perhaps only a small fraction of the Senate), with the House as an institution remaining a bystander or at best acting as the agent of the government, and with Representatives attempting to exert whatever influence they can through their fellow partisans in the government or the Senate, as the case may be.

Admirers of the House of Representatives, not surprisingly, bristle at such assessments, and reject them as coarse over-simplifications that fail to appreciate the much more complex and nuanced relationship that exists between the government and its majority in the House. Be that as it may, it does seem fair to say that the most prominent and knowledgeable advocates of legislation that passes the Australian House are the government's ministers, not House members without ministerial rank. In Washington, the congressional 'experts' on a bill usually are the senior members of the House and Senate committees that may have conceived of it in the first place, and that were very likely to have been instrumental in formulating the detailed provisions of the separate versions of the bill that the House and Senate passed. The President may have put the issue on the congressional agenda and proposed a version of the bill that influenced the subsequent legislative deliberations. However, his specific legislative proposal sometimes is almost unrecognisable when the final version of the bill is written in conference. Successful presidents make a habit of settling for what often is less than half of the proverbial loaf, and then stepping before the cameras to claim victory.

It is natural and appropriate, then, for the final texts of US national laws to be written in conferences composed of senior House and Senate committee members who would pass legislative paternity tests with flying colours. Who would be their counterparts in Canberra? Conference committees have not thrived in the Commonwealth Parliament because they would involve negotiations between the Senate and the House when, in truth, the House is a minor player when compared with the government. Conference committees are not a suitable forum for final-stage legislative negotiations because, when such negotiations are necessary, they usually involve government ministers and Senators. Furthermore, the negotiations may include only minor party and Independent Senators when a mutually acceptable agreement between the government and the Opposition is not a realistic possibility.

There is a second, related explanation that also is plausible. Conference committees in the US Congress involve negotiations between representatives of two institutions, the House and the Senate, that enjoy virtually the same powers and legitimacy. A natural tendency, therefore, is for their negotiations to result in split-the-difference compromises. Even if a middle ground is neither sought nor found on every individual disagreement, the final package of compromises usually allows the representatives of each house to claim that they won more than they lost in the conference negotiations. To submit final legislative decisions to a House-Senate conference in Canberra, or even a government-Senate conference if such a thing could be envisaged, would require the government to accept the Senate as an equal partner in policy-making. And this is something that I doubt any Commonwealth government would be prepared to do.[195]

---

195 In a somewhat broader context, another American observed that negotiation is not exactly at the heart of the Australian legislative process: 'What seems odd to me ... is that after fifty years of proportional representation in the Senate and the states, Australian governments have still not internalised the art of negotiation. ... Negotiation is dragged out of governments here like pulling teeth. The experience of parliaments in Europe is that a proportional representation election generally precedes a period of negotiation. It is not a prelude to a slanging

Perhaps for these reasons, conference committees have not developed in Canberra to supplement or replace the formal exchanges of messages, positions, and amendments as the only procedure for resolving legislative disagreements.[196]

match between people who need each other, which is the Australian way because political relationships are dominated by the customary confrontational behaviour of government and opposition in the lower house.' (Ward 2000a: 14)

196 There is another consideration. If a bill dies in Washington because the House, the Senate, and the President cannot agree on the final version of its text, months (and as much as two years) of effort largely go to waste because the entire legislative process must begin again, and usually not until the next Congress convenes with somewhat different political divisions and a somewhat different cast of characters. In Canberra, there can be advantages to the government if it cannot reach agreement with the Senate on a bill. As we saw in Chapter 3, the House can pass the bill again and if the same deadlock occurs, the government gains the trigger it needs to secure a double dissolution.

9

Mandates and reforms

There has been no dearth of proposals for reforming the Senate. As we would expect, some of them have been thoughtful and carefully argued; others have not. However, all these proposals have two things in common. First, all are predicated on assertions or assumptions about why the Senate exists and what role, if any, it should play in Australia's political system; and, second, all conclude that there is something that needs to be reformed—that there is some significant misfit between the reformers' assertions or assumptions and their assessments of the status quo.

When thinking about proposed changes affecting the Senate that politicians themselves have made, it is worth bearing in mind that their judgments about political institutions often are colored by the political situations in which they find themselves at the moment. If an institution serves their purposes, they may conclude that it deserves to be respected and protected. If it poses an obstacle to their ability to achieve their goals, they may discover that the institution is in need of 'reform'.

Conflicting statements by many political leaders, in Australia and elsewhere, could be adduced to illustrate this point, but we need look no further than Prime Minister Howard. In June 2003, the Prime Minister began floating proposals to make it easier for the government and the House of Representatives to override Senate objections to a government bill. The proposal would eliminate the need for a double dissolution, followed by an election for all members of both chambers, before a joint sitting could be convened to vote on a bill that the Senate had refused to pass in a form acceptable to the government. One proposal would permit a joint sitting after the dissolution and election of the House of Representatives, but not the entire Senate as well. An alternative would allow the government to convene a joint sitting without any intervening dissolution and election at all. Why? According to the Prime Minister, 'Tragically for Australia, the Australian Senate in recent years, so far from being a states' house or a house of review has become a house of obstruction.'[197]

In commenting several months later on Prime Minister Howard's proposals, Senator John Faulkner, the ALP's Leader of the Opposition in the Senate, noted that Howard had spoken of the Senate in much more complimentary terms in 1987, before he became Prime Minister.[198] The Senate, he had argued, was:

> one of the most democratically elected chambers in the world—a body which at present more faithfully represents the popular will of the total Australian people at the last election than does the House of Representatives. *Commonwealth Parliamentary Debates* (House of Representatives), 8 October 1987:1022

Faulkner also quoted Howard's 1997 opinion about the Senate's exercise of its legislative powers:

> The Senate has a perfect right to determine the way in which it will process legislation … If those opposite [the ALP] had behaved with a little more respect towards the rights of minorities in this parliament over the years, then perhaps they would not be facing the attitude that is now being taken by the Senate. If they had not insulted the Senate, if they had not sought to undermine the Senate, if they had not described the Senate as 'unrepresentative swill', if members of the Labor Party did not contain within its ranks people who still want to destroy the Senate, they would not be faced with this situation. *Commonwealth Parliamentary Debates* (House of Representatives), 19 August 1993: 330

With this reminder that 'reform' is in the eye of the beholder, we will review in this chapter several recent proposals to illustrate their variety, comment on their merits, and illuminate the theories of Australian government implicit in them. First, though, we will examine one of the most familiar and powerful collections of assertions and assumptions about how Australia's national policies are supposed to be made and how its parties in Parliament are supposed to behave. This theory of sorts, which many Australian politicians have seemed to endorse when it has been to their advantage to do so, goes to the heart of Australia's political order and implies a minimal and largely passive role for the Senate within that order.

---

197 John Howard. 'Closing Address to the Liberal Party National Convention— Adelaide SA', 8 June 2003. Available electronically at www.pm.gov.au/news/ speeches/2003/speech2331.htm

198 John Faulkner. 'Reform of the Senate', 16 August 2003. ALP News Statement. Available electronically at www.alp.org.au//media/0803/20005358.html.

The matter of mandates

One way in which many politicians and some scholars have tried to clarify the respective roles and powers of the House of Representatives and the Senate is by resorting to claims of electoral mandates. So much sweat, if not blood and tears, already has been shed in arguments about the existence and meaning of mandates that I enter the fray only because of the implications of the theory of mandates for the centrality of the House and the marginality or illegitimacy of the Senate, especially when it actually exercises its constitutional powers.[199]

The principles of responsible government, conventionally understood, imply that a majority in the Parliament, or the lower house of a bicameral parliament, will prefer the existing government to any available alternative. These principles do not necessarily require that the government can and should prevail in the Parliament on all occasions and on all matters. In the Commonwealth Parliament, the government always *can* prevail because its supporters command a majority in the House and they are united in a single disciplined party (or an almost equally disciplined coalition of parties). However, to conclude that the government always *should* prevail requires a further justification that emerges from the mandate theory of democratic governance.

Briefly put, the mandate theory asserts that the government has both the responsibility and the right to have the Parliament enact the legislative proposals that its party or parties had championed during the preceding election campaign. If the government fails to pursue enactment of those proposals, it fails in its obligation to the electorate and it breaks the links of democratic governance. Those links involve a clear and simple logic: a party seeks support from the voters for its program; the voters endorse that program by voting for the party and giving it enough seats to form the government; and the party then has the *responsibility* to enact its program into law. Furthermore, the verdict of the electorate gives the winning party, now in government, the *right* to enact its program. It would seem, therefore, that any constitutional arrangement, parliamentary procedure, or Opposition stratagem that might prevent the government from implementing its plans is, to that extent, illegitimate.

This is essentially the argument that Prime Minister Howard made after the 1998 election:

---

199 The best discussion of this issue, certainly in the Australian context, is Goot (1999a).

I have a very simple view about the political process in this country. And that view is that elections are opportunities for opposing political forces to lay their plans in detail before the Australian people and when the Australian people have made a decision it is the obligation of the victor in that political contest to implement the plans laid before the Australian people. There is nothing complicated about it. (quoted in Nethercote 1999: 16)

Notice that there is no mention here of the fact that the Australian people had made a decision to leave the Senate under non-government control. Howard was speaking to a Liberal Party meeting, so he can be excused for attempting to rally the faithful. Nonetheless, he was unquestionably right in saying that he was expressing a very simple view about the Australian political process.[200]

The Prime Minister was not alone in claiming for his government a mandate to govern. That theme was a favourite among Australian editorial writers in the days following the 1998 election, as this sampling attests:

The Senate has no right to thwart a newly elected government's election program. In our Westminster system, the authority of government lies in the House of Representatives. (*Sunday Mail* (Adelaide), 4 October 1998, p. 16)

John Howard has won government and now has the right and duty to present to Parliament the program on which he was re-elected. Anyone who challenges that … should go sit in a corner and not annoy the rest of the country. (*Daily Telegraph* (Sydney), 5 October 1998, p. 12)

No assertions from Labor … can alter the fact that John Howard and the Coalition won the 1998 Federal election with an unquestioned mandate to govern. (*Sydney Morning Herald*, 5 October 1998, p. 12)

[O]ur Westminster convention decrees that the party with the majority of seats in the House of Representatives enjoys the right to govern. (*Herald Sun* (Melbourne), 5 October 1998, p. 18)

Australia made its choice with its eyes open and the Government should now be allowed to deliver. (*Australian Financial Review* (Sydney), 7 October 1998, p. 18)

[T]he second Howard Government, like its predecessors, is right to insist that it does have a mandate to implement its electoral program. (*Age* (Melbourne), 10 October 1998, p. B9)

---

200 There are more nuanced conceptions of mandates; see, for example, Emy (1996, 1997). Our interest, however, is with how the concept is used in political discourse, not in what political theorists think it should mean or how they think it should be used.

We will find this same theory reflected clearly in a current minister's critique of the Senate and the influence that minor parties can exercise in it. In a 1999 paper (Coonan 1999b) revised and republished in 2000,[201] Senator Helen Coonan, a Liberal Senator from New South Wales and Assistant Treasurer in the Coalition Government from November 2001, canvassed a variety of proposals to change the Senate, including abolishing the equal representation of the states in the Senate and authorizing a joint sitting of the two houses to resolve a legislative deadlock as soon as it occurs (not only after a double dissolution election and a third unsuccessful attempt to pass the bill). She did not directly endorse any such proposal because each would require a constitutional amendment, and Australia's track record of approving amendments by referenda made her very dubious about securing approval of any constitutional change, especially one that would be interpreted as reducing the political leverage of some of the states. Instead, she expressed most interest in a way of reducing the numbers of minor party Senators, or eliminating them altogether, by imposing a minimum percentage of first-preference votes that any party would have to win before it could receive transferred preferences and, therefore, hope to win seats in the Senate.[202]

Her underlying argument begins with the assertion that the Senate has become, or is in danger of becoming, 'an obstructional competitor in the government of the country, frustrating or at least substantially delaying urgently required responses to national problems and regional and world crises,' and so 'is disabling Australia from realising and enjoying its full potential.' Instead of acting as 'a great institutional safeguard for all Australians', 'The Senate safeguard has in fact become a handbrake on progress.' This situation has arisen for reasons with which we have become familiar: the adoption of proportional representation in 1948 for Senate elections and increases in the size of the Senate, in 1948 and again in 1983, combined to facilitate the election of minor party Senators and to increase the likelihood that no government party would have 'the numbers' in the Senate.

The result has been that, when the government and the Opposition disagree, minor parties hold the balance of power in the Senate and can use their leverage to secure changes in government policies. The

---

201 This paper was presented as an address to the Sydney Institute on 3 February 1999. The quotes that follow are taken from the web version, available through [www.onlineopinion.com.au/May/hand.htm].

202 However, Coonan's own analysis showed that the imposition of even a relatively high five per cent threshold would not have prevented election of any of the 16 minor party or Independent Senators who were elected in 1993, 1996, or 1998.

current system for electing Senators 'permits the election of minor parties on a fraction of the national vote who may then be in a position to exercise on behalf of their minority interests not just a voice, which indeed should be able to find expression in a healthy democracy, but in effect to have a casting vote on national legislation.' Therefore, the election laws should be amended to make it more difficult for minor parties to win Senate seats. Coonan's argument assumes that the government and the Opposition are routinely arrayed against each other which, as we have seen, is not at all the permanent condition in the Senate. But for the sake of argument, let us accept her assertions as to the leverage that minor parties have enjoyed and how they have used it. What is the problem that needs to be solved, other than the obvious inconvenience this situation poses for the government of which she is a member?

In using their votes to force changes in government legislation, she argues, the minor parties in the Senate are engaging in 'political opportunism that reduces any sense of common purpose to the lowest common denominator,' because they are interfering with implementation of the government's electoral mandate. The government's lack of a majority in the Senate requires the government to compromise which, she clearly implies, is a bad thing in parliamentary government:

> [P]roportional representation has ensured that neither of the major parties will have a working majority in the Senate. At the very best that means that government will be by compromise. That, in turn, means at least delay, at worst inability on the part of Government to respond in what it considers to be effective and necessary ways to crises in the national and international spheres.

But is not compromise a virtue in democratic government? Evidently not in parliamentary government, because compromise intrudes on the government's exercise of its mandate to govern:

> [I]f responsible government is to function according to convention, in my view it requires the authority of the people … to govern generally and in accordance with the specific promises and responsibilities spelt out in its policies. In our system, this authority is delivered to the party that wins a majority of seats in the House of Representatives and forms the Government.[203]

---

203 Not all Members and Senators agree, at least not all the time. Senator Amanda Vanstone, a fellow Liberal Party Senator and minister, offered a different view of what democratic politics, and the Senate, are all about: 'In politics I don't get what I desire most of the time, but you don't want a system where people get everything they want. People who go into politics have a degree of megalomania. You're there, Jack, you can do whatever you like. That's why the Senate is there, that's why the

Here is the mandate theory in full bloom. What need is there for any deliberative legislative process at all? The election determines a winner, so the winner—the government—has the right and responsibility, and should have the power, to do anything and everything that it said it would do. The government allows the Opposition to criticize its proposals, but the government would be violating its commitment to the public if it allowed itself to be swayed by the merits of the Opposition's arguments. In reply, as we shall find, the non-government parties may argue that they are the ones that really have the mandate because the government failed to receive the support of a majority of voters. This 'overall majority argument,' according to Senator Coonan, 'conveniently overlooks the fact that our present system awards government to the party that secures a majority of seats in the House of Representatives.' The obvious rejoinder, of course, is that her argument conveniently overlooks the fact that the same present system awards control of the Senate to the party or parties that secure a majority of seats in that house.

The second and more serious problem is that Senator Coonan only pays attention to the parts of her Constitution that she likes and not to those that are the ultimate source of difficulties for her government. We have heard her argue about what is needed 'if responsible government is to function according to convention,' and her argument might well be sound if she were a member of the House of Commons. But in Australia, the same Commonwealth Constitution that says not one word about responsible government, much less about the conventions surrounding it, is explicit in its grant of authority to the Senate to amend legislation. If Coonan is prepared to draw inferences about responsible government from what the Constitution does not say, advocates of Senate power are that much more justified in drawing the inferences that, if the Senate has the right to amend bills, it also has the right not to pass them until the House has responded to its amendments in a manner satisfactory to the Senate, or not to pass those bills at all.

As I have said, underlying Senator Coonan's argument is an uncomplicated and linear concept of democracy: (1) the party presents a program to the people; (2) the people vote for the party; (3) this constitutes an endorsement of the program; so (4) the party enacts the program. This understanding of how a democracy should work calls to mind the aphorism usually attributed to H.L. Mencken, that 'there is always an easy solution to every human problem—neat, plausible, and

---

states are there. It's frustrating, but the citizen should be grateful for this.' (quoted in Terrill 2000: 287)

wrong',[204] except that here we have a solution that is worse: it is neat and plausible—and dangerous.

For better or worse, the mandate theory in Australia is something else that was transported and transplanted from Great Britain. The most explicit endorsement of the theory is found in the 'Salisbury Convention', by which the House of Lords committed itself not to block legislation to implement commitments that the government, with its majority in the House of Commons, had made in its most recent election manifesto. The convention dates back to 1945 after Britain elected its first majority Labour Government, which confronted a weak but not powerless House of Lords that was composed overwhelmingly of Conservative Party supporters. It was the Conservative leader in the House of Lords, Lord Salisbury, who agreed to the convention. Had he not done so, and had the unelected hereditary peers delayed enactment of Labour's legislation (to the extent the Lords still could do so under the Parliament Acts of 1911 and 1949), a powerful movement might well have developed for legislation to reform or abolish the House of Lords.[205]

The Salisbury Convention was justified on two grounds. First, the House of Lords was not elected and so was not able to claim any democratic legitimacy. Second, the political composition of the Lords always favoured the Conservatives to an overwhelming degree. The consistent result was an imbalance in party composition compared with the Commons, and especially, of course, during periods of Labour government. Neither of these conditions holds true in Australia. The Commonwealth Senate always has been directly elected, and it can make its own claim to being as representative as the House of Representatives. The House claims that it is the representative body because seats in the House are allocated to, and within, the states on the basis of population. In the Senate, of course, each state enjoys equal representation regardless of its population; so, the House argues, it cannot claim to be a truly representative body. Defenders of the Senate reply, however, that the Senate actually is *more* representative than the House, in that electing Senators by proportional representation has produced a closer correspondence between seats and votes in the Senate than in the House. In other words, the distribution of seats among parties is closer in the Senate than in the House to the distribution of votes among the parties in the national electorate (Evans 1997b: 22–23). A party that receives 40 per cent of the vote, for example, is more

---

204 *The New York Evening Mail,* 15 November 1917.
205 As we recently have observed, such a 'constitutional' reform can be achieved in the UK by ordinary legislation.

likely to win more or less 40 per cent of the seats in the Senate than in the House.

Notwithstanding these differences between the situations in London and Canberra, Australian governments have adopted the mandate theory with great enthusiasm. In his review of the 1975 crisis, Gough Whitlam laid out a formulation of this misguided and pernicious theory that is so stark and strong as to merit quotation at some length:

> [T]he mandate of 1972 was the most positive and precise ever sought and ever received by an elected government in Australian history. The program was the most comprehensive, its promulgation and popularisation the most intensive and extensive in our political history. Its central elements had been developed not in the three weeks of an election campaign … but over a period of half a decade and more. Three successive conferences of the Labor Party, in 1967, 1969, and 1971, had rewritten two-thirds of the Party's platform. The program's crucial reforms in the three great areas of schools, hospitals and cities had been presented to the people not once but four times, at elections in 1967, 1969, 1970 and 1972, each time more precisely, each time more successfully, until their unequivocal endorsement on 2 December 1972. I deliberately ignore in this context our equally clear mandate on matters related to international affairs—the ending of the Australian commitment in Viet Nam, our recognition of the People's Republic as the sole government of China, the interment of the already moribund South East Asia Collective Defense Treaty Organisation (SEATO), the independence of Papua New Guinea and the ending of conscription for military service in Viet Nam or anywhere else. (Whitlam 1979: 5)

> We believed that the precision of the program reinforced the strength of the mandate and that so strong a mandate would meet with no more than token resistance from a Senate which had no mandate at all. We were grievously wrong. The strongest resistance came on the very matters upon which we were most entitled to believe our mandate to be the most explicit. (Whitlam 1979: 5–6)

> As leader of a reform government, I placed the strongest interpretation on the meaning of the mandate given at an election by the majority of the people. Conservatives naturally prefer its restricted interpretation—that an election win confers a mandate to govern but is not an instruction to implement an election manifesto to its last detail. The weaker interpretation is not, I believe, acceptable for a party and government of reform. Our minority position in the Senate confirmed my determination to interpret the mandate in the strongest sense. (Whitlam 1979: 7)

The ALP had campaigned on a clear and comprehensive policy program, and the voters had approved that program by voting for the

ALP, which gave the ALP a mandate—a right and a responsibility—to implement its program 'to its last detail.'[206]

Whitlam is to be forgiven for the enthusiasm that he and his Labor colleagues brought to his Ministry after the ALP's 23 years in the political wilderness, just as he is to be forgiven for the righteous indignation he continued to feel several years after his dismissal. Nonetheless, the factual assumptions of his argument are breathtaking.

To accept his argument requires us to accept, first, that the Australian electorate was fully aware of each and every one of the elements of the Labor Party program. This is an assertion for which Whitlam offers no evidence, of course—his book is political argument, not political science—nor can I offer any evidence to the contrary. However, what political scientists have learned about the public's interest in and its attention to the positions of political parties leads me to believe this claim to be entirely implausible (McAllister 1998; Goot 1999a).[207] Here, for instance, is Jaensch's assessment of the situation in Australia as of 1986:

> A summary of survey findings suggests that most Australians are not informed, not interested, and show a very low level of knowledge of personalities, institutions, issues or policies. Few voters even know the names of their local members, or the candidates they voted for at the last election. Many do not distinguish between state and national politics, and many of the voters have no idea of the policies of the party they supported, or of the issues at the election. (Jaensch 1986: 148)

Yet Whitlam—and, more important, contemporary advocates of electoral mandates, whether in Parliament House or universities—would have us accept that Australians voted for the ALP in 1972 *because* they supported the Labor program *in its entirety*, and in particular because the voters supported in 1972 key proposals that, by the same kind of logic, they must have rejected on three prior

---

206 This was not just a post hoc formulation. Nethercote (1999: 13) quotes a lecture that Whitlam gave in August 1975, several months before his dismissal, in which he asked rhetorically whether his government's mandate in 1972 and again in 1974 had been 'a grant of permission to preside or a command to perform'. Not surprisingly, he concluded that it was the latter.

207 After the Republican Party took control of the US House of Representatives in 1995 for the first time in 40 years, its leaders immediately claimed a powerful mandate to enact immediately a specific catalogue of bills, known as the 'Contract with America,' that many of its candidates had supported during the campaign. Survey research subsequently revealed that relatively few voters knew about this 'Contract' or paid much attention to it or could identify its elements. Could it fairly be said, then, that the Republicans really had a mandate to enact their treasured agenda after 40 years as the seemingly permanent minority party?

occasions. The voters had been presented with the party's 'crucial reforms in the three great areas of schools, hospitals and cities' in the elections for the Senate in 1967 and 1970, and in the intervening election for the House of Representatives in 1969. Labor did not emerge from any of these elections with a working majority in the chamber that was contested. But when Labor then won in 1972, it was supposedly because the voters now approved those same reform planks. In each of the four elections, the reforms were presented to the people 'more precisely' and 'more successfully,' so the 1972 election constituted an 'unequivocal endorsement' of them. Any reader who has no difficulty imagining average voters deciding to support Labor because they agreed with Whitlam that SEATO was moribund is welcome to accept the other assumptions his argument requires.

These assumptions are (or were) subject to empirical examination. Although it is too late to interview a random sample of Labor voters to learn why they voted for the ALP, what they knew of the party's program, and which elements of that program they supported and which they opposed, it would be possible to ask those same questions of Labor voters today and then extrapolate backwards, on the plausible assumption that the basis for voter choice is probably not that much different now than it was 30 years ago, and that the level of public knowledge about parties and politics was probably not much greater then (and quite possibly less then) than it is today. Lacking such evidence, I cannot prove that Whitlam's implicit theory is wrong. I would wager, however, that (1) public comprehension of Labor's program was far, far more shallow and less widespread than he would like to believe; (2) support for specific policy commitments was only one among many reasons—Whitlam's personality and style being prominent among them—that led Australians to vote for Labor in 1972; and (3) most Labor voters who supported some ALP policies also opposed others of the party's policies—or they would have opposed them if they had known about them.

There are two other reasons for questioning the empirical basis of the mandate theory. First, the theory assumes that voting is prospective, not retrospective—that voters make their decisions on the basis of what the competing parties promise to do in the future, not on the basis of voters' evaluations of what the parties have done in the past. In many instances, I suspect, Australians, like Americans, cast their votes in order to 'throw the bums out.' That kind of cliché about democratic politics implies that voting is retrospective. The same inference also has to be drawn from much of the rhetoric of the Opposition, whether that happens to be the ALP or the Coalition. The Opposition is constantly criticizing the government. In fact, we may say that the Opposition spends most of its time for several years trying to convince Australians that the incumbent government deserves to be kicked out of office. Then it spends only a matter of weeks explaining what it will do if elected to replace the government. If voting is prospective and based on a comparison of the parties' policy promises for the future, why do all parties devote most of their time and energy to criticizing the evils and errors of what their competition did in the past or is doing now? There can be no such thing as an electoral mandate (and this is true by definition) unless elections are decided on the basis of parties' promises for the future, not their record of performance in the past. The parties' own strategies and rhetoric strongly imply that they do not believe this to be the basis for voters' choices—at least until the morning after a party wins the House and then discovers that it has won a powerful mandate after all!

A second, related reason is that the mandate theory assumes that voters are voting *for* a candidate or party and not *against* a candidate or party. Yet consider Solomon's (2001: 185) claim that 'The way people vote at election time is mainly influenced by their dislike of one side or the other, rather than their attraction to particular policies.' To the extent that voting is retrospective, it is a verdict on the performance of the party or coalition in government. If voters are satisfied with the government's performance, they are likely to vote to retain it in office. If not, they are likely to vote against it. In either case, the basis for voter choice is *the government's record* and what it portends for the future, not the policies espoused by the Opposition. Furthermore, this is a perfectly rational basis for choice. The government's record is there to be evaluated, and it is reasonable for voters, like investors, to extrapolate from past performance to future results. How are voters to evaluate the Opposition's promises, especially if it has been out of power for some years and its current leaders have no record of performance as government ministers? This is not to say that all voting is retrospective instead of prospective or that voters are less likely to vote for the party they support than to vote for an alternative to the party they oppose. However, both are reasonable ways for voters to make their decisions, and there is no room for either in the theory of electoral mandates.

In addition, there are at least two other, more normative, reasons for rejecting the mandate theory. First, as I have argued, the theory posits that the government has a responsibility as well as a right to enact its program. The government made promises to the people during the last campaign, and the electorate voted for the government on the basis of those promises. Now the government must fulfill its promises. How, therefore, can a government justify failing to do its best to implement one or more of its campaign promises?

Paul Kelly recounts that, after the 1975 election, 'The most crucial early decision of the Fraser government was the reversal of its previously stated stand in favour of wage indexation':

> In a day Fraser had repudiated one of the central campaign promises on which he went to the electorate. The key economic proposals he put to the people were the implementation of tax indexation backed by wage indexation. This was explained throughout the campaign in the clearest possible terms in speech after speech. ... Fraser was not terribly concerned about repudiating a key section of his policy platform if other factors came into play. He believed that the government was elected by the people in an act of trust to take the best decisions possible at any given time, rather than be tied to a specific set of promises. He claimed that dogmatism would inevitably lead to bad government. (Kelly 1976: 324–325)

Was he wrong? Surely under some circumstances, a government's failure to live up to one of its commitments can be condemned as misrepresentation and dishonesty. Under other circumstances, though, the same decision not to implement a campaign commitment must be recognized as an adjustment to changing circumstances or to the discovery that policy choices that looked simple when in Opposition are revealed to be more complicated when in government.

For our purposes, the point is simple. The more a government insists on its responsibility as well as its right to implement each and every one of its campaign promises, the more it must accept condemnation whenever it does not try its best to do so. A government may respond by seeking to distinguish between electoral commitments that were at the heart of its appeal to the voters and others that were of lesser significance, arguing that it is at liberty to ignore the latter.[208] That argument has merit, however, only if voters know, before making their voting decisions, which of its promises each party is committed to honouring and which it is not. But, it will be argued, conditions change, so it would be unreasonable to demand that a government keep all its

---

208 Emy (1997: 74) has proposed that 'It would be desirable for the parties to agree to make a clearer distinction between core promises, on which each was seeking specific electoral endorsement, and non-core promises which would have the status rather of good intentions.' This strikes me as impractical. No party would want to lose the flexibility that an explicit distinction between core and non-core promises would compel it to forsake. And no group of Australians would be happy to learn that the promise a party has made to meet the group's needs or advance its interests was really just a non-core promise, a statement of good intentions. The pressure on parties to move almost all its promises into the 'core' would become intense and irresistible.

promises when some of them no longer suit the needs of the na
That is exactly right; it would be destructive to demand consistenc, at
all costs. But is it only the government that has the right to make such
judgments? Surely the non-government parties have an equal right—
and responsibility—to evaluate whether government promises continue
to make as much sense as they did on election day.

Finally, consider once again Whitlam's claim to have had a right
and responsibility to implement all of Labor's electoral program. The
ALP emerged from the 1972 election with a majority of only nine seats
in the House of Representatives. Although it had won its first House
election after 23 years in opposition, its victory was something less than
overwhelming. Yet Whitlam's mandate theory had nothing to offer all
those who voted for non-Labor candidates. They had lost; there was
nothing more to say. They would have to wait three years and then try
again, just as Labor had waited and tried again, and then waited some
more and tried once more, again and again throughout the seemingly
endless era that Menzies had defined. Whitlam offers a winner-take-all
approach to politics that evidently places no value on the concepts of
compromise and accommodation, and finds nothing to be gained by
giving a little in order to at least recognize the legitimacy of one's
opponents' interests and preferences. In fact, Whitlam's concept of an
electoral mandate, like that of his political soulmate, Senator Coonan,
de-legitimates compromise and accommodation. After all, the voters
had endorsed the Labor program, not some diluted version of it. So
those voters had a right to have that program enacted as it had been
offered during the campaign. For Labor to have done anything else—to
have agreed to compromises in the interests of finding common ground
with the Opposition—would have constituted a breach of its trust with
the electorate.

Why does the government insist on strict party discipline in the
House? Not only because it can, but also because it should. Party
discipline is needed to win, and the government must win because it has
a mandate that gives it the responsibility as well as the right to win.
And why does the government become so upset when the Senate
delays, amends, or even defeats one of its bills? Not only because it
frustrates the government's policy preferences, but because it also
interferes with the implementation of the government's electoral
mandate. A government is put in an untenable position when it has the
right and responsibility to win, but not, because of the Senate, the
ability to win—or at least to win as it should, without having to
compromise. So, it is not difficult to argue, the Senate should not
exercise its constitutional powers or the Constitution should be
amended to strip it of those powers when they challenge the

government's ability to enjoy the fruits and meet the obligations of its mandate.

It is very easy to understand why any party that has won an election would want to claim that it has a clear and unequivocal mandate to implement its program. Perhaps the best response to a government's claim to have such an electoral mandate is to fight House fire with Senate fire. If the government lacks a majority in the Senate, does that not mean that the non-government parties and Senators enjoy a mandate of their own: a mandate derived from two elections over a six-year period; a mandate for them to oppose the government, especially because the parties' shares of votes at elections are more accurately reflected in the distribution of Senate seats than House seats?[209]

> When the balance of power in the upper house is held by a few members none of whom belong to the largest two parties, we have the most complicated situation of all—everyone can claim to have a mandate for something. The government claims it has a mandate because it has won a majority of seats in the lower house. The opposition claims that it has a mandate to oppose the government's legislation because that is what oppositions are for, and because more voters voted against the government than voted for it. And the minor parties and independents in the Senate can claim that they were elected precisely because their supporters wanted to modify the government's legislative program. (Sharman 1998: 154)

That was the kind of argument made in 1995 by Senator Cheryl Kernot, then Leader of the Democrats in the Senate:

> [W]hile [the Democrats] do not have a mandate to govern the country or to over-ride the Government's political or economic agenda, we do have a mandate … to ensure the Government is made accountable and that its legislation is properly scrutinised and debated … (quoted in Lipton 1997: 200)

And then again, after the 1996 election:

> Voters opted to take out an insurance policy by giving balance of power to the Democrats … [M]ore than half the people who deserted Labor gave their primary votes to candidates other than the Coalition … . Clearly, there are two mandates resulting from this election: one for government to be changed, and one for a balance of power check on that Government in the Senate. (quoted in Sugita 1997: 171)

---

209 'In declaring their opposition to the privatisation of Telstra as a major part of their election policy, the Democrats claimed that they had secured a mandate to oppose the sale of Telstra in the Senate. The incoming coalition government, on the other hand, argued that only governments could have mandates and that the Senate should respect its mandate to sell.' (Mulgan 1996: 197)

In the 1996 election, five of the Democrats' seven Senators were elected, one in each of five states. In light of the claim that Senator Kernot made after that election (just quoted), it is fair to observe that, of those five Senators, none received as much as 15 per cent of the first-preference votes cast, and five of the six were the last in their state to achieve the quota of votes required to win a seat, thanks to the distribution of preferences. The Democrats won their seats according to the rules of the game, to be sure; whether the magnitude and manner of their victories justified any claim to having received a mandate is a different matter entirely.

If we accept Senator Kernot's arguments, then I think it is fair to say that the concept of electoral mandates contributes nothing useful to prescribing what constitutes appropriate, even legitimate, uses of constitutional powers by either the government or its parliamentary opponents. If everyone has a mandate, then no-one does. Let Sharman continue:

> The issue may be simply the extent to which governments must compromise when they make new laws—from this perspective no-one has a mandate to do anything except enter into negotiations. The present situation in the Commonwealth Parliament requires governments to compromise so that a larger group than the governing party, perhaps even a body of parliamentarians representing a real majority of voters, supports a proposed measure. This means that, quite apart from any amendments that may be required, legislation is closely scrutinised, and the government of the day and its supporting bureaucracy must publicly justify every proposed law to a legislative body whose support cannot be taken for granted. (Sharman 1998: 154)

All claims of electoral mandates should be viewed with profound suspicion unless it can be verified that they accurately reflect the knowledge, preferences, and intentions of the voters. Most often we can expect to find that mandates are mirages, the wishful thinking of those claiming to have received them—a commonplace rhetorical device that most or all parties can use in attempts to convince themselves and others that they are acting in the name and in the interests of the voting public. Claims of mandates become dangerous, however, when they are invoked to support a claim that the government has a right to govern without hindrance and, therefore, that any hindrance by the Senate is undemocratic and illegitimate. For all the constitutional, electoral, and political reasons that we have explored, no one party is likely to enjoy such a mandate in Australia, nor should we want it to. Sharman is correct in concluding that 'no-one has a mandate to do anything except enter into negotiations,' and that is something to be welcomed, not deplored.

Complicating this discussion is a distinction sometimes drawn between a general mandate and a specific mandate.[210] The general mandate is a license that the voters are supposed to have given the government at the last election to do as it thinks best, as circumstances require but within the parameters of the party's known philosophy. The voters then will review the government's performance at the next election and decide whether or not to extend its mandate. The specific mandate, on the other hand, is a directive that the voters are supposed to have given the government at the last election to enact and implement certain specific proposals that it enunciated during the election campaign. At the next election, the voters will evaluate the new sets of proposals presented by all the parties and decide which of them will receive the electorate's directive to proceed with its program. In either case, the relationship posited between voters and governors requires that the government be able to do what it thinks best (in the case of a general mandate) or what it has promised to do (in the case of a specific mandate). And in either case, the relationship is understood to be between the electorate and the party or parties that control the House and, therefore, comprise the government.

There is no place here for the Senate. By implication, therefore, the Senate should not do anything that impedes, delays, or prevents the government from fulfilling its mandate with the people—except to act as the House of Review, whatever that may mean—no matter what powers the Constitution gives the Senate.

> Governments are likely to claim that the mandate covers a general right to govern which gives them a right to determine policy as they see fit, subject only to the eventual verdict of the voters. They also claim a specific mandate which confers a right, *and a duty*, to enact policies contained in their election program. In 1993, these two aspects of the mandate came into conflict over the budget. The government held that its (general) mandate entitled it to enact the budget as it stood (with consequent damage to financial confidence if this mandate was interfered with). The coalition, on the other hand, argued that the budget was in breach of the government's (specific) mandate in so far as it increased taxes. (Mulgan 1996: 196; emphasis added)

With both mandates in hand, the government cannot lose. It can insist on enactment of the policies it advocated during the campaign because of its specific mandate, but it also can claim the right to enact policies inconsistent with its campaign pledges, or which were not

---

210 This is a distinction for which Goot (1999a) has considerably less sympathy than Mulgan (1996).

discussed during the campaign, because the voters also have bestowed on it a general mandate—'a general right to govern.'

In fact, any government needs to insist that it has both mandates. Take the case of Australia's present Coalition Government. Its 1998 re-election campaign emphasized its support for enactment of a Goods and Services Tax (GST). So after its victory, it naturally claimed what was in effect a specific mandate to enact that policy into law. Then, in 2003, the same government decided to involve Australia's defence forces in the war against the government of Iraq, a position that could not possibly have been in the minds of voters at the last election as well as a position that, if opinion polls are to be believed, did not enjoy the support of most Australians when the decision was made.

Some mandate theorists would argue that, when such a critically important issue arises in this way, the government should call an election to have its policy endorsed before committing itself to a course of action. Although that actually could have been done in the case of the war in Iraq, the Howard Government did not do so. In fact, the government made it clear that it would decide on its policy without recourse to the electorate and that it would make its decision *before* it scheduled a full-dress debate on the issue in Parliament. The government must have been relying, even if implicitly, on its conviction that it held a general mandate. Furthermore, that is precisely what Australian governments often must be doing. It simply is not practical to hold new House elections every time a major new issue requires a governmental response before the end of the current government's three-year term. Yet even in these circumstances, governments still insist on having their own way, claiming that this is their right because they have a mandate to govern, so non-government Senate majorities should not try to make them compromise on policies that never have been presented to the electorate.

But even though governments need to claim both mandates, the two are incompatible with each other. The concept of a general mandate posits that voters put their faith in a party, trusting it to do what is wise and right, whatever the government decides, after the election, that may be. On the other hand, the concept of a specific mandate is predicated on voters choosing a party because it has produced a manifesto of specific policies that it has pledged itself to implement. The voters select that party because they agree with its menu of policy choices, not because of some generalized trust they have in the common sense, good judgment, and rectitude of the party's leaders.

Presumably recognizing the problem, Mulgan proceeds to try to define it away:

Neither aspect of the mandate depends, as is sometimes thought ... on any conscious intention on the part of voters. ... the general mandate follows from the support for a government of a majority in the lower house; the specific mandate follows from the inclusion of a policy in the government's election program, *regardless of whether any voters knew of it, let alone whether their votes were determined by it.* Inclusion in the manifesto has been recognized as both necessary and sufficient for the recognition of such a mandate. (Mulgan 1996: 196, emphasis added)

In the process, the logical and empirical underpinnings of the specific mandate disappear entirely because voters now are able to prefer one party over another on the basis of policies of which they are unaware. There no longer is any necessary connection between specific voter preferences and specific government policies.[211] And the general mandate seems to mean little more than 'we won, which gives us the power to govern, which gives us the right to govern.' Mandate is reduced to mantra.[212]

Certainly representative government assumes and requires that those whom the people elect to represent them in government make a good faith effort to do what they have promised to do, in so far as they are able to do it and unless their policy commitments made during the election campaign are overtaken by events. There can be no argument with the second condition: we would not want our representatives to continue pursuing the policies they had announced without regard to how circumstances may have changed since election day. The real question concerns the first condition. Does the fact of a democratic election then require that those elected should be able to implement their campaign promises whenever and however they choose, or that they should pursue implementation of those promises within the rules of the game as already established by the Constitution?

From the way in which I have formulated the question, it will be obvious that I support the latter interpretation. Imagine, for example, that, in its manifesto or policy speech, a party promises to 'take whatever steps are necessary to protect the nation against terrorism', a

---

211 However, Mulgan later argued, with cause, that what is important is not the empirical or logical underpinning of mandate claims, but what claims politicians make and with what effect. From this perspective, 'The mandate is understood as a convention which allows a government after winning an election to proceed with a policy it has clearly announced during the preceding election campaign.' (Mulgan 2000: 319)

212 Uhr (1997: 74) speaks of mandates as magic. 'Mandate is a magic word in the sense that it is used just as magicians use special words to conjure up extraordinary effects to reinforce their spellbinding authority.' Both the concept and the consonance are the same.

not unlikely promise in today's world. If that party wins, surely it does not now have carte blanche to take *whatever* steps it decides are necessary; its policies and actions still must conform with basic principles of human rights, civil liberties, and democratic freedoms. By endorsing the party's commitment to fight terrorism, the electorate certainly has not somehow nullified the constitutional authority and responsibility of the High Court to invalidate the government's new laws as unconstitutional if that need should arise. No, the only mandate that the electorate can give to any government is one to proceed within the limits of the established constitutional order, and, in Australia, that established constitutional order includes the Senate with its virtually co-equal legislative authority, just as it includes the High Court and its authority. Whether these constitutional arrangements are good or bad is another question. For our thinking about mandates, what matters is that these arrangements exist, and no election result can set them aside or should be used as an excuse for trying to do so.

A democratic constitution establishes a set of procedures and institutions that, collectively, lay out the rules of the game in which advocates of different public policies compete to have their preferred policies enacted as law. No election victory, no matter how sweeping, can sweep away the rules of the governance game. In Australia, those rules include the constitutional powers of the Senate and the statutory procedures for electing Senators.[213]

The electorate bestows two things on the winner of a free and fair democratic election for parliament (or for president and congress). First, it bestows the advantage of numbers. If the winning party gains a majority of seats in parliament, it gains an obvious advantage in its efforts to see its policies enacted. Under most parliamentary standing orders, it also gains effective control of the legislative agenda, so that it

---

213 What that election victory may do, however, is enable one team of players to change the rules of the game, if it is willing and able to do so. A theme to which we shall return in the next chapter is that the continuing non-government control of the Senate, which has been critical to the contemporary revitalization of the Senate, depends on continuing to elect Senators in much the same way they are elected now. This makes the Senate vulnerable to an agreement between the government and the Opposition to change the rules of the game. There are several ways in which this might be done without appearing to change the electoral system in a fundamental way. As Senator Coonan suggested, for example, there could be a threshold imposed of some percentage of first preference votes that a minor party would have to win before it would be eligible to have any of its candidates elected to the Senate with the benefit of voters' second and later preferences. Or states could be divided into a number of districts in each of which only one or two Senators would be chosen at each half-Senate election, which would make it far harder for any minor party or Independent candidate to secure election.

decides what proposals will be considered seriously, as well as when they will be considered and for how long. Second, the electorate bestows a sense of legitimacy on the party's policies. The party can, and certainly will, claim that the election demonstrates the public's support for its program. Even if there is no evidence that most voters know very much about that program and that they voted for the party because of that program—in other words, there is no basis for a specific electoral mandate—at least the winning party can argue that the voters prefer its program to any of the other party programs that were on offer at the election.

Notice that neither of these advantages is dichotomous; the winning party enjoys them to greater or lesser degrees. A close election may give the winning party only a slight numerical advantage in the parliament. (In fact, one of the major complaints about some election systems is the degree to which they produce a disparity between seats and votes, with the winning party receiving a percentage of seats that is considerably larger than its percentage of votes.) That advantage may not be enough to produce winning majorities on all parliamentary votes. It may suffice, for example, to pass legislation by majority votes, but not to take any actions that require a higher majority such as a two-thirds vote. Or, if more than two parties have won seats, the 'winning' party may win only a plurality of the seats, so it still will need to find parliamentary allies in order to create winning majority voting coalitions.

By the same token, the persuasiveness of the winning party's claim to have the public's support for its programs also depends on the magnitude of its election victory. A party that wins a 51 to 49 per cent victory hardly can make a convincing claim that 'the people' have endorsed its program wholeheartedly when almost every second voter opposed it. 'John Howard claimed victory on the night of the [1996] election, publicly noting his 'very powerful mandate' arising from his remarkably large forty seat majority. The Coalition's share of the final two-party preferred vote for the house was very large by historical standards: just under 54 per cent.' (Uhr 1997: 74) In that election, the government won 46.9 per cent of the first preference vote (Goot 1999a: 327). Are we simply to ignore the facts that a majority of Australians gave their first preference votes to other parties or candidates, in effect voting against the government, as did the voters who gave the Coalition only half of the Senate seats that were contested in that election? Instead of claiming a mandate from the people, would it not have been more accurate for the Prime Minister to have claimed a mandate from half the people?

It is tempting to dismiss all talk of mandates as nothing more than self-serving wishful thinking, and to invoke an old axiom of American politics—that where you stand depends on where you sit. It was Prime Minister John Howard who did not hesitate to claim a mandate after the 1996 election, so perhaps it was some other John Howard who, as a member of the Opposition in 1987, had asked during a House debate why the Labor Government of the day did not agree to a public referendum on its Australia Card legislation:

> [W]hy do they not put that belief [that the public supported the bill] to a test at a referendum and not hide behind the argument that there is some kind of mandate out of the last election? That suggestion is invalid not only in terms of the number of votes cast but also on the simple proposition that when people vote at an election they do not vote on only one issue. *The mandate theory of politics from the point of view of proper analysis has always been absolutely phoney.* (*Commonwealth Parliamentary Debates* (House of Representatives), 15 September 1987: 57, emphasis added)

Governments inevitably will continue to claim electoral mandates (no leader of a winning party could possibly resist the temptation) and, on that basis, argue that the Senate, if it has a non-government majority, should respect the government's mandate by not delaying or rejecting government bills and by not insisting on Senate amendments that are unacceptable to the government and the House. Not so, we learn from the same John Howard, this time speaking in the House in 1993:

> The Senate has a perfect right to determine the way in which it will process legislation. If under the constitution the Senate has coextensive powers with the House of Representatives, except in relation to certain designated matters, does that not mean that the Senate has a perfect right to say in which circumstances, in what time, through what process and through what procedure it will deal with legislation that comes to it from the House of Representatives? (*Commonwealth Parliamentary Debates* (House of Representatives), 19 August 1993: 332)

I doubt that many readers will be shocked to encounter such inconsistencies, and I would be surprised if we could not discover that an ALP leader had made similarly inconsistent statements about mandates. Yet it would be a mistake to become *too* cynical about mandate claims because, after all, there is supposed to be a discernible linkage between electoral choice and parliamentary decisions. It would be wrong, in several senses of the word, for the non-government majority in the Senate to refuse to pass any of the major legislation proposed by a government that has just won a landslide victory in the House. But it would be equally wrong for the Senate to passively endorse every bill sent to it by a government that had barely been able to scrape together a House majority after an election almost three years earlier.

More judgment is required, of course—more political nous—when the political situation falls somewhere between these two extremes, as it usually will. Still, it is worth bearing in mind a conventional principle of statutory construction: that there is presumed to be a reason why a law gives someone the authority to do something and, therefore, that there is presumed to be some circumstance under which it is proper for that authority to be exercised. So too for interpreting a constitution: if it grants, even by necessary implication, a government institution—the Senate, for example—a power to do something, it must have been with the expectation that, under some circumstances, it would be proper for the institution to do what the constitution empowers it to do. If the Senate acts to block or dilute government legislation that most Australians actively support, the government has an obvious recourse: to go to the people during the next election campaign and ask the voters to punish those Senators who were responsible for thwarting the will of the nation. Parties and politicians have a wonderful facility for anticipating such attacks and protecting themselves against them by accommodating themselves to what they are convinced their voters want.

If *Odgers' Australian Senate Practice* (2001: 13) is any indication, the Senate itself is well aware that deciding how much deference to give to government bills requires the exercise of judgment; it is more complicated than a simple 'yes or no' proposition. In developing the theme that the Senate should use its constitutional powers 'circumspectly and wisely,' its author, Harry Evans, identifies a number of factors for Senators to consider, including:

> A recognition of the fact that the House of Representatives represents in its entirety, however imperfectly, the most recent choice of the people whereas, because of the system of rotation of senators and except in the case of simultaneous dissolution of the two Houses, one-half of the Senate reflects an earlier poll.
>
> The principle that in a bicameral parliament one house shall be a check upon the power of the other.
>
> Whether the matter in dispute is a question of principle for which the government may claim electoral approval; if so, the Senate may yield. The Senate is unlikely to resist legislation in respect of which a government can truly claim explicit electoral endorsement, but the test is always likely to be the public interest.

The third of these factors recognizes, in all but name, that sometimes a government can claim a mandate for specific legislation and that, in those cases, the Senate generally should defer to the government. However, there also is a loophole: the Senate may act otherwise if it decides that doing so is likely to be in the 'public interest.' This last phrase, obviously enough, is so broad and imprecise as to open a loophole through which the Senate could drive a roadtrain when it decides to be governed by its own judgment instead of the government's legislative program.

As John Uhr reminds us, by referring back to the Salisbury Convention (discussed above), the mandate theory was born and raised during the course of a constitutional and political debate over the respective powers of the elected House of Commons and the hereditary House of Lords:

> The misleading model of 'mandate' is drawn from the British parliament at Westminster, where the mandate theory developed in the pre-First World War struggle between the House of Commons and the unelected House of Lords. The irony is that it was the Lords which foolishly taunted the Commons with the charge that a range of contentious government bills on social policy lacked a mandate. The Commons successfully curtailed the power of the unelected Lords to obstruct government bills, and adopted the strategy of claiming a mandate for every contentious bill. ... Mandate theories derive from the inter-cameral disputes of Westminster, and seem an inappropriate response to the realities of parliamentary power in Australia ... (Uhr 1997: 75–76)

In Great Britain, no credible claim then could be made that the House of Lords enjoyed democratic legitimacy; in Australia, no credible claim now can be made that the Senate does not. This difference is no mere detail. Any Australian government that would claim that its electoral mandate gives it a right and responsibility to enact its program without hindrance or delay must concoct a satisfactory explanation why Australian national policy should be determined solely by the outcome of free and fair elections affecting one side of Parliament House but not influenced at all by the outcome of equally free and fair elections affecting the other side of the same building.

In earlier chapters, experts on the Commonwealth's election laws have been heard to argue that it is virtually impossible for either the ALP or the Coalition to win control of the Senate. To be more specific, for either protagonist to win the Senate outright, it would have to win electoral landslides that would be unprecedented in modern Australian history. Whether a government majority in the Senate is impossible or merely unlikely, the fact remains that, as each election campaign begins, both sides know that the winner is almost certain to confront a Senate that it does not control. This leaves each of the major party protagonists with two choices.

One choice is for the ALP and the Coalition each to proclaim all the fine and wonderful things it will do if it receives the people's mandate to govern. Then, if it wins a majority in the House of Representatives, it must attempt to convince non-government Senators that, in exercising their constitutional authority, they should defer to the government instead of exercising their own best judgment even though they too were elected to legislate. If the government does not succeed, it may berate the Senate, bemoan its fate, seek a double dissolution, or do all three. The other choice is for both major parties to accept and acknowledge that, whichever of them wins the election for the House, its victory will be incomplete, and, therefore, that it needs to moderate its campaign promises accordingly. Perhaps if Australia's political leaders spent less time in campaigns making promises that they know they may not be able to keep, there would be less talk after elections of expectations unfulfilled, promises broken, and commitments unkept. Perhaps there also might develop a better public understanding of the practical realities of the Commonwealth political system.[214]

I wonder what the citizens of the state of Victoria make of a recent amendment to their Constitution. Section 12 of the *Constitution (Parliamentary Reform) Act 2003*, assented to on 8 April 2003, amended the *Constitution Act 1975* by adding a new Section 16A for the purpose of 'improving the relationship between the Houses':

16A. *The principle of Government mandate*
> (1) It is the intention of the Parliament that regard should be given to the following principle—
> The Council [i.e., the Legislative Council, which is Victoria's equivalent of the Commonwealth Senate] as a House of Review will exercise its powers in recognition of the right and obligation of the current Government to implement—
>> (a) the Government's specific mandate—the policies, promises and initiatives which were publicly released by or on behalf of the Government during the last election campaign; and
>> (b) the Government's general mandate—to govern for and on behalf of the people of Victoria.
> (2) The principle in sub-section (1) is not to be construed as limiting the powers of the Council, the Assembly or the Parliament.

---

214 The same argument can just as well be made about American presidential campaigns. The danger, of course, is that the voters of either nation may punish a candidate (or party) who resists telling them what they want to hear.

I admit to having no idea what this section is intended to mean and what effect, if any, it is intended to have. In one brief section, the Constitution now gives constitutional standing and sanction to a collection of concepts that we already have reviewed critically: the upper house as a House of Review, the government's obligation as well as its right to implement its program, and both its specific and its general mandate to do so. By itself, sub-section (1) seems to be sending a message to the Legislative Council to be more circumspect. Sub-section (2), however, seems to be saying that sub-section (1) is not intended to effect any changes in the powers of either house or in their exercise of those powers. In that case, I can only think that if this new section has any effect at all, it will be to increase confusion, not clarity, about the respective roles of the Legislative Assembly and the Legislative Council. Worse yet, it will embolden Victorian governments to claim that they now have an affirmative constitutional obligation always to win in their Parliament.

Politics is a complicated and subtle business (though rarely depicted as such by Australia's politicians), and those who offer simple answers are likely to be wrong. That is true with regard to the Senate and the exercise of its legislative powers. In deciding when and how and how much to exercise those powers, it must respect the judgment of the voters and what the results of the last election imply about their policy preferences. This involves making thoughtful and informed judgments about which issues and proposals seemed to capture voters' attention and their fancy, and which were less important to them. What an election says about public support for a specific policy proposal depends on how much emphasis the party gave to that proposal during the campaign, how clearly the party articulated its proposal, and how much that one proposal dominated the party's approach to the campaign.[215] The Senate also must respect the principles of responsible government as they apply to the creation and survival of the government and its relationship with the House of Representatives. But the Senate also must respect itself and the Constitution that gave birth to it. Balancing all these things is not easy; there is no formula for calculating the right balance. But then anyone who thinks that making a political system work is easy has never spent much time in Canberra— or Washington or Paris or Tokyo or Brasilia or ...

---

215 'If a general election is fought on a single issue, in such a way as the whole election seems to turn on the question of whether or not a particular policy ought to be adopted, the victorious party can meaningfully claim to have a mandate to follow its known policy in that particular matter.' (P.A. Bromhead, quoted in Goot 1999a: 330)

Proposals for reform

Having disposed of the matter of mandates, let us turn now to a review
of the merits and broader implications of several proposals affecting the
Senate that would require either statutory or constitutional change.

Blocking the Senate from blocking supply

Senator John Faulkner, Leader of the Opposition in the Senate for the
ALP, wrote (1999: 126) that 'Labor is committed to constitutional
reform to prevent the Senate rejecting, deferring or blocking
appropriation bills,' and that he thought there might well be a multi-
party consensus in favour of doing so. In an obvious response to the
events of 1975, Faulkner argued that:

> The real problem [concerning the Senate] arises with regard to the Senate's
> power to deny financial sustenance to a government, particularly when such
> power is exercised not because of any objection to the content of the
> legislation appropriating the funds, but to bring down the government. This
> flies in the face of one of the basic principles of our system of government,
> that a government is responsible to the House of Representatives and
> continues in office only so long as it has the confidence of that House.
> (Faulkner 1999: 125)

Faulkner, of course, is not the first to make such an argument, and
certainly not the first ALP leader to do so in the aftermath of 'the
troubles' of 1975. Whitlam proposed at the 1976 Australian
Constitutional Convention in Hobart, for example, that 'this convention
recommends that the Constitution be amended so as to remove the
power of the Senate to reject, defer, or in any other manner block the
passage of laws appropriating revenue or moneys or imposing taxation.'
And in 1979, the ALP proposed at its federal conference that the Senate
should not be able to delay any money bill and that it should not be able
to reject any bill or delay any other bill for more than six months
(Hutchison 1983: 147–148). This proposal clearly was reminiscent of
the Parliament Act of 1911 in the UK. More recently, in 1988, a
commission on constitutional reform recommended:

> that the Constitution be altered by the inclusion of sections to limit the
> power of the Senate to reject, or refuse to pass, Bills it cannot amend. In
> particular we recommend that the Constitution be altered to provide that:
>> If at any time during the first three years of a parliament the Senate
>> rejects, or fails to pass, within 30 days of its transmission, a Bill it
>> cannot amend, the Bill shall be presented for the Royal assent. (quoted
>> in Jaensch 1997: 61)

I argued in Chapter 4 that the Coalition majority in the Senate should not have used the Senate's constitutional power to block supply because its essential reason for doing so was to serve its short-term political advantage, so I sympathize with Faulkner's objective (but not with Labor's far more draconian 1979 plan). The question, though, is whether the necessary solution to the problem is a constitutional amendment that reduces or nullifies the Senate's power under sec. 53 of the Constitution.

Such an amendment would deny the Senate its most powerful constitutional weapon on the grounds that, like nuclear weapons, the power to deny appropriations to the government is a power so drastic and damaging that its use never can be justified. Even if that is true, however, that does not necessarily leave us with a choice only between a Senate that has been constitutionally castrated and a Senate that can force a government to resign. There are more benign alternatives.

One could amend the Constitution to give Representatives, like Senators, a fixed term of office of, say, three or four years unless the requirements for a double dissolution are met. If the Constitution were amended in this way, it would transform the consequences of blocking supply. A non-government majority no longer could take this step with the hope or expectation of forcing the government to call an early election because there could be no early election for the House alone. Senators would have to convince the government to seek a double dissolution which, of course, would put every Senator at electoral risk as well. However, such a constitutional amendment would affect the dynamics of politics and governance in other and less predictable ways. It may or may not be desirable to prevent governments from calling elections at times that are expected to work to their electoral advantage. Any constitutional amendment that would have this effect needs to be evaluated and approved on its own merits, not as a means to achieve some other purpose that can be achieved more directly.[216]

Another related proposal that also is more benign than reducing the Senate's legislative powers would amend the Constitution to provide that, if the Senate fails to pass budget legislation, a double dissolution must ensue. (Recall that in 1975, the Governor-General was able to grant a double dissolution only because other bills, unrelated to the

---

216 In 1981, a Labor-supported bill in the Senate would have established a fixed term of four years for both houses, prevented the Senate from blocking supply in the future, and barred the Governor-General from again dismissing a government—all obviously in reaction to the events of 1975 (Souter 1988: 580–581). Faced with opposition from the Fraser Government, only the first of the three provisions survived the Senate's deliberations. But even this truncated bill died in the House.

crisis over supply, already had met the requirements of sec. 57.) In this way, Senators would exercise their greatest and most extreme constitutional power, and thereby force an election on an unwilling government and House, only if they were prepared to put all of their own seats at risk. On its face, this proposal has the virtue of promoting fairness. Appealing though it may be, however, I question the practicality of this proposal.

First, the poor track record of past proposals for constitutional amendments, as well as the virtue of constitutional continuity and stability, argue that a 'solution' that involves amending the Constitution should be the last resort chosen. Second, it is doubtful that a constitutional amendment could be drafted in a way that would eliminate all doubts as to if and when the Senate actually has refused to pass legislation that would trigger a double dissolution. Recall the questions that have arisen in the past about what constitutes 'failure to pass.'[217] Third, if the amendment applies only to bills funding the ordinary annual services of government, the Senate would be free to block every other spending and revenue bill. Alternatively, there is a danger that the coverage of the amendment would be so broad, covering any bill with any significant spending or revenue provision, that the cure would prove more injurious than the illness. Fourth, there is no guarantee that the double dissolution would produce a new Parliament that would not be inclined to continue the same party battle, but now with fresh troops in the ranks of each.

Fifth, a period of some weeks, at a minimum, would necessarily intervene between the Senate's action and, after the double dissolution and the election that follows, the convening of the newly-elected Parliament. So if the 'crisis' is not to continue during that time, the double dissolution may have to occur early enough so that the electoral process can be completed before the money runs out. But that would require a determination, presumably by the government, that a constitutionally sufficient blockage has occurred when more than ample time remains for further negotiations and for a political solution to the impasse to be reached. Any observer of democratic politics appreciates the importance of timing in political negotiations and the tactical value of resorting occasionally to brinkmanship. Political solutions often are found for what seem to be even the most intractable disagreements, but only when an unavoidable deadline looms. The political process in a

---

217 An approach to this difficulty might be to amend the Senate's standing orders to require it to vote on approving covered legislation within a specified period of time. But this requirement would be effective only if it could not be suspended, amended, or repealed by majority vote.

democracy often is messy and replete with uncertainties, and I doubt that this proposed amendment could make it otherwise.

There are other, less drastic, alternatives to be considered, one of which derives from recent American experiences.

As I mentioned in the context of the 1975 crisis, it has become almost commonplace for the departments and agencies of the American federal government to run out of money to continue their normal operations, or teeter on the brink of doing so, because the President and the Congress are unable to reach agreement on the necessary appropriations bills for the new fiscal year. Almost invariably, the response is for the President and the Congress to agree to a temporary funding bill—a new law that temporarily continues the availability of funding for what usually is a matter of days or a few weeks in the hope that a long-term agreement can be reached before the end of that time. If that hope proves a forlorn one, another continuing resolution, as these stopgap appropriations laws are known, is enacted.

Typically, a continuing resolution allows one or more departments and agencies to continue spending but only at the same rate they could spend during the fiscal year just ended (perhaps with an adjustment for inflation) and only for the purposes for which they could spend during the prior year. This is the most obvious and 'prominent solution' (to use Thomas Schelling's famous phrase) to determining a generally acceptable temporary funding level. Sometimes, though, more complicated formulas are used, or certain exceptions are allowed for implementing new program initiatives on which both the President and the Congress, and both political parties, agree. One or more such continuing resolutions have been enacted in most recent years. Yet the Congress has been unwilling to approve any bill that would create what is in effect a permanent continuing resolution by stating that whenever a funding deadlock occurs, the affected departments and agencies may continue to spend, for existing purposes only and at last fiscal year's level, until the deadlock is resolved without the necessity for Congress to enact a targeted continuing resolution on each occasion.

The reason lies in the fact that any funding level that is established in advance introduces a bias into the political contest in that it gives one side or the other in the dispute an incentive not to resolve it because that contestant finds the status quo under the permanent continuing resolution to be preferable to any alternative solution it is likely to negotiate with the other side. If, for example, there is a deadlock over the bill appropriating funds for defence, with the President seeking to increase defence spending significantly and the Congress wanting to cut it marginally, the Congress might well prefer no agreement to any agreement that the President is likely to accept. In short, no automatic funding mechanism can be devised that is policy neutral and, therefore, politically neutral. It would work to the advantage of either the President or the Congress, though who benefits, of course, would vary from issue to issue and from year to year.

What is a problem in Washington, however, might not be considered a problem in Canberra. Appropriating funds permanently, not annually, is a practice already well-known to the Parliament.[218] The government might be reasonably content with a mechanism that allowed it to continue spending at the same rate at which it had been able to spend under its own budget for the previous year.[219] In fact, if the automatic spending mechanism was triggered on more than rare occasions, a government might even begin building into its budget for each year a cushion to ensure that it would have adequate funding levels if it had to continue operating under that budget during part of the following year. In any event, a law providing automatic spending authority would avoid the danger that a deadlock between the government and the Opposition, manifested in a deadlock between the House and the Senate, would bring the Commonwealth to a halt. It also would allow the Senate to retain its existing constitutional power to refuse to pass an appropriation bill, but only to dramatize its policy disagreements with the government. The Opposition could not use a deadlock over appropriations for short-term partisan advantage, as Fraser and associates did in 1975, because it could no longer be argued, as it was in 1975, that a government that cannot ensure supply has no choice but to resign.

I am not the first to suggest such a mechanism for Australia. On 23 September 1987, Senator Michael Macklin, Australian Democrat from Queensland, presented his Constitution Alteration (Appropriations for the Ordinary Annual Services of the Government) Bill 1987, which proposed to add the following new paragraph to sec. 53 of the Constitution:

> If the House of Representatives passes a proposed law appropriating revenue or moneys for the ordinary annual services of the Government in respect of a year, and at the expiration of sixty days after the day on which the proposed law is transmitted to the Senate the Senate has not passed the

---

218 As of the mid-1980s, according to Reid and Forrest (1989: 350–352), roughly two-thirds of annual expenditures from the Consolidated Revenue Fund and Loan Fund were authorized by permanent appropriations, leading them to conclude that 'Nowadays the greater bulk of public expenditure escapes annual approval by Parliament.' According to *Odgers' Australian Senate Practice* (2001: 310) the proportion had increased to 78 per cent in 2001.

219 Some accommodation might be necessary during the first year of a government's life, when the budget for the prior year was not its own.

proposed law, there shall be deemed to be in force, until the Parliament makes a law appropriating revenue or moneys for those services in respect of that year, a law appropriating for those services in respect of that year an amount of money equal to the amount appropriated for those services in respect of the year immediately preceding that year.

In short, his constitutional amendment would have allowed the government to spend during a financial year at the same rate as during the prior financial year if the Senate failed to pass the appropriation bills for the ordinary annual services of the government within 60 days after receiving those bills from the House.

My suggestion is for a law, much like the one that Senator Macklin proposed, that would be triggered on the first day of a new financial year if the basic annual appropriations bill for that year had not already been enacted. Senator Macklin's proposal, by contrast, would have given the Senate 60 days to act on that appropriations bill, once passed by the House. If the bill were not enacted by the end of the 60-day period, funding at last year's level would become available for the coming financial year, even if time remained for additional negotiations and legislative action before the new financial year actually began. More important, Senator Macklin proposed a constitutional amendment, whereas I doubt that is necessary.[220]

Ministers in the Senate

David Hamer, former Representative and Senator, has offered an array of reform proposals for the Senate (Hamer 1996). Assessing some of them, such as giving Senators four-year fixed terms and resorting to referenda to resolve House-Senate deadlocks instead of the current procedures involving double dissolutions and joint sittings, require far more analysis than he was able to offer in his brief essay. Other proposals that he made, though, are misguided on their face, at least if the American experience has anything to offer. Particularly noteworthy is his insistence (1996: 72) that 'The Senate should ... pass the Budget as a package. The Budget is such an interwoven mix of economic, political and social measures that to have a Parliament tinkering with its details is a recipe for disaster.' This, of course, is the present practice in both houses, and one that deprives them of their most effective possible

---

220 If this proposal would require a constitutional amendment, it probably would be doomed unless it had strong bipartisan support. It is too easy to imagine the amendment being criticized on the grounds that it would allow the government to continue spending the people's money, year after year after year, without anyone taking responsibility by voting for appropriation bills.

way to hold government accountable and make it more responsive to the Parliament. Nothing concentrates the mind of a US department or agency head more effectively than the knowledge that if the Congress is unhappy with his policies or performance, it has both the opportunity and the will to react by cutting his budget. Surely an Australian minister would be sensitive to the same prospect if he knew that parliamentary review of the budget amounted to more than an extended debate followed by a single vote on the entire package, without change.

Furthermore, the 'details' to which Hamer refers are the amounts that the party in power intends to spend to carry out the activities of the Commonwealth government (or some of them; many are funded indefinitely or permanently, as we have seen). A national budget may be presented as a mass of numbers and details, but in fact it is the single most important documented statement of the government's priorities for each year. It cuts through all the rhetorical commitments that governments make and the assurances of sympathy and support that they offer, and answers one of the most basic questions of politics: who gets what. In the same volume in which Hamer's essay appears, for example, John Langmore, a former Labor MP and minister, discusses several policy commitments that recent Labor governments made but then failed to fund adequately or at the levels they had promised. If a legislative body is denied the opportunity to tinker with those details of the budget, as is usually the case in parliamentary regimes, it is powerless to propose even marginal adjustments in the government's priorities. There is no more dramatic or consequential manifestation of the legislative weakness of parliaments.

The change that Hamer described as the key step that he would take is to remove all ministers from the Senate. Let Hamer make his own argument:

> The Senate will not become a really effective legislature until ministers are removed from it. If this might be thought a remarkable act of self-abnegation by senators, the compensation should be that the chairs of major Senate committees are given the status and privileges of ministers, for they are, or should be, at least as important. It would not be difficult to gain these benefits for the chairs of major Senate committees because the Senate has to approve any increase in the number of ministers. This would give it considerable leverage in due course, if not immediately.
>
> If the chairs of Senate committees were fairly divided between the various parties—and the Senate has recently made a start in that direction—there would be a situation where the major Senate figures owed their positions not to which party was in government but to their own standing in the Senate. The Senate would start to develop as an important legislature. But while ministers remain in the Senate, the Senate will continue to spend too much of its time duplicating the electioneering role of the House of

Representatives and, in the process, handing far too much legislative power to the minor parties and independents who hold the balance of power. (Hamer 1996: 74)

Other observers have come to the same conclusion. Four years later, for instance, Solomon (2000: 11) noted the argument that selecting some Senators as ministers actually weakens the Senate:

> The idea is that the Senate is corrupted by containing members of the government of the day. Senators, it has been argued, would be better able to perform the legislative tasks if they were able to debate proposed laws in the absence of ministers. If people who were elected to the Senate were prevented from winning ministerial rank, the Senate would then be filled with people who wanted to be legislators, not members of the executive government. The proposal [to bar Senators from appointment as Ministers] has won the approval of many supporters of the Senate, but not of most senators. They still aspire to be ministers. And governments do not want to surrender the power they have over the members of the government party in the Senate, even if they do not control the whole of the Senate.

Hamer acknowledges that requiring all ministers to come from the House of Representatives would narrow what already is a modest talent pool from which prime ministers must assemble their governments. If the House is closely divided, the majority may have fewer than 80 members. If there are as many as 30 ministers, then three of every eight eligible members would have to be ministers if all ministers came from the House. Add to that the need to find ministers who are experienced, who know something about the portfolio they receive, and who represent the various states in reasonable proportions, and it becomes clear why it may be necessary for governments to find ministers among Senators, whether they might want to or not.[221] In turn, the presence of ministers on the government bench in the Senate, as well as shadow or former ministers on the Opposition bench, lends weight and credibility to Senate proceedings that they otherwise might not enjoy (Uhr 2002: 9–10).

Still, Hamer (1996: 74) argued, so long as Senators can hope to become ministers, 'The whole political aspiration pyramid is skewed in the wrong direction.' Nor is he alone in making this argument. Blewett (1993: 12) too contends that:

> perfecting the Senate as a House of legislative review and as the body for effective scrutiny of the Executive … would require the elimination of all

---

221 However, that concern did not dissuade the House Standing Committee on Procedure from expressing the opinion in 1986 that all ministers should be Members of and responsible to the House of Representatives. (*House of Representatives Practice* 2001: 58–59)

ministers from the Senate. For while the ambition of most of the leading
and abler players in the Senate is to retain or secure ministerial office, as it
is today, then the capacities of the Senate will be distorted to service those
ends.

To those who think that increasing the capacity of Senate
committees would be a very good thing, it is an appealing prospect to
change the incentive structure in the Senate so that the personal
ambitions of Senators would be tied to the health and influence of the
committees on which they serve and especially the committees they are
selected to chair. At least ambitious Senators would have a choice
between career paths—to take the chance of running for the House and
securing appointment as minister if their party is in government, or to
remain in the Senate and build their influence through service on
committees. It is unclear, however, exactly how and why any governing
party would permit any 'reforms' that would strengthen the Senate
committee system, and thereby undermine the strength of parties and
party discipline in the Senate. Most Senators will use their committee
positions most of the time to promote the policies of their parties so
long as they know that their continued service in the Senate depends on
how highly their party organization places them on their party's list for
the next Senate election. Under the current electoral system, just about
all it takes to put a Senator's career in jeopardy is for his party to move
him or her down from second or third to fourth place on the party list.

If there no longer are ministers in the Senate, the government and
the Senate would have to compensate in some way. Just as Senate
ministers now speak, at Question Time for example, for House
ministers who cannot be present to speak for themselves, government
Senators somehow would have to be designated to represent every
minister. Otherwise, there would be no-one for the Opposition to
interrogate. Whatever accountability now takes place through debate
and questions in the Senate chamber would dissolve if only the Leader
of Government Business in the Senate and the Government Whip could
claim to speak for the government.

Hamer's proposal also points to a related issue that he does not
discuss but that also merits review: who speaks for the government
before Senate committees? There recently has been a debate about
whether Senate committees can and should require the appearance of
ministerial advisors who are political appointees and advisors, not
career public servants. There also is ongoing discussion about what
kinds of questions it is proper to put to senior public servants when they
testify before committees and what questions public servants should
decline to answer and instead refer to their ministers. But what has
received less attention is the wisdom and even the practicality of

continuing to observe the convention that Senate committees may not insist on receiving testimony from ministers who are members of the House of Representatives, as most ministers are.

The argument underlying this convention is that whatever bicameral harmony there is in Parliament House would be seriously damaged if one house decided that it had the right to interrogate members of the other house. The principle is sound and one that is respected in the US Congress as well. The problem, however, is that allowing this convention to continue to operate in Canberra seriously impedes any efforts Senate committees may make to evaluate government legislation or review government performance. Today a Senate committee can hear from a minister if that minister happens to be a Senator or if the minister chooses to accept the committee's invitation to testify. Otherwise, the committee must content itself with hearing from whichever government Senator is designated to speak for a minister from the House, or with hearing from public servants who are not supposed to be asked to defend government policy because that is the domain of the minister—who, of course, cannot be obligated to attend and offer that very defence.

Not all governments that are responsible to a parliament or its lower house draw their ministers from among the ranks of MPs. But in all those that do, ministers by definition wear two hats. With the merging of the legislature and the executive, ministers are at one and the same time members of the Parliament and members of the government. As MPs, they should be protected from demands from the other house for their appearance and testimony. However, this immunity that they enjoy in their capacity as MPs should not also immunize them from being held accountable in their capacity as ministers. It certainly would be inappropriate for a Senate committee to question members of the House about any of their actions or positions taken as the representatives of their electorates. But it should be appropriate for the Senate to insist that they answer questions about the actions and positions they have taken as government ministers. Surely there will be instances in which committees and ministers will disagree as to whether a particular line of inquiry crosses this border. In those cases, let the committee and the minister make their cases and let the public (and the media) decide whether the Senate is intruding into matters that are none of its business or whether the minister is stonewalling.

As long as the convention remains unchanged, Senate committees simply cannot provide the kind of scrutiny that accountable government requires. And, by the way, removing all ministers from the Senate would move all ministers beyond the reach of Senate committees which, of course, would only hamper the committees' accountability efforts.

Installing presidential-congressional government

In his *Coming of Age: Charter for a New Australia* (1998), David Solomon, the author of two informative books on the Parliament cited elsewhere in this study, rejects precisely the kind of reform that we encountered Senator Coonan advocating during our discussion of electoral mandates. Specifically, he objects to a proposal floated but not yet pushed by leaders of Coonan's Liberal-National Government that would transform the Senate into a two-party house. Under this proposal, each state would be divided into six electoral regions, with two Senators to be elected from each, one at each half-Senate election that takes place every three years. At any one half-Senate election, only one Senate seat would be contested so inevitably it would be won by one of the major parties. Even in the case of a double dissolution, when two seats would be contested in each electoral region, the major parties almost certainly would win both seats and, what is more, they almost certainly would split them, with the ALP winning one and the Coalition winning the other. As a result, Solomon argues, minor parties soon would shrivel and die. Just as third parties never have thrived in the United States because they have no chance to win the ultimate electoral prize, the presidency, minor parties in Australia would lose their attraction to voters if they could not make a plausible argument that they had a chance to win representation in the Senate.[222]

In explanation of the proposal, Solomon quotes the Liberal Party official who had developed it as saying that its purpose was to enable the government to govern 'and not have interminable debate and compromises and committees and inquiries.' (quoted in Solomon 1998: 90) There we have it again: compromises as things to be avoided, but now linked with other undesirables which just happen to be staples of effective democratic legislatures: debate, committees, and inquiries. Perhaps the moral is to ignore proposals for political 'reforms' when they are made by people whose professional interest is only in winning power, not in the purposes to which that power is put.

One possibility is that implementing this proposal would produce a Senate that is evenly divided between the ALP and the Coalition.

---

222 Another version would divide each state into three regions. During each normal half-Senate election, each region would select two Senators—almost inevitably one from Labor and one from the Coalition. The consequences for minor parties and Independents would be the same.

Another possibility is that the result would be a House majority of one party and a Senate majority of the other, a possibility that cannot be dismissed in light of the fact that half the Senators would have been elected at the preceding election, three years earlier. The frequency of divided government in the United States, with a president of one party occupying the White House and a Congress with majorities from the other party, or even a Congress with one party controlling the House of Representatives and the other party controlling the Senate, should make clever Australian political operatives contemplate that the same thing could happen in their country. This proposal, and variations on the same theme, would remove from the Senate the minor parties and Independents and the leverage they now often have, but at a considerable risk to any government's ability to function, and at the cost of substituting direct confrontation in the Senate between government and Opposition for the greater flexibility that the presence of other non-government Senators now provides.

Solomon's rejection of the Liberal Party plan would seem to cast him as a conservative who finds acceptable the current process for electing Senators and the distribution of Senate seats that it produces. Far from it, though. In fact, Solomon is the revolutionary in that his proposal for reforming the Senate is to abolish it in the process of scrapping everything that goes by the names of parliamentary or responsible government or the Westminster model in favour of an American-style presidential-congressional system.

His diagnosis and prescription are easily summarized: 'the real problem is that the executive government has come to completely dominate the lower house of parliament. That problem cannot be overcome unless the executive is moved out of the parliament altogether.' (Solomon 1998: 60) The discussion that follows is replete with disparaging observations about the House and what happens in it, typified by his claim that 'The only purpose of the house is to do the government's bidding.' (Solomon 1998: 72) In their current incarnations, the House and even the Senate are beyond salvaging as either legislative or oversight bodies because no government will permit them to work effectively:

> [A]ll Australian governments reject and resist any suggestion that they should not be able to put into law any proposal which they have determined upon. In effect, they do not accept the notion that the parliament (or some part of it) has a role independent of government to consider independently and fashion the laws, to question and demand answers about the way in which the government is conducting the affairs of government, and to provide a form of public accountability. They will not acknowledge the extent to which they are supposed to be accountable to the parliament, let

alone surrender to the parliament the power to fulfil its theoretical responsibilities. Governments have preferred to forget that the people elect members of parliament to represent them. (Solomon 1998: 77)

Solomon (1998: 85) contrasts this diagnosis with a rather idealized vision of the American Congress and presidential-congressional relations and, not surprisingly, concludes that the Australian political system requires radical reform:

> Governments, having taken control of parliament in the twentieth century, are not willingly going to surrender their powers and increase the ability of oppositions to upset their legislative programs or question their actions. Governments are not going to allow proposals for parliamentary reform to reduce the power of governments over parliament or make governments more responsible to parliaments.
>
> The only way in which genuine reform will be achieved is through the adoption of something like the American system of separation of powers.

At this point, his vision for what this new political system would look like becomes rather fuzzy. But even if he had spelled it out in detail, we would not assess it here because long books have been written, and are needed, to fully compare, contrast, and evaluate parliamentary versus presidential-congressional regimes. No, what is more problematic is that Solomon fails to lay out any plan for getting from here to there. Given the government's control of the House through strict party discipline, why should we expect any government in Canberra to support such a radical change that is designed to confront it with an assembly that it is much less likely to control? Today the government does not control the Senate; tomorrow, if Solomon has his way, it would not control the parliament (or perhaps now best called the legislature) at all. Indeed, Solomon's critique has the ring of a *cri de coeur*: a diagnosis that he cannot avoid of a debilitating illness for which he has no practical remedy.

Is the situation as dire as Solomon believes? In theory, no. In theory, so long as non-government parties (and Independents) control the Senate, they have the leverage they would need to transform the Senate into an independent legislative body that holds the government to strict account for its actions, that reviews its legislation with a critical eye, and that even feels free to initiate its own bills—but only if they are truly, truly determined to make all this happen. The non-government majority has the ability to force any reform proposals it chooses onto the Senate's agenda and have them adopted over the government's opposition. Doing so would constitute a peaceful coup d'etat of sorts, but it could be done. The government might respond, through its control of the budget, by trying to starve the Senate of resources to actually implement its new ambitious plans, and as we know, the Senate cannot directly amend the budget. However, the Senate has the clear constitutional power to hold any and all government legislation hostage until it agrees to accommodate the Senate's demands (or secures a double dissolution).

All this could happen, but it is very unlikely, for at least two reasons. First, I suspect that most of Australia's Senators have been inculcated with the idea that parliamentary government is not only the best form of government, it is the natural and naturally right form of government for Australia. Most of them probably would be terminally uncomfortable with both the kinds of revolutionary changes in the Senate that are possible and also with the methods that would be required to bring them about. Second, any transformation of the Senate that would strengthen it vis-a-vis the government must, by necessity, be led by the Opposition. And I expect that any Opposition would be at best ambivalent about such a program because it sees itself as the Government-in-Waiting. As John Uhr (2002a: 15) has argued from a slightly different perspective, 'The major parties share a particular interest in ensuring that Senate power does not generate permanent gridlock adversely affecting their next turn in executive office. ... Given this very regular alternation in office, the major parties' own political ambition is an important constraint on Senate power.'

The role of the Opposition in Canberra, as in any parliamentary system, must be extraordinarily frustrating. Naturally, therefore, the Opposition must view its exile to the wrong side of the chamber as temporary, as aberrational, as an unnatural state of affairs that the next election is certain to cure. And equally naturally, therefore, that Opposition will be skeptical of any institutional reform that would work to its advantage today but would then cripple it during all those many coming years that it hopes and expects to be in government. It is all too likely, then, that any programs for major institutional change in the Senate—changes that would speak to Solomon's critique and obviate the need for the even more radical change he proposes—would fail because they would fail to find a champion in the Senate, certainly not on the government side and probably not on the Opposition side either. I will return to this calculus toward the end of the next chapter.

A head of state for a republic?

First, though, I will conclude this chapter by considering a proposal that has received far more attention than any of those discussed earlier: whether Australia should become a republic and, if so, what form that republic should take. I venture some personal observations on the subject because I anticipate that, sooner or later, it will again occupy parliamentary and public attention as it did in the late 1990s.

On 6 November 1999, Australia rejected by referendum a set of constitutional amendments that would have replaced the office of the Governor-General with a President, elected by a two-thirds majority of the members of the Parliament, who would have exercised essentially the same powers that the Governor-General has enjoyed, and subject to essentially the same constraints. Since Federation, 44 constitutional amendments have been put to national referenda and only eight have succeeded. So it was not particularly surprising that this amendment also was rejected (as was another to add a preamble to the Constitution). Irving and McAllister (2001) are among those to point out, however, that, as Irving (2000: 111) puts it, 'The result was ... even worse than most had predicted. Majorities in every State rejected both questions ... . The national count of just over 45% in favour put the republic question in among the lowest third of all referendum results.'

Although the explanation of this result is not our concern here, surely some Australians preferred the status quo while others preferred to have a President directly elected by the people instead of one chosen by the Parliament.[223] Still others would have been justified in voting 'no' because of the specific new constitutional language that was proposed (though I certainly do not suppose that many did so). Although that text now is primarily of historic interest, one provision of the proposed new sec. 59 deserves mention in light of our discussion in Chapter 4 of the 1975 crisis and in anticipation of matters that we will take up in the next chapter. The final paragraph of sec. 59, as proposed, stated that:

> The President shall act on the advice of the Federal Executive Council, the Prime Minister or another Minister of State; but the President may exercise a power that was a reserve power of the Governor-General in accordance with the constitutional conventions that related to the exercise of that power by the Governor-General.

This new section would have established both reserve powers and conventions in the Constitution itself, but without defining either of them. Had this section been part of the Constitution in 1975, it would not have offered Governor-General Kerr any clear guidance as to whether his reserve powers extended to dismissing a government that

---

223 McAllister (2001: 256) reports survey results showing that 'combining those who wanted a directly elected President with those favouring appointment by the Parliament—a large majority of the electorate were actually in favour of the introduction of a new system of government. Indeed, according to the survey, just 24% of those interviewed favoured the retention of the current system.'

still enjoyed majority support in the House of Representatives and, if they did, whether the governing constitutional conventions justified his dismissal of the Labor Government under the conditions prevailing on 11 November of that year. Almost exactly 24 years later, the Australian people were asked to create a presidency without knowing exactly what powers they were investing in that office.

As we shall see in Chapter 10, the approach taken by the drafters of the proposed sec. 59 has been justified on the grounds that both reserve powers and conventions cannot be defined and delimited precisely enough to reduce them to writing. If so, this inability to specify the powers of an office can be taken as reason enough not to establish it. On the other hand, it can be argued, and with force, that contention over the events of 1975 should not detract from the fact that Australia has lived quite comfortably for a century with understandings (or a lack of understandings) of both reserve powers and conventions that have remained unwritten. Later in this chapter, I will put forward a proposal that defines this problem out of existence. For the moment, though, let us simply set it aside and proceed on the assumption that it poses no insurmountable obstacle to having a president as Australia's head of state.

The first question, of course, is whether or not replacing the Governor-General with a President would be a good thing to do. This is a value-laden question that is not particularly susceptible to social scientific analysis. Is it desirable for Australia to have a continuing connection with the Queen and her successors? If the question were whether or not Australians should prefer a monarchy to a democracy, then political theorists and empirical political scientists would have something to contribute. Because the connection now is essentially symbolic, I have little to offer as a political scientist. Still, I will offer my own opinion that I tend to agree with whose who believe that Australia derives no particular benefit from retaining that vestigial umbilical cord that the monarchy provides. One of my first vivid memories is watching the Queen's coronation on television. I have a certain admiration and affection for her. But if I were an Australian, I would be a republican.

This conclusion raises more questions than it answers. The 1999 referendum proposed a minimal agenda for change, essentially replacing the Governor-General with a President while transferring the powers of the former to the latter without substantive change. As we have just seen, this intention extended to an explicit attempt to transfer applicable reserve powers and constitutional conventions as well. For what undoubtedly was a mixture of reasons, the opportunity for a more encompassing re-examination of the Commonwealth's structure of government was foregone. Some advocates of a republic, for example, would have liked to preclude any future President from exercising the kind of reserve power on which Governor-General Kerr relied in 1975. Others would have preferred to expand the powers of the President well beyond those of the Governor-General, with the goal either of having the executive power shared between the President and the prime minister and Cabinet, or of moving part or all of the way to an American-style presidential-congressional system.

Any such major re-design of the constitutional system is not something to be undertaken lightly. First, and inescapably, it involves value judgments—for instance, how important is governmental efficiency in making decisions when weighed against the breadth of support for the decisions made? Second, it requires a clear statement of exactly what is wrong and precisely how and why any proposed constitutional reform is going to fix it, and a convincing explanation why the problem cannot be solved without resorting to constitutional amendment. And third, it involves predictions about how certain institutional arrangements, whatever their theoretical virtues, will work in a particular set of circumstances. Ultimately it is pointless to argue the relative merits of parliamentary and presidential systems in the abstract because there are so many other factors that influence how they work in practice. Lijphart (1999a), for instance, argues that what he calls consensus democracy has advantages over the alternative, majoritarian democracy. However, either a parliamentary or a presidential system can lean toward either form of democracy, depending, for instance, on the electoral law in effect, the number, size, and unity of political parties, and whether the legislative and executive power is concentrated in the hands of one party or whether it is divided among parties in a way that necessitates compromises among them.

The discussion that follows takes as its starting point the kind of minimal agenda for change that was presented in the 1999 referendum without also assuming that this is what most Australians do want or should want. A decision about how a President should be elected cannot be made without taking into account what powers the President would be entitled to exercise—both the powers explicitly assigned to the office and whatever reserve powers may accompany them. So in asking whether a President should be directly elected, my answer depends on the assumption that the powers of that office would be no greater than those of the Governor-General. A different assumption probably would produce a different answer.

A directly elected president?

If there is to be a President who assumes the existing powers of the Governor-General, how should he or she be chosen? I instinctively prefer allowing the people to choose those who represent them. In this case, however, and notwithstanding drafting problems with the 1999 proposals, I would prefer to have the President of Australia, if there is to be one, elected by the Parliament. My primary concern is that a popularly-elected president some day might emerge as a competing centre of democratic legitimacy. I have seen no evidence that there is much sentiment in Australia for trading in the current political system for one that more closely resembles the French mixed system or any similar systems in which there is both a president and a prime minister, both directly elected and both of whom can legitimately claim to be the freely-elected choice of the people. Yet that is precisely the possibility that would remain if the President of Australia retained even some of the powers that the Constitution now vests in the Governor-General, to say nothing of whatever additional reserve powers may be found in the bottom drawer of the president's desk (and that the 1999 referendum sought to recognize without defining them).

As I write this, Australians are debating whether or not Australian military forces should participate in an anticipated war against Iraq. Let us imagine a similar situation arising sometime in the future, when a popularly-elected president resides at Government House in Canberra. Suppose that there is an armed uprising in the Indonesian province of West Papua, which shares the island of New Guinea with the former Australian territory of Papua New Guinea. The indigenous Melanesian population of West Papua rebels, seeking independence from the rest of non-Melanesian Indonesia. Memories of East Timor are revived, and there is real concern that Papua New Guinea may be drawn into the conflict, transforming a domestic insurrection into a war on Australia's doorstep. Indonesia's overwhelming advantages in manpower and weaponry create the prospect of devastation across both halves of the island, and Australians speak of an impending genocide if Australia does not intervene. Opponents of intervention, however, emphasize the delicacy of Australian-Indonesian relations and raise fears that any intervention in the New Guinea conflict almost certainly will lead to a wider war.

The Australian Government decides that Australia must intervene militarily and, however reluctantly, most Australians seem to concur. But now also imagine that Australia's elected President is a beloved poet of international renown whose poetry has connected with Australians better than anyone since Henry Lawson and Banjo

Patterson. For several years, he has been an ideal representative for the nation, appearing at events at home and abroad to express with eloquence how Australians see themselves and what makes Australia unique. Both the government and the Opposition have had good reason to be pleased with the President whom Australians had elected two years earlier. At that time, however, it was not known that the President opposed any commitment of Australia's military for any purpose other than the immediate self-defence of the island-continent. The concern of Australians was Australia, he believed; it was a conviction that had pervaded his thinking and his poetry for decades. This conflict, however tragic, is an internal matter for Indonesians, including the West Papuans, to resolve for themselves. Australia has no business intervening in the internal affairs of any other nation, he argues, and especially not a neighbouring sovereign state and certainly not one with such an enormous and largely Muslim population distributed over hundreds of islands.

The President consults his copy of the Commonwealth Constitution and discovers that he can prevent what he is absolutely convinced would be a national calamity. There it is, in the clear, unambiguous language of sec. 56:

> A vote, resolution, or proposed law for the appropriation of revenue or moneys shall not be passed unless the purpose of the appropriation has in the same session been recommended by message of the Governor-General [now the President] to the House in which the proposal originated.

So he informs the Prime Minister, in a statement that he immediately makes public, that he will make no such recommendation for the appropriation of any 'revenue or moneys' to fund any military operations outside Australia's national borders. Furthermore, if the government uses funds that it already has available to pay the costs of military intervention in Indonesia or Papua New Guinea, he will exercise his constitutional discretion by refusing to recommend appropriations for selected other purposes, and even withhold his assent from other laws, until the government commits itself explicitly to withdraw from conflict or not to become involved in it in the first place.

The government is furious, of course, and the Prime Minister immediately consults his legal advisors who assure him that the President is acting within his constitutional powers. While it is true that he was never expected to exercise this power in this way, the High Court is very unlikely to compel him to recommend an appropriation because the government wants it, nor is it likely to sanction any attempt by the government to circumvent sec. 56. So the Prime Minister poses another set of questions to his legal advisors: Can he sack the

President? Can he do it because the President has exercised one of his constitutional powers in this way and under these circumstances? Assuming the government can dismiss the President immediately, how is he to be replaced? How quickly can a replacement be installed? Who, if anyone, can exercise the powers of the office while it is vacant? Which of these questions might give rise to litigation that could tie the government's hands until the High Court rules on them?[224]

Meanwhile, the popular and charismatic President is travelling across Australia, from Hobart to Broome and Cairns to Kalgoorlie, reciting his poems, making his case, and closing his speeches by declaiming:

I speak for Australia! My friends, that is what you chose me to do. You elected me because you know that I share your values, the values that unite all true Australians. Today I am here to speak for those values that make Australia such a special place. I ask you now to raise your voices and speak with me. If we all speak with one voice, we will be heard, even by the bureaucrats and politicians in Canberra, and we will prevail.

They do not want to listen. Our Prime Minister tells us that there will be a debate in Parliament, but only when it is too late to make a difference— only after he has decided what the policy of Australia will be. That is not democracy, my friends, when one little man from one corner of our country can meet in secret with his cronies and send the future of Australia to its death.

---

224 As I read the Constitution Alteration (Establishment of Republic) 1999 Bill, as passed by both houses (but then rejected by the voters), the prime minister could remove a President at any time and for any reason (proposed sec. 62). However, that bill provided for Parliament to select the President. If the President were directly elected instead, the Constitution surely would not permit any President to be removed from office without cause and without a formal proceeding that leads to a vote in Parliament. But assume for the moment that the proposed sec. 62 was in force. Then once the prime minister removed our hypothetical President, the longest-serving state governor, regardless of party, would act as President until the Parliament approved his successor or unless the Parliament had made some different arrangement to fill presidential vacancies (proposed sec. 63). It is quite possible, therefore, that invoking these provisions would not solve our prime minister's legal problems, and certainly not his political ones. He could find himself faced with an acting President who also opposes his government's policies. He also would have to go through the procedures of the proposed sec. 60 before a new President could take office. These procedures involve receiving the report of a nominating committee and then convening a joint sitting of both houses of the Parliament, all of which could become time-consuming. Moreover, the choice of any President would require the concurrence of the Leader of the Opposition in the House, who could withhold his approval, arguing that the voters need to resolve the policy conflict by electing a new government and that the new prime minister should be the one to nominate the new President (subject, of course, to the approval of the new Leader of the Opposition, who might well be the former prime minister).

Did you elect the Prime Minister to speak for you? No, of course not. He is the choice of other politicians. I am your choice to be your voice.

My friends, the Prime Minister may be able to ignore the voices of our so-called representatives, but he cannot ignore the voice of the people. Join with me, Australians, so the government finally will hear us. I speak for Australia! We speak for Australia!

After watching the government's public support plummet by the day, the embattled Prime Minister counter-attacks, arguing that this is a decision that the Australian people elected the government to make. The President responds that he has a mandate from the people who put their trust in him as a person, not in some party label. Meanwhile, the Opposition, quiescent until now, points to the public opinion polls that overwhelmingly support the President, and pronounce that the government has lost the confidence of the Australian people and that the government must resign so the voters can decide this question that literally involves the life or death of who knows how many young Australian men and women. If the government refuses to resign, the Opposition announces, perhaps the time has come for the non-government majority in the Senate to invoke the Senate's power of legislative veto over any and all legislation relating to the powers of the government in international affairs.

Such a series of developments are unlikely, of course, but they certainly are possible, and to me, they make a compelling case for preferring a President elected by the Parliament to one elected directly by the people. It is true that an indirectly elected President could do much the same things—and I will return to the implications of this argument—but at least he would not be able to invoke a popular mandate for his actions.

A transition to the presidency?

The results of the 1999 referendum suggested that many Australians were uneasy with cutting the last ties to the monarchy and were unsure how happy they would be with a President, however chosen, as their head of state.

With this uncertainty in mind, I offer the possibility of an incremental transition that would allow Australians to become comfortable with the new arrangement and assuage the unhappiness of those who oppose it, as well as allowing the transition to take place even before a constitutional referendum is scheduled to ratify it and embed it in the Constitution. Let the Parliament enact a law, tomorrow or whenever, that establishes the office of the President, and let that law assign to the President ceremonial and representational responsibilities only. So long as the statutory powers of the President do not conflict with the constitutional authority of the Governor-General, I see no constitutional impediment to such a law.[225]

I would then expect that the President who is selected under the terms of this law would become increasingly visible in the public eye, playing whatever public role the Governor-General now plays, and probably a more active one than that. In consequence, the Governor-General almost certainly would become far less visible to the public and soon would fade into obscurity as his public role disappears and he is reduced to attending the meetings and signing the papers that are necessary to satisfy the constitutional formalities. Assuming that a wise government makes a popular selection for Australia's first President (or that the electorate makes an equally popular choice), I suggest that the government arrange for the President also to be named the Governor-General when the latter office next needs to be filled. The same person will wear two hats, at least temporarily, but the British bowler will largely disappear from view, and the primary reminder of the formal constitutional connection between Australia and the monarchy will be the coins in Australians' pockets.

If this transition is complete before the Queen leaves the throne, that would be an appropriate time to make the formal constitutional change which, I suspect, at that point would occur without trauma. Meanwhile, this transitional period should allow Australia's best minds to concentrate on resolving all the related issues such as the meaning and future of reserve powers and whether the Constitution should continue to assign powers in ways so very much at odds with how the Australian political system actually works and what the Australian people surely would accept. The goal of this constitutional re-examination should be to ensure that the head of state acts only in a symbolic and representational capacity and exercises no governmental powers.

A head of state at all?

Campbell Sharman (2001: 173–175) has argued that, where the head of government is not also the head of state, the likelihood of tension between the two offices depends on the legitimacy of the head of state and the powers vested in that office. From this perspective, the Australian Constitution creates a mis-match by providing for 'a head of

225 Irving (2000: 114) has made a similar suggestion with regard to the office of Governor-General. 'It would be quite possible constitutionally to have a parliamentary choice, even a direct popular election, for the Governor-General, leaving the Constitution itself undisturbed, with the name of the chosen candidate going forth as the Prime Minister's nominee to the Queen … '

state, the governor-general, with relatively low legitimacy and very extensive constitutionally specified powers.' So, he concludes (2001: 179), if Australia's Prime Minister is to remain the head of government, then 'Whatever one's preference for a republican head of state— appointed, indirectly chosen through parliament, or directly elected, a prerequisite is the formal reduction of the powers of the head of state.'[226] My only quarrel with this contention is that I would not reduce only the formal powers of the head of state; Sharman's argument applies with at least equal force to reserve powers.

However, let me carry the argument one step, though a major step, further by suggesting that we really have been considering two separate questions: first, whether Australia should be a republic; and second, how should its head of state be selected. Let me now pose a third question: whether it is either desirable or necessary for Australia to have a head of state who is not also the head of government. Perhaps it is not surprising that Gough Whitlam (1979: 184) wrote in his memoir of 1975 that 'Experience has shown that a Head of State who is anything more than an ornament is a menace.' Although Whitlam obviously was not the most detached commentator on this matter, his contention still merits consideration.

There are three primary arguments for having a separate head of state. First, the head of state performs various time-consuming ceremonial functions and so allows the head of government to concentrate on the job of governing. If there were no Governor-General, or if there were to be no President, it would be the prime minister or other government ministers who would be under pressure to attend all the various civic functions and international events (such as funerals of foreign leaders) that require recognition in the form of the presence of a senior representative of the nation. Yet when there was a memorial service for those who died in the 2002 Bali bombing, it was thought right that the prime minister himself should attend. And when there is political credit to be gained by attending an event such as one, for example, to demonstrate support for Australia's embattled farmers or those who fought the bushfires that savaged Canberra in early 2003,

---

226 There is an alternative, he acknowledges, but not an appealing one. '[T]he combination of low legitimacy and high powers has the bad effect of making tension between the head of state and the head of government a matter which has the potential to raise serious constitutional disputes. The question of a remedy to this situation can be approached by either increasing the legitimacy of the office or reducing its powers. ... Increasing the legitimacy by having the head of state directly elected, while leaving the powers of the governor-general/president as they are, would create the monster of a United States presidency coupled with a parliamentary executive ... ' (Sharman 2001: 176–177)

the PM does not send the head of state in his place or in place of another senior minister. So we could expect that the presence of a head of state would continue to make life only somewhat easier for the prime minister and his Cabinet than it otherwise may be. That may be a good reason for having a head of state, but it hardly is a sufficient one.

Second, the head of state can stand as a symbol of the nation, a figure of special legitimacy who transcends the cut and thrust of the political arena. The best example, of course, is the Queen. But an Australian President would not necessarily enjoy the same respect and deference. Imagine if the President were to be elected by the Parliament with no direct public participation in the choice. Would the person selected automatically rise in the public's estimation to become someone accepted as the spokesperson for the nation, much less an embodiment of all that is best about the Australian people? That would depend very much on the personal characteristics of the person chosen; his or her elevation to the status of national symbol certainly would not be an inevitable consequence of having been chosen by one of Australia's least respected classes, its politicians. On the other hand, imagine that the President is elected. If it is to be a meaningful election, there must be a choice. And if it is a meaningful choice, we can expect that at least 40 per cent or more of Australians will have voted for someone else. Do we expect those Australians to accept the President as speaking for and representing them, as symbolizing their nation, even though they voted against him or her?

The best way to maximize the likelihood that a President will gain wide acceptance as national spokesperson is to select someone who does not come from the world of politics. A poet, perhaps, as I assumed in my hypothetical scenario, or a scientist, community leader, or sports figure. But that brings us to the third, and perhaps the most important, supposed benefit of having a head of state—having someone to act as defender of the Constitution in exceptional cases of emergency by exercising the reserve powers, on the scope or very existence of which Australia's best and brightest so far have been unable to agree, and by exercising them within the constraints of accepted constitutional conventions, on the definition of which there has been no universal accord.

Here is the dilemma. Although most Australians, and most Americans for that matter, might not believe it, governance is not for amateurs. The effective exercise of political power requires a knowledge of public affairs, an instinct for understanding people and their motives and intentions, an understanding of law and history, an appreciation of the importance and nuances of public rhetoric, and, among other aptitudes, the wisdom to know when to do nothing. And so, shocking as it may seem, the people best equipped to exercise those mystical reserve powers and understand those uncertain conventions are people who have been in the political arena. It would be rash to assume that the qualities and experiences that have made someone a great poet, scientist, or athlete will have prepared that person to exercise great power at times of national crisis. Quite the opposite, in fact. He or she is likely to make a mess of it, despite the best of intentions.

Ah, but we say, our President will have his or her advisors to offer the benefit of their knowledge, their experience, their understanding of the complex world of governance. But who are these advisors to be? Public servants or parliamentarians, or alumni of either corps, or perhaps scholars who themselves lack any direct experience of their own? What other alternatives are there? If the President is chosen from outside the world of public affairs in order to find someone widely acceptable to the nation, is it not very likely that decisions of great national moment will be made by someone who is sadly bereft of political nous, or that they will be made, in fact but not in name, by people at his or her side whom no one elected to stand there?

Taking all this into account, I suggest that Australians think some more about the concept of responsibility—not only the responsibility of the government to the Parliament, but the responsibility of government ministers, and especially the prime minister, to the nation. The ceremonial and symbolic roles of the head of state can be performed perfectly well by the head of government. In this era of televised politics, any prime minister who cannot speak as effectively to the nation as he can speak to his parliamentary colleagues across the dispatch boxes is unlikely to succeed at the job.

Sharman (2001: 178) has argued that if a President does not have all the explicit powers that the Constitution now assigns to the Governor-General, the result could be to 'create a vastly more powerful prime minister, whose office would be subject to almost no institutional checks.' His argument would have that much more force, of course, if there were no President or Governor-General at all. The prime minister presumably would become the commander-in-chief of Australia's armed forces, for example, and he (or the Cabinet) would be able to convene sessions of Parliament, schedule half-Senate elections, and effect double dissolutions. If the authority to dissolve the House before the end of its three-year term is not given to the prime minister or the Cabinet, it could be decided by vote of the House itself, just as the House could approve the choice of a new prime minister, minister, or Cabinet through a vote of investiture. I see no serious practical problems in re-assigning the powers that the Governor-General now exercises only at the request of the government of the day. In fact, I see it as a positive gain because it would make assignment of the formal authority of government that much more commensurate with the actual responsibility for how that authority already is exercised. The government now effectively controls the exercise of the Governor-General's authority; let it take formal responsibility for those decisions as well.

That leaves us with the issue of reserve powers—in other words, whether Australia requires a *deus ex machina* to descend from above the political stage and intervene in cases of direst emergency to resolve crises that mere mortals have created for themselves and the nation. I am inclined to answer in the negative. Perhaps I have more confidence in the good sense of politicians than most have, or maybe I have more confidence in the ability of politicians to understand what is ultimately in their own best interests. I believe that if elected politicians create a mess for themselves, as they did in 1975, they are perfectly capable of finding their way out of it, and they will do so as they continuously reassess and recalculate how they can emerge from that mess in a way that leaves them with the fewest possible stains and that maximizes their public support. Finally, as for the need for a President or Governor-General to intervene when the government is alleged to have acted illegally or unconstitutionally, let the matter be resolved instead by the jurists on the High Court, who are almost certain to have the benefit of better training and more experience for the task. I would rather leave the interpretation and enforcement of the law, including the Constitution, to those trained for the task than put it in the hands of a President appointed or elected for entirely different reasons.

10

The Senate in the balance

In her engaging book, *Platypus*, Ann Moyal chronicles the debates among Nineteenth Century scientists and naturalists that followed their first acquaintance with what one of them called 'This paradoxical quadruped' (Moyal 2001: 7). At first some thought that it was a hoax, an artificial construction—a carefully stitched together amalgam of parts that were impossible to imagine as elements of a single natural organism. Once these suspicions were proven wrong and it became accepted that there really was such a thing as the platypus, attention then turned to efforts to determine the creature's essential nature. For example: 'How did this curious animal from the Antipodes produce its young? If it was not "viviparous", producing its young like other mammals, was it in truth "ovoviviparous" like some lizards with eggs formed and hatched within the female's body? Or was it, perhaps, "oviparous", hatching its young from eggs laid outside its body, like a bird?' (Moyal 2001: 14)

The answers to these questions were critical to resolving another quandary: how was the platypus to be fitted into the existing taxonomical schemes for organizing all living things into what came to be phyla, classes, orders, families, genera, and species? Taxonomy was proving to be a very useful device not just for organizing knowledge, but for identifying relationships and predicting traits that had not yet been observed. Moyal concludes that 'each naturalist sought to shoehorn the little animal into their [sic] different prescriptive forms. Each sought to accommodate it within fixed and long established categories.' But none succeeded. 'No animal ... was to rub more strenuously up against the prevailing taxonomic categories than the paradoxical platypus.' (Moyal 2001: 41)

So too the Commonwealth Parliament. Perhaps no other national assembly in a truly democratic nation rubs more strenuously up against the prevailing taxonomic categories that shape and underlie political and constitutional analysis. Yet ironically, even that assertion may be vehemently contested by some who profess no doubt about where

Australia's national constitutional regime fits into the range of democratic alternatives.

If we take 'democracy' to be one of several alternatives at the most fundamental level of categorizing political systems—the political equivalent of animal, vegetable, and mineral—the other alternatives may be oligarchy, dictatorship, and perhaps more. More relevant for our purposes than the alternatives to democracy are the phyla and classes to which different democracies can be assigned, based on fundamentally important criteria that distinguish among them. So at the phylum level, we might distinguish between direct democracy and representative democracy. And more important still, we might accept a division of representative democracies into two broad classes: to use the familiar shorthand, parliamentary and presidential (or presidential-congressional) systems. But observers of contemporary democratic governments would be quick to point out that, even putting aside the varieties of parliamentary and presidential systems, there are others that are unarguably democratic but neither quite one nor the other. Instead, they are described as mixed systems, hybrid systems, or semi-presidential systems, among other labels. What typically characterizes this third class of representative democracies is some significant degree of sharing of executive power between a president, who may or may not be directly elected, and a prime minister (or prime minister-plus-cabinet), who is appointed and removable by the president, the parliament, or both.

But when we come to Canberra, where do we fit the Commonwealth constitutional system into this schema? Is it even possible to fit the Australian regime comfortably into any one of these three classes? In this final chapter, first we shall explore this question, which is essentially descriptive and analytical. Then, I propose to venture an assessment of the Australian system and the Senate's place in it, and offer a personal perspective on whether the people of Australia should view their system with dismay, alarm, or satisfaction (indifference being an unacceptable alternative). We will conclude with some speculations about what is to come.

What kind of creature?

It is easier to say what the Australian system is not. Obviously it is not a presidential system, and I argue that it also is not a hybrid system in which executive power is shared in significant ways between president and prime minister (a simplification admittedly, but a useful one, of what characterizes these hybrid systems). Some may well disagree, contending that Australia's prime minister and cabinet share executive

power with another executive in the person of the Governor-General—
or perhaps more accurately, that the former derive their executive
power by delegation from the Governor-General.

In support of this contention, there are, first, the black letter of the
Constitution and the formal powers it vests in the Governor-General,
and from which derive his reserve powers; and second, Governor-
General Kerr's undoubted exercise of power during the famous or
infamous events of 1975 that I have reviewed at some length. But I find
this point of view unpersuasive because, as a matter of political
practice, not constitutional abstractions and speculations, it rests almost
entirely on that dramatic and controversial dismissal of Prime Minister
Whitlam and his government. I strongly suspect that the Governor-
General's reserve or potential powers rarely would be thought worth
discussing, except among legal scholars, if, in 1975, the incumbent had
announced that the impending crisis was a dispute between Labor and
the Coalition, between the government and the Senate, that needed to
be resolved through the political process, and so was a matter in which
it would be inappropriate for the Governor-General to intervene.

That leaves us with a third possibility—that the Commonwealth is a
parliamentary system—a possibility that, to many past and present
observers, is obviously, even self-evidently, correct. The
Commonwealth Constitution, after all, is a direct second-generation
descendant of the British constitution, home of the Westminster model,
which is the mental image that most of us probably have in mind when
we think of 'parliament.' The colonial constitutions of what became the
six Australian states were modelled in many of their fundamentals on
the British system of government and, in turn, provided the model that
the creators of the Federation knew, admired, and adapted to the
somewhat different requirements of a continental and federal state. And
if this historical argument is not persuasive, look at the basic elements
of the system at work. The government comprises members of the
Parliament who are chosen by the Parliament and remain in office only
as long as they retain the confidence of the Parliament. Those are
precisely the core relationships, even the definition, of a parliamentary
system.

Consider the following argument from *House of Representatives
Practice* (2001: 461):

> One of the features of the Westminster system of government is the
> existence of a clear line of representation from the people through the
> Parliament to the Executive Government. This in turn results in a clear line
> of responsibility in reverse order from the Executive to the Parliament to
> the people. Once this clear line of responsibility is interfered with (as with
> the intervention of the Senate which is not an equitably representative body

in the sense that the House is) the powerful concept of representative and responsible government is weakened.

Note that 'the Parliament' is distinguished here from the Senate, so it must be synonymous with the House of Representatives only. But that is a semantic quibble. What is more interesting is the undefended assumption that 'the Westminster system' (or the 'Westminster syndrome', Parker's (1980b) more flexible and accommodating formulation) provides the appropriate basis for understanding how the Australian government should work. In fact, that assumption is true, but it is only half of the truth—and then only if we are prepared to ignore the absence of parliamentary sovereignty in Australia (discussed below) and the widespread conviction that the Parliament is more responsible to the Executive than vice versa.

It is fair to apply the label of Westminster model, system, or syndrome to the relations between the government and the *House of Representatives* but not to the relations between the government and the *Parliament*, which, by explicit constitutional definition, includes the third institution that shares Parliament House: the Senate. However well or poorly the somewhat idealized formulation just quoted actually describes the relations between the government and the House of Representatives, it fails to take account of the contemporary Senate which is elected by a form of proportional representation that has made it very unlikely—almost impossible, according to many—that any government ever will have a majority in the Senate under the present electoral system. In truth, the legislative powers of the Senate simply cannot be reconciled with the contention that Australia has a parliamentary form of government, pure and simple.

The Senate's constitutional authority to reject any or all bills, coupled with an electoral system that stacks the deck against the government's control of the Senate, is incompatible with a fundamental principle of parliamentarism: that the government can remain in office to enact and implement its legislative program because (and only as long as) it has the support of a majority in the government-creating and -destroying house of the Parliament. That condition is both necessary and sufficient. The government cannot enact and implement its program unless it has the support of that majority. And the support of that majority enables the government to enact and implement its program.

The argument why this principle does not apply in Canberra can take either a weak or a strong form. The weak form of the argument is that non-government majorities in the Senate can defeat government bills or force the government to accept changes in them as the price of passage. For some of the reasons we will consider later in this chapter, the Senate may be very restrained in exercising these powers (perhaps because the non-government parties disagree among themselves), but that is a decision to be made on the non-government side of the Senate. It may be subject to the government's influence, but not to the government's control. As Reid and Forrest (1989: 479) put it, 'The Senate is plainly the Executive Government's hair shirt.'

The strong form of the argument is that, as the events of 1975 demonstrated, an intransigent Senate has the power to force a government to resign, even though it retains its majority in the House. I argued in Chapter 4 that the Fraser-controlled Senate should not have refused to vote supply for party political reasons, and that Kerr should not have dismissed Whitlam when he did. But assuming the Senate had remained intransigent (a dubious assumption, I argued), and even if Kerr had done nothing, Whitlam would have had no choice but to resign, sooner or later, after the money ran out, after government activities ground to a halt, and after Australians noticed the difference. I think it highly unlikely that anything like the events of 1975 will be repeated in the foreseeable future, but unless and until the Constitution is amended (or the statutory solution I proposed in the preceding chapter is enacted), a non-government Senate majority can force a dissolution of the House or a double dissolution if it is willing to pay the price for the damage it is almost certain to inflict on itself and the nation.

As a general proposition for the comparative study of politics, parliamentarism is not necessarily incompatible with bicameralism, because we understand the former to mean that the government must have a majority in the only house of Parliament that matters, the only one that has the constitutional writ to approve or disapprove the government's legislation. In London and Ottawa, that means only the House of Commons. But in Canberra, both houses matter, and that fact matters for the argument that Australia has a parliamentary government. It does not. Nor does it have a mixed or hybrid system of the kinds that have become increasingly familiar throughout Europe, including the new or proto-democracies of eastern Europe and the former Soviet Union. Australia is a different place in the form of its national government, just as it is a different place in the form of its fauna. Parliament as platypus.

It is not difficult to understand why this conclusion may be bothersome to many Australians—for example, to those who associate democracy with their understanding of the 'Westminster model' and the practices of the British Cabinet and Parliament, and to those who were taught as children that they lived in a parliamentary democracy defined by responsible cabinet government ('although, oh yes, we also have the Senate, don't we?'). The mixed nature of the Commonwealth

Constitution creates ambiguity and uncertainty; it is considerably easier and more convenient to suppose that Westminster is alive and well in Canberra than it is to understand and explain the more complex and confusing reality.

So a natural enough response is to look for ways to show that the Commonwealth is a parliamentary regime after all. One way is to argue that the Senate really does not have the legislative power that the Constitution appears to give it, and to search the debates of the constitutional Conventions for evidence that its authors could not possibly have meant what the Constitution clearly says. How could these children of Westminster, these products of colonial systems of responsible government, have intended anything but to recreate what they knew and what they had inherited? The question answers itself, so if we look at the Commonwealth Constitution through this historical prism, it is possible to see the Senate's legislative powers becoming more and more insubstantial.

Another way is to argue that the Senate's apparent legislative powers must be understood in the context of the unwritten conventions on which Westminster government rests. The Senate, according to this line of argument, may have the written constitutional power to defeat important government legislation, and even to reject an essential appropriation bill, but it would be unconstitutional for the Senate to do so because that would violate an absolutely fundamental convention of responsible government. The Constitution vests executive power in the hands of the Governor-General, but everyone knows that is not what its authors really intended. By the same token, the authors surely did not intend for the Senate actually to use to their fullest the legislative powers that the Constitution assigns it. David Mayer (1980: 51), for example, identifies 'two defensible, but contradictory, interpretations of the Australian Constitution—a literal, federalist interpretation, and a constitutionalist interpretation which gives primacy to responsible government.' When confronted with the choice between 'literalism' and 'constitutionalism', it is not difficult to guess which interpretation he believes to be the proper one.

Unfortunately for these arguments, scholars have documented that leaders of the constitutional Conventions knew precisely what they were doing. They knew perfectly well that they were creating a federal system with the voluntary consent of the six colonies, and that this required institutional arrangements that had no counterpart in London (or in the colonial governments themselves, for that matter). As we have seen, some of them acknowledged in debate that the arrangements they were creating were inconsistent with responsible government. Recall Samuel Griffith's statement that 'the experiment we propose to try has never yet been tried,' and Baker's recognition that 'The essence of federation is the existence of two houses, if not of actually co-equal power, at all events of approximately co-equal power. The essence of responsible government is the existence of one chamber of predominant power.' The solution for them was not to pretend that they were doing something other than what they did. No, their solution was to rely on the prudence, self-restraint, and common sense of those who would operate the system they were creating, so that the contradiction inherent in their creation would remain of theoretical interest—which it has, with few exceptions, ever since.

Still another way to discover a parliamentary regime in Canberra is to revise how we define such a regime. For instance, Ward offers an alternative path to the conclusion that 'Australia is a relatively orthodox parliamentary state' which involves defining away the main objection to this conclusion. One of his criteria for identifying such a state is that, if the parliament is bicameral, 'one chamber has primacy.' Contrary to Barwick and Kerr, he posits that 'The parliamentary model rejects the proposition that a government can be responsible to two chambers, because they might be controlled by different majorities.' So, the question becomes, what constitutes 'primacy'? Ward responds by proposing four criteria:

> First, the government is formed by the party or coalition which has a majority in the lower house. Second, the Prime Minister is a member of the lower house. Third, a majority of ministers sit in the lower house. And fourth, the lower house, or effectively the government that controls the lower house, possesses legislative initiative. Financial bills originate there, and most other legislation begins there too. Furthermore, legislation that originates in the upper house is most often government legislation, introduced there because of time constraints in the other house. In most parliamentary states, the upper house may only delay, not deny, legislation, but even where an upper house has the power to deny all, or certain, bills, as in the German and Indian federations, there is a presumption that the government will determine the bulk of the legislative program. This is certainly true of Australia ... (Ward 2000a: 65)

What is most interesting about this analysis is the criterion that is missing: the capacity to control legislative outcomes. According to Ward's analysis, if the constitutional and electoral systems combine to compel the government to engage in legislative compromise or face the rejection of its legislation, that awkward fact does not detract from characterizing the regime as 'a relatively orthodox parliamentary state.' I would have thought that in such a state, the governing majority can expect to secure enactment of its legislative program, or at least the priority items of its program, so long as it retains majority support in the lower house to which it is formally responsible. Not so, Ward tells us. The electoral mandate that we encountered in the last chapter and that gives a responsible parliamentary government both the right and responsibility to implement its program without significant hindrance or delay, here is reduced to a 'presumption that the government will determine the bulk of the legislative program.' Would John Howard or Paul Keating or, better yet, Margaret Thatcher, be content with such a minimalist conception of parliamentary orthodoxy? I think not.

The problem or the solution?

I now propose to conclude what began as a kind of diary of ideas and understandings with my own reaction to what I have learned about the Commonwealth Parliament and the regime of which it is a part.[227]

It is interesting and informative to explore what the authors of the Constitution intended in the 1890s or what the proponents of the 1948 electoral law expected to follow in its wake. Ultimately, though, those questions are primarily of historical interest. For one thing, what's done is done. For another, debates over such questions frequently are as inconclusive as debates over the 'original intent' of the authors of the US Constitution. Quotations often can be adduced to sustain conflicting positions, and may be offered to support conclusions that comport with the analyst's preconceived notions or the advocate's prior preferences. Also, when many people come together to make a decision, almost invariably they will have different reasons for making their decision, even if they agree on what it should be. Sometimes a single individual even has mixed motives for his or her own decision, especially when it is possible to point to reasons of principle for a decision that just happens to advance self-interest as well.

So there comes a point at which the question to be asked is not why a decision was made or why an action was taken long ago, but whether that decision or action has proven to be a good thing or something less. When that question is posed about the current design of the Commonwealth political system, my answer, and my interpretations and evaluations of Australian government and politics, unavoidably are filtered through the prism of my experiences in Washington, especially as those experiences have shaped my understandings of how political institutions work and what motivates politicians. In fact, it will become

227 The discussion that follows draws heavily and freely on my paper, 'A Delicate Balance: the Accidental Genius of Australian Politics,' presented at Parliament House, Canberra, on 28 February 2003, as part of the Australian Senate Occasional Lecture Series. http:www.aph.gov.au/Senate/pubs/occa_lect/transcripts/280203.pdf.

clear almost immediately that my perspective on governance in Canberra is very much a reflection of my American heritage.

Emy (1995: 25) has written that the Senate is an aspect of the Australian constitutional system that is 'essentially contested', which Mulgan (1996: 191) takes to mean that it is 'subject to opposing interpretations and evaluations based on conflicting and irreconcilable political values.' Let me begin by foreshadowing my own general interpretation and evaluation. In much of what has been written about the Australian political system, the Senate is depicted, either explicitly or implicitly, as a problem. Sometimes the Senate is portrayed as a conceptual problem—as an institution that does not quite fit into Australia's intended constitutional design. Often it is presented as posing a continuing practical problem for the government of the day, when the Senate interferes with the government's ability to fulfill its self-proclaimed electoral mandate by enacting its legislative program. My perspective is a contrary one. For me, the Senate is not the problem, it is the solution—or, perhaps I should say that the Senate is the potential solution for a problem that has not yet had the most dire consequences to which it could give rise. Now let me try to explain what I mean and reveal the political values on which my position rests.

For more than 30 years, as I explained in the Preface, I earned my living by worrying about the United States Congress, which was, most assuredly, a full-time job. And for more than 20 years, my office in Washington was in the James Madison building. Madison, as some readers will know, often has been proclaimed as the 'father' of the United States Constitution. He also was one of the authors of *The Federalist Papers* which, to my mind, remain the most compelling example of practical political theory since Machiavelli, and unquestionably an effective piece of political advocacy, which was their essential purpose.

In the fifty-first of those essays, Madison offered a rationale for the US Constitution and, in the process, revealed a posture toward power and the powerful that continues to resonate in American political thought. It is an attitude that many Americans continue to share, even if they would not phrase it so felicitously. Here is how Madison begins his defence of the separation of powers as we know it in America:

> But what is government itself but the greatest of all reflections on human nature? If men were angels, no government would be necessary. If angels were to govern men, neither external nor internal controls on government would be necessary. In framing a government which is to be administered by men over men, the great difficulty lies in this: you must first enable the government to control the governed; and in the next place oblige it to control itself. A dependence on the people is, no doubt, the primary control

on the government; but experience has taught mankind the necessity of auxiliary precautions.

Those 'auxiliary precautions' take the form of a set of checks and balances imbedded in a system of separation of powers. I fear that phrase, the separation of powers, is being claimed and then distorted by defenders of such different constitutional systems that it is in danger of losing any real meaning. So let me make clear that I use it in the sense that was explicated in a classic of American political science, *Presidential Power* by Richard Neustadt, which was published at just about the time John Kennedy was elected President. Neustadt's book probably is best known today for two insights. One is his understanding of presidential power, which was roughly this: that the power of the President is the power to persuade others that what he wants them to do is what they should want to do in their own interests—in other words, that the most persuasive way for anyone, not just the President, to elicit the support of others is to shape their own sense of their own self-interest. Notice that this conception is entirely compatible with Madison's doubts about the essentially altruistic nature of humanity.

More to the point is Neustadt's other insight, which is that the American political system is *not* one in which each of the different powers of government is neatly and clearly assigned to one of the different institutions of government: the legislative power to the Congress, the executive power to the President, and the adjudicative power to the courts. Instead, as Neustadt explained, the American regime is characterized by a separation of institutions that share the powers of government. The core of the legislative power is assigned to the Congress, but it is shared with the President, primarily through his enormously potent veto power. The core of the executive power is assigned to the President, but it is shared with the Congress that must approve the organization, procedures, and most senior personnel of the executive departments, just as the executive power also is shared with the courts that have the authority to invalidate executive actions inconsistent with the law or the supreme law of the land, the Constitution. And the adjudicative power is centred in the courts, but it also is shared with the President who chooses all federal judges, and with the Congress which must approve those choices and which, through legislation that is subject to the President's veto, controls the organization, resources, and budgets of the courts, even the Supreme Court. It is in this complex sharing of powers that are to be found the checks and balances that provide many of the 'auxiliary precautions' to which Madison referred.[228]

Madison then extends his argument in a way that, from today's perspective, is striking for both its lack of prescience and its lack of application to the Commonwealth Parliament. First he explains that the protection of individual rights ultimately lies in the competition for influence that the Constitution creates among institutions that share the legislative, executive, or judicial powers of government. Those who serve in any one of these institutions have an incentive to preserve its institutional power not for reasons of abstract principle, but in order to protect their own influence—so that 'the private interest of every individual may be a sentinel over the public rights.' Harness individual self-interest to preserve the balance among institutions. So far so good. Then he continues:

> But it is not possible to give to each department an equal power of self-defence. In republican government, the legislative authority necessarily predominates. The remedy for this inconveniency [legislative dominance, that is] is to divide the legislature into different branches; and to render them, by different modes of election and different principles of action, as little connected with each other as the nature of their common functions and their common dependence on the society will admit.

---

228 The concept of checks and balances is distinguishable from beliefs about the appropriate range and scale of governmental activity. Some authors of the Constitution certainly preferred the most limited government, and especially the most limited central government, that was practical. However, I believe that Sawer (1977: 139) was partly mistaken in asserting that '"checks and balances" is an eighteenth-century American notion based on a suspicion of all government, and *a desire to ensure that governments performed the minimum of functions.*' (emphasis added) The challenge to modern democratic life, as Sawer recognized, is the product of the widespread belief that Twenty-first Century governments need to be much more powerful, and have a far broader reach, than Eighteenth Century governments. This does not mean, however, that checks and balances have become outmoded. To the contrary, they are more essential than ever before. Sawer (1977: 140) argued that a modern democratic government 'committed to economic management and a multitude of welfare services ... is not possible if the initiatives of a government based on a House of Representatives majority are to be constantly "checked" by a hostile majority in the Senate, as the American Founders expected their two Houses of Congress and President, elected separately and at different intervals, to "check" each other *so that laws would be few and administrative activity negligible.*' (emphasis added) It is true that checks and balances sometimes can slow the wheels of government and certainly can require governments to make compromises that are distasteful to them, and it also is true that the reach of the Australian central government may be greater than that of the American. Still, I doubt that any observer of American society would contend that the checks and balances built into the US Constitution prevented an extraordinary expansion of federal powers and activities during the Twentieth Century.

Here, then, is a theoretical rationale for the Senate of the United States and, if you choose, for the Commonwealth Senate as well: to protect against the uncontrolled exercise of power by a naturally predominant legislature.[229] And here also is a world-class example of one of a skilled politician's most valuable traits: the ability to transform a necessity into a virtue, to discover a principled reason for doing what self-interest and necessity dictate. We will never know if Madison would have found such compelling virtues in bicameralism if he were not selling to the state ratification conventions the 'Grand Compromise' that made agreement on the US Constitution possible.

This Madisonian fear of power and suspicion of the powerful—the idea that Lord Acton may have been on to something when he posited that power tends to corrupt, though not necessarily in terms of dollars and cents—seems eminently sensible to me. It justifies a system of government that can entail costs of government delays, sometimes inaction, and even occasionally deadlock. These costs sometimes may be high but, considering the alternative, they are well worth paying. The same emphasis on the risks created by government power also highlights the dangers of what, during our current era of post-Soviet democratization, sometimes has been called plebiscitory democracy as distinguished from liberal democracy. In the former, a president is chosen in what satisfy, more or less, the standards of free and fair elections, but then encounters few effective restrictions on his actions in office until the next election. The limits on his exercise of power are electoral only. In the latter, free and fair elections are accompanied by various checks and balances, through a system of separation of powers or by other means, that constrain the president or the parliament in their exercise of power between elections.

This is why talk of presidential emergency powers that are justified as being inherent in the Constitution, and not grounded in statutory grants of power, tends to make many Americans nervous. And it is why I doubt that Americans ever would be very comfortable with the concept of 'reserve powers.' Furthermore, 'conventions' are not a staple of American political discourse, unless we are referring to the quadrennial presidential nominating extravaganzas. The American political system, as well as its legal system, places great weight on there

---

229 In addition to the other rationales for bicameralism that it offers, *Odgers'*
    Australian Senate Practice (2001: 4) holds that 'Bicameralism is also an assurance
    that the law-making power is not exercised in an arbitrary manner. Such an
    assurance is of considerable practical significance in parliaments where the house
    upon which the ministry relies for its survival is liable to domination by *rigidly*
    regimented party majorities.' (emphasis added)

being knowable rules of law to govern and thereby constrain the authority of power-holders, even democratically-elected power-holders. So speak not to me of reserve powers unless you can tell me what they are. And speak not to me of unwritten conventions that stand on equal footing with the words of the Constitution. In the United States, a constitution that fails even to acknowledge some of the core institutions and relationships of government would be a source of dismay and concern, not a source of pride.

In one essay about the 'troubles' of 1975, two distinguished Australian academics denigrated their written Constitution as a mere 'selection of legal rules'. They contended that there was no 'qualitative distinction between written and unwritten constitutions', and argued that to give precedence to the Constitution when it conflicted with unwritten convention would be 'to deny a democratic foundation to Australian politics.' (Archer and Maddox 1985: 56–59)[230] It is difficult to conceive such a statement being made in the United States by analysts of comparable repute. To endorse giving the greatest weight to a convention, defined as 'a rule of behaviour accepted by those involved in public life' and a 'tradition of past conduct which experience has shown to work,' as the authors were prepared to do, strikes me as being breathtaking in its complacency.[231]

The notion that 'we really can't define our conventions of parliamentary governance well enough to commit them to paper, but never mind, we all can recognize a convention when we see one, and we all know what they are' presumes and depends on a degree of political consensus that is enviable beyond words. There may have been just such a consensus in the Australia of 1900, and maybe it remains today. In multicultural Australia of the Twenty-first Century, however, it may require an extraordinary effort, and quite possibly a futile effort, to maintain that consensus—a universally shared understanding of what the essential customs and practices of political life are and a universally shared agreement to accept as them as binding.

Millions of people, especially in post-Communist nations, are struggling to create for their own benefit and protection what they often

---

230 In similar fashion, a New Zealand government publication even listed, as the first of the major elements of the Westminster model, that 'important parts of the constitution remain unwritten.' New Zealand Electoral Commission (1996), *Voting Under MMP*. GP Publications.

231 I am hardly reassured by de Smith's observations (quoted by Hughes 1980: 41) that 'Some conventions are clear-cut; some are flexible; some are so elusive that one is left wondering whether the "convention" is an ethereal will-o'-the-wisp. It is often particularly hard to say whether a political practice has crystallized into a constitutional convention and, if so, what is its scope.'

call 'rule-of-law societies'. So it is both ironic and paradoxical that Australia has flourished for more than a century, with only one truly painful hiccup in 1975, under a political regime governed by rules that have not been codified and, for that reason, perhaps cannot be enforced. If Australia ever decides to become a republic (as I expect it will, sooner or later), that will require that the Constitution be amended. Opening a constitution to amendment is the political equivalent of opening Pandora's Box, so there is a wise and natural reluctance to make amendments that are not absolutely necessary. The litany of constitutional amendments defeated in Australian referenda demonstrates what seems to be an instinctive constitutional conservatism on the part of the Australian people, or a profound cynicism about the motives of Australian politicians (as well as the difficulty of the requirements that sec. 128 imposes for amending the Constitution).

On the other hand, I am unpersuaded by the argument that the conventions (and reserve powers, for that matter) that are thought to be so central to responsible government are simply too complex, subtle, and full of nuance to be codified. Ward (2000b) reports that other parliamentary democracies have succeeded in doing so quite well, especially if the task is limited to incorporating into the Constitution those now-unwritten rules that are truly essential.[232] I think it would be more in keeping with what I have come to know and admire about

---

232 Ward (2000b: 121) argues that some of the Australian attempts to codify conventions foundered because too many practices of government were included on the lists of conventions that required codification. He reports, for example, that one such effort included among the conventions to be codified the practices that 'the Governor-General [is] to appoint a Prime Minister he judges to have the support of a majority in the lower house,' and that he is 'to consult the outgoing Prime Minister about a successor.' Surely such common-sense practices do not require or deserve constitutional standing. All that matters ultimately is whether a new prime minister and government enjoy the confidence of a majority in the House of Representatives. The process of forming that new government is expedited and simplified, of course, if the Governor-General has the good sense to consult with those who best understand the mind of the House and if he then selects the obvious candidate, but it hardly is necessary to transform such obvious practices into constitutional requirements. If the Governor-General should fail, for whatever reason, to appoint the House's choice for a new prime minister, a majority in the House would have little difficulty in securing the House's consideration and adoption of a resolution expressing its will to the Governor-General. That is just what the House did in the first hours after Whitlam's dismissal in 1975 when the House voted, too late as it turned out, to express its lack of confidence in the caretaker Fraser Government and called upon the Governor-General to ask Whitlam to form a new government.

Australians if the Commonwealth Constitution were amended so that, in more respects, it means what it says and says what it means.

Perhaps there is an underlying difference in the American and Australian political cultures as well as in the two societies' respective approaches to constitutional law. Perhaps Australians have a more positive view of government and a more optimistic view of human nature, despite their cynicism about politicians generally and their disrespectful attitude toward individual political leaders. If so, there may be less concern in Canberra than in Washington over the question of 'who guards the guardians.' Ian McAllister (1997: 9) of the Australian National University wrote several years ago that, in Australia, 'the state exists primarily in order to resolve problems and disputes, not to preserve individual liberty,' and he quoted W.K. Hancock in 1930 to the effect that 'Australians have come to look upon the state as a vast public utility, whose duty it is to provide the greatest happiness for the greatest number.' This view is consistent with the first point that Lord Bryce (1905: 298–299) thought to make almost a century ago when considering the new Commonwealth Constitution and comparing it with its American counterpart:

> When that instrument [the US Constitution] was enacted, the keenest suspicion and jealousy was felt of the action of the Government to be established under it. It was feared that Congress might become an illiberal oligarchy and the President a new George the Third. Accordingly great pains were taken to debar Congress from doing anything which could infringe the primordial human rights of the citizen. ... The English, however, have completely forgotten these old suspicions, which, when they did exist, attached to the Crown and not to the Legislature. So when Englishmen in Canada or Australia enact new Constitutions, they take no heed of such matters, and make their legislature as like the omnipotent Parliament of Britain as they can ... . Parliament was for so long a time the protector of Englishmen against an arbitrary Executive that they did not form the habit of taking precautions against the abuse of the powers of the Legislature; and their struggles for a fuller freedom took the form of making Parliament a more truly popular and representative body, not that of restricting its authority.

This benign attitude persisted. La Nauze (1972: 227) recounted that Sir Owen Dixon, one of Australia's pre-eminent jurists and Chief Justice of the High Court during 1952–1964, once was asked to explain to an American audience why Australia's Constitution lacked the protections of individual rights offered by the Bill of Rights and the Fourteenth Amendment. Dixon responded:

> Why, asked the Australian democrats [and authors of the Constitution], should doubt be thrown on the wisdom and safety of entrusting to the

chosen representatives of the people sitting either in the Federal Parliament or in the State Parliaments all legislative power, substantially without fetter or restrictions?

The same attitude was reflected years later in former Prime Minister Robert Menzies' statement, made after leaving office, that 'the rights of individuals in Australia are as adequately protected as they are in any other country in the world' because of 'our inheritance of British institutions and the principles of Common Law.' Menzies was quoted to this effect by Brian Galligan; we have relied on Galligan's scholarship in earlier chapters, so it is worth taking account of his rejoinder:

> Menzies' defence of the Australian system was seriously flawed in a number of respects. The independence of parliament, particularly the House of Representatives, had been undermined by disciplined political parties so that the prime minister and his senior ministers controlled the house and not vice versa. Whether a minister resigned depended on retaining the prime minister's and not parliament's confidence, provided the prime minister retained control of his ruling party. The growth of 'big government' served by large bureaucracies meant that government had become more pervasive with many policy decisions being taken in the executive branch outside parliamentary scrutiny. In other words, parliament was no longer a sufficient check on prime ministerial and ministerial conduct nor an adequate means of protecting rights, despite Menzies' claims. (Galligan 1997: 27)

The formation of the Commonwealth may have been guided by a sunnier attitude toward government and governors than is to be found in the writings of Madison or other theorists of American government (or in the views of Lord Acton, for that matter). In fact, if we are to take Menzies' boast as indicative, that sunnier attitude persisted for decades. I wonder, however, if that attitude is equally widespread today. I also wonder whether Americans have ever been quite so suspicious of government and Australians quite so trusting as Madison and Menzies would lead us to expect. I would guess that the average American, if she exists, has more sympathy with the view of government as problem-solver and utility-enhancer than a reading of Madison might have us predict, just as I suspect that many Australians are more sceptical and suspicious of how governmental powers are exercised, and for whose benefit, than the 'public utility' imagery would imply.

What does all of this imply about the Commonwealth Constitution and the Australian polity? The implications I am about to draw should not be too difficult to predict. But since I already have referred in passing to Lord Acton, let me allow my argument to be introduced by Lord Hailsham, who was Lord Chancellor of the United Kingdom when he became famous, or infamous, for describing the British political system as an 'elective dictatorship'. As Harry Evans (1982), among others, has pointed out, what he actually had in mind is not what often has been attributed to him. It is the doctrine of parliamentary sovereignty that gives rise to elective dictatorship.

> The point is not that all other nations have what is called a written constitution in the literal sense. After all, much of our own is in writing and much more could be reduced to writing if we wished without making any appreciable change. No, the point is that the powers of our own Parliament are absolute and unlimited. In this we are almost alone. All other free nations impose limitations on their representative assemblies. We impose none on ours. (Hailsham 1976: 4)

Traditionally in Britain, all governmental authority ultimately resides in Parliament and, within Parliament, in the House of Commons. In some cases, Parliament itself acts to exercise its sovereign power. In other cases, others act on its behalf and are accountable to it. In all cases, the authority of government belongs to Parliament as the directly elected representative of the people. Parliament determines its own constitutional powers; there is no court that can intervene and restrain Parliament in order to enforce the sovereignty of a constitution from which parliamentary powers derive and by which they are limited. Similarly, Parliament is accountable to no authority other than the voters (and today, perhaps, the largely unaccountable institutions of the European Union).

Referring to this doctrine of parliamentary sovereignty, which he understands to be a defining characteristic of the 'Westminster model' of democratic governance, Lord Hailsham concluded that:

> There is nothing quite like it, even among nations to whom we have given independence. They believe of course that they have inherited the so-called Westminster model. In fact, the Westminster model is something which we have seldom or never exported, and, if we had tried to do so, I doubt whether any nation would have been prepared to accept it. (Hailsham 1976: 3–4)

On this basis alone, we could dismiss contentions that the Commonwealth political system comports with this model. First, Australia, like most other democracies but unlike Britain, has a written Constitution to which the Commonwealth Parliament, like all other institutions of government, is subordinate. Parliament may not do things and may not make decisions that contradict the Constitution. Second, the High Court, which is independent of the Parliament, has the constitutional power to overrule it by declaring its acts unconstitutional and, therefore, null and void. Third, the Constitution grants specific powers to Parliament and the authority to legislate on an enumerated list of subjects (as interpreted by the High Court); all other matters are beyond Parliament's legitimate reach and belong to the states, or are beyond the reach of government at any level. And fourth, there is the Senate and its powers, which we already have discussed and to which we will return shortly.

What is important for our purposes here is what had come to worry Lord Hailsham because, after all, parliamentary sovereignty was not exactly a recent innovation. He later wrote that:

> human nature being what it is, every human being and every human institution will tend to abuse its legitimate powers unless these are controlled by checks and balances, in which the holders of office are not merely encouraged but compelled to take account of interests and views which differ from their own. ... It is the absence of balance and effective checks which has destroyed established regimes by bloody revolution, which has overthrown democracies which have proved ineffective or aggressive. It was this which corrupted political societies hitherto distinguished for their success. (Hailsham 1982: 293)

And this from the Lord Chancellor of the United Kingdom, who reigned but did not rule over the British Senate!

What is the connection between Lord Hailsham's view of human nature and his assessment of the British political system?

> [T]he sovereignty of Parliament has increasingly become, in practice, the sovereignty of the Commons, and the sovereignty of the Commons has increasingly become the sovereignty of the government, which, in addition to its influence in Parliament, controls the party whips, the party machine and the civil service. This means that what has always been an elective dictatorship in theory, but one in which the component parts operated in practice to control one another, has become a machine in which one of those parts has come to exercise a predominant influence over the rest. (Hailsham 1976: 8)

He elaborates:

> Until fairly recently influence was fairly evenly balanced between Government and Opposition, and between front and back benches. Today the centre of gravity has moved decisively towards the Government side of the House, and on that side to the members of the Government itself. The opposition is gradually being reduced to insignificance, and the Government majority, where power resides, is itself becoming a tool in the hands of the Cabinet. (Hailsham 1976: 7)

Unconstrained parliamentary sovereignty had been acceptable because Parliament's exercise of its unchecked power was constrained by checks imposed by the operations of Parliament itself and by the relations between Parliament and its government. But now, he argues, those non-constitutional checks have succumbed to the combined increase in the powers of government and the strength of party.

In other words, the combined growth of government and party has produced an *elective* dictatorship (his phrase) that can be exercised by an *elected* dictatorship (my phrase). The potential for elective dictatorship has existed for as long as parliamentary sovereignty; it has been transformed into a more real threat to democratic governance by the emergence of strong political parties that, once in government, are not subject to effective checks and balances. The Opposition in Parliament may oppose government legislation, but its ability to do so is effectively at the sufferance of the government majority which can suspend or amend the Parliament's rules of procedure at will. For these reasons, he concluded that 'the absence of any legal limitation on the powers of Parliament has become unacceptable.' And of course, Lord Hailsham was referring to Great Britain, where party discipline is not nearly as strict as it is in Australia.

In light of what I already have said, it should not be surprising that I have come to view the Australian political system with both admiration and apprehension. My admiration is for a political system that has several important advantages over the American system.[233] In a democratic polity, no government should be able to dominate the political debate and control the legislative agenda to the exclusion of other issues and alternatives. Still, a parliamentary system, as manifested in Canberra in the relationship between the government and the House of Representatives, provides a clarity of voice and direction that American Presidents rarely are able to achieve. In Washington, there always are a myriad of forces and interests, in government and outside of it, advocating this and demanding that, with the result that the policy-making process often seems to lack any sense of direction or priorities. So many issues are being studied and so many bills are being debated, all at the same time, in the committees of the House and Senate, in the executive branch's 'corridors of power', and in the pages of the few newspapers that pay much attention to such things, that it

---

233 My admiration also extends to the many fine men and women whom I have come to know and who have dedicated their professional lives to the service of the Senate and the House of Representatives, sometimes under rather trying conditions, such as the evening sessions which must strain the family lives of those who actually make Canberra their home, not a place they visit for a few weeks of some months. I especially want to make it clear that I would not want my qualms about the House of Representatives to reflect in any way on the skills and dedication of the people who serve it.

becomes difficult for even the most interested and conscientious citizen to know what to worry about first.

In Canberra, the daily contests in the chambers of the House of Representatives and the Senate constantly define and redefine the partisan and policy alternatives that will be available to the voters at the next election. In the American system, by contrast, there often is a serious disconnect between elections and governance. Individual Representatives and Senators are running for re-election all the time. In doing so, they are promoting their own personas and, to a lesser extent, their individual records in office. Their campaign activities are not overtures for the next presidential campaign. Although those campaigns also never seem to end, it is hard to think of them as natural extensions of governance. The party out of power has to select its leader every four years, and the anointed one often has to introduce himself to the American people. One of the worst positions from which to run for the White House is that of party leader in the House or Senate. The names of congressional party leaders and committee chairmen who sought, or who would have liked to seek, their party's presidential nomination and failed, just since World War II, would constitute an impressive cast of characters. However, the skills required of an effective House or Senate leader and the demands of their positions almost disqualify congressional leaders from becoming successful presidential candidates. There is a connection between elections and governance in parliamentary regimes in Canberra that is admirable—and absent in America.

Responsibility and accountability

What concerns me about the House of Representatives in the Commonwealth political system—and, to a lesser extent, about other parliamentary regimes in which party discipline is not as strong—is that it may yield responsible government without accountable government. In Canberra, the House of Representatives continues to make governments and, in principle, retains the power to dismiss them. But I believe that the concept of responsible government should entail more than that.[234] A responsible government has been described as being the executive committee of the Parliament. The Parliament chooses some of its members in whom it has confidence to act as its agent—to administer the government on its behalf and only for so long as that

---

234 I acknowledge, but from a safe distance, the disagreements about the meaning of 'responsible government'. On this, see the essays by Archer, Parker, and Thompson in Weller and Jaensch (1980).

confidence remains unbroken. For this relationship to work, the Parliament must be able and willing to make informed, independent, and, when necessary, critical judgments about what the government is doing and how well the government is doing it.

It is an appealing theory, but only so long as we do not allow some awkward practical considerations to intrude. As both Madison and Lord Hailsham would remind us, it is only human for those elected to this (or any other) Parliament to have their own self-interest in mind. So if I were a Member of the House of Representatives, or the Senate for that matter, I first would understand that my continued service in the Parliament depends on the support of my party. In fact, this is probably more true of the Senate, with its list system of elections, than it is of the House. Second, I also would understand that my prospects for advancement in the Parliament are limited indeed—that there are few if any positions in the House of true power and influence that do not carry with them the title of minister. In Congress, the position of committee chairman is one to which all members aspire and a position with which most are perfectly content as constituting the pinnacle of a successful and fulfilling political career. If I truly seek political advancement in the Australian Parliament, on the other hand, I must look for a ministerial appointment, and those appointments are dependent on the good will of my party leaders. And third, I would understand that I am less likely to achieve my first goal—political survival—and I cannot achieve my second goal—political advancement to ministerial office— unless my party remains in government or becomes the government. In short, it is very much in my interests to be a loyal and obedient member of my party.

The government is responsible to the House, but it is not accountable to the House in the sense of having to face parliamentary scrutiny of its decisions and actions that is sufficiently intense and regular to protect against unwise or inappropriate uses of its power or even abuses of power. Although the House's standing orders provide regular opportunities for Opposition members to make speeches and ask questions, the majority party or coalition ultimately controls the proceedings of the House, and that majority has a powerful incentive to avoid holding the government to account in ways that are likely to undermine popular support for their party at the next election.

Under these circumstances, what does it mean to say that the Parliament effectively holds the government accountable for its decisions and actions? What are the incentives for the Parliament to hold the government accountable after installing it in office? Where are those subordinate distributions of power to which Madison referred, 'where the constant aim is to divide and arrange the several offices in such a manner as that each may be a check on the other'? And where are those checks and balances of which Lord Hailsham wrote, 'in which the holders of office are not merely encouraged but compelled to take account of interests and views which differ from their own'?

When I look only at the House of Representatives, I have difficulty answering these questions to my satisfaction. It is not that I charge any individual prime minister with undemocratic ambitions, but I do charge that the government and the House in Canberra fail to offer a satisfactory answer to that core question of democratic governance to which I referred earlier: who guards the guardians? It is difficult to predict what effects the acquisition of power will have on men and women. What if an apparently benign and honorable person is selected as party leader, becomes prime minister, and the people of Australia wake up one day to encounter their own version of Joseph McCarthy or Richard Nixon? Is that likely? No. Is that possible? Of course. The Washington system, for all its faults, and it has many, is designed, however imperfectly, to protect against the consequences of such a worst-case development. The Westminster system, for all its virtues, and it has many, is not.

Furthermore, again recall Lord Hailsham's concern that 'the holders of office are not merely encouraged but compelled to take account of interests and views which differ from their own.' In the House, those other interests and views are expressed, to be sure, and often very loudly. But being heard is not the same as being listened to, as being taken into account. There is nothing in the mechanisms of parliamentary government that requires the government to moderate or modify its legislative program to accommodate in any way those who have objections to it and those who believe they will be injured by it. In fact, in claiming their electoral mandates, the winners of parliamentary elections even make a great virtue of their determination to enact their legislative program without change, implying that doing otherwise would constitute a breach of faith with their supporters. This is representative democracy at its best, we have heard them argue. A party presents a clear program to the voters and pledges to enact it; a majority of the voters endorses that program with their votes; and the party then redeems its pledge by promptly moving its program through the Parliament. Last year's campaign manifesto becomes this year's new package of laws. The legislative process is a smooth and efficient assembly line.

Well, perhaps. But perhaps we should be less impressed with how quickly a bill can be made into a law and more impressed with whether that law addresses an acknowledged national problem in a way that is likely to achieve widespread social acceptance. A parliamentary regime that is dominated by what effectively are two disciplined political parties provides inadequate protections against a democratically elected government abusing its powers. But a greater source of daily concern is that it also offers inadequate incentives for policy compromises. The true challenge of the legislative process is not to distinguish right from wrong, but to acknowledge that there are legitimate differences of interests in a diverse society such as America's or Australia's, and then to decide how best those interests can be taken into account, even if they cannot be fully reconciled.[235] In the political world that I wish to inhabit, compromise is not only a necessity, it is very much a good thing. Protect me from those who claim to know the Truth, however well-intentioned they may be.

And so we come to the Senate of Australia.

When I first read the Commonwealth Constitution, I thought that my copy was incomplete because it failed to do what I expect a constitution to do—to define the essential relationships among the core institutions of government. After reading the Constitution, I decided that it was a conceptually incoherent document, and I found myself nodding in agreement with that oft-quoted (see Chapter 5) prediction of Winthrop Hackett in 1891 that 'either responsible government will kill federation, or federation ... will kill responsible government.' I understood the reasons why the Constitution was designed as it is, but I thought the authors' institutional concoction was a recipe for disaster. Then I began

---

235 This argument is compatible with Harry Evans' advocacy of 'distributed majorities'. 'If institutions require, for the making of major political decisions, the support of majorities distributed across different groups in society and different regions, factious government and the growth of alienated and disaffected minorities are discouraged, and government is made more acceptable and stable.' At first, the equal representation of states in the Senate created the need for majorities that were distributed geographically. Later, the adoption of PR came to require 'an ideologically distributed majority for the passage of legislation through the Senate, a majority distributed over the political parties which receive a significant share of votes.' (Evans 1994: 28–29) Actually, what creates the kind of distributed majority to which Evans refers is the fact that *different* majorities control the two houses. So legislative decisions must take account of the preferences of more parties than those constituting the majority in the House. The basis of Senate representation or the mode of Senate elections is less important than that the two houses are constituted sufficiently differently so as to produce, as a matter of course, different majorities in each. Consider Brennan's (1999: 1) thesis that, 'If one believes ... that good government is, like the amateur golfer's swing, a mass of compensating errors, then a good case might be made for the use of PR in the Senate without requiring one to decide on whether PR is, in a global sense, a better electoral system than the single-member electoral district system that characterises the House of Representatives. One might take the view that there is something to be said for both multiple-member (PR) and single-member districts, and conjecture that the Australian bicameral system serves to exploit the advantages of each.'

to read about the events of 1975, and I found myself again nodding my head, but this time smugly, at the naive if benign arrogance of those in the 1890s who recognized the contradiction they were building into the Constitution, but who were confident that its dangers could be avoided by relying on the 'prudential restraint' of Australia's politicians, or 'their rugged sense of British constitutionalism and parliamentary politics,' as Brian Galligan has put it.

It took some time for me to decide in my own mind how to allocate the responsibility for the events of 1975. It took even longer for me to appreciate the importance of the fact that events such as those had not happened before nor have they happened since—and, in fact, that one effect of the 1975 crisis undoubtedly has been to make any political combination in the Senate much less likely to force such a confrontation again, at least in my lifetime.[236] The authors of the Constitution were fundamentally justified in their hopes or expectations that the good sense of Australia's politicians would suffice to prevent the Constitution's conceptual fault lines from causing repeated political earthquakes.

Generally, I have come to appreciate that the Australian system of government *works*. Even though it cannot easily be labelled, even though it is difficult to explain, even though most Australians may not understand it very well, and even though it is a recurring source of heartburn for prime ministers and their Cabinets, it has served the people of Australia reasonably well. In light of the track records of governments around the world, that is enough to ask.

In 1990, Campbell Sharman, a distinguished Australian student of parliamentary affairs, lamented the lack of a theory to explain and justify his system of government—to resolve 'the tension between those institutions deriving from the liberal tradition manifest in the United States constitutional structure [which would include the Senate, of course], and those from the collectivist tradition of the contemporary British parliamentary system [especially responsible party government].' (Sharman 1990a: 1) That is fair, though any such theory would be something imposed after the fact rather than one discovered in the thinking of the Constitution's authors, often described as a collection of men distinguished by their practical experience.

---

236 This was not necessarily assumed at the time. Epstein (1976: 27), for example, wrote that, 'in the immediate aftermath of the 1975 election, there is good reason to accept the widespread assumption that the Senate has established its power to force a general election. ... [I]n political practice, the 1975 election result provides sufficient indication of popular acquiescence to serve as a precedent for subsequent blockage of supply by the Senate.'

Principles are sometimes used to determine compromises. But this is rare. The whole point of a compromise is that two or more parties have principled reasons for their stances and modify them for no other reason than the desirability of an agreed conclusion. The (conflicting) principles are what provide the *need* for compromise rather than the compromise itself. (Sampford 1989: 359; emphasis in original)

By this reasoning, the absence of a unifying theory of Australian government should be no surprise. What is more interesting is the inference, as Sharman (1990a: 2) encapsulates it, that 'Australian government is thus portrayed as an imperfect structure, a mongrel, defective and without coherent justification.' I have just acknowledged that I am among those who think the Commonwealth Constitution, in its marriage of federalism and responsibility, is conceptually incoherent. But even if the document might make Montesquieu wince, that does not necessarily mean that, for the practical purposes of democratic governance, it is imperfect or defective—'a mongrel'. Indeed, the refutation is inherent in the very terms of the claim. I put the matter to a professional veterinarian who later became a political scientist, and who confirmed my impression that 'mongrels' often are more vigorous and healthier than their pure-bred cousins. In fact, veterinarians recognize the concept of 'hybrid vigor', especially in first-generation hybrids. I rest my case for Australia.

That often denigrated system may be serving Australia better now, since the emergence of seemingly permanent non-government Senate majorities, than ever before, and certainly better than before the advent of proportional representation. Since Federation, we have seen democracies rise and fall in many parts of the world, and never take root at all in others. Now we are witnessing many nations confront the discovery that democracy depends on both the words of their constitutions and the values of their leaders. Under these circumstances, the people of Australia should not under-value what they and their chosen leaders have built, even if their construction sometimes looks less like the Old Parliament House with its modest stateliness and more like the new Federation Square in Melbourne with its unusual and confusing design.[237]

---

237 I have been told that many Australians admire the US Constitution more than they appreciate their own, and that they may be better able to identify the drafters who met in Philadelphia than those who divided their time among Adelaide, Melbourne, and Sydney. It is undoubtedly true that, for many Americans, their constitution has been elevated to the status of a sacred though secular text, but one that very few have read since their early school days. In the midst of the 1975 crisis, Gareth Evans wrote in *The Australian* (29 October 1975: 11) that 'The Australian Constitution is not a blood-stirring document. Unlike its United States counterpart,

In earlier chapters, we encountered the Senate being described as a House of the States or a House of Review. Having found the first label inaccurate and the second label unhelpful, let me offer labels of my own. The House of Representatives remains the site of responsible government—the House of Responsibility—and the Senate is becoming more and more the site of accountable government—and so, the House of Accountability. In this respect, I agree with Mulgan (1996: 201) when he says that 'A division of labour is emerging with the two major parliamentary functions, the provision of government and the holding of government to account, being increasingly divided between the two houses.'

In my usage here, 'responsibility' and 'accountability' are by no means synonymous.[238] When I refer to the House as the House of Responsibility, I am using 'responsibility' in a narrowly technical sense, but one appropriate to the real dynamics of Australian government. When I refer to the Senate as the House of Accountability, I am using 'accountability' in an unconventionally broad sense (compare, for example, Aldons 2001), and I am thinking as much about what the Senate could become as about what it now is.

By 'responsibility', I mean that the government is responsible to the House in and only in the dual sense that the House creates the government and retains the ultimate power to destroy it. It is true that, in Australia, there is no suspense about what government the House will create. Yet the act of creation remains both an essential one and an essentially defining one that distinguishes a parliament from a congress that confronts an independently elected president. It also is true that there is little likelihood of the House engaging in an act of destruction (by voting no confidence in the government it created), but that does

---

it has never been much recited in schoolrooms or bar-rooms.' I suppose he was mistaking the Constitution for the Declaration of Independence (the preamble of which I did have to recite as a schoolboy), but even in that case, I would be truly amazed—and equally disappointed—to learn that such bar-rooms actually exist.

238 I think it is useful to maintain a distinction between the two. Otherwise, meanings and arguments can lose their clarity. In *Odgers' Australian Senate Practice* (2001: 10), it is argued, for example, that 'The representative character of the Senate has enabled it to uphold the *responsibility* of governments to Parliament. ... [Because of the unusually strong party discipline in Australia,] the need for alternative parliamentary avenues for holding a government *to account* is pronounced, and this need in Australia is supplied by its elected Senate. ... The Senate when functioning as a repository of and forum for *responsibility* is thus more than a mere venue for a clash between government and Opposition working on the basis of pre-determined numbers. Governments have therefore been held *to account* in the Senate more effectively than in a house where they are always supported by a party majority.' (emphasis added)

not make this second sense of 'responsibility' unimportant. Again, it
defines the formal relationships between institutions of governance and
it remains available as the ultimate weapon of control that governments
can never entirely ignore. In this sense, it is much like the impeachment
power in the United States. The fact that only twice has the US House
of Representatives actually impeached a President (and would have
done so in a third case if Richard Nixon had not resigned) cannot be
taken to mean that the power is of little consequence. Anyone who
thinks this is the case might ask Bill Clinton for his opinion.

This is what I mean by responsibility. What I do not mean by the
term is that the House monitors, oversees, constrains, and controls on a
daily basis what the government does and how the government does it.
Instead, that is part of what I mean by 'accountability' and what I have
in mind when I label the Senate as the House of Accountability. This
post facto sense of accountability is a familiar one. Especially in the
Australian context, however, it is appropriate to adopt a more expansive
definition that includes holding the government accountable for what it
proposes to do as well as for what it already has done. Accountability
that is limited to looking backward carries the risk of coming too late.
Holding the government to account also should mean reviewing and
evaluating its proposed primary legislation as well as its proposed
secondary legislation (functions performed in part by the Senate
Committee for the Scrutiny of Bills and the Committee on Regulations
and Ordinances, respectively). This sense of accountability, therefore,
includes the process of evaluating government bills (always), amending
them (sometimes), and refusing to pass them (infrequently).[239]

For me, then, the genius of the Australian political system lies in the
way in which it can combine the virtues of parliamentary government
with the means to control its vices—how its constitutional and electoral
systems can combine to make the government responsible to the House
but accountable to the Senate.

This is the opportune moment to introduce the remedy that Lord
Hailsham offered in reaction to his critique of the House of Commons.
Being a responsible statesman, he was not satisfied with criticizing the
status quo; he thought it his responsibility to offer at least a general
sketch of the changes he hoped to see take place in the British political
system. After opting for a written constitution, he proceeded to identify
some of the essential elements that document should contain:

239 To students of the US Congress, this is an unconventional notion of accountability.
     The study of Congress often—too often, actually—tries to separate the legislative
     work of Congress from its oversight activities.

I would myself visualise a Parliament divided into two Chambers, each elected. The one, the Commons, would, as now, determine the political colour of the executive Government and retain control of finance. Preferably, in my view, it would be elected as now by single member constituencies. The other, you might call it a senate, but I would prefer the old name, would, like the Senate of the United States, be elected to represent whole regions, and unlike that Senate, would be chosen by some system of proportional representation.

The powers of Parliament, so formed, would be limited both by law, and a system of checks and balances. Regions would have devolved assemblies, and the respective spheres of influence of these and of Parliament would be defined by law and policed by the ordinary Courts. (Hailsham 1976: 14–15)

Welcome to Canberra, Lord Chancellor.[240] Having found that the Westminster model, in contemporary British practice, has 'moved towards a totalitarianism which can only be altered by a systematic and radical overhaul of our constitution,' he concluded that the elements of the remedy lie in precisely those elements which now distinguish the Australian from the British constitution, and especially in the potential of the Senate. Instead of viewing the Australian Senate as a constitutional appendage of doubtful value and questionable legitimacy that is fundamentally incompatible with the purity of Commonwealth parliamentarism, Lord Hailsham would encourage us to view the Senate as a protection against the weaknesses and dangers of parliamentary government in an age of executive dominance and party discipline.

As I have said, the Commonwealth Parliament's combination of capacities for responsibility and accountability, centred in the House and Senate respectively, seems theoretically contradictory, and it may be so. Having just introduced my own labels, let me also say, at the risk of seeming to contradict myself, that the Australian polity, taken in its entirety, does not readily lend itself to labels and capsule characterizations—'a parliamentary system', 'the Westminster model', 'the Washminster mutation', and so on. I prefer my emblem: the platypus. It may be implausible, but it works. The fact that no more conventional label fits very well must make it more difficult to explain to new or young Australians how their government works and for the House and Senate to explain themselves to the public. So be it. One sign of maturity is the acceptance of ambiguity. I have sometimes heard it said that Australia, as such a young nation, still lacks a sense of its own identity. I have seen no evidence of that. But in any case, perhaps

240 I do not mean to suggest that he was not aware that his prescription closely tracked the Commonwealth Constitution. He was. It also should be noted that his constitution also would incorporate an entrenched Bill of Rights.

one sign of Australia's growing maturity as a self-confident nation will be its growing acceptance of the ambiguity that is inherent in its constitutional system.

A delicate balance

This is the genius of the Australian political system, but it is an accidental genius. I do not believe that it really was intended to work this way. I especially doubt that the distinction I have drawn between responsibility and accountability would have resonated well at the constitutional Conventions. Instead, I suspect that most of the Constitution's authors would have argued that it is precisely by holding governments responsible that the Parliament holds them accountable. I also accept the judgments of scholars that the Chifley Government in 1948 did not intend to make it almost impossible for future governments to have 'the numbers' in the Senate. Finally and most important, I am sure that many inhabitants of each of the three parts into which Parliament House is divided—the Senate, the House of Representatives and the Government—would not fully accept my appraisal and characterization.

If, as I have just argued, what makes the Australian political system special is its capacity to balance principles of responsible government (as manifested primarily in the House of Representatives) with the principles of controlled government embodied in checks and balances (and manifested primarily in the Senate), then it is a delicate balance. By this I mean four things, two of which by now will be familiar. First, I mean that the Australian political system is an unusual and probably unique combination of elements that do not fit together comfortably. So the balance among them is not necessarily a sturdy one. Second, I mean that those elements can combine to create a functioning political system that avoids some of the deficiencies of more 'pure' versions of both parliamentary and presidential regimes by balancing some characteristics of each against the other.

Third, I also mean that the balance requires constant maintenance and, when necessary, adjustment. In practice, this requires that the stronger the bonds that tie the House to the government, the more important it becomes for the Senate to increase its own capacity and willingness to demand accountability from the government. The Senate has yet to develop fully the capacities and, more important, the sense of itself that it will need if it is to provide the accountability that once was expected to accompany the relationship of formal responsibility between the lower house and the government. The Senate rightly prides itself on a more deliberative legislative process (and a more energetic committee system, an important subject that I have not addressed)[241] than is to be found in the House of Representatives or, for that matter, in perhaps any other 'upper house' that is part of what otherwise is a parliamentary regime. But my argument suggests that the Senate should begin asking not whether its glass is half-full, but whether it remains half-empty, and whether it has further to go before it is willing and able to enforce the degree of accountability that my conception of democratic governance requires.

The future direction of the Senate and the prospects for it evolving into an even more effective House of Accountability rest primarily in the hands of the Opposition, whether it be the ALP or the Coalition.

The government party can make a rational calculation that a weak Senate, or a Senate no stronger than it is today, is in the government's interests. A Senate that interferes with passage of the government's legislative program and a Senate that second-guesses the government's administration of existing policies and programs is a distraction and a hindrance. Only a government that knows that it is almost certain to lose the next House election, as the Chifley Government evidently did in 1948, would have a self-interested reason for supporting a strengthened Senate. Otherwise, even if the government party accepts the argument that the Commonwealth needs a better system of checks and balances and that the Senate is the key to meeting that need, I am happy to predict that the government (whether Coalition or Labor) usually will find a compelling reason that this simply is not the best time for reform. A more suitable time surely will come, even if it just so happens that time does not arrive until the governing party has been exiled to the Opposition side of the House and the Senate.

For minor parties, on the other hand, their incentives are to preserve the Senate or strengthen it. With no foreseeable hope of becoming part of government, the institutional base of minor parties will remain the Senate; it is there that they will exercise whatever influence they can. The influence they can exert, therefore, depends on the powers of the Senate—not only its formal constitutional powers, but its capacity and willingness to exercise those powers. So we should expect that, more often than not, the minor parties will react sympathetically to proposed enhancements in the Senate's authority, practices, and resources that

---

241 The scrutiny activities of Senate committees have become well enough entrenched to have entered popular culture. A recent novel centering around Aussie Rules football opens with the hero/narrator speculating on espionage in sports and imagining himself 'giving evidence before a senate committee, how approaches were made, cash dangled under my nose … ' (Wearne 1997: 1) This may not qualify as scientific proof, but it is a telling example of what have been called 'unobtrusive measures' of social phenomena.

356 PLATYPUS AND PARLIAMENT

the government is just as likely to oppose. Furthermore, the minor parties should be especially sensitive to proposed changes in the rules for electing Senators. It was the switch to proportional representation that made it possible for minor parties to secure representation in the Senate, and it is no secret that the best way to deprive them of their seats and their 'balance of power' is through carefully designed and calibrated changes in the electoral laws as they affect the Senate.

The Opposition is the key. Whether the ALP or the Coalition is the Opposition of the day, it can view the Senate in several different ways. It can view the Senate as its bastion of power; the place where it has opportunities to create alliances against the government and defeat it— opportunities that are not available in the House. From this perspective, the Opposition also should be an advocate of strengthening the Senate; by joining forces with the minor parties, it could institute changes that serve their separate but coinciding interests. Alternatively, the Opposition can view the Senate from the vantage point of the future government. From this perspective, the Opposition would evaluate any proposal to change the Senate by asking not only if that change would work to the Opposition's advantage today, but whether that same change would make its life even more difficult—unacceptably difficult—when it returns to power, presumably in the very near future.

There is another alternative. The government and the Opposition could decide to join forces, as early as tomorrow, to amend the electoral law to rid both of them of minor party and Independent Senators and the leverage they now can have. The major parties could agree to scrap proportional representation altogether or, as I already mentioned, to divide each state into divisions—perhaps three divisions with two Senators to be elected from each of them at each half-Senate election. That 'reform' should just about ensure a two-party Senate. Another approach would be to retain the current electoral system but add to it a requirement that a minor party would have to win some significant percentage of first preference votes before it would be eligible to hold any Senate seats. In other words, a minor party could not win a seat through the distribution of second and subsequent preferences unless it could demonstrate that it was the first choice of a sufficient share of the electorate. By such means the Coalition and the ALP could implement an agreement that the pivotal place of minor party and Independent Senators simply makes legislative life in the Senate too complicated and unpredictable, and that they would rather take the risk of a winner-takes-all system that would allow one to govern and the other to oppose, without the negotiating and compromising and temporizing that non-government majorities in the Senate impose on them both. Were that to happen, I suspect that it would be a decision that would prove difficult to reverse.[242]

In this respect, the balance is delicate indeed, and there is no guarantee that any change affecting the Senate is going to be change for the better. For the Opposition to join with the minor parties in promoting a stronger Senate today would create problems for it in the future, when it becomes the government. But for the Opposition to join with the government in weakening the Senate would be detrimental to the Opposition's short-term interests and, by making it easier for the government to enact its program and protect itself against searching scrutiny, might even make it more difficult for the Opposition to discredit the government and replace it in power. In the longer term, a government-controlled Senate would have the same political incentives to treat the government gently—too gently—that the House majority has. It is likely that sooner or later, and probably sooner, the Senate would be no different from the House if the government held a majority of seats there as well. An Opposition-controlled Senate, on the other hand, might undertake energetically to hold the government accountable, but it would be motivated by the natural desire to help promote the Opposition to majority status in the House. The risk, therefore, is that the Senate would become another instrument in the electoral contest, not an instrument of effective governance.

A likely result of all these calculations and considerations is a perpetuation of the status quo, with only incremental and unintended changes taking place to strengthen or weaken the Senate at the margins. Incremental changes or changes with unintended consequences may be what the future holds for the Senate, and this is not necessarily a bad thing. The consequences of major or rapid changes in institutions are very difficult to predict, which is the source of the truism that today's reform becomes tomorrow's problem. For a complicated institution of democratic governance, gradual change may be best. What may be more important than the pace of change is a clear sense of the direction that change should take.

---

242 Bennett (1996: 82) has pointed out that, in recent decades, PR has been introduced for upper house elections in New South Wales, South Australia, and Western Australia (and proposed in Victoria). 'It is now close to an Australian norm,' he argues, 'that preferential voting is used for lower houses and PR for upper houses, and a government that attempted to alter this pattern might find many voters antagonized by what would be portrayed as a government attempting to distort the electoral system for its own ends.' As the proposal for multi-member Senate districts or regions indicates, however, there are ways to reshape electoral outcomes while arguing that PR is not being abandoned, and that only the form of PR is being changed.

The fourth respect in which the Australian political system embodies a delicate balance lies in the fact that making the system work to its potential requires a degree of self-restraint as well as a tolerance for institutional complications and political inconveniences. These are things that do not come naturally to impatient politicians whose instinctive interests are in maximizing their power and in subordinating concerns with government institutions and procedures to their desire to get things done—now. This last meaning of balance merits some elaboration.

Nowhere is self-restraint more necessary than in the Senate itself. Harry Evans, Clerk of the Senate and editor of the tenth edition of *Odgers' Australian Senate* Practice (2001) is not shy about claiming for the Senate its rightful place in the sun. At first he makes a relatively modest argument based on the virtues of bicameralism:

> In every walk of life—be it medicine, science, or day-to-day family problems—the second opinion is sought and valued. So is it in government, where a second House acts so as to ensure proper consideration of all legislation, imposes a period for reflection and provides an opportunity for anyone to voice an opinion, support or protest regarding proposed legislation, after which the second House may make or suggest amendments to proposed laws. (*Odgers' Australian Senate Practice* 2001: 11)

Later, though, he asserts the legislative primacy of the Senate, if only by default:

> Section 1 of the Constitution vests the legislative power of the Commonwealth, that is, the power to make laws subject to the limitations provided by the Constitution, in the Parliament, which consists of the Queen represented by the Governor-General, the Senate and the House of Representatives. The agreement of each of the three components of the Parliament to a proposed law is required to make a law of the Commonwealth. In practice, with the ministry, the executive government, initiating most legislation in the House of Representatives, controlling that House through a party majority, and advising the Governor-General, the task of exercising the legislative power falls upon the Senate. (*Odgers' Australian Senate Practice* 2001: 251)

Almost by necessary implication, the Senate is all that stands between the Australian people and an electoral parliamentary dictatorship. Even if that is so, it does not imply that the Senate should exercise its constitutional powers fully and at will. When push comes to shove, the Senate is well-advised to show deference to the House. In this context, we should revisit for a moment the trio of considerations (introduced in the last chapter during the discussion of mandates) which it is proposed that the Senate take into account as it decides how to use its powers 'circumspectly and wisely':

> A recognition of the fact that the House of Representatives represents in its entirety, however imperfectly, the most recent choice of the people whereas, because of the system of rotation of senators and except in the case of simultaneous dissolution of the two Houses, one-half of the Senate reflects an earlier poll.
>
> The principle that in a bicameral parliament one house shall be a check upon the power of the other.
>
> Whether the matter in dispute is a question of principle for which the government may claim electoral approval; if so, the Senate may yield. The Senate is unlikely to resist legislation in respect of which a government can truly claim explicit electoral endorsement, *but the test is always likely to be the public interest*. (*Odgers' Australian Senate Practice* 2001: 13; emphasis added)

It is interesting to compare these statements from 2001 with what the then Clerk of the Senate, J.R. Odgers, wrote in 1966:

> The House of Representatives is, and must always be, the policy making chamber. The worst thing that could happen to the Senate is for it to attempt to compete with the House of Representatives as a policy maker. If it did, it would, in the process of time, risk emasculation, as the House of Lords was eclipsed. ...
>
> If it disagrees with policy, the Senate has the right, indeed the duty, to project its viewpoint by the process of amendment or suggestion, but it is submitted that the Senate should not—except where state interests are seriously threatened—insist upon amendments disagreed to by the policy making Chamber. The will of the House of Representatives should prevail and, if that House errs, it can safely be left to the sanction of the people at election time. (quoted in Solomon 2000: 11)

In 1966, the standard for the Senate acting to thwart the government was a serious threat to 'state interests'. In 2001, it was the arguably weaker standard of what is likely to be in the public interest, presumably as determined by the Senate. Although we should not subject these phrases to too fine an examination, it is not difficult to discern in them a less deferential tone in 2001 than in the mid-1960s.

For a moment, let us ignore the advice to the Senate in both quotations, think only of the Senate's formal constitutional authority, and imagine what might happen if the Senate were willing and able to exercise that authority to its fullest.[243] The Senate could reject, or amend

---

243 I put aside as unknowable how the High Court might rule on the boundaries of Senate power, and if, when, and why it might invoke conventions as the basis for limiting that power.

beyond recognition, any and all government legislation that did
accord with the policy preferences of stable or shifting maj.
coalitions of non-government Senators. The Senate also could init
its own legislation and, if there was a sufficiently stable n
government majority on that side of Parliament House, it could deve.
and seek enactment of its own legislative agenda in competition w
that of the government. The government's ability to impleme
whatever electoral mandate it tried to claim would be at the mercy o
the majority will of the Senate. And in effect, the Senate could, at any
time and on any issue, force the government to choose among
compromise, capitulation, or a double dissolution. In response, a
sensible government would ensure, as soon as possible, that at least one
bill had satisfied the requirements of sec. 57, and so could be invoked
to trigger a double dissolution whenever the government decided the
time was right. In turn, an intransigent Senate could try to force the
government's hand by refusing supply and compelling the government
to resign, in order to provoke simultaneous elections at a time more to
the liking of the non-government parties in the Senate.

Fortunately, this is a nightmare scenario that so far has remained
just that: a bad dream. But why? Why were the events of 1974–1975 so
much more the exception than the rule? Although governments often
complain about the Senate, it becomes clear that its non-government
majorities have exercised great self-restraint when we compare what
they do and have done with what they could do if they threw caution
and good judgment to the winds. More than half a century ago, Denning
(1946: 64–65) suggested four reasons for the Senate's self-restraint: (1)
the responsible attitude of Senators 'towards the proper working of the
machinery of government'—in other words, respect for what both
parties take to be the principles underlying the Constitution; (2) the
recognition that 'capricious use' of their power would seriously damage
the public standing of the Senate; (3) the non-controversial character of
much legislation; and (4) the recognition, or hope, that the party in
government today soon will be in Opposition, so that neither party has a
long-term interest in encouraging bicameral practices that increase the
likelihood of stalemate.

These arguments, which are interconnected in many ways, remain
plausible today. Although Odgers did not explain exactly what he
meant when he wrote in 1966 that a too-assertive Senate would 'risk
emasculation,' he presumably was suggesting a recognition by the
Senate that, to some Australians, its position in the constitutional order
was and remains questionable or ambiguous. Reid and Forrest (1989:
479) recite various ways in which the Senate has arranged its
procedures to suit the interests of the government, even when the

government lacks a Senate majority. This leads them to conclude that 'Senate majorities have taken an enlightened attitude towards protecting the Government's interests in the Senate, and *in doing so they have protected the Senate in the eyes of the public.*' (emphasis added) I believe, as they evidently did, that there remains an ambivalence or uncertainty among many Commonwealth politicians as well as the Australian public as to what is appropriate for the Senate to do and under what circumstances, notwithstanding its formal constitutional powers. If so, the Senate has to be somewhat concerned that if it becomes too assertive too often, it may find itself without the public support it needs to sustain that role. The too vigorous exercise of its powers could produce a backlash that would inspire greater support for attempts to reduce its powers.

Goot (1999b: 338–341) reports surveys showing that the Australian public does not necessarily prefer unified government (i.e., the government party or coalition also controlling the Senate), that there is no consensus that the Senate should refrain from blocking bills or that its constitutional powers should be curbed, and that 10–15 per cent of voters have split their tickets in recent House and Senate elections. These findings lead him to conclude that 'all the evidence points to a better educated, more politically aware electorate, welcoming the check on executive power and wanting the Senate to stay.' That must be reassuring for the Senate's advocates and defenders. However, practicing politicians will ask how stable public support for the Senate would be if and when the government accuses it, as it was accused in 1975, of being used by the Opposition in an attempt to bring the government to its knees in contravention of all that is most familiar about how Australia's political system works.

Denning's fourth argument is mirrored in Melissa Langerman's much more recent observation (in Bongiorno et al. 1999: 167) that 'Perhaps the only certainty for political parties, particularly in recent years, has been that whatever procedures they introduce as a stumbling block for the government while they are in opposition, almost certainly become a stumbling block for themselves in government.' As I already have argued, major 'reforms' in the Senate are most unlikely without the active support of the Opposition. However, the Opposition, of whatever party, always wants to convince itself that it is the Government-in-Waiting that will regain power within the next three years at most. With that happy prospect in mind, today's Opposition will think more than twice about pressing for changes in the Senate that may work to its immediate advantage but that soon will come back to haunt it.

When Denning wrote, there had been only one double dissolution and that had occurred more than forty years earlier. So it is not surprising that he failed to add to his list of arguments favouring senatorial self-restraint the fact that non-government Senators always must remember that if they refuse to pass a government bill, they may be creating the basis for a double dissolution and an election at which they all must face the voters. As Reid and Forrest (1989: 74) put it, 'In many cases the Senate's opposition to the government of the day has been limited not by the Constitution but by its willingness to face the possible electoral repercussions of its actions.' Furthermore, the non-government parties must ask themselves whether they are likely to be penalized at the polls precisely because their assertions of Senate power are thought to violate an essential principle of the constitutional system.

In practice, therefore, the question for a non-government majority in the Senate is whether or when the public will think it is legitimate for that majority to use its voting strength to block enactment of legislation unless the government makes satisfactory policy concessions, or whether the public will decide that doing so is incompatible with the governing principles of Australian democracy as it understands them. Under what circumstances is it appropriate for the Senate to exercise its right to amend or veto legislation? When should its non-government majority rest content with questioning, reviewing, and even investigating and exposing government policies and actions in a far more independent manner than can be expected in a House that the government controls through strict party discipline? In turn, the question for the government and its House majority is whether or when it should be flexible enough to accommodate the Senate's amendments to its legislation instead of allowing that legislation to die in the face of Senate opposition (and become a double dissolution trigger).

More often than not, the result is a reasonably effective working relationship between the House with its government majority and the Senate with its non-government majority. Sharman (1998: 8–9) concluded that 'governments can usually get most of what they want through both houses of parliament, given strong justification and the time necessary for proper scrutiny. It is only when governments are impatient or see partisan advantage in passing legislation without amendment that they become openly hostile to the actions of the Senate in forcing compromise.' Even more recently, Ward (2000a: 69) came to much the same conclusion: 'the evidence is strong that governments still hold the legislative initiative and get most of what they want, and certainly most of what they absolutely need, out of the upper house.' The problem for Australia is that this may not be the impression that an Australian citizen would get from reading media reports and listening to government leaders in the House and non-government Senators chastise each other.

Some concluding thoughts

Some readers may try to discern in this chapter a hidden diagnosis and agenda. The diagnosis? That the underlying problem with the Australian political system is that it differs from the American system. The agenda? To move the Australian system further down the road from Westminster to Washminster to Washington. Not guilty, I argue. My goal is not to argue for a transformation of the Australian Senate into the United States Senate, nor to advocate that the Commonwealth move toward a US-style presidential-congressional system (as some Australians recently have proposed). On the contrary, my interest is in strengthening the capacity of the Parliament so that it is better able to fulfill its part of the bargain of parliamentary government. A core purpose of requiring the government to be responsible to the Parliament is to ensure that it is accountable to the Parliament. If the development of disciplined parties makes it unlikely that the House of Representatives will hold the government accountable, it would remain consistent with the underlying purpose of responsible government for the Senate to do so. In other words, to claim that the Senate acting as the House of Accountability contradicts the fundamentals of responsible government is to emphasize form over function.

Ward has written that 'the potential for conflict between a government responsible to the lower house and a powerful, federal upper house ... has been ... resolved in favour of the government. The threat to responsible government by an American-style Senate has not materialised.' (Ward 2000b: 119) I disagree on all counts. First, I disagree that the 'potential for conflict' has been 'resolved'—or at least I hope that the Senate will prove him wrong in the years to come. Second, I disagree with the implication that conflict between the Senate and the House (and government) is a 'threat to responsible government.' To the contrary, as I have argued, an assertive Senate is necessary to prevent 'responsible government' from remaining or becoming little more than an empty formalism.[244] And third, I disagree with his implication that the alternatives are an ineffectual Senate and an 'American-style Senate'. There is a middle ground, but finding and maintaining it may prove to be the greatest challenge of all.

Although I have come to admire the Australian regime, I doubt that I would recommend it to anyone else, precisely because of the delicate

---

244 This certainly is not an original argument; see Uhr (2002a), among others.

balance that it requires. Australians have made it work in Australia, however, and I now share the benign arrogance of the Constitution's authors in believing that Australians can make it work still better in the future. But that is most likely to happen if there is a clear understanding of what constitutes the problem and what constitutes the potential solution.

How likely is this analysis to be of anything more than historical interest ten or twenty years from now? Barring overwhelming victories by the same party in two successive Senate elections or any change in the election rules, non-government majorities in the Senate are likely to persist. The relatively balanced popular support for the two main contestants; the election of Senators, six or twelve at a time in each state, on a state-wide basis; the election rules that allow minor party and independent candidates to win Senate seats by meeting a fairly low quota requirement and doing so primarily on the basis of voters' second and third preferences—these and like factors combine to explain why some informed observers go further and contend that continuing non-government majorities in the Senate are a virtual certainty.

Of that I am not quite convinced. Landslides are known to happen and, given a good streak of luck and a strong economy, I can conceive of a landslide victor being rewarded two or three years later by another equivalent success. One obvious question, then, is whether a government (of either political persuasion) that finds itself with majorities in both chambers would take advantage of the opportunity to change the rules of the game to the detriment of the minor parties and Independents. The goal presumably would be to make it far more likely that, in the future, whichever party wins the House also will win control of the Senate.

There is no certain answer to this question because the governing party would confront conflicting incentives. On the one hand, there would be the obvious incentive to take 'control' of the Senate away from the inconvenient handful of Senators who, after all, represent such a small fraction of the national electorate.[245] On the other hand, a government can gain control of the Senate only after two successive election victories. If it then changes the rules of the game, the new rules would take effect only at the next election. So the governing party would have to win a third successive election before it would be able to take advantage of its control of what now would be a two-party Senate. Under these circumstances, a government would have reason to fear

---

245 Jackson (1995: 46) cites a newspaper report of Prime Minister Keating saying in 1994 to Senator Kernot, Leader of the Australian Democrats, that 'We can get rid of you lot, that little tin pot show you run over there.'

that the 'reforms' it made actually would work to the advantage of the Opposition, which would stand an equal or better chance of winning that third election. It is quite possible, therefore, that even if and when a government does have majorities in both houses with which it could legislate a change in the system for electing Senators, it might decide not to do so out of fear that it might not be the immediate beneficiary of that change.

Alternatively, we can imagine the Coalition and the ALP forming a temporary coalition of convenience, agreeing that it is in their mutual interests to amend the electoral laws to squeeze minor parties and Independents out of the Senate. Then, with the battlefield cleared, they could contest with each other, and only with each other, for control of the Senate—winner take all. Yet there several reasons to doubt that this actually will happen. First, if it were such an appealing idea, why has it not already happened? Governments have faced non-government majorities in the Senate for most of the past five decades. During that time, either they have not sought to ally with the Opposition against the minor parties, or they have tried but been rebuffed. Perhaps the reason such a temporary alliance has not already been formed is the level of distrust between Labor and the Coalition. Each may fear that any 'reform' proposal that either makes somehow would work to the disproportionate benefit of the other, even if it is not clear how that could happen. Almost by definition, any proposal that was acceptable to both sides would have to guarantee that neither party would benefit at the expense of the other.

Change would entail political risks that one side or the other might decide are too great to run. Under the current system, both the government and the Opposition know that they usually are only a handful of votes away from victory in the Senate, and there are reasonable people with whom to negotiate for those votes. By contrast, the only reason to change the Senate's electoral system would be to make it much more likely that one of them, either Labor or the Coalition, would win control of the Senate at each election and the other would lose. However, the kind of 'reform' that both sides are most likely to accept is one that gives each of them an equal chance of winning in each state, a system that is likely to result in the Coalition and the ALP splitting the six or twelve votes that are on offer at each Senate election. And what could be worse than the realistic possibility of a two-party Senate in which the two parties are tied?

Finally, both the government and the Opposition must ask whether they prefer the inconveniences that the status quo creates for the government and the opportunities it creates for the Opposition when compared with the alternatives that significant electoral change almost certainly would bring. Any reform that effectively precludes the election of minor party or Independent Senators would produce a Senate that is controlled either by the government or by the Opposition; there could be no third force to hold the balance of power. If the government controls the Senate, we could expect it to stagnate or degenerate. Just as governments have no incentive to strengthen the House, they would have no self-interested reason to support a Senate that reviews and even challenges and occasionally rejects its primary and secondary legislation, and that makes a serious effort to monitor its implementation of the laws. If the Opposition controls the Senate, we could expect it to become a forum for inter-party conflict that could make the House today resemble a tea party by comparison. Perhaps an apt comparison for the Parliament would become the Cold War or, even more frightening, a rugby union match in which blood flows freely but few tries are scored by either side.[246] A government would not be able to enact *any* legislation without the support or at least the acquiescence of the Opposition. I would expect that after only a few years of enduring the frustration that would ensue, a government of either political complexion would try to reduce the Senate's powers by constitutional amendment or, if that proved impossible, as would be likely, to amend the election laws once again.[247]

It is not unreasonable, therefore, to assume that there will continue to be non-government majorities in the Senate. How that situation will affect the outcomes of Senate decision-making and the political dynamics in the Senate will depend very much on a complex of factors that include the policy distance that separates the government from the Opposition and where the 'balance of power' Senators stand, in policy terms, in relation to both of the 'major powers'.

Late Twentieth Century German experience offers a good example.[248] For years, the Bundestag comprised the two major parties—the Social Democrats (SPD) and the Christian Democrats (CDU)—and a minor party, the Free Democrats (FDP). Ideologically, the three parties could fairly easily be positioned on a single left-right spectrum,

---

246 Note to American readers: it would take another book to explain this comparison adequately; suffice it to say that what I envision would not be a pretty sight.

247 Sec. 128 of the Constitution allows the Governor-General to submit a proposed constitutional amendment to a national referendum if the proposal is passed twice by either house, even if the other house rejects it on both occasions. In these matters the Governor-General would be expected to act on the advice of the government. Thus it is highly unlikely that a proposal passed by a hostile Senate and rejected by the House of Representatives would be put to a referendum.

248 Though I ask readers familiar with German politics to forgive the simplifications in what follows.

with the SPD to the left of centre, but not too far left, and with the CDU to the right of centre, but not too far right, and with the FDP in between. This situation made the FDP available as a plausible coalition partner with either of the major parties when neither won a majority in its own right, which was always the case.

Then, in the 1980s and 1990s, the situation changed. The status of the FDP as the third force in German national politics was challenged first by the emergence of the Greens and then, after German reunification, by the Party of Democratic Socialism (PDS). In their early years, at least, the Greens were not particularly interested in coalition politics and the compromises such politics entail, and neither the SPD or the CDU was interested in publicly choosing the PDS as its political bedfellow in the national parliament. This made life more difficult for both major parties, but especially for the CDU because it was further ideologically from either of the two new minor parties than it was from its primary opponent, the SPD. In terms of ideological compatibility, a grand coalition with the SPD made more sense for the CDU than a coalition with either the Greens or the Democratic Socialists.

Now return to Canberra, and recall that the first minor party to secure and retain Senate seats after the switch to PR beginning with the 1949 election was the Democratic Labor Party (DLP). The DLP usually voted with the Coalition; it even has been argued that the DLP's raison d'etre was to keep the ALP away from power. For as long as the DLP remained in the Senate, therefore, the Labor Party often found itself opposed by a triad of the Liberals, the Country/National Party, and the DLP. The Senate's new, minor party was not often said to hold the balance of power. Then the DLP faded from the scene and the Australian Democrats emerged instead. At least at first, the Democrats fitted easily enough between Labor and the Coalition on a left-right continuum (though that changed as the new millennium began). And anyway, the Democrats claimed to be less interested in using their Senate leverage to promote their own social, economic, or international agenda than to 'keep the bastards honest'—a posture that emphasized the process of government as least as much as its policies.

Now, in mid-2003, the conventional wisdom is that the Democrats are in the process of imploding because of philosophical and strategic differences, and may not survive the next election. The more people assume this will happen, the more skeptical I become. But for the sake of argument, let us suppose that, after the election of 2004, the 'balance of power' in the Senate will be held by the Greens, not the Democrats. What difference will that make for the political dynamics in the Senate and for how much pain the Senate causes the government?

The answers are that (1) we do not know, and (2) it all depends. The first answer reminds us that things are obvious in politics only after the fact. The second answer is short-hand for saying that the Coalition could be expected to have more difficulty than Labor in coping with a larger Green presence in the Senate. It also is uncertain whether or not the Greens, for reasons of habit or conviction, might prefer remaining a force in opposition to whichever party is in government, so it might be reluctant to form government-Green winning coalitions. We have seen that the Greens in the late 1990s frequently voted with the Labor Opposition; what we cannot know is whether the Greens voted in this way because they chose to ally themselves with the *Labor* Party or with the *Opposition* party. In other words, that track record of the 1990s holds no guarantees about how often an enlarged Green contingent would be prepared to vote with a Labor Government (or a Coalition Opposition), much less another Coalition Government.

I offer no predictions about election outcomes or their consequences for what then happens in Parliament House. The purpose of these speculations is to emphasize two points. First, in politics as in finance, what has happened in the past is no guarantee of what will happen in the future. Politics is a human activity, an intensely human activity. Therefore, it is unpredictable. If it were otherwise, it would be boring. What we can say is that what will happen is going to depend to a significant though not necessarily determinative degree on what the rules of the game are and who the players are. But second, while the answers may change, the questions do not, or at least they do not change nearly as much. The same questions we have asked about the Senate in the 1990s, and the modes of analysis we have applied, will continue to remain relevant so long as the Commonwealth Parliament remains the platypus of the Australian political system.

Bibliography

ALDONS, MALCOLM. (2001) 'Responsible, Representative and Accountable Government,' *Australian Journal of Public Administration*, v. 60, n. 1.

ARCHER, JEFFREY, AND GRAHAM MADDOX. (1976) 'The 1975 Constitutional Crisis in Australia,' *Journal of Commonwealth and Comparative Politics*, v. 14. Reprinted in Woodward et al. (1985).

ARCHER, J.A. (1980) 'The Theory of Responsible Government in Britain and Australia,' in Weller and Jaensch (1980).

ARONEY, NICHOLAS. (2002) 'Imagining a Federal Commonwealth: Australian Conceptions of Federalism, 1890–1901,' *Federal Law Review*, v. 30, n. 2.

BANNON, JOHN. (1997) 'Towards Federation: the Role of the Smaller Colonies,' *Papers on Parliament* n. 30, November 1997.

BARTLETT, ANDREW. (1999) 'A Squeeze on the Balance of Power: Using Senate "Reform" to Dilute Democracy,' in Sawer and Miskin (1999).

BARWICK, GARFIELD. (1983) *Sir John Did His Duty*. Serendip Publications.

BAUME, PETER. (1991) 'Senate Estimates Committees—Do These Watchdogs Bite or Only Bark?' *Papers on Parliament* n. 12, September 1991.

BEAHAN, MICHAEL. (1996) 'Majorities and Minorities: Evolutionary Trends in the Australian Senate,' *Papers on Parliament* n. 27, March 1996.

BEAN, CLIVE. (1988) 'Politics and the Public: Mass Attitudes Towards the Australian Political System,' in Jonathan Kelly and Clive Bean (eds) (1988) *Australian Attitudes*. Allen & Unwin.

BEAN, CLIVE, AND MARTIN P. WATTENBERG. (1998) 'Attitudes Toward Divided Government and Ticket-Splitting in Australia and the United States,' *Australian Journal of Political Science*, v. 33, n. 1.

BEAN, CLIVE, AND IAN MCALLISTER. (2002) 'From Impossibility to Certainty: Explaining the Coalition's Victory in 2001,' in John Warhurst and Marian Simms (eds) *2001: the Centenary Election*. University of Queensland Press.

BENNETT, SCOTT. (1971) *The Making of the Commonwealth*. Cassell Australia.

—— (1996) *Winning and Losing: Australian National Elections*. Melbourne University Press.

BLACK, JOHN, MICHAEL MACKLIN, AND CHRIS PUPLICK. (1992) 'How Parliament Works in Practice,' *Papers on Parliament* n. 14 February 1992.

BLEWETT, NEAL. (1993) 'Parliamentary Reform: Challenge for the House of Representatives,' *Australian Quarterly*, v. 65, n. 3.

BLICK, BILL. (1992) 'Accountability, the Parliament and the Executive,' *Papers on Parliament* n. 18, December 1992.

BOLTON, GEOFFREY. (1962) 'The Choice of the Speaker in Australian Parliaments,' *Parliamentary Affairs*, v. 15.

BONGIORNO, PAUL, MICHELLE GRATTAN, AND MELISSA LANGERMAN. (1999) 'Reporting the Senate: Three Perspectives,' in Sawer and Miskin (1999).

BRENNAN, GEOFFREY. (1994) 'Australian Parliamentary Democracy: One Cheer for the Status Quo,' *Papers on Parliament* n. 22, February 1994.

——— (1998–99) 'The "Unrepresentative Swill" Feel Their Oats,' *Policy*, v. 14, n. 4.

——— (1999) 'The Senate and Proportional Representation: Some Concluding Observations,' in Sawer and Miskin (1999).

BROOME, RICHARD. (2002) *Aboriginal Australians*. (3rd ed.) Allen & Unwin.

BROWNING, H.O. (1985) *1975 Crisis: an Historical View*. Hale & Iremonger.

BRYCE, JAMES. (1905) *Constitutions*. Oxford University Press.

BUTLER, DAVID. (1973) *The Canberra Model*. St. Martin's Press.

BUTTON, JOHN. (1980) 'Federal Parliament: Decision Making in a Bizarre Working Environment,' in Mayer and Nelson (1980).

——— (1992) 'The Role of the Leader of the Government in the Senate,' *Papers on Parliament* n. 14, February 1992.

CABINET HANDBOOK (5TH ED.) (2000) Department of the Prime Minster and Cabinet. [www.dpmc.gov.au/pdfs/cabineted5.pdf]

CHANEY, FRED. (1988) 'Bicameralism Australian Style: Governing Without Control of the Upper House,' *The Parliamentarian*, v. 69, n. 3.

——— (1999) 'Should Parliament Be Abolished?' in Sawer and Miskin (1999).

CHILDS, BRUCE. (1992) 'The Truth About Parliamentary Committees,' *Papers on Parliament* n. 18, December 1992.

CLARK, MANNING. (1981) *A Short History of Australia*. The Macmillan Company of Australia.

CODY, HOWARD. (1988) 'Australian Small State MPs and Senators as Representatives,' *Australian Quarterly*, v. 60, n. 2.

——— (1996) 'Australia's Senate and Senate Reform in Canada,' *Papers on Parliament* n. 27, March 1996.

COGHILL, KEN AND DESPINA BABBAGE. (1991) 'Seating in Legislatures,' *Legislative Studies*, v. 5, n. 2.

COLLINS, HUGH. (1985) 'Political Ideology in Australia: the Distinctiveness of a Benthamite Society,' in Stephen R. Graubard (ed.) (1985) *Australia: the Daedalus Symposium*. Angus and Robertson.

COMANS, C.K. (1985) 'Constitution, Section 57—Further Questions,' *Federal Law Review*, v. 15, n. 3.

CONSTITUTION OF THE COMMONWEALTH OF AUSTRALIA [*Commonwealth of Australia Constitution Act 1900*], as amended to 1977. Various editions; available online at www.aph.gov.au/Senate/general/Constitution/index .htm

COONAN, HELEN. (1999a) '"Survival of the Fittest": Future Directions of the Senate,' in Sawer and Miskin (1999).

——— (1999b) 'Safeguard or Handbrake on Democracy?' Address to the Sydney Institute, 3 February 1999. Published in revised form in Costar (2000).

COSTAR, BRIAN (ED.). (2000) *Deadlock or Democracy? The Future of the Senate*. University of New South Wales Press.

CRISP. L.F. (1983) *Australian National Government* (5th ed.). Longman Cheshire.

DALE, WILLIAM. (1993) 'The Making and Remaking of Commonwealth Constitutions,' *International and Comparative Law Quarterly*, v. 42, n. 1.

DAVIS, S.R. (1983) 'What Price Upper Houses in Australia?' in Reid (1983).

DENNING, WARREN. (1946) *Inside Parliament*. Australasian Publishing Co.

DETMOLD, M.J. (1985) *The Australian Commonwealth: a Fundamental Analysis of Its Constitution*. Law Book Company.

DISNEY, JULIAN, AND J.R. NETHERCOTE (EDS). (1996) *The House on Capital Hill: Parliament, Politics and Power in the National Capital*. Federation Press.

EDWARDS, J.E. (1943) 'The Powers of the Australian Senate in Relation to Money Bills,' *Australian Quarterly*, v. 15, n. 3.

—— (1948) 'P.R. : Application of the System in Electing the Senate of the Commonwealth of Australia,' *Journal of the Society of Clerks-at-the-Table in Empire Parliaments*, v. XVII.

ELLICOTT, R.J. (1977) 'The Blocking of the Budget and Dismissal of the Government: Commentaries,' in Evans (1977).

ELLINGHAUS, M.P., ADRIAN BRADBROOK AND A.J. DUGGAN (EDS). (1989) *The Emergence of Australian Law*. Butterworths.

ELLIOTT, CLEAVER. (1997) 'Less than Optimal Outcomes: Fraser and Keating Without the Numbers,' *Legislative Studies*, v. 11, n. 2.

EMY, HUGH. (1974) *The Politics of Australian Democracy*. Macmillan.

—— (1996) 'The Mandate, the Senate, and Responsible Government,' *Australia and World Affairs*, n. 30.

—— (1997) 'The Mandate and Responsible Government,' *Australian Journal of Political Science*, v. 32, n. 1.

EPSTEIN, LEON. (1976) 'Australian Bicameralism: a Comparative Perspective,' *Politics*, v. 11, n. 1.

EVANS, GARETH. (1975) 'The Senate's Rights Can be Wrong,' *The Australian*, 29 October 1975, p. 11. Reprinted in Mayer and Nelson (1976).

EVANS, GARETH (ED.). (1977) *Labor and the Constitution 1972–1975*. Heinemann.

EVANS, HARRY. (1982) 'Australia and the "Westminster System,"' *The Table*, v. 50.

—— (1984) 'Party Government Versus Constitutional Government,' *Australian Quarterly*, v. 56, n. 3.

—— (1992a) 'Parliamentary Reform: New Directions and Possibilities for Reform of Parliamentary Processes,' *Papers on Parliament* n. 14, February 1992.

—— (1992b) 'Parliament: an Unreformable Institution?' *Papers on Parliament* n. 18, December 1992.

—— (1993a) 'Party Government: the Australian Disease and Australian Cures,' *Legislative Studies*, v. 7, n. 2.

—— (1993b) 'Constitution, Section 53—Amendments and Requests—Disagreements Between the Houses,' *Papers on Parliament* n. 19, May 1993.

—— (1994) 'Essentials of Republican Legislatures: Distributed Majorities and Legislative Control,'. *Papers on Parliament* n. 24, September 1994.

—— (1995) 'Restructuring the Senate's Committee System,' *Canberra Bulletin of Public Administration*, n. 78.

—— (1997a) 'Federalism and the Role of the Senate.' Paper presented at the Samuel Griffith Society Conference, Canberra. [www.aph.gov.au/senate/pubs/griffith.htm]

—— (1997b) 'Government and Parliament,' in Gwynneth Singleton (ed.). *The Second Keating Government.* Centre for Research in Public Sector Management, University of Canberra and Institute of Public Administration Australia.

—— (1998) 'The Other Metropolis: the Australian Founders' Knowledge of America,' *The New Federalist*, n. 2.

—— (1999) 'Accountability Versus Government Control: the Effect of Proportional Representation,' in Sawer and Miskin (1999); also published in Costar (2000).

—— (2000a) 'The Howard Government and the Parliament,' in Singleton (2000).

—— (2000b) 'The Australian Constitution and the 1911 Myth,' *The House Magazine*, 6 September. Reprinted in Murray (2001).

—— (2001) 'An Elected President for an Australian Republic: Problems and Solutions,' in Murray (2001).

FARRELL, DAVID, AND IAN MCALLISTER. (1995) 'Legislative Recruitment to Upper Houses: the Australian Senate and House of Representatives Compared,' *Journal of Legislative Studies*, v. 1, n. 2.

FAULKNER, JOHN. (1999) 'A Labor Perspective on Senate Reform,' in Sawer and Miskin (1999): 119–129; also published in Costar (2000).

FUSARO, ANTHONY. (1966) 'The Australian Senate as a House of Review: Another Look,' *Australian Journal of Politics and History*, v. 12.

—— (1967) 'The Effect of Proportional Representation on Voting in the Australian Senate,' *Parliamentary Affairs*, vol. 20, n. 4.

GALLIGAN, BRIAN. (1980a) 'The Founders' Design and Intentions Regarding Responsible Government,' in Weller and Jaensch (1980).

—— (1980b) 'The Kerr-Whitlam Debate and the Principles of the Australian Constitution,' *Journal of Commonwealth and Comparative Politics*, v. 18, n. 3.

—— (1984) 'Interpreting the Constitution After 1975,' *Australian Quarterly*, v. 56.

—— (1991) 'Senate Committees—Can They Halt the Decline of Parliament?' *Papers on Parliament* n. 12, September 1991.

—— (1995) *A Federal Republic: Australia's Constitutional System of Government.* Cambridge University Press.

—— (1997) 'The Constitutional System,' in Galligan, McAllister, and Ravenhill (1997).

GALLIGAN, BRIAN, AND JAMES WARDEN. (1986) 'The Design of the Senate,' in Gregory Craven (ed.), *The Convention Debates, 1891–1898: Commentaries, Indices and Guide.* Legal Books.

GALLIGAN, BRIAN, AND JOHN UHR. (1990) 'Australian Federal Democracy and the Senate,' *Public Law Review,* v. 1, n. 4.

GALLIGAN, BRIAN, AND JOHN S.F. WRIGHT. (2002) 'Australian Federalism: a Prospective Assessment,' *Publius: the Journal of Federalism,* v. 32, n. 2.

GALLIGAN, BRIAN, IAN MCALLISTER, AND JOHN RAVENHILL (EDS). (1997) *New Developments in Australian Politics.* Macmillan Education Australia.

GOOT, MURRAY. (1999a) 'Whose Mandate? Policy Promises, Strong Bicameralism and Polled Opinion,' *Australian Journal of Political Science,* v. 34, n. 3.

—— (1999b) 'Can the Senate Claim a Mandate?' in Sawer and Miskin (1999).

—— (2000) 'Debate: Mulgan on Mandates,' *Australian Journal of Political Science,* v. 35, n. 2.

—— (2002) 'Distrustful, Disenchanted and Disengaged? Public Opinion on Politics, Politicians and the Parties: an Historical Perspective,' *Papers on Parliament* n. 38, April 2002; also published in David Burchell and Andrew Leigh (2002) *The Prince's New Clothes.* University of New South Wales Press.

GOULD, STEPHEN JAY. (1991) 'To Be a Platypus,' in his *Bully for Brontosaurus.* W.W. Norton & Company.

GRATTAN, MICHELLE. (2002) 'Greens' Vote May Echo Nationally,' *Age* (Melbourne), 27 November 2002.

GRIFFITH, GARETH, AND SHARATH SRINIVASAN. (2001) *State Upper Houses in Australia. Background Paper* n. 1/2001. New South Wales Parliamentary Library Research Service.

GRIFFITH, J.A.G. AND MICHAEL RYLE. (1989) *Parliament: Functions, Practice and Procedures.* Sweet & Maxwell.

A GUIDE ON KEY ELEMENTS OF MINISTERIAL ACCOUNTABILITY. (1998) Department of the Prime Minister and Cabinet [www.dpmc.gov.au/pdfs/Key_Elements_Ministerial_Responsibility.pdf]

HAILSHAM, QUINTIN HOGG, BARON. (1976) *Elective Dictatorship: the Richard Dimbleby Lecture, 1976.* British Broadcasting Corporation.

—— (1982) 'The Role of an Upper Chamber in a Modern Parliamentary Democracy,' *The Parliamentarian,* October 1982.

HAMER, DAVID. (1979) 'Some Proposals for Senate Reform,' in Geoffrey Hawker et al., *Working Papers on Parliament.* Canberra College of Advanced Education.

—— (1989) 'Australia's Commonwealth Parliament,' *Legislative Studies,* v. 4, n. 2.

—— (1991) 'Senate Committees—Keeping Parliament Responsible,' *Papers on Parliament* n. 12, September 1991.

—— (1994) *Can Responsible Government Survive in Australia?* University of Canberra Press.

—— (1995) 'Can Responsible Government Survive in Australia?' *Papers on Parliament* n. 26, August 1995.

—— (1996) 'Parliament and Government: Striking the Balance,' in Disney and Nethercote (1996).

HIRST, JOHN. (2000) *The Sentimental Nation: the Making of the Australian Commonwealth*. Oxford University Press.

—— (2002) 'The Distinctiveness of Australian Democracy,' *Quadrant*, December 2002.

HOUSE OF REPRESENTATIVES. (1999) *Guide to Procedures*. Department of the House of Representatives [www.aph.gov.au/house/pubs/gtp/text/gtp.pdf]. Cited in the text as *House Guide*.

HOUSE OF REPRESENTATIVES. *Infosheets*, 1–21 (April 2002). Available at [www.aph.gov.au/house/info/infosheets/index.htm]

HOUSE OF REPRESENTATIVES. *Standing and Sessional Orders*, as of 16 September 2002. Department of the House of Representatives. [www.aph.gov.au/house/pubs/standos/index.htm] Cited in the text as HR.SO (#).

HOUSE OF REPRESENTATIVES PRACTICE (4TH ED.). (2001) Edited by I.C. Harris. Department of the House of Representatives. [www.aph.gov.au/house/pubs/PRACTICE /Index.htm]

HOWARD, COLIN. (1976) 'The Constitutional Crisis of 1975,' *Australian Quarterly*, v. 48, n. 1.

HOWARD, COLIN AND CHERYL SAUNDERS. (1977) 'The Blocking of the Budget and Dismissal of the Government,' in Evans (1977).

HUGHES, COLIN. (1980) 'Conventions: Dicey Revisited,' in Weller and Jaensch (1980).

HUGHES, COLIN (ED.). (1968) *Readings in Australian Government*. University of Queensland Press.

HUNT, ERLING. (1930) *American Precedents in Australian Federation*. Columbia University Press.

HUTCHISON, JENNIFER. (1976) 'The Australian Senate 1901–1972.' PhD Thesis, Australian National University.

—— (1983) 'The Senate,' in Lucy (1983).

IRVING, HELEN. (1997) *To Constitute a Nation*. Cambridge University Press.

—— (2000) 'The Republic Referendum of 6 November 1999,' *Australian Journal of Political Science*, v. 35, n. 1.

JACKSON, ROBERT J. (1995) 'Foreign Models and Aussie Rules: Executive-Legislative Relations in Australia,' *Political Theory Newsletter*, v. 7, n. 1.

JAENSCH, DEAN. (1986) *Getting Our Houses in Order: Australia's Parliament: How It Works and the Need for Reform*. Penguin.

—— (1991) *Parliament Parties & People: Australian Politics Today*. Longman Cheshire.

—— (1992) *The Politics of Australia*. Macmillan Education Australia.

—— (1997) *The Politics of Australia* (2nd ed.). Macmillan Education Australia.

JAENSCH, DEAN, AND DAVID MATHIESON. (1998) *A Plague on Both Your Houses: Minor Parties in Australia*. Allen & Unwin.

KELLY, PAUL. (1976) *The Unmaking of Gough*. Angus & Robertson Publishers. Reprinted in 1983 as *The Dismissal*.

—— (1995) *November 1975.* Allen & Unwin.

—— (1996) 'The Dismissal, Twenty Years On,' *Quadrant,* v. 40, n. 1–2. Reprinted in Lovell et al. (1998).

KERNOT, CHERYL. (1995) 'For Parliament or Party: Whose Democracy Is It, Anyway?' *Papers on Parliament* n. 25, June 1995.

—— (1997) 'Balancing Acts—Wielding the Balance of Power,' *Australian Journal of Public Administration,* v. 56, n. 2.

KERR, SIR JOHN. (1975) 'Statement by His Excellency, the Governor-General,' 11 November 1975. Reprinted in Mayer and Nelson (1976).

—— (1978) *Matters for Judgment: an Autobiography.* Macmillan.

KINLEY, D. (1985) 'Governmental Accountability in Australia and the United States,' *University of New South Wales Law Journal,* v. 18, n. 2.

KIRBY, MICHAEL. (2001) 'A Centenary Reflection on the Australian Constitution: the Republic Referendum, 1999,' *The Round Table: The Commonwealth Journal of International Affairs,* n. 361.

KNIGHTLEY, PHILLIP. (2000) *Australia: a Biography of a Nation.* Random House.

KUKATHAS, CHANDRAN. (1990) 'Democracy, Parliament and Responsible Government.' *Papers on Parliament* n. 8, June 1990 [full issue].

LA NAUZE, J.A. (1972) *The Making of the Australian Constitution.* Melbourne University Press.

LEES, MEG. (2000) 'Parliamentary Reform: the Baby and the Bathwater,' in Costar (2000).

LIBERAL PARTY OF AUSTRALIA. (1975) *Why the Government Should Face the People Now.* Reprinted in Mayer and Nelson (1976).

LIJPHART, AREND. (1999a) *Patterns of Democracy.* Yale University Press.

—— (1999b) 'Australian Democracy: Modifying Majoritarianism?' in Sawer and Miskin (1999).

LINDELL, GEOFFREY, AND BOB BENNETT (EDS). (2001) *Parliament: the Vision in Hindsight.* Federation Press.

LIPTON, JACQUELINE. (1997) 'Responsible Government, Representative Democracy and the Senate: Options for Reform,' *University of Queensland Law Journal,* v. 19, n. 2.

LOVELL, DAVID W. (1994) *The Sausage Makers? Parliamentarians as Legislators.* Department of the Parliamentary Library.

LOVELL, DAVID W. ET AL. (EDS). (1998) *The Australian Political System* (2nd ed.). Addison Wesley Longman.

LUCY, RICHARD. (1991) 'How American is the Australian Division of Powers?' *Legislative Studies,* v. 6, n. 1.

LUCY, RICHARD (ED.). (1983) *The Pieces of Politics* (3rd ed.). Macmillan.

LYNCH, ANNE. (1988) 'Legislation by Proclamation: Parliamentary Nightmare, Bureaucratic Dream,' *Papers on Parliament* n. 2, July 1988.

—— (1999) 'Personalities versus Structure: the Fragmentation of the Senate Committee System,' in Sawer and Miskin (1999).

MACINTYRE, STUART. (2002) '"A Parcel o' Rogues in a Nation": Australian Attitudes to Politics and Politicians.' Paper presented as the 2002 Reid Oration at the University of Western Australia, 16 October 2002.

MARGETTS, DEE. (1999) 'The Contributions of the Greens (WA) to the Australian Senate,' in Sawer and Miskin (1999).

MARSH, IAN. (1995) *Beyond the Two-Party System*. Cambridge University Press.

—— (1999) 'Opening Up the Policy Process,' in Sawer and Miskin (1999).

MAYER, DAVID Y. (1980) 'Sir John Kerr and Responsible Government,' in Weller and Jaensch (1980).

MAYER, HENRY, AND HELEN NELSON (EDS). (1976) *Australian Politics, a Fourth Reader*. Cheshire Publishing.

MAYER, HENRY, AND HELEN NELSON (EDS). (1980) *Australian Politics, a Fifth Reader*. Longman Cheshire Publishing.

MCALLISTER, IAN. (1997) 'Political Culture and National Identity,' in Galligan, McAllister, and Ravenhill (1997).

—— (1998) 'Civic Education and Political Knowledge in Australia,' *Australian Journal of Political Science*, v. 33, n. 1.

—— (2001) 'Elections Without Cues: the 1999 Australian Republic Referendum,' *Australian Journal of Political Science*, v. 36, n. 2.

MCKEOWN, DEIDRE, AND ROB LUNDIE. (2002) 'Free Votes in Australian and some Overseas Parliaments.' *Current Issues Brief* n. 1 2002–03. Department of the Parliamentary Library.

MCMULLIN, ALISTER. (1959) *An Introduction to the Australian Federal Parliament*. Angus and Robertson.

MOORE, W. HARRISON. (1910) *The Constitution of the Commonwealth of Australia*. (2nd ed.). Charles F. Maxwell.

MOYAL, ANN. (2001) *Platypus*. Allen & Unwin.

MULGAN, RICHARD. (1996) 'The Australian Senate as a "House of Review,"' *Australian Journal of Political Science*, v. 31, n. 2.

—— (2000) 'Debate: the 'Mandate: a Response to Goot,' *Australian Journal of Political Science*, v. 35, n. 2.

MURRAY, ANDREW (ED.). (2001) *Trusting the People: An Elected President for an Australian Republic*. Optima Press.

NETHERCOTE, JOHN. (1987) 'The Senate, the House of Representatives and the Condition of the Commonwealth Parliament,' *Legislative Studies*, v. 2, n. 2.

—— (1999) 'Mandate: Australia's Current Debate in Context.' *Research Paper* n. 19, 1998–99, Department of the Parliamentary Library.

NEUSTADT, RICHARD E. (1976) *Presidential Power: the Politics of Leadership, with Reflections on Johnson and Nixon*. Wiley.

OAKES, LAURIE. (1976) *Crash Through or Crash*. Drummond.

ODGERS, J.R. (1948) 'The Senate: Case for the Defence,' *Australian Quarterly*, v. 20, n. 4.

ODGERS' AUSTRALIAN SENATE PRACTICE (10TH ED.). (2001) Edited by Harry Evans. Department of the Senate. [www.aph.gov.au/senate/pubs/Html/index.htm]

O'KEEFFE, PETER. (1996) 'Amending Legislation in the Australian Senate,' *Statute Law Review*, v. 17, n. 3.

PAPADAKIS, E. AND C. BEAN. (1995) 'Minor Parties and Independents: the Electoral System,' *Australian Journal of Political Science*, v. 30.

PARKER, R.S. (1980a) 'The Evolution of British Political Institutions in Australia,' in A.F. Madden and W.H. Morris-Jones (eds) (1980) *Australia and Britain.* Frank Cass.

—— (1980b) 'Responsible Government in Australia,' in Weller and Jaensch (1980).

PARKIN, A. (1980) 'Pluralism and Australian Political Science,' *Politics,* v. 15, n. 1.

PARLIAMENTARY HANDBOOK (29TH ED.). (2002) Department of the Parliamentary Library.

PARTRIDGE, P.H. (1952) 'The Politics of Federalism,' in Geoffrey Sawer (ed.) (1952) *Federalism: an Australian Jubilee Study.* F.W. Cheshire.

PATTERSON, SAMUEL C., AND ANTHONY MUGHAN (EDS). (1999) *Senates: Bicameralism in the Contemporary World.* Ohio State University Press.

PAUL, J.B. (1996) 'Paul Kelly on the Dismissal,' *Quadrant,* v. 40, n. 12. Reprinted in Lovell et al. (1998).

PEARCE, DENNIS. (1997) 'The Legislative Power of the Senate,' in Zines (1997).

QUESTIONS & ANSWERS ON THE COMMONWEALTH PARLIAMENT (5TH ED.). (1977) Australian Government Publishing Service for the Department of the Senate.

QUICK, JOHN, AND ROBERT R. GARRAN. (1901) *The Annotated Constitution of the Australian Commonwealth.* Angus and Robertson. Reprinted in 1995 by Legal Books.

RAE, PETER. (1990) 'The "Revolutionary Proposals" of 1970,' *Papers on Parliament* n. 12, September 1991.

RATNAPALA, SURI. (1995) 'Westminster Democracy and the Separation of Powers: Can they Co-exist?' *Papers on Parliament* n. 26, August 1995.

REID, G.S. (1964) 'Australia's Commonwealth Parliament and the "Westminster Model,"' *Journal of Commonwealth Political Studies,* v. 2, n. 2.

—— (1977) 'The Double Dissolutions and Joint Sitting: Commentaries,' in Evans (1977).

—— (1982) 'Parliament and Delegated Legislation,' in J.R. Nethercote (ed.) (1982) *Parliament and Bureaucracy.* Hale and Iremonger.

REID, G.S. (ED.). (1983) *The Role of Upper Houses Today. Proceedings of the Fourth Annual Workshop of the Australasian Study of Parliament Group.* University of Tasmania.

REID, G.S., AND MARTYN FORREST. (1989) *Australia's Commonwealth Parliament, 1901–1988.* Melbourne University Press.

RICHARDSON, JACK. (2001) 'Resolving Deadlocks in the Australian Parliament,' in Lindell and Bennett (2001).

RODAN, PAUL. (1983) 'The House of Representatives,' in Lucy (1983).

—— (1983) 'The Prime Minister and Cabinet,' in Lucy (1983).

RUSSELL, MEG. (2001) 'Upper House Reform in the United Kingdom and Australia,' *Australian Journal of Political Science,* v. 36, n. 1.

RYDON, JOAN. (1983) 'Upper Houses—the Australian Experience,' in Reid (1983).

—— (1985) 'Some Problems of Combining the British and American Elements in the Australian Constitution,' *Journal of Commonwealth and Comparative Politics,* v. 23, n. 1.

—— (1986) *A Federal Legislature: the Australian Commonwealth Parliament, 1901–1980.* Oxford University Press.

SAMPFORD, C.J.G. (1987) 'The Australian Senate and Supply—Some Awkward Questions,' *Monash University Law Review*, v. 13.

—— (1989) 'Reconciling Responsible Government and Federalism,' in Ellinghaus (1989).

SAWER, GEOFFREY. (1956) *Australian Federal Politics and Law, 1901–1929.* Melbourne University Press.

—— (1963) *Australian Federal Politics and Law, 1929–1949.* Melbourne University Press.

—— (1977) *Federation Under Strain: Australia, 1972–1975.* Melbourne University Press.

SAWER, MARIAN. (1999) 'Dilemmas of Representation,' in Sawer and Miskin (1999).

—— (1999) 'Overview: Institutional Design and the Role of the Senate,' in Sawer and Miskin (1999).

SAWER, MARIAN, AND SARAH MISKIN (EDS). (1999) *Representation and Institutional Change: 50 Years of Proportional Representation in the Senate. Papers on Parliament* n. 34, December 1999.

SAWER, MARIAN, AND GIANNI ZAPPALA (EDS). (2001) *Speaking for the People.* Melbourne University Press.

SEKULESS, PETER, AND FRANCIS SULLIVAN. (1999) 'Lobbying the Senate: Two Perspectives,' in Sawer and Miskin (1999).

SENATE. *Standing Orders and Other Orders of the Senate* as at February 2003. Department of the Senate. [http://www.aph.gov.au/Senate/pubs/standingorders.doc] Cited in the text as S.SO (#)

SHARMAN, CAMPBELL. (1986) 'The Senate, Small Parties and the Balance of Power,' *Politics*, v. 21, n. 2.

—— (1988) 'Constitutional Politics in Australia (1900),' in Vernon Bogdanor. (1988) *Constitutions in Democratic Politics.* Gower Publishing Company.

—— (1990a) 'Australia as a Compound Republic,' *Politics*, v. 25, n. 1.

—— (1990b) 'Parliamentary Federations and Limited Government: Constitutional Design and Redesign in Australia and Canada,' *Journal of Theoretical Politics*, v. 2, n. 2.

—— (1998) 'The Senate and Good Government,' *Papers on Parliament* n. 33 (May 1999).

—— (1999) 'The Representation of Small Parties and Independents,' in Sawer and Miskin (1999): 149–158. Revised version published in *Australian Journal of Political Science,* v. 34, n. 3.

—— (2001) 'Over Powered and Under Legitimized: Redesigning the Australian Head of State,' in Murray (2001).

SINGLETON, GWYNNETH. (1996) 'Independents in a Multi-Party System: the Experience of the Australian Senate,' *Papers on Parliament* n. 28, November 1996.

—— (2000) *The Howard Government.* University of New South Wales Press.

SINGLETON, GWYNNETH, DON AITKIN, BRIAN JINKS, AND JOHN WARHURST. (2000) *Australian Political Institutions* (6th ed.) Pearson Education Australia

SOLOMON, DAVID. (1978) *Inside the Australian Parliament.* Allen & Unwin.

—— (1986) *The People's Palace.* Melbourne University Press.

—— (1998) *Coming of Age.* University of Queensland Press.

—— (2000) 'A Single-Chamber Australian Parliament?' *Papers on Parliament* n. 36, June 2001.

—— (2001) 'Parliamentary Reform Under a Republic,' in Murray (2001).

SOUTER, GAVIN. (1988) *Acts of Parliament: a Narrative History of the Senate and House of Representatives, Commonwealth of Australia.* Melbourne University Press.

STONE, BRUCE. (1998a) 'Size and Executive-Legislative Relations in Australian Parliaments,' *Australian Journal of Political Science,* v. 33, n. 1.

—— (1998b) 'Small Parties and the Senate Revisited: the Consequences of the Enlargement of the Senate in 1984,' *Australian Journal of Political Science,* v. 33, n. 2.

—— (2002) 'Australian Bicameralism Beyond the Senate: Potential and Performance in the State Upper Houses.' Paper presented in the Department of the Senate Occasional Lecture Series, Parliament House, Canberra.

SUGITA, HIROYA. (1997) 'Parliamentary Performance in the Senate,' in Warhurst (1997).

SUMMERS, JOHN. (1985) 'Parliament and Responsible Government in Australia,' in Woodward et al. (1985).

TERRILL, ROSS. (2000) *The Australians.* Doubleday.

THOMPSON, ELAINE. (1980) 'The "Washminster" Mutation,' in Weller and Jaensch (1980).

—— (1999) 'The Senate and Representative Democracy,' in Sawer and Miskin (1999).

UHR, JOHN. (1989a) 'The Canadian and Australian Senates: Comparing Federal Political Institutions,' in B.W. Hodgins et al. (eds) (1989) *Federalism in Canada and Australia: Historical Perspectives, 1920–1988.* Frost Centre for Canadian Heritage and Development Studies, Trent University.

—— (1989b) 'Public Expenditure and Parliamentary Accountability: the Debatable Role of Senate Estimates Committees,' *Papers on Parliament* n. 6, March 1990.

—— (1992) 'Prime Ministers and Parliament: Patterns of Control,' in Weller (1992).

—— (1995a) 'Proportional Representation in the Australian Senate: Recovering the Rationale,' *Australian Journal of Political Science,* v. 30 (special issue).

—— (1995b) 'Keeping Government Honest: Preconditions of Parliamentary Effectiveness,' *Papers on Parliament* n. 29, March 1997.

—— (1996) 'Reshaping Parliament: a Republican Agenda,' *Australian Quarterly,* v. 68, n.4.

—— (1997) 'Parliament,' in Galligan, McAllister, and Ravenhill (1997).

—— (1998) *Deliberative Democracy in Australia: the Changing Place of Parliament.* Cambridge University Press.

—— (1999a) 'Generating Divided Government: the Australian Senate,' in Patterson and Mughan (1999).

—— (1999b) 'Why We Chose Proportional Representation,' in Sawer and Miskin (1999): 13–40. A revised version is at [www.aph.gov.au/Senate/pubs/pops/pop34/c02.htm]

—— (2001a) 'Rules for Representation: Parliament and the Design of the Australian Electoral System,' in Lindell and Bennett (2001).

—— (2001b) 'What is a House of Review?' Opening Address presented at the First Public Seminar of the Constitution Commission of Victoria. [www.constitution.vic.gov.au/librarydocs/UhrSeminar.pdf]

—— (2001c) 'Evaluating Parliamentary Scrutiny: the Business of Benchmarks.' Paper presented at the 2001 Annual Conference of the Australasian Study of Parliament Group, Canberra.

—— (2001d) 'Parliament and Public Deliberation: Evaluating the Performance of Parliament,' *University of New South Wales Law Journal*, v. 24, n. 3.

—— (2002a) 'Explicating the Australian Senate,' *Journal of Legislative Studies*, v. 8, n. 3.

—— (2002b) 'Parliament and the Executive.' Paper presented at a 2002 conference at the Centre for Comparative Constitutional Studies, University of Melbourne.

WARD, ALAN J. (2000a) 'Australia and Parliamentary Orthodoxy: A Foreign Perspective on Australian Constitutional Reform,' *Papers on Parliament* n. 35, June 2000.

—— (2000b) 'Trapped in a Constitution: the Australian Republic Debate,' *Australian Journal of Political Science*, v. 35, n. 1.

WARHURST, J. (ED.). (1997) *Keeping the Bastards Honest: the Australian Democrats' First Twenty Years*. Allen & Unwin.

WEARNE, ALAN. (1997) *Kicking in Danger*. Black Pepper.

WELLER, PATRICK (ED.). (1992) *Menzies to Keating: the Development of the Australian Prime Ministership*. Melbourne University Press.

WELLER, PATRICK, AND DEAN JAENSCH (EDS). (1980) *Responsible Government in Australia*. Drummond Publishing.

WEST, FRANCIS. (1976) 'Constitutional Crisis 1975—an Historian's View,' *Australian Quarterly*, v. 48, n. 2.

WHEARE, KENNETH. (1963) *Legislatures*. Oxford University Press.

WHITINGTON, DON. (1969) *The House Will Divide: a Review of Australian Federal Politics*. Lansdowne Press.

WHITLAM, GOUGH. (1979) *The Truth of the Matter*. Penguin Books.

WILSON, WOODROW. (1885) *Congressional Government*. The World Publishing Company. Reprinted 1956 by Meridian Books.

WINTERTON, GEORGE. (1983) *Parliament, the Executive and the Governor-General*. Melbourne University Press.

WOOD, D. (1989) 'The Senate, Federalism and Democracy,' *Melbourne University Law Review,* v. 17, n. 2.

WOODWARD, DENNIS, ANDREW PARKIN, AND JOHN SUMMERS (EDS). (1985) *Government, Politics and Power in Australia* (3rd ed.). Longman Cheshire.

WRIGHT, JACK F.H. (1986) 'Australian Experience with Majority-Preferential and Quota-Preferential Systems,' in Bernard Grofman and Arend

Lijphart (eds) (1986) *Electoral Laws and Their Consequences.* Agathon Press.

WRIGHT, JOHN S.F. (2001) 'Anglicizing the United States Constitution: James Bryce's Contribution to Australian Federalism,' *Publius: the Journal of Federalism,* v. 31, n. 4.

WRIGHT, RAYMOND. (1992) *A People's Counsel.* Oxford University Press.

YOUNG, LIZ. (1997) *Minor Parties ... Major Players? The Senate, the Minor Parties, and the 1993 Budget.* Department of the Parliamentary Library.

—— (1999) 'Minor Parties and the Legislative Process in the Australian Senate: a Study of the 1993 Budget,' *Australian Journal of Political Science,* v. 34, n. 1.

—— (2000) 'Parliament and the Executive: the Re-emergence of Parliament as a Decisive Political Institution,' in Paul Boreham, Geoffrey Stokes, and Richard Hall (eds) (2000) *The Politics of Australian Society.* Pearson Education Australia.

ZINES, LESLIE. (1977) 'The Double Dissolutions and Joint Sitting,' in Evans (1977).

ZINES, LESLIE (ED.). (1997) *Commentaries on the Australian Constitution.* Butterworths.

Index

Quotas for Senate elections
  calculation of quota, 47
    for double dissolutions, 52

R

Referenda. *See* CONSTITUTION,
  AUSTRALIAN—ALTERATION OF
Republic, Australian
  debate on, 313–25
  referendum on, 1999, 101, 314,
    315, 319n
Reserve powers. *See under* GOVERNOR-
  GENERAL
Responsible government, 3, 12, 14n,
  16–25, 89, 90, 93, 99, 102, 103,
  105–6, 110, 112, 120–29, 124, 133,
  134, 135, 139, 143, 152, 184, 185,
  240, 244, 276, 299, 300, 328, 331,
  332, 345–54, 363
  divided government and, 4
  dual responsibility theory of, 111–
    20
  party discipline and, 55
  responsibility defined, 351–52
  Senate and, 5

S

Salisbury Convention, 281, 297
Senate
  as house of accountability, 351–52
  as legislature, 246–48
  balance of power in, 174, 183–88,
    235, 237
  casual vacancies, 88, 95
  coalition building in the chamber,
    157–88, 231–34
  committee of the whole, 202
  committees, 8, 190–92, 212n, 251,
    306, 308, 352
    House ministers and, 255
    ministers as witnesses, 308–10
  composition
    nexus with House of
      Representatives, 15, 77
  continuing nature of, 14
  cooperation and compromise in,
    190–92
  democratic legitimacy of, 142, 281,
    297

elections for. *See under* ELECTORAL
  SYSTEM
enforced reasonableness in, 249
geographically distributed majority
  and, 54n, 141, 144n, 348n
half-Senate elections, 14
impact of minor parties and
  Independents, 82
increased in size in 1984, 47
legislative programming in, 257–58
Macklin motion, 257–58
mandate theory and, 288, 295–98,
  299
media reporting of, 235–36, 253,
  256. *See also* MEDIA REPORTING
  OF PARLIAMENT
ministers in, 254, 305–10
modus operandi 1901–09, 58–60
Opposition role in. *See* OPPOSITION
party affiliations of senators
  historical table, 54
  in 2002, 158, 163
powers, 16–25, 129–35, 280, 331,
  358–63. *See also under*
  FINANCIAL LEGISLATION
reform of, proposals for, 300–313
  removal of power to block
    supply, 300–305
relations with House of
  Representatives. *See* Parliament,
  Commonwealth—relations
  between the houses
representative character of, 248,
  252, 281
reputation of, 189, 247, 252, 361
  before 1949, 76
role of
  house of review, 148–56
  representation of the states,
    139–48
rotation of senators, 14, 157
senators' terms of office, 14, 46–54
states represented equally, 141, 144
televising of, 253
votes on party rather than state
  lines, 55n, 144–47
voting in, 193, 208n
  analysis of patterns of, 1996–
    2001, 189–237
  party affiliation and, 157–88
  position-taking, 210, 224, 226,
    227, 233

- party discipline trumps any sense of obligation to support the position of one's chamber

- H of Reps - different ambitions - hope to become ministers - even PM

- Senate - few ministerial posts - only once has a Senator become PM & he quickly sought a seat in H of R

p 242 compromise & consensus seeking are part of the culture of the Senate

p 251 - Speaker's ruling in H of R. that it would be inappropriate for a Senate estimates committees to examine the finances of the H of Rep.

p 254 - TV coverage of Senate began in 1990 put pressure on H. of R. to allow coverage of floor proceedings

- usually about 1/3 of ministers are drawn from the Senate

- no provision in S.O.s of two chambers to allow ministers from the other place to appear.

p 256 motions of censure of ministers in Senate, have a political impact - but lack const'l significance